THE
CRESCENT CITY
LYNCHINGS

THE
CRESCENT CITY
LYNCHINGS

THE MURDER OF CHIEF HENNESSY, THE NEW ORLEANS

"MAFIA" TRIALS, AND THE PARISH PRISON MOB

TOM SMITH

THE LYONS PRESS
An imprint of The Globe Pequot Press

All dialogue appearing in this book is taken from accounts contemporary with the events.

The Lyons Press is an imprint of The Globe Pequot Press.

10 9 8 7 6 5 4 3 2 1

Printed in the United States of America

ISBN-13: 978-1-59228-901-1
ISBN-10: 1-59228-901-0

Library of Congress Cataloging-in-Publication Data is available on file.

To Vic and Karen, for many kindnesses

The people's safety is the supreme law.

—LATIN PROVERB

A mob is the scum that rises upmost when the nation boils.

—JOHN DRYDEN

☽

CONTENTS

LIST OF KEY CHARACTERS

General Algernon S. Badger, *chief of the Metropolitan Police*

James G. Blaine, *United States Secretary of State*

Thomas N. Boylan, *chief of the New Orleans police and owner of Boylan's Detective Agency*

CARUSO BROTHERS:
Jim Caruso, *Matranga stevedore and suspect in Hennessy murder*
John Caruso, *suspect in Hennessy murder*
Vincent Caruso

Pasquale Corte, *Italian Consul in New Orleans*

Lemuel Davis, *Orleans Parish Prison warden*

Thomas Devereaux, *police chief of aids*

Giuseppe Esposito, *Sicilian bandit*

ESPLANADE AMBUSH VICTIMS:
Tony Matranga, Frank and Tony Locascio, Vincent Caruso, Rocco Geraci, Bastian Incardona, Salvatore Sunzeri

ESPLANADE AMBUSH SUSPECTS:
Joseph Provenzano, Peter Provenzano, Tony Pellegrini, Nick Guillio, Tony Gianforcaro, Gaspardo Lombardo

ESPLANADE AMBUSH TRIALS:

JUDGES:
Joshua G. Baker, *first trial;* Robert Marr, *second trial*

PROSECUTORS:
Assistant District Attorney John Finney, Lionel Adams, A. D. Henriques

DEFENSE ATTORNEYS:
First Trial:
J. C. McMahon, J. M. Pratt

Second Trial:
William Lloyd Evans, Arthur Dunn, James C. Walker

Baron Saverio Fava, *Italy's ambassador to the United States*

Dexter S. Gaster, *appointed police superintendent, January 1891*

David C. Hennessy, *New Orleans Police superintendent and chief*

Mike Hennessy, *detective and Dave's cousin*

HENNESSY MURDER TRIAL:

DEFENDANTS IN FIRST TRIAL:
Antonio Bagnetto, *night watchman at Poydras Market;* Bastian Incardona,

laborer; **Joseph P. Macheca,** *fruit importer;* **Antonio Marchesi,** *fruit seller;* **Gasperi Marchesi; Charles Matranga,** *labor manager;* **Pietro Monasterio,** *cobbler;* **Emmanuele Polizzi,** *street vendor;* **Antonio Scaffidi,** *fruit seller*

DEFENDANTS SCHEDULED FOR SECOND TRIAL:
James Caruso, *stevedore;* **John Caruso,** *stevedore;* **Loretto Comitz** *(or Comites), tinsmith;* **Rocco Geraci,** *stevedore;* **Pietro Natali,** *laborer;* **Charles Patorno,** *merchant;* **Charles Pietzo,** *grocer;* **Frank Romero,** *ward politician;* **Salvatore Sunzeri,** *stevedore;* **Charles Traina,** *rice plantation worker*

JUDGE:
Joshua G. Baker

DEFENSE ATTORNEYS:
Lionel Adams, A. D. Henriques, Thomas J. Semmes, Arthur Gastinel, Charles Butler; Fernand Armant *(for Patorno);* Charles Theard *(for Polizzi);* John Q. Flynn *(for Polizzi)*

PROSECUTORS:
District Attorney Charles H. Luzenberg, William Lloyd Evans, Arthur Dunn, James C. Walker

John Journée, *New Orleans Police captain, acting police superintendent, October 1890–January 1891*

Joseph P. Macheca, *suspect in Hennessy murder, partner in Macheca Brothers firm, stepbrother to John and Michael Macheca*

MARCH 14, 1891 MOB LEADERS:
Walter Denegre, *lawyer;* **James D. Houston,** *politician and New Orleans waterworks administrator;* **William S. Parkerson,** *lawyer;* **John C. Wickliffe,** *editor of the* **New Delta** *newspaper*

MATRANGA BROTHERS:
Charles Matranga
Tony Matranga
Salvatore Matranga, *patriarch*

William J. "Billy" O'Connor, *Hennessy's friend and Boylan agency detective*

Dominick C. O'Malley, *private detective*

PROVENZANO BROTHERS:
George Provenzano
Joseph Provenzano, *defendant in Matranga shooting*
Peter Provenzano, *defendant in Matranga shooting*
Vincent Provenzano

J. C. Roe, *Boylan agency officer assigned to guard Hennessy's home*

Joseph A. Shakspeare, *mayor of New Orleans*

George Vandervoort, *Hennessy's secretary*

TIMELINE

1869

February 26—*David Hennessy Sr. is killed in New Orleans.*

1876

November—*John Forester Rose is kidnapped and ransomed in Sicily.*

1881

JULY

6—*Sicilian suspected to be Giuseppe Esposito is secretly taken into custody by New Orleans police detectives David and Michael Hennessy. Prisoner is sent to New York the following morning.*

July 18 to September 14—*Esposito extradition hearing in New York City. The prisoner is extradited to Italy on September 21.*

OCTOBER

4—*New Orleans mayor Joseph Shakspeare suspends police chief of aids Thomas Devereaux.*

13—*Mike Hennessy is wounded in a gun battle with Devereaux, who is killed by Dave Hennessy.*

DECEMBER

22—*Esposito is sentenced to "life servitude" after a two-week trial in Palermo, Sicily.*

26—*The Hennessy cousins are acquitted of murdering Devereaux.*

1886

September 29—*Mike Hennessy is murdered in Houston, Texas.*

1888

May 2—*As the second Shakspeare administration begins, Dave Hennessy accepts post of superintendent and chief of police.*

1890

MAY

5—*Stevedores employed by Matranga & Locascio are ambushed.*

6—*The ambush victims accuse six men as their assailants: Joseph Provenzano, Peter Provenzano, Tony Pellegrini, Nick Guillio, Tony Gianforcaro, and Gaspardo Lombardo.*

JULY
15 to 19—*The Provenzano trial.*

AUGUST
9—*The Provenzanos are granted a retrial, which is scheduled to start on October 17.*

OCTOBER
15—*Hennessy is shot and dies the following morning. Mass arrests of Italian Americans and Italian migrant workers follow.*

17—*Antonio Scaffidi is shot in Orleans Parish Prison.*

18—*Joseph Macheca, Frank Romero, and Charles Patorno individually surrender to police. Mayor Shakspeare appoints a Committee of Fifty to investigate the Hennessy murder.*

27—*Committee of Fifty defines its mission to the public at a mass meeting in Lafayette Square.*

NOVEMBER
20—*Grand Jury indicts nineteen men for Hennessy's murder: Antonio Bagnetto, James and John Caruso, Loretto Comitz (or Comites), Rocco Geraci, Bastian Incardona, Joseph Macheca, Gasperi and Antonio Marchesi, Charles Matranga, Pietro Monasterio, Pietro Natali, Charles Patorno, Charles Pietzo, Emmanuelle Polizzi ("Manuel Politz"), Frank Romero, Antonio Scaffidi, Salvatore Sunzeri, and Charles Traina.*

1891

JANUARY
6—*Accused counterfeiter Antonio Ruggiero is arrested in Amite, Louisiana, and taken to the Orleans Parish Prison.*

12—*The Provenzano retrial begins.*

22—*It is agreed to try the nineteen defendants in the Hennessy case in two successive trials to speed the jury selection process. A trial date is set for first nine. Police officer Dexter Gaster is appointed superintendent and chief.*

23—*The Provenzanos are acquitted of some charges in the Esplanade ambush case.*

26—*Antonio Ruggiero is released from prison.*

28—*The remaining charges against the Provenzanos are dismissed.*

FEBRUARY
16—*The Hennessy trial begins.*

27—*Jury selection is completed.*

28—*Testimony begins.*

MARCH
12—*After two days of closing arguments, the case goes to the jury at 6:32 p.m.*

13—*Verdicts are announced at 3 p.m.*

14—*Mass meeting in Canal Street at 10 a.m. By noon, ten of the nineteen men charged with Hennessy's murder are dead, and one is critically injured.*

31—*Baron Saverio Fava, Italy's Ambassador to the United States, is recalled.*

APRIL
3—*Dominick O'Malley is charged with jury tampering.*

MAY
5—*The grand jury exonerates the mob leaders.*

7—*O'Malley responds to his enemies in the* Times-Democrat.

JUNE
The trials of the alleged jury bribers take place.

NOVEMBER
The last jury bribery charges are dismissed.

1892

April 13—*President Benjamin Harrison orders a U.S. government payment of $25,000 to the families of the Italian citizens who were lynching victims.*

1893

December 19—*Gasperi Marchesi is awarded $5,000 in damages after filing a lawsuit against the city of New Orleans.*

ACKNOWLEDGMENTS

I am extremely grateful to the New Orleans Public Library's Louisiana Division, especially the 1989–1990 desk staff, without whose assistance the research for this book would have stalled permanently. I owe special thanks to Karen Konnerth and Vic Shepherd, without whose years of friendship and hospitality my time in New Orleans would be much poorer. Lucinda and Dr. David Shields at the University of South Carolina, Dr. Eleanor M. Lang at Southern Connecticut State University, Twig Holland, Nick Trenticosta, Pam Haring, Ralph Colalillo, Nan King, and Heleri Ziou provided much appreciated advice, help, and encouragement along the way. I also wish to thank the librarians of Cheshire and Wallingford, Connecticut, as well as Suzanne Christoff, archivist at the U.S. Military Academy at West Point; Jim MacDonald at Connecticut College's Shain Library; Dale Johnson and Seth Godfrey at the New Haven Free Public Library; and Maryetta Russell and Suzanne Lorimer at the Yale University Library.

I want to thank Ed Knappman at New England Publishing Associates for his goodhumor, persistence, and editorial advice, not to mention keeping me busy until the book saw daylight. It was a pleasure working with the excellent Lyons Press staff and editor Rob Kirkpatrick, who pointed out loose ends and patiently allowed me to find the best ways to tie them. And as always, I thank my family, whose love and support make all things easier.

Prologue:

THOSE PEOPLE CAN'T KILL ME

AFTER THE KILLING STOPPED AND CURIOSITY ABOUT THE AFFAIR faded, only an insult remained alive, a strange and childish taunt: *who killa de chief?* A generation passed before a callus formed to protect against the hurtful words, long after the people of New Orleans had resumed what they considered to be normal life.

Life was mercifully quiet in 1890, as if the city was at last catching its breath after a hard century. Shoppers browsing along Canal Street that year heard voices in wax cylinders spinning on Edison's new talking machine. Relief from smothering summer humidity might come in a 5¢ bottle of Coca-Cola, touted as "The Ideal Brain Tonic (A Priceless Boon to Ladies)." Men cultivated mustaches and sporting gents cocked their derby hats at rakish angles before heading out to see local baseball games. Pugilist John L. Sullivan was in his prime. His fellow Irishman James O'Neill, seeking a rest from eight years portraying the Count of Monte Cristo in the glow of the nation's footlights, was coming to town to play the Bonanza Prince. Barnum & Bailey's circus was coming too, with *Nero, or the Destruction of Rome*, a three-ring "Grand Terpsichorean Divertissement" recently performed for Queen Victoria and England's royal household.

Music in New Orleans meant arias in the French Opera House on Bourbon Street or, more frequently, gay burlesques in the Grand Opera House, a popular Canal Street variety theater. The world beyond the limits of Orleans Parish knew nothing then about second-lining, dancing the Hog Face, or enjoying brass bands at ball games. Buddy Bolden was a thirteen-year-old schoolboy without a cornet and there was no jazz, not even in the city it would consume within a generation. Pianists stroked sentimental melodies by dependable, dead Stephen Foster to entertain customers in the city's bordellos.

Mules pulling city streetcars on the greatest thoroughfare in the South would soon be gone, replaced by electricity. Plans to bring electric light to the Algiers Point neighborhood across the river from the French Quarter with a cable dropped under the waters of the Mississippi were drawn and ready. Even though New Orleans was one of the best-lit cities in the nation, it was still learning about electricity's unpredictable current. The parish prison executioner decided to keep his rope after hearing of a condemned man in Sing Sing slowly burning to death in a brand new contraption called an electric chair.

The Civil War was twenty-five years in the past. Confederate veterans reunited in New York and the Grand Army of the Republic took rail trips into the South for reunion conventions. Each side decorated the graves of the other with flowers on their respective Memorial Days. The immediate trauma was healing, even if a generation of young Southerners, deprived of their war by only a few years, felt the loss with a passion lacked by many of their elders who had personally lived the horror. With a new century just a mere decade away, the modern-day struggle was for money.

Although the Civil War left the port intact and the docks remained the heart of New Orleans's economy, its eminence as a trading center had been shaken. Daily life was less attractive than city boosters wished. Taxpayers couldn't decide if they wanted a paid fire department, teachers' wages amounted to a pittance, and the reeking streets didn't smell much better than sewers. Citizens were tight with a buck, and you couldn't blame them, considering how much of their money disappeared into the seemingly bottomless pockets of corrupt politicians. It was mighty hard to find any man in New Orleans public life without at least a thin line of grime under his fingernails. Francis Tillou Nicholls ruled the state, if not the city. The governor, for whom Hospital Street would later be renamed, was a Confederate veteran who had lost his left arm at Winchester, then recovered to lose his left foot at Chancellorsville. "Vote For What's Left of Nicholls" was one of the few jokes allowed in the hot-tempered world of Louisiana politics. Republicans sat in the White House but were the "outs" of Louisiana politics. Two political factions—both filled with Democrats—jousted for power in New Orleans, attacking each other without mercy. Bullets had flown on election days within recent memory.

The city was not as unpredictably dangerous for African Americans as the rest of the South. Beneath the placid surface of daily life, however, New Orleans remained a mostly divided city. Black New Orleanians still possessed social freedoms and voting rights they had gained during Reconstruction, but white state lawmakers were plotting new rules. Crafting a clause to disenfranchise blacks would be tricky, but it was not impossible and would happen very soon, delivering segregation laws that would trouble the country for another three-quarters of a century. The notion that Southern women of any color would want to vote was considered to be so scandalous that only a few discreet individuals seriously suggested it. Women were thought only to be interested in Parisian millinery and the identity of next season's Mardi Gras queen. Prostitutes working Customhouse Street, later renamed Iberville Street, might share an interest in Flanders lace and Sicilienne sleeves with their customers' wives and mistresses, but they lived in a world profoundly different from the prosperous universe upriver from the dark side streets of the French Quarter.

All news came by word of mouth or from newspapers. New Orleanians were tickled when they read a story about a married couple arrested for kissing on a Boston street. There was less sanctimony in the Crescent City, even beneath Uptown's prim and proud veneer. The once familiar practice of dueling had been forbidden for years. Formal duels did not occur often, but occasionally two enraged gentlemen would accord the prohibition the same respect that less well-heeled classes showed a city ordinance banning bets on rat fights. At times it felt as if all of New Orleans were armed. Perhaps it was, as a pistol cost only a dollar or two. Campaigns to outlaw prostitution and gambling limped along, as they had for generations, and Governor Nicholls was fighting bitterly to destroy the corrupt Louisiana State Lottery. Secret cockfights, dogfights, and human prizefighting were all criminal enterprises under current law. So was selling beer on Sundays.

On October 15, 1890, the last disciplinary item on the New Orleans Police Board agenda was the case of Sergeant Lynch and Stableman Thibodaux of the Eighth Precinct. The pair was accused of barging into Algiers shops, ordering drinks, then demanding cash to prevent any charges that the Sunday closing law was being violated. The Sunday prohibition of liquor sales was Mayor Joseph Shakspeare's pet project, which was enough to make the sergeant and the stableman nervous. The blackmail charge interested Police Superintendent and Chief David C. Hennessy more. The accused men did not need to look at their boss to know they were in trouble.

"I'm not guilty," Sergeant Lynch protested. "I haven't had time to prepare a defense."

"The people charging the officers have been put through a deal of trouble coming over from Algiers this evening in such terrible weather," Mayor Shakspeare replied sternly as rain tattooed the windows. "I suggest we hear the prosecution now and continue the case until the defense witnesses can be summoned at a later date." Hennessy and the four civilian members of the board agreed.

John Michel testified that Lynch and Thibodaux entered the back of his closed grocery and bar to tell him that he had violated the Sunday law. The grocer knew the officers, who were out of uniform. Michel said Lynch suggested that a little cash would square the case. Michel told them he was closed, but as arguing was pointless, he emptied his till of all he had, about $3.50. The cops next visited the shop of Phil Bennerrette, who swore that Lynch demanded $5 to avoid being reported. Bennerrette refused, but his wife gave them some money. He saw Lynch's badge flash under his overcoat as the sergeant stuffed the cash into his pocket. The grocer admitted selling liquor on Sunday, "just like everyone else does."

"That man and me have had words before," Italian saloonkeeper Philip Geraci said as he leveled a finger at Thibodaux. "He told me once he was going to fix me! They came to my store and said 'Give us some change!'"

Chief Hennessy asked if the men were dressed as policemen when they came to Geraci's store.

"Not this time," Geraci said. "But I knew the other one is police too."

When Hennessy asked when it happened, Geraci answered, "Seven o'clock, two Sundays ago." Glaring at Thibodaux, he added, "You did not ask me for money, but you threatened to do me before, cursed me, and called me a 'dirty dago.' Everybody knows you are a bulldozer and a tough, and I was never in trouble until you forced me into it!"

Hennessy and the board decided that nothing Lynch or Thibodaux could say would rebut such charges, so the men were fired.

"The Algiers precinct seems to be wholly without discipline," the mayor groused as the sacked officers left the room.

Assuring Shakspeare that more attention was being paid to discipline daily, the chief was eager to move on to more mundane improvements. As rain lashed the window, he began his report, asking for $75 to make repairs at the Seventh Precinct station.

Long after the police board adjourned, Hennessy lounged in his office, shooting the breeze with an older colleague, William J. "Billy" O'Connor of Boylan's detective agency. Both men had been cops most of their lives and both had policed world's fairs. O'Connor served with the Savannah, Georgia, and New Orleans police forces before becoming the Boylan Agency's superintendent. Hennessy was also a longtime commercial partner in the agency and planned to return to it full-time when his public term as police superintendent and chief ended.

The two men talked for an hour before they lifted their umbrellas in the doorway of the Central Station and stepped into the waning twirls of rain. It was late, just after eleven o'clock. The Basin Street gutters between Common Street and Hennessy's home on Girod Street would be flooded by now, spilling over badly kept banquettes. Treading through the miry streets was out of the question.

"Let's take Rampart Street," suggested one of the men. "The sidewalks on Basin are too bad."

The lights of Dominic Virget's saloon shone ahead, and Hennessy proposed a stop. The men stepped into the warmth of Virget's place and ordered a dozen oysters. Hennessy washed his down with a glass of milk.

After their late snack, Hennessy and O'Connor bid each other good night at the corner of Rampart and Girod, in front of the neighborhood's McDonough School. As O'Connor headed down Girod toward the river, Hennessy turned up the street toward his home, holding his umbrella against the blowing mist.

Hennessy could see a figure across the street, a block distant, but paid him little mind. It looked like J. C. Roe, the Boylan security officer detailed to watch his house. Hennessy didn't care much about the added protection. He didn't need one of his men or friends like Billy O'Connor to walk home with him every night. Sure he had enemies—any chief of police had more than a human share—but he was safe enough here. He knew most of his neighbors, at least by sight, and after all, remembering faces was part of his business. John Petersen, who had joined Boylan's force seven or eight months ago, lived across the street with his mother. Another neighbor, Officer Charles Dayton, a city cop, shared half of the Thames family's shotgun cottage below the corner. Hennessy strode past the Thames's door, anxious to get home out of the damp. He did not make it.

He felt the bullets before he heard them. Cuts in his face and arm stung, as a deeper pain tossed him off balance and crackled along his ribs. Hennessy grabbed his Colt from his waistcoat. The walls of the buildings around him shuddered as he turned toward the flashes. Losing his breath, he hurried to the corner, firing back at the dark figures coming for him.

O'Connor was almost to the corner of Dryades, two dark blocks below the Thames home, when the first explosion resounded. He turned to see two more flashes from the uptown side as the report of heavily charged shotguns rumbled through the wet night, punctuated by the cracks of a revolver.

O'Connor ran toward the flashes, but the shooting had stopped by the time he covered the first block. He saw a Boylan officer named Kotter about twenty feet from the McDonough School.

"Which way did they run?" O'Connor puffed.

"I believe it was uptown," Kotter said.

O'Connor ran on, and by the time he reached the corner of Basin, there were five or six people on the street, but no sign of Hennessy. Then he heard it.

"Billy. Oh . . . Billy."

O'Connor looked down the dilapidated Basin Street sidewalk toward the center of the city. Hennessy sat alone on a doorstep, bleeding from his face, hands, and legs. The left side of his coat was ripped into a dark red tangle, and his Colt hung from his hand, the pearl grips smeared with blood. "They gave it to me, but I gave 'em back the best I could."

Hennessy's vest and collar were loosened. A cop and a Boylan officer rushed up, holding a frightened black laborer they caught running down Basin Street after the shooting. O'Connor wasn't listening to them. He was bending toward the chief. Over a dozen police officers and neighbors now surrounded them.

"Who gave it to you, Dave?"

"Put your ear down here," Hennessy gasped. O'Connor bent nearer. He could feel Hennessy's breath on his face as the answer came, driven up by punctured lungs, but loud enough for O'Connor, one of the cops, and one of Hennessy's neighbors to hear the word "dagos."

The officers rang the nearest doorbell furiously and lifted the wounded man as O'Connor ran to a nearby grocery to telephone for an ambulance. Then he called the Central Station. A *Times-Democrat* reporter installed in the Central Station lobby to catalog incoming drunk and disorderly mugs was dozing when O'Connor's call came in. The room froze.

"The chief's been shot at the corner of Basin and Girod streets!" the police operator yelled a second time before anyone moved.

The *Times-Democrat* reporter dashed outside, intending to run to Girod Street, but he spotted police Captain John Journée standing on the corner and blurted out the news. Journée blew his whistle, trying to stop a patrol wagon galloping away in the wrong direction. The whistle shrieked in the night, but the wagon did not turn, leaving Journée to make his own way to the Gillis house where Hennessy had been taken. When Journée pushed his way into the Gillis family's lamplit parlor, he found the chief on the floor in a creeping pool of blood.

"I've been shot," Hennessy said, as if stating the obvious would somehow bring the situation under control. He sensed his subordinate's horror. "I'm all right, Captain," he said. "Hurry it up. Don't let me stay here long."

Auguste Gillis and her mother fanned Hennessy. "Do you want us to send for your mother?" one of them asked.

"No! For God's sake, don't do that . . . my poor mother," Hennessy groaned. "Can you take off my cuffs?"

Auguste Gillis pulled back his sleeves and removed his cuff studs. Blood poured from the once stiff, white cuffs, now pliant and dark. Miss Gillis untied Hennessy's cravat, handed it to her mother, and gently pulled the starched collar from beneath his neck, careful not to disturb his head. One of the men removed the chief's muddy shoes.

"I feel a little better now," Hennessy said, trying to hide his agony. He asked his neighbor Mike Healy to take his watch and chain.

Two men appeared over the wounded chief and wrapped him in a heavy blanket. He closed his eyes as they hurried him outside to the waiting ambulance, past neighbors and policemen rushing into the neighborhood.

When he opened his eyes again, he was in the operating amphitheater of

Charity Hospital. Slowly he propped himself up on his elbow, and doctors stepped forward to restrain him. Hennessy waved them away with his other hand. "Someone help me take off this coat, please." Interns removed his coat, and he sank back with a sigh.

House surgeon J. D. Bloom entered with two student physicians. "Doctors, how are you?" Hennessy breathed politely.

"Fine, Chief," Dr. Bloom answered with a professional smile. Hennessy's bloodstained shirt and undershirt were cut away. The doctors left a thin, coral necklace with a gold clasp around the chief's neck.

Bloom began to squeeze clotted blood from the dark wounds in Hennessy's left side to examine the damage. The surgeon had seen more appalling wounds, but was not encouraged by what he found. A bullet had passed through both lungs. Two others struck near Hennessy's heart, but had not penetrated deeply enough to be dangerous; one had merely pushed his handkerchief out of his breast pocket. Another slug had torn the left side of his abdomen from behind to leave a long, bleeding rip.

"Does your stomach hurt much?" Bloom asked.

"No, sir," Hennessy said. "Not much, only a little. You know, I had my hand at my side when they shot me."

The chief's burly friend Tom Anderson burst past the doctors and grasped his hand. "This is terrible. How are you?"

"Hello, Tom. I'm all right, I ain't going to die . . . all I care about is my poor old mother."

The doctors told Anderson to step back. The bruises and flesh wounds that covered Hennessy's trunk and arms caused Dr. Bloom to suspect buckshot.

"Yes, they did it with shotguns . . . it's hard to breathe."

Bloom put his head to Hennessy's heart and listened.

"There are in reality six wounds," the surgeon told reporters later as interns behind him continued to wash away blood. "Only the one through the lungs is dangerous. It is too near the heart sack, or pericardium, for us to remove the bullet at this time. There is also a bullet lodged in the bone of the right leg, below the knee. Another penetrated the elbow joint of the left arm. The other wounds entered the flesh, but did not penetrate."

Police Sergeant Richard Walsh arrived from the scene of the shooting, where he and Captain Journée were commanding a search party. Walsh pulled Bloom aside. "Can I speak with the chief?"

"It wouldn't be advisable," Bloom answered. He wished the interns would finish, so that the wounded man could be removed from the amphitheater, out of an accumulating circus of policemen, city officials, and reporters. It had become impossible to keep them out. Bloom relented, but warned the persistent Walsh to be brief.

Walsh leaned toward the chief and whispered something.

"The dagos shot me," Hennessy said aloud. Walsh whispered again. "The dagos shot me," Hennessy repeated.

"Do you know who did it?" Walsh asked.

Hennessy shook his head from side to side and closed his eyes.

"Don't you know?"

The chief moved his head, breathing heavily.

When Hennessy opened his eyes again, Bloom was taking his pulse. Staring men surrounded them, breaking the silence with whispers. Hennessy knew the look; they thought they were watching a dying man.

"I'm all right," he announced. "I don't feel much pain, and I know I'm going to live. I can tell you that."

He turned his head toward the door as Mayor Shakspeare entered with members of the police board. They spoke with the doctors for a moment before coming to the operating table.

"How do, Your Honor," Hennessy said, taking Shakspeare's handshake. The chief saw his friend William Beanham, a police board commissioner, who asked how he felt.

"God is good," Hennessy exhaled. "Thank God I'm all right."

The big-cheeked Beanham, a nervous, curly-haired man with wild arching brows, said, "Dave, it does not look good. I've sent for your mother. Is there anything you want to tell us?"

"Captain, I'm not going to die," Hennessy said firmly. "I'm going to get over this."

"I am certain you will," Beanham lied. "We simply want to bring the men who did this to justice."

"Those people can't kill me. God is good and I will get well . . . Captain, I want some milk."

Beanham shook his head, mindful of the wound in Hennessy's abdomen. "I'd do it with the greatest pleasure, but the doctors say it would not be good for you to have any right now."

"Is that orders?" Hennessy asked. "If it is, I won't take any . . . can you give me some water?"

"No, Dave, for the same reason I can't give you any milk. I can give you some cracked ice," Beanham offered.

As Hennessy worked the cold flakes around his dry mouth, he said, "There is some money in my pants pocket. Take care of it."

Beanham reached into the chief's trousers. "No," Hennessy instructed calmly. "In the left pocket, the left one."

Beanham removed a neat roll of bills as two interns began to wrap the chief's torso in medicated cotton bandages.

At 12:45 a.m. Father O'Neill arrived with two Sisters of Charity. Bloom cleared the amphitheater as the priest and sisters knelt by the chief's side to pray. Father O'Neill stood and asked that Hennessy's steel gray socks be removed. The priest kissed the stricken man's feet, anointed him, administered the last rites, and departed.

Hennessy's mother tried to compose herself as she waited with friends in the hospital library. When Anderson led her into the amphitheater, she calmly put her arms around her son's neck and kissed him repeatedly.

"Don't get excited, Mother," Hennessy said heavily.

"I'm not, my boy."

"Mother," Hennessy said, "Now go home and keep quiet. I'll be with you soon."

As his mother left the room, Hennessy spoke as if from a great distance. "It's for her alone I'm troubled. For myself I don't give a thought. It's she who will suffer if I'm lost."

"Chief, we are going to move you upstairs now."

When Hennessy was settled in a room on the second floor of the hospital, Judge David Hollander, assistant recorder, appeared with his notebook. Hennessy recognized Hollander and that book—the recorder was there to take a declaration about the shooting. The chief knew that such statements were the last weapon of the dying.

"Chief, your mother has just left," Hollander said softly. "You know who I am and my capacity. Do you wish to make a declaration?"

"No, I don't think I am that bad off. Oh yes, I am going to be all right."

Hollander stepped back. The doctors prepared a needle, and Hennessy's mind slipped into opiated warmth.

Doctors examined Hennessy throughout the night, and when questioned about his condition, he answered coherently each time. At 2:30 a.m. the doctors told reporters that the chief's condition was very dangerous, but not necessarily fatal. Newspapermen began to leave for the night, wending their way through a corridor filled with police officials and friends. By 4:00 a.m. Hennessy's laborious breathing was steady, and he seemed to be resting peacefully. At least that is what the remaining newsmen were told.

Beanham did not like the way the way his friend's face looked. At six o'clock he sent for the doctors. An hour later they told him he was right. Beanham sent policemen for Mrs. Hennessy, the mayor, and Recorder Hollander. "Dave, I do not think you will live," Beanham whispered. "Do you have anything to say?"

"No. I am not going to die."

Mrs. Hennessy had never wanted to leave the hospital in the first place and was having a bad time withholding her grief. When she bent to kiss her son, he opened his eyes. "Why do you come, Mother? It's no use for you to be here. I'm all right now. You mustn't fret. Just go home and stay there. I'm going to get well, and I'll be there after a while."

Mrs. Hennessy wanted to believe her son. She had a confusing impulse to show her faith by walking out of the hospital, but the reality of the situation rooted her tired body in the antiseptic little room. Tears slipped from her eyes.

Beanham broke the spell. "If you have any family matters to discuss . . ."

Mrs. Hennessy understood and began to ask her son about his affairs. He answered with a clear voice, detailing each of his investments and the location of all of his personal effects and property. When he finished, Margaret Hennessy let her son fall asleep with a smile on his face. She wept, smoothing his hair. "God be merciful," she said. "I lose in you, Davey, a good boy. I thought I would be the first to go, but they have taken you from me."

As the rain clouds outside lightened in the morning sky, the doctors allowed Hennessy's friends to join his mother. They tried to comfort her as the mayor, Hennessy's loyal young driver, and ten police officers stood by. The members of the police board the chief had met with just a few hours before crowded silently around the bed, holding their hats.

"I'm all right," Dave Hennessy said again and again.

At eleven minutes past nine, a wail destroyed the calm of the hospital corridor. Recorder Hollander arrived a few moments later, realizing instantly that he never should have left.

City shops opened under a dreary sky. Wagons began to roll in earnest through the cold, muddy streets. Talk of the attempted murder of Chief Hennessy was everywhere. People awaiting the latest news from the hospital crowded street corners outside the Central Station. Inside, Journée called his fellow captains into the chief's office. Tears streamed down his face as he read:

> *D. C. Hennessy, Superintendent of Police, expired at 9:00 a.m. this morning from wounds received last night. Capt. Journée has assumed command of the police force.*
>
> *G. W. Vandervoort, Sec'y*

Journée handed the message to the police operator. "Send it to all stations."

When New Orleanians buried their chief of police, they shared in the biggest funeral in the city since the death of Confederate President Jefferson Davis.

Tales of Hennessy's murder began to take form even as his coffin rolled to the cemetery. He was described as the orphaned son of a brave Union army officer turned policeman who had been murdered while serving at a courthouse. Young Hennessy followed his father's footsteps into the ranks of the New Orleans Police where he earned a spotless reputation and the undying enmity of Sicilian criminals for capturing the fugitive leader of a previously unknown organization called the Mafia, which was trying to introduce the concept of revenge murder to a peaceful and law-abiding American city.

His experience with the capture of the Sicilian bandit made Hennessy a natural choice to later keep public order by mediating a dispute between two families of immigrant stevedores. When he tried to prosecute one faction for its misdeeds, he was targeted, placed in the murderers' gunsights by a running boy who announced the chief's approach with a "Mafia whistle," and killed. The plotters—all foreign-born Italians—were captured and tried. Thanks to a bribed jury, however, they were not convicted, even though one of the suspects confessed. Justice arrived in the form of a regrettable but popular uprising, the public lynching of the accused murderers, which restored order and banished the Mafia from New Orleans forever.

This was the enduring tale of the Hennessy killing for nearly a century. As later generations of historians began to discover it, however, the incident took a different shape. In these later incarnations, Hennessy was variously a murderer, extortionist, or partner in a French Quarter brothel, following in the footsteps of corrupt police commanders. According to some versions, the men accused of his murder were all law-abiding Italians or Italian Americans, the hapless victims of conspiracies to expel them from both the shipping docks and the voting rolls, with New Orleans's city fathers, police, commercial elite, newspapers, and prison guards unanimously colluding to slaughter innocents and then whitewash the crime.

What was the real story?

From deadly details to the greater panorama of the bloodiest civics lesson in Louisiana's history, the truth would long depend upon who was telling the tale.

☽

THE
CRESCENT CITY
LYNCHINGS

PART I:
VENDETTAS

One

A SOLID LAD

THE IRISH TEASE THEMSELVES THAT A GOOD BOY'S GOT MUCH
in common with the Savior: he lives at home until he's thirty, he goes into his
father's profession, and his mother thinks he's the Son of God. That's the solid
Irish lad. Wags could have added that the Almighty chose to erase any doubts
in Hennessy's case by making him police superintendent as well.

Young David Hennessy might never have become chief if it hadn't been
for his father, David Hennessy Sr., although the son's career was decided neither by privilege nor by a wise guiding hand. The elder David Hennessy had
been a different sort of cop.

Like their immigrant countrymen in the North, many of the Irish of New
Orleans saw the Civil War as an opportunity. They had been harassed throughout the 1850s, when American-born members of secret "Know-Nothing" societies preached that arriving Irish Catholics were a dirty, quarrelsome, and
inferior race, hell-bent on enthroning the pope in the White House. Memo-
ries of Know-Nothing beatings of the New Orleans Irish were fresh when the
first cannonballs exploded against Fort Sumter. After a decade of being threatened, murdered, and legislated out of much participation in American society
beyond manual labor, many Irish immigrants in the South and the North were
glad for a chance to prove their patriotism when recruiting drums rolled.

Confederate New Orleans Irish regiments were fighting in Virginia when
their city fell in 1862. The Union army of occupation raised its own local regiments, both black and white. David Hennessy Sr. threw in with the Union
and the party of Lincoln.

Union soldiers in the same position as Hennessy quickly realized what an
uncomfortable choice they had made. They were on the winning side, but for all
their bravery, their hometown considered them neither loyal nor likable. New

Orleanians who sided with the Confederacy and suffered under the occupation were not about to reward an immigrant soldier for saving the Union. Old shame and insecurities returned, sometimes assuming a bitter, dangerous mask. Some of the pro-Union Irish left town. Others like Hennessy joined the Metropolitan Police, as the force was then called, whose power was delegated by state authorities allied with the federal government, not by the city. A job serving as a "special officer" with the Metropolitans was political in nature, based upon outspoken loyalty to the Union and an absence of service to the Confederacy. Republican politics made you a "special" like Dave Hennessy Sr. Brawn helped keep you alive.

A year after the war ended, Officer Hennessy was drinking in a bar with fellow specials when a fight broke out. Rumors said that the specials jumped a man named Fred Gruber when he cursed one of the cops for being an Irishman. Gruber was stabbed to death. When the case came to trial, it was established that Hennessy and the others were present during the ruckus, but no proof was offered that they took part. All the specials were acquitted.

The people of New Orleans seldom respected their policemen, who were too often appointed and used as muscle by whatever political party was in power, even before the war. Reconstruction politics turned this popular mistrust into outright hatred, but Hennessy remained a Republican, despite his crude outspoken contempt for black citizens being elected into Louisiana's government for the first time with the party's backing. His reputation as a bully and a hard-drinking loudmouth worsened after the Gruber killing. At midnight on Christmas Eve of 1868, he smelled smoke and rushed his family into the street. An arsonist had tried to incinerate them all.

"The Eighth District Court" was a St. Ann Street bar and coffeehouse, frequented by lawyers and clerks who worked in the real Seventh District Courthouse nearby. One February afternoon in 1869, the elder Hennessy stepped into the bar with a character named Arthur Guerin. This was an odd couple. Hennessy had a reputation as an overbearing drunk, but Guerin, a former cop dismissed from the force in the prewar years for violent behavior, cut a much darker figure. In 1853 Guerin killed a man in the Louisiana Ball Room. In 1854 he killed an Indian known as Red Warrior in the French Market, another man in election-day violence between the Irish and Know-Nothings, and a third at the fruit market. Two years later he killed a Greek sailor. In 1860 he shot to death a man named Fanning, and in 1868 he killed yet another man, a black worker in the French Market. These murders were allowed or sanctioned because of chaos in the courts, complained those who called Guerin an insane thug. All alleged but never proven, said his friends and family, although even Guerin's pals steered clear when his "spells" overcame him.

Every dead man who had not known Guerin well enough to keep his distance was a natural target of the "Native American" cause of the Know-Nothings. Why in the world did a son of Erin like Hennessy invite this crazy bastard to take a drink?

In the logic of courts and newspapers, the answer was simple. Hennessy and Guerin had been feuding for some time and pulled pistols on each other two months earlier in a different coffeehouse. Hennessy could have killed Guerin easily then, but customers stopped the fight. On this winter Saturday, however, they seemed friendly. They met on a street corner in the French Quarter and discussed their differences, then went into the Eighth District Court together for a drink. As the afternoon wore on and the drinks flowed, Hennessy grew louder. When Guerin left the bar to join friends at a lunch table, Hennessy roughly buttonholed a stranger, a court officer named Freeman.

"Are you an Irishman or an Englishman?" Hennessy demanded, leaning hard into Freeman's face.

"I was born across the water," Freeman replied. Hennessy asked if Freeman was Guerin's friend. No, answered Freeman, cautiously adding that he hoped he was a friend to all men.

"You ought to know me," Hennessy instructed. "Everybody in town here ought to know me, for I'm accused of killing Fred Gruber." Hennessy pointed a finger at Guerin. "If that man had done it, nothing much would be said about it. I'm as good an Irishman as any man ever knew." Hennessy threw out his chest and glared at Guerin. "I am an Irishman, and I don't care a damn for any man!"

Guerin rose and came to the bar. He suggested yet another drink. The barman poured, then placed the whiskey and brandy bottles back on his shelf, turning just in time to see Guerin tranquilly fire three bullets into Hennessy's chest.

"Oh my God, what did you do that for?" Hennessy gasped as his legs buckled. He was dead before his face hit the floor.

When the coroner came, Hennessy's heavy body was lugged into the courtyard for an autopsy. He was laid out on an unhinged door and hacked apart, baring tubercular lungs and a scarred liver for inspection by the coroner and bar patrons.

Guerin, whose pistol was found under the bar safe, was quickly arrested. Police had confiscated the gun three months earlier when he tried to kill the barkeeper of the Crescent Billiard Saloon. They had noted the serial number, but clearly did not hang onto the gun long enough.

Guerin went free two weeks later, as he had so many times before. Much was made of Hennessy's reputation as a bully at the homicide hearing. Some witnesses said Hennessy had made no threatening move, although one claimed Hennessy was fumbling in his trouser pockets when the shots rang out. As usual, he was carrying two derringers, a revolver, and a sword cane. His history of trouble with Guerin, his threatening manner, and his reach into a pocket were enough to produce a verdict of justifiable homicide.

Hennessy would lend you the shirt from his back if he owned only two in the world, said a brother officer following the funeral cortege. Such testimony was small comfort to Margaret Hennessy and her boy, whom the *New Orleans Crescent* described as a bright little lad of twelve. Police pensions for officers killed outside the line of duty did not exist, and before the year was over, mother and son had nothing left between them and the city poorhouse. Mrs. Hennessy threw herself on the mercy of General Algernon S. Badger, superintendent of the Metropolitan Police. When Badger agreed to hire the boy as a messenger, Hennessy's studies at the local Jesuit school ended, and his life with the New Orleans Police began.

☽

Two

THE MAN FROM SICILY

WINTER SUNSHINE PEELED THE MORNING CHILL FROM railway coaches as the locomotive chugged into the hills of western Sicily. Twenty-two-year-old John Forester Rose of the prosperous firm of Gardner, Rose & Co. felt the train climb. The strapping Rose was returning to the sulfur mine he managed for his family at Lercara, twenty miles into the *campagna* south of Palermo. The operation was a minor concern, one of dozens owned by English entrepreneurs harvesting fortunes from the island's groves and mines.

Two horsedrawn carriages were available to take Rose and his elder brother George to Lercara in the hills above the station, but Forester's horse and groom were waiting when he arrived. Wishing to avoid a long ride in a crowded omnibus, Forester Rose told his brother he would meet him in town and set off up the steep hill, accompanied by the groom and a clerk. Along the way, two men appeared on the hillside path, dressed like Sicilian country gentlemen and riding fine horses. The men saluted Rose and asked if he was traveling to Lercara. Yes, answered Rose. Would he mind a little company on the climb? Not at all, replied Rose with his best British manners.

Good, said one of the Sicilians, a little man with a bushy mustache, short beard, and puckish grin. Rose and his employees continued up the rough track with the Sicilian gentlemen a short distance behind them.

They had not gone far when two men stepped into the middle of the mountain trail, holding several horses by the reins. Rose's clerk sensed trouble when the two men on foot demanded the names of the Rose party. The clerk swiftly gave a false name. The young mine manager, however, was not as wise. The clerk tried to give his employer an alias, but Rose interrupted with his real name.

Rose's bridle was seized, and he was ordered off his horse. The two Sicilian gentlemen riders trotted up from behind with drawn weapons. The little grinning man suggested that Rose do as he was told. Then no one would be hurt.

Rose knew in an instant that he was the world's greatest idiot.

Brigands from the hills had been kidnapping wealthy Sicilian landowners for ransom. There had been murders when dealmaking went sour. A few threats were received by non-Sicilians like the Roses, but the threats were never taken seriously by the English, whose decades of doing business on the island had given them enough power to deal their way out of such situations privately. No foreigners had ever been kidnapped or "sequestered," as the Sicilians called it. Rose mounted one of the brigand's horses with the unpleasant realization that he was the first.

As he was led away, Rose noticed two carriages on the main road below, straining up the hill. His brother would be in one of them. Rose suddenly launched himself backward over the horse's rump. He began to run as fast as he could, stumbling down the rocky hillside as bullets buzzed over his head.

Rose fell into the Lercara road and hailed the lead carriage, winded but relieved as George Rose and the other passengers spilled out to surround the breathless young Englishman. As he gasped what had happened on the trail above, horses rounded the bend, galloping into the passengers and scattering them about the cramped roadway.

"I am Leone!" bellowed the little man, no longer grinning. His notorious name removed any thoughts the stampeded passengers had of defending themselves. Leone nonchalantly wiggled the double barrels of a breechloader at Rose and chastised him for leaving without saying good-bye. Back on the horse, the brigand ordered.

Rose hoped someone in the crowd might pull a gun to defend him. No one moved. Rose did not dare to catch his brother's eye.

"You must not blame us," Leone apologized with mock courtesy. "You must blame the government, which for so many years has been trying to catch us or to kill us."

It was painfully clear to Rose that no one was going to help him. For the safety of his brother, whose identity no one had betrayed, and out of sheer helplessness, Rose remounted and allowed himself to be led away.

Leone and his captive soon rejoined the groom, the clerk, and the other brigands. Together they rode toward Palermo, taking one of the high mountain roads. At the edge of the Valley Fiume Torto, they stopped.

Leone ordered Rose's employees to go back. If the army came into the mountains, he warned, things might go badly for the Englishman. Rose would fare very well otherwise, if the ransom was paid. Ah yes, ransom would be demanded.

The clerk and the groom rode away as fast as their horses would take them. When they felt safe, they turned and looked back. In the distance they could see their boss and Leone's band descend into the deep valley. They did not see Leone and his men turn out of the valley later and head high into the desolate Sicilian hills, where *carabinieri* had never been able to find them.

The British of Palermo were furious over the Rose kidnapping. It was bad enough that one of their own, the son of one of the most respected families on the island, had been snatched. The fact that no one had been manly enough to lift a finger in his defense bolstered their feeling that Sicilians refused to interfere in matters which did not concern them, no matter how dire the situation. The Italian government appeared reluctant to send troops after the bandits or to prosecute them when they were caught. The local populace, which seemed to admire bandits as folk heroes, became even more loathsome to the British.

News of the affair spread quickly to England. Angry words flashed between London and Rome. The boiling English knew the solution to the problem. Find the bandits and shoot them. Hang them or send them to the guillotine. Send them to the galleys for life. A pity Sicily was not part of the Empire. A regiment of Highlanders would sort things out quickly enough. It was shameful to do nothing but pay Rose's ransom and wait.

Yet that is exactly what happened. Money changed hands. An understanding was reached.

Two weeks after John Forester Rose vanished into the mountains of Sicily in the winter of 1876, the mine manager was released unharmed by the bandit Leone, who sent the young English bachelor on his way with a chummy farewell and a train ticket home.

Sitting in his office on a summer day in 1881, Thomas N. Boylan, chief of the New Orleans Police, studied the photograph of a short, thick-faced man with a mustache and a slight indentation between the eyebrows. The chief returned the photograph to his visitor, an Italian diplomat. Speaking in French, Boylan said that he did not recognize the man in the picture, but that he could have officers show the portrait around the Italian community and make some inquiries.

That was not necessary, the diplomat replied, but it would be helpful if the chief could find the photographer who took the image; discreetly, of course. Boylan promised to have one of his men look into it.

With relative ease, the picture was traced to a studio near the French Market, and the chief secretly contacted the Italian consulate. Pleased with the intelligence, Boylan would later say, the Italian diplomat returned the favor by illuminating his mysterious inquiry.

The man in the picture, explained the diplomat, was Giuseppe Esposito, a former brigand chieftain. He was in New Orleans, and the Italian government wanted him. Five years before he had helped to kidnap the Reverend John Forester Rose, an English clergyman traveling in Sicily. The diplomat said that Rev. Rose was forced to write a ransom letter to his wife and family in England, demanding that they send thousands of pounds to secure his release. To make sure there was no mistake over the kidnappers' intentions, one of the Reverend's ears was mailed with the letter.

Rose's family had no such sums and appealed to the English government for help. The English appealed in turn to the Italian government, which, the diplomat was sorry to say, could not be of effective assistance. Before the money could be found, the brigands grew impatient. They cut off the Reverend's other ear and mailed it to his poor wife! The British were so outraged that the Italian government was compelled to send troops into the Sicilian mountains. The brigands, who were led by a bandit named Leone, were destroyed, and this man Esposito, the diplomat said pointing to the portrait, was captured. Esposito was brought to trial, but before justice could be dispensed, he escaped in a most sensational manner to America, to New Orleans.

Boylan studied the picture. A fugitive vicious enough to chop off a helpless clergyman's ears certainly merited the attention of the New Orleans Police. Boylan would be glad to find the man and shadow him, which pleased the diplomat. The consulate, he said, would make a copy of the photo from the plate and send it to Italy for confirmation of Esposito's identity. Until then, the diplomat asked Boylan to keep the matter a secret.

That was no problem, Boylan assured the diplomat, for only the detective who retrieved the photographic plate knew anything about the inquiry. Meanwhile, Boylan had a trustworthy young fellow on the force who could watch the man in the portrait.

The man Boylan had in mind for this Italian business was Dave Hennessy, now a twenty-four-year-old veteran detective. Hennessy had grown from a skinny, delicate boy into a muscular young man who was recklessly headstrong about the law. While in his teens, the young messenger hired by General Badger after his father's death had literally collared two adult thieves and dragged them to the nearest station house. Hennessy's politeness and industry made him one of Superintendent Badger's favorites. When Badger left the police, he dismissed his entire force except for the eighteen-year-old Hennessy and one other veteran officer, so that the incoming chief would be free to make his own appointments. Hennessy was made a detective with patrolman's pay, but his aptitude for analyzing and remembering physical peculiarities quickly earned him a promotion to full detective. The promotion meant a lot to young Dave Hennessy. The force was his teacher, his family, and his savior. He had grown up in it. It had rescued him and his mother from the poorhouse, and he was repaying the favor with a devotion no one else but his mother would enjoy.

There was also a corporeal family tie to the force in Dave's partner and older cousin, Mike Hennessy. Together they worked on murder cases, tracked waterfront firebugs, and did anything else requiring more subtlety than the billy clubs that settled many police problems. Mike, like Dave, was named for his father. The two cousins were as loyal to each other as brothers, but the pair were hardly twins. Dave was much taller than his cousin. Little Mike Hennessy was shrewd and brave, but he could turn into a bulldog after a few drinks. As a cop, Mike resembled his dead uncle, while his sober cousin with the big fists, clever Dave, at least knew how to keep his mouth shut. Chief Boylan told Dave Hennessy to keep an eye on the man he had been told was the Sicilian bandit, Giuseppe Esposito.

In early July of 1881, soon after these secret meetings, a private detective from New York named James Mooney sauntered into the Italian consulate in New Orleans. When he was admitted to see the consul, Mooney threw a pair of steel handcuffs on the desk and coolly announced that he had come to pick up Esposito.

The consul was insulted and astonished by Mooney's brash behavior. He had notified his superiors in New York that he was sure Esposito was in New Orleans, but he was not in a position to deliver the brigand himself, particularly to a lout like Mooney. If the detective wanted to make an arrest of some sort, advised the consul, perhaps he ought to call upon the chief of police.

Mooney wasted no time. He called on Chief Boylan, who directed him to the U.S. Marshal's Office. The marshal ruled that since the papers that Mooney called arrest warrants were improperly issued, they were not official documents. Mooney returned to Boylan, who suggested a visit to the U.S. Attorney in New Orleans. Mooney tried this, but was told that only the marshal could judge the legitimacy of the warrants. The proprietor of Mooney's Detective & Patrol Agency was forced to cool his heels as his blood pressure rose.

Dave Hennessy soon appeared in Boylan's office and asked the chief's permission to help Mooney arrest the Sicilian they had been following.

Mooney was in a peculiar position, Boylan replied, for Mooney's warrants were informal to the point of being useless. If the suspect was picked up and managed to challenge those warrants, everything could fall apart. The Italian consulate was sure that Esposito had powerful friends who could secure his release on a writ of habeas corpus, giving him just enough time to disappear. Even if he was held long enough to get him on a train, an attempt might be made to spring him at one of the stops on the way north. The only unassailable route to New York was by sea.

That could be managed, Hennessy observed. If Esposito was allowed to escape the law, it would be a tragedy.

Chief Boylan agreed. He was certain they were watching the right man and had no objections to Mike and Dave making an arrest. The chief wanted it understood, however, that whatever the Hennessys did would be entirely their responsibility. City authorities would not stand behind them if anything went wrong.

Dave Hennessy thanked his boss and went looking for his fiery little cousin and the New York detective.

Night was arriving when the man from Sicily reached the peaceful flagstone plaza outside St. Louis Cathedral in the French Quarter. White pools of sun evaporated from the tiles of the old Spanish Cabildo, dissolving in the ascending twilight. The Sicilian crossed the square, past the statue of American General Andrew Jackson waving his hat from atop a blind, rearing steed. The day's heat still warmed the foliage, teasing orange scents through the iron fence.

The Sicilian felt the two men on him. They spoke as their hands tightened on his arms, but he did not understand as he struggled to pull free. Two more men stepped in to surround him. He was hustled into a waiting carriage that bucked as the four Americans wedged tightly around him, drawing the curtain to cut off the view from the streets. The heat in the dark cab was stifling. The silent Americans had guns.

When they stopped, the Sicilian was hurried into a police station. Night passed and he saw no one but his guards. When morning came, two of the men who had taken him from the street came to his cell. Again he was pushed into a dark carriage that dashed away with drawn blinds. When the door finally bobbed open, his heart sank. The two Americans grabbed him by the coat and yanked him down the gangplank onto a steamship. By noon he was in the Gulf of Mexico.

The capture of a genuine Italian brigand in the heart of New Orleans was a welcome melodrama for the city's newspapers. The captured fugitive was Esposito, a henchman of the famed Sicilian bandit Leone who had cut the ears off an English cleric. Esposito had been captured in Jackson Square and hustled into the Second Precinct Police Station, where he spent the night incommunicado so that news of his capture would not reach those who might attempt a violent rescue. With the utmost secrecy, he was put aboard a steamer at dawn and was now on his way to New York, where the Italian government would try to secure his extradition on charges of murder and kidnapping.

Reporters were told that the operation was flawless work, a masterpiece of cooperation between New Orleans Police detectives and the Italian government. Acting on a tip sent to Washington by detectives Dave and Mike Hennessy, U.S. marshals had come to the city with arrest and extradition warrants, which the U.S. Circuit Court and the U.S. district attorney had ruled to be in perfect order. With the help of the Hennessys, who had shadowed the fugitive and obtained a drawing and photograph resulting in the bandit's positive identification, Esposito was taken into custody and spirited away on the steamer *City of New Orleans*.

The prisoner was said to have been a fruit and vegetable dealer, a short man with a full, black beard, a "low forehead," and "a small mark between the eyes at the apex of the nose." He was "popular" among the Italians of the French Quarter for his audacity: in plain sight of everyone, he bought an oyster lugger and flew a flag on it emblazoned "Leone," the name of his late chief, who was alleged to have been killed in Algeria. The Italians of the Quarter were said to be agitated over the clever way Esposito had been removed from the city. They believed, added the papers, that he had been betrayed by one of his own countrymen.

Mooney got no credit in the New Orleans press for the arrest. There was a little editorial grumbling about the man's rights being violated. Even in a city used to exotic crimes, however, the Esposito affair lit up a full column, an amount of space reserved for crimes committed only by the wealthy or the unspeakable. The facts of the drama seemed hideously clear to the press, especially in light of the fugitive's past. Who could lament the loss of a fiend who would slice the ears from a helpless man of the cloth?

There was plenty of talk among the cops. Detractors hoped aloud that Chief Boylan and the Hennessys got a good pile of change for jerking that New York detective around: after all, a big reward was rumored to be involved and that New York dick was loaded with cash, just waiting to throw it at anyone who'd help him put the Sicilian on the boat. Nonsense, said David Hennessy's friends. Hennessy was saying he did the job for free. He's that sort of fellow, his friends agreed.

Cops weren't the only ones talking about the arrest.

In the French Market, for all the world to hear, Tony Labruzzo screamed curses in the face of lemon dealer Gaetano Ardotta, accusing him of the *infamia* of delivering the famous Sicilian prisoner to the police. Labruzzo yelled his accusations from behind a large knife and an even bigger pistol.

When Ardotta grabbed the oysterman's knife hand, Labruzzo swung, smashing Ardotta in the face with his pistol. The bleeding Ardotta broke free, ran home, and returned to the market with a gun even more enormous than the piece with which Labruzzo had pistol-whipped him. By then, officers from the Harbor Precinct had arrived to investigate the first tussle. The waterfront cops confiscated a large-bore dueling pistol and a Remington cavalry revolver before herding the two combatants to the station. The next morning, the pair was charged with disturbing the peace, and they were each placed under a $1,000 peace bond, then released. They were still furious. "I'll kill that man anyhow," Labruzzo spat as he left court.

The increasing ruckus prompted Ben Onorato, one of the city's prominent Italians and a respected Royal Street auctioneer, to call a public meeting. Onorato was a well-educated man with a northern Italian impatience and disdain for Sicilians. The situation is getting desperate, he thought as he hurried to the meeting. Perhaps the community could organize to stop all of this nonsense.

Onorato did not like the look of the assembly when he arrived at Zimmerman's Coliseum Saloon on Bienville. Too few of the men he wanted to see and too many toughs were in the hall, including Tony Labruzzo. Onorato invented an excuse at the podium and rescheduled the meeting. As the gathering broke up, he stopped Labruzzo and politely but firmly told the lanky oysterman that it would be best for everyone if he and his friends were not present when the meeting reconvened.

Onorato was tired of impudent trash causing trouble, making every Italian in the city look bad. He got Labruzzo's promise not to attend the next gathering.

That Friday, Onorato returned to Zimmerman's for the rescheduled meeting and immediately spotted Tony Labruzzo at the bar. Onorato stiffly asked what had become of their understanding.

Labruzzo assured the auctioneer that he was just making sure none of his friends attended the meeting.

"In that case, I have no more to say," Onorato replied. "The saloon and the street are indeed free to all." As Onorato walked upstairs, Labruzzo drained his drink and went outside.

Old man Zimmerman's daughter watched the Sicilian cross the street to the corner of Exchange Place. She sat outside, fanning herself in a chair by the gutter, trying to cool off while the sour notes of an organ grinder struggled down the block. The grinder was probably an Italian, she thought, like the men gathering at her bar. She vaguely remembered the one crossing to the corner, Labruzzo, the one with the little beard. She could not hear him, but watched him speak and gesture to new arrivals heading for her saloon. Miss Zimmerman thought he was giving them directions.

A peddler named Adolph Wieland was also walking toward Zimmerman's saloon when he saw two shapes move in the twilight shadows of Exchange Place. Suddenly the horrified Wieland saw one of the shapes stoop forward to steady a shotgun across the iron fence.

Hot buckshot tore through Tony Labruzzo before continuing over Miss Zimmerman's head to blow in the saloon windows, shattering bottles behind the bar. Labruzzo fell, riddled and bleeding.

In the shadows across the street, the taller of the two armed men rose and fired a pistol at his kneeling companion with the shotgun, then fled as men poured down the Coliseum Hall saloon stairs into Exchange Place.

A hysterical Italian ran up with a small sawed-off shotgun in his hand. A private watchman snatched the gun away and arrested him. While waiting for the ambulance, the watchman also detained the peddler Wieland and the organ grinder.

Gaetano Ardotta, the kneeling man shot by his companion across the street from the Coliseum, lay behind the iron railing, bleeding from a back wound. He was taken to the hospital, where he asked for saloon owner Tony Matranga. Labruzzo's corpse was taken to the nearest police station and laid out on the floor. Shrieks rang through the building as his relatives and friends viewed the bloody body, some kneeling beside Labruzzo, hissing under their breath. Cops and newspapermen muttered among themselves that this was far from over.

The police produced a motley group of suspects. The tall man who shot Ardotta in the back was identified as Vincent Vasso, who was carrying a loaded pistol with one fired chamber when arrested. The Italian who rushed forward with the sawed-off shotgun turned out to be a tipsy shoemaker who was merely trying to help by turning in a weapon he had found. He was placed under a $1,500 bond, an unreachable sum for him. Typically for a city where things were seldom as they appeared, the organ grinder was not an Italian at all, but a down-on-his-luck American steamboatman trying to lose himself under a false name. Wieland was the state's only eyewitness. Two weeks after the shooting, authorities suspected the peddler of wanting to leave town. He was placed under a $500 bond and locked in the rank parish prison for "safe-keeping," the law's custom of detaining material witnesses until trial, sometimes for months—the very same prison where Vasso and Ardotta were being held without bail for murder.

The Labruzzo killing was the only public violence in New Orleans linked to the man accused of being the Sicilian brigand Esposito. In New York, however, the battle over the man's future was just beginning.

When the Sicilian arrived in New York, he faced half a dozen charges filed against him by Coudert Brothers, the Italian government's American law firm, which had dispatched Mooney to New Orleans. The prisoner was arraigned and questioned while an extradition hearing was scheduled. The small bearded man spoke very softly, telling everyone who would listen that he was an uneducated fruit dealer, a native of Messina who had left his poor farm four years earlier to find the better life described in the letters of friends working in America. He was told that a woman claiming to be his wife was seen weeping at the New Orleans dockside. "I've never been married," the prisoner replied. "I wish that they would let me go home," he sighed. Why did he think he was arrested? He said the detectives had made up the case to get a $5,000 reward offered by the Italian government for Esposito's capture.

The prisoner was represented at his extradition hearing by Dr. Lorenzo Ullo and two American judges, William D. Shipman and William G. Choate. Dr. Ullo insisted that his client was not Esposito, but Vincenzo Rebello, an innocent peddler who had been selling fruit in New Orleans for years. Prince Camporeale, the Italian Consulate's Charges d'Affaires, replied with a telegram announcing that *carabinieri* who could identify Esposito were en route from Palermo. The hearing was postponed for three weeks pending their arrival, despite Dr. Ullo's protests that this was too long for an innocent man to wait. Dr. Ullo unsuccessfully demanded that the prisoner be returned to New Orleans, so that witnesses there could testify as to his identity.

Despite the disagreement over whether or not the prisoner was Esposito, everyone could agree that the man in Ludlow Street Jail did not have his story straight in the matter of his wife. An Italian woman was now on her way to New York with a ten-month-old baby in her arms, claiming that he was the father, but the prisoner continued to deny that he was married. When the woman arrived in New York in mid-August, however, the prisoner agreed to see her. Watching reporters described their meeting as warm and affectionate.

When the hearing resumed, court galleries filled with spectators from Little Italy, including many women with babies. They listened as prosecutor Paul Xavier Fuller offered a deposition from Palermo in which five Sicilians, including Esposito's jailer and a vice chancellor of the Italian government, swore that a photograph sent from New York was "extremely like" the Esposito who had escaped two years earlier. Dr. Ullo argued that the document proved nothing.

Meanwhile, the two *carabinieri* from Sicily arrived and pointed out the prisoner among the other inmates of the Ludlow Street Jail. One of the Italian officers knew Esposito as a labor gang foreman known as Randazzo or Randazza and had guarded him at the Palermo barracks. The other officer claimed he had once visited the famous brigand whose criminal exploits had made him a celebrity in the barracks. Both *carabinieri* testified through an interpreter that they were sure the prisoner from New Orleans was Esposito.

When the prosecution closed, the defense called several New Orleans fruit dealers. Joe Provenzano, Tony Pellegrini, and Rocco Geraci testified that they knew the prisoner by the name Vincenzo Costanzo and had first seen him prior to the yellow fever epidemic of 1878, a year and a half before the Italian government's last sighting of Esposito in Sicily. Palermo-born printer Vincenzo Mondini similarly testified that he had seen Esposito tried with twenty less famous brigands in 1878 and that this prisoner only resembled the notorious bandit. Mondini further accused his boss at the newspaper *Il Progresso Italo-Americano* of trying to bribe him to finger the prisoner from New Orleans, but prosecutor Frederick Coudert was ready with a different view of Mondini's accusation. Coudert tried unsuccessfully to get the printer to admit that he was scared of being stabbed to death if he appeared in court and that $200 his boss had offered him was not a bribe, but an offer to help him relocate if he was afraid to stay in New York. Editor Maurice Mauris was called to rebut Mondini's testimony, recalling that the printer had positively identified the prisoner at the U.S. Marshal's office. A clerk and two marshals agreed, adding that Mondini was considered reliable enough to have been considered as a prosecution witness.

When the woman sitting behind the prisoner during Mondini's testimony was called, she gently handed her baby to the prisoner. The child began to bawl. The woman took the baby back and carried it with her to the witness chair. Sarah Castagno had been a washerwoman when she first met the prisoner, three months before the epidemic of '78. He hired her to wash his clothing, but soon he began to court her and they married. The Italian government's lawyers showed no interest in cross-examining the prisoner's wife, but objected when the defense produced affidavits from people in New Orleans, who swore that they had been doing business with Rebello the fruit seller at the same time Esposito was on trial several thousand miles away in Palermo. The entire bundle of affidavits was ruled inadmissible because the persons who made them could not be cross-examined. Before the next witness was called, Commissioner Osborn noted for the record that the prisoner had two scars on his forehead, including one between his eyebrows.

Ullo and Shipman were still trying to get the prisoner transferred to New Orleans for a hearing when summations began. If there was any reasonable doubt about the prisoner's identity, they argued, he should be allowed to return home where he could provide witnesses. As for the extradition itself, all allegations of the prisoner's alleged criminality in Italy should be ruled inadmissible. Arguing for the Italian government, Coudert replied that not one line of evidence had been offered to prove that the man claiming to be Rebello was not Esposito. If the prisoner arrived in America legally before 1878, written records would exist to prove on which day he sailed, the name of the ship, and the hotel or lodging where he stopped upon his arrival. This was a serious case, Coudert emphasized—weren't the kidnapping and mutilation of the Reverend Rose and the testimony of three witnesses in Sicily who had seen Esposito murder another man enough to warrant an extradition?

In the end, Commissioner Osborn decided that the prisoner was Esposito. He acknowledged that there was doubt, but evidence existed of complicity in the Rose kidnapping and no conclusive evidence had been offered to establish the prisoner's true identity.

> There is a great mystery as to who this man is if he is not Giuseppe Esposito, alias Randazzo, because he gave his name when arrested as Rebello, married, and doing business under the name of Costanzo. He has not offered any evidence, through his counsel, why he used these two names. Neither has he offered, in the face of testimony identifying him with Esposito, when he came to this country, what ship he came in, where he landed, and what he has been doing here.

In spite of all the "doubtful features" of the case, Commissioner Osborn declared that it was his conscientious belief that the prisoner was Giuseppe Esposito. The prisoner was put into the custody of U.S. marshals pending an order from the State Department to deliver him to the Italian government. The defense waived the prisoner's right of appeal in the courts, testily declaring that they would appeal directly to the State Department for a reversal.

They never got the chance. Osborn's decision was sent to Washington, DC, on a Saturday night. An extradition order was signed at the State Department and returned to New York on Monday. On Tuesday the Italian Charges d'Affaires handed Coudert a mandate for immediate extradition, along with a dispatch from Rome warning that an organized attempt at rescue would be made. Events in New Orleans and New York made this seem probable to Coudert. The prisoner was handcuffed and swiftly delivered to the two *carabinieri* on Wednesday, and by that afternoon they were steaming toward Sicily.

The deported man's lawyers were outraged. They protested to Secretary of State James G. Blaine that the stealth with which their client had been hustled out of the country had nothing to do with threats of forcible rescue. This was kidnapping, an unlawful seizure made to wreck any chance of an appeal to the State Department. They demanded their client's immediate return.

Coudert Brothers also wrote to Blaine. Their actions and the State Department's extradition papers were entirely in order, especially under the threat of attempted rescue. As to the cruelty of not allowing the prisoner a chance to bid his family goodbye, the jail was not closed to the prisoner's wife. If the prisoner was Esposito, Coudert added dryly, another wife and child were waiting for him in Sicily. Ullo and Shipman had no one to blame but themselves for the backfire of their appeal strategy. "You may be puzzled to decide," Coudert told Blaine, whether the outraged demand for their client's return was "seriously meant or merely thrown out as a sop to a credulous public whose good opinion counsel are eager to obtain."

One week to the day after the deportation, peddler Adolph Wieland told a New Orleans court that Gaetano Ardotta was the man who shot Casimino "Tony" Labruzzo to death in Exchange Alley. Wieland did not recognize Vincent Vasso as the standing man who shot Ardotta, nor did John Kenney, the steamboatman moonlighting as an organ grinder. All he knew was that a man serving time for assault and battery had approached him and said that Ardotta would "do good" for Kenney when he got out.

Vasso was acquitted after a quick trial. Ardotta was found guilty and sentenced to life imprisonment. His lawyers, Lionel Adams and W. L. Evans, appealed the conviction. Ardotta watched silently, understanding only that the English words flying in the courtroom might, with luck, prevent him from swinging a penitentiary sledgehammer until the day he died.

For New Orleans authorities, Ardotta's conviction closed the Labruzzo case. Federal authorities were equally sure that the Esposito extradition had put a foreign criminal into Italian hands where he belonged. A decade would pass and more people would die before anyone again debated whether the two cases were truly that simple.

By that autumn, however, the Esposito affair was nearly forgotten in New Orleans, especially by police, who were scrambling to contain a new vendetta—within their own ranks.

☽

Three

A POLICE MUDDLE

ONE MIDNIGHT BACK IN FEBRUARY 1876, SPECIAL OFFICER Thomas Devereaux ducked a shotgun blast as he unlocked his front door. Luckily for him, the shotgun exploded and was found smoking behind a fence, alongside part of the shooter's hand. A suspect was charged with attempted murder when he checked into a hospital with a wound matching the lump of flesh. Former detective Robert Harris was standing on a street corner a few days later when a man in a light-colored suit put a bullet in the back of his head and strolled away. Devereaux, who was nearby wearing a light-colored suit as he customarily did, was detained. A fully loaded pistol and a spring dirk were found in his pockets, and he was arrested for carrying concealed weapons. Witnesses who saw the Harris killing from a nearby soda fountain recalled the killer's light clothing, but none identified Devereaux.

Like other special officers whose employment arrived or disappeared on political tides, Devereaux soon found himself out of a job. In 1881, however, politics swept him back into the police department thanks to New Orleans city councilmen who were inventing new ways to circumvent and antagonize the new reform-minded mayor, Joseph Shakspeare. One of the council's inventions was a novel position called chief of aids. This administrator would oversee all police detectives, who were called "aids" for their work in aiding the chief's office. Shakspeare's city council enemies chose Devereaux for the job.

Naming Devereaux to command the detectives office did not look like a change for the better to anyone wishing for an improvement in the weak police force's performance. Chief Boylan might not be perfect, but his authority was being reorganized away at a time when many New Orleanians were hoping that the professional, less political trend of Boylan's force would last.

Devereaux's appointment was a sore spot with Boylan, who resented a political hack being handed such a plum.

Boylan had his detractors, but he was usually criticized on ethical grounds, not political or professional ones. A son of Irish immigrants, the balding chief had made police lieutenant by the time the Civil War started, and he served in the Confederate Army as a detective. When the conflict ended, he came home to the force, but turned down an offer to be police chief during Reconstruction. Instead, he and two fellow detectives quit to take a citywide bank security contract. Boylan eventually accepted the post of chief of police in 1877, leaving control of the bank protection agency to his partner, Mike Farrell. When bankers and merchants of the city's powerful Cotton Exchange concluded three years later that Boylan's underfunded city police were not up to the job of protecting freight during a rash of arson cases, the business leaders asked Boylan if he would quit the police and organize a private force to guard the docks. Boylan declined, saying he would not resign a public post for personal gain. He suggested, however, that they talk to his civilian partner, and Farrell's Harbor Protection Police was soon patrolling the riverfront, armed with full police powers granted by the city council. The Farrell agency's client list grew to include ship agents, railroads, businesses, and private residences.

Between them, Boylan and Farrell controlled the lion's share of police work in the city, and their close relationship left them open to conflict-of-interest charges. Whenever the city's police were assailed for being ineffectual, which was often, Boylan was accused of hobbling the force to keep his partnership with Farrell supplied with rich clients concerned about their property. There was never a shortage of crime in New Orleans, but the collusion accusation surfaced whenever anyone had a bone to pick with Boylan. The same charge would one day be leveled at Dave Hennessy as well.

On July 2, 1881, the same day the nation learned that President James A. Garfield had been shot, the power struggle between Boylan and Devereaux spilled into the newspapers and confirmed for the public what every cop and politico in the city already knew. Chief Boylan told the *Daily States* that there was animosity and chaos in the detectives' office and he emphatically denied encouraging the tension between Devereaux and his men. If there were bad apples in the ranks, Boylan suggested that Devereaux use his own power to throw them out.

Devereaux countered that the trouble was caused by two problems, "one public, the other quiet." The "quiet" problem was a spat over the proper use of a jailed informer. Boylan wanted the stool pigeon in the state penitentiary and was criticizing Devereaux's efforts to have the jailbird's sentence commuted. Devereaux huffed that he knew the man was a crook, but wanted to use him on the streets, just as other detectives—including Mike Hennessy—had done for years. More seriously, Devereaux publicly accused Boylan of wanting to keep the detectives department weak to ensure more business for Farrell's Harbor Protection Police. "The more degenerate the police become, the more profitable for the agency," Devereaux charged, adding that certain officers under his command were recipients of "gift cases" and "favored matter."

Much of this was disingenuous wind. Chief Boylan was less than candid in disclaiming responsibility for discord in the detectives' office. His loyal officers did not need to ask his permission to scorn an outsider like Devereaux. As for Devereaux, he seldom got along with fellow officeholders, which had contributed to his bouncing in and out of various municipal jobs before landing in his present position. Even if they were true, his charges of favoritism within the department were hypocritical, considering that his own position was a pure political invention.

Detectives Mike and Dave Hennessy kept mum. Theirs was the most deft side step, for they openly hated Devereaux. The common assumption that Dave Hennessy might become the next chief of police when Boylan decided to step down did little to lessen the tension. Yet it was Mike Hennessy who most despised Devereaux. They had publicly squared off, twice outside polling places and once at a Mardi Gras ball. Chief of Aids Devereaux had recently charged Mike with insubordination, causing the police board to censure the detective. Mayor Shakspeare himself rebuked Mike, although the board added a compliment for Mike's "zealous and efficient" service.

In the end, Devereaux's career began to collapse when he tried to use his position to sink the Hennessys. He charged Mike with drunkenly assaulting a citizen in a house of ill repute on Basin Street, drawing a revolver, using language unbecoming of an officer, and entering a "palace of sin" to behave in a disgraceful manner. Dave faced a less sensational but equally career-killing charge of being absent from his post. The problem with Devereaux's charges was that no one seemed to have witnessed the offenses, and Devereaux did not claim to have actually seen Mike's alleged debauchery. When Devereaux arrived for the inquiry before the Police Board of Commissioners alone, he said his witnesses had all decided to stay at home because they were not legally bound to appear. Someone had tampered with them, he said.

Mike Hennessy was better prepared. He submitted a note from the man he had allegedly assaulted, who declared that he and Mike were personal friends. It was true that Hennessy had visited a "palace of sin" on the night in question, but this was hardly unusual in 1881, let alone a criminal offense. The establishment's madam and one of her prostitutes both testified that Hennessy was sober and well-behaved when he visited. The charges against Mike ebbed when police commissioners examined Devereaux's own visit to this house of ill repute, and when Devereaux protested the change of focus, he was ordered out of the hearing room. Mike Hennessy capped his defense with a clipping from a morning paper titled DETECTIVE IN TROUBLE. Devereaux was seen coming out of the newspaper office the night before, Hennessy claimed, proving that there was a plot afoot to "prejudice the public mind" against him. The commission wanted to think this over and passed a motion to continue Hennessy's case.

By then Devereaux knew that he was in trouble. He hedged when he was called back inside to present his charge against Dave Hennessy, saying it was all a misunderstanding. Angry police commissioners saw it differently when they learned that Devereaux had been informed by Chief Boylan, Hennessy's doctor, and even the ailing detective's mother that Dave Hennessy was absent from duty because of illness. That case was dismissed.

The mayor and police commissioners concluded that Devereaux's charges were prompted by malice and passed a resolution charging him with "oppression in office, insubordination, and unofficerlike conduct." Mayor Shakspeare told Chief Boylan to suspend Devereaux from duty until he could be tried, an order Boylan must have been delighted to execute. As the stink leaked from city hall, the *Daily Picayune* dubbed the conflict THE POLICE MUDDLE and declared that creating the chief of aids position was a regrettable political act.

Devereaux's attempt to rid himself of the Hennessys slid further into disaster a week later during his defense against the council's charges. When the first witness was called, Devereaux jumped to his feet and blurted out that he had once personally arrested a certain aid for robbery. Although Devereaux named no one, he meant Mike Hennessy, who had been arrested and cleared of robbing a U.S. senator years before when Mike was a young cab driver. The outburst was Devereaux's last official mistake. Convicted of "oppression in office," the state of his career and his relations with other detectives couldn't get any worse, or so most people thought.

At eleven o'clock on October 13, 1881, the morning after his devastating police board trial, the suspended chief of aids was in John W. Fairfax's brokerage at the corner of Gravier Street and St. Charles Avenue. Devereaux was discussing city bond investments with Fairfax when Mike Hennessy appeared on the sidewalk outside. Seconds later, Fairfax and his clerks dove behind a steel safe door for cover, as bullets smashed the windows and split the woodwork.

Devereaux's heavy English Tranter revolver dropped Mike Hennessy with one shot to the mouth, splintering teeth and the left side of Mike's jaw and stopping in his neck. Hennessy stumbled and fell hard on a stone doorstep. Devereaux stepped from behind an iron pillar and leveled his Tranter at the bleeding detective who had caused him so much trouble. He did not see another man coming swiftly from the front of the barbershop two doors away or the glint of nickel rising into the sunlight. Dave Hennessy put his gun to the back of Devereaux's head and fired.

Devereaux pitched forward, his outraged brain commanding a last shot out of his pistol. The slug went wild as Devereaux fell to the banquette. Dave Hennessy calmly put his pistol into his pocket, and as he pulled Mike to his feet, Mike fired again at the prostrate Devereaux, hitting the office door. Dave hailed a cab and hurried his wounded cousin to Charity Hospital as onlookers from banks and brokerages crowded around the dying Devereaux.

By nightfall, Devereaux's friends were calling it an ambush, while the Hennessys' friends denied that Dave had fired the fatal shot. When Dave was arrested, he handed over a nickel-plated Colt .38. The revolver was rumored to have been presented to him by the widow of Bob Harris, the detective Devereaux allegedly gunned down five years earlier. Mike was stitched up, too proud to grimace as doctors pulled shards of teeth and bone out of his face. He complained of pain in his side from his fall, but he was expected to recover. His wife told waiting reporters that her husband would rather die a thousand deaths than live under Devereaux's accusations. By midnight, Mike was resting comfortably, and Dave sat in the parish prison.

An unrelated incident caused two other men to be locked up that night. The owners of Matranga's bar near Poydras Market—Sal Matranga and his son, Tony, whom Gaetano Ardotta had requested to see after the Labruzzo shooting—were brought in after a brawl in their saloon. Hennessy and the Matranga family would come to know each other well.

A coroner's jury met and charged the Hennessys with murder, but Mike's wounds became infected. Expecting him to die, prison officials allowed him to be moved home. Dave remained in prison, surrounded by burglars and murderers, some of whom he had personally delivered there. Perhaps he had saved his cousin's life, and if Mike lived, Dave could console himself with having manfully proved his family loyalty. It would be a hollow victory if Mike died. Either way, it looked as if Dave Hennessy's career with the New Orleans Police—his way of life itself—was over.

A small, bearded man with a shuffling gait arrived in Sicily in mid-November 1881. Police escorts and government officials awaiting his arrival identified the man as Giuseppe Esposito, the notorious bandit. Brought to trial in December, he was charged with six crimes including murder and the kidnapping and attempted ransom of John Forester Rose.

Esposito, found guilty and sentenced to a life of servitude, was led to his cell in Palermo, while Dave Hennessy, the American who captured him was imprisoned in New Orleans, awaiting trial for murder.

Mike recovered by the time he and his cousin went on trial in April 1882. Fairfax testified that Mike's gun was already drawn when he appeared outside the brokerage. Maurice Hart, an influential contractor who was discussing bonds with Fairfax and Devereaux, at first agreed with Fairfax. In court, however, Hart testified that Hennessy and Devereaux drew and shot simultaneously. Other witnesses thought the shot that felled Mike Hennessy came first.

It was unclear who started the fireworks, but there was no doubt who put the bullet in Devereaux's head. Mike's role in the incident faded as the trial concentrated on the fatality. Dave claimed he was on his way to a meeting with his former boss, Mike Farrell, whose office was upstairs from Fairfax's brokerage. Witness after witness testified to Dave's good reputation for peace and quiet while Devereaux was remembered as an irritable, quarrelsome man who would not hesitate to kill if provoked. Devereaux's defense attorneys Adams and Evans, who had defended Ardotta in the Labruzzo killing, called Chief Boylan, who said that his problems with Devereaux were official, not personal. Three witnesses said they had heard Devereaux threaten to blow the Hennessys' heads off with a shotgun if they bested him in the police board mess.

No one accused Devereaux of being a coward, but the constant testimony about his pugnacity moved prosecutor Henry Castellanos to protest that even if the chief of aids was the worst of men, it did not justify shooting him down like a dog. Castellanos and assistant district attorney Joshua Baker must have known their case was lost when Judge Charles H. Luzenberg told jurors that threats did not justify the taking of a life. If an overt act like the drawing of a gun showed that a threat was an imminent reality, however, the threatened party was justified in killing in self-defense.

Jurors decided that shooting Mike was sufficient proof of Devereaux's intentions toward both Hennessys. After nineteen hours of deliberation, Mike and Dave were acquitted and set free. Yet it appeared that their police careers were over. Mike moved to Texas with his wife, and Dave went back to work for Farrell as a bank detective. If the Hennessys were the upright characters they claimed to be, their departure into new jobs was timely, for the Crescent City's police force was about to sink into murkier depths of corruption.

☽

Four

THE RING AND SILK STOCKINGS

Of course the police do not interfere; it does not seem to be their business to interfere in anything. They are a mild and feeble folk, the New Orleans police, apparently harmless and useless. They are mostly under-sized men, go about with common stiff felt hats, blue coats, generally unbuttoned, and they slouch along, often smoking comfortably and chatting pleasantly with corner groups and doorway idlers. They enter barrooms freely and stay at pleasure. Sauntering into a concert hall the other night, I saw half a dozen policemen smoking, drinking and chattering with frequenters and the waiter girls. They are the only visible embodiment of city authority, and are said to represent very fairly its dignity, discipline, and efficiency under a combination of boss and hoodlum rule.

—*New York Times*, December 29, 1884

ON A MILD, BRIGHT DAY TWO YEARS AFTER HIS ACQUITTAL, Dave Hennessy listened as the guns of the Washington Artillery discharged a salute to dignitaries docking at an upriver levee. The fanfare trumpeted the opening of the World's Industrial and Cotton Centennial Exposition, the 1884 World's Fair, touted as the greatest event of the age. Thousands of curious visitors arrived to see fantastic exhibits from around the globe and from all thirty-eight American states. Pickpockets drifting through the crowds, sizing up the trade, were Hennessy's meat. Following two years as a Farrell agency bank detective, he was managing security for the exposition.

Running this force was complicated but uneventful. There were the usual "footpads" or pickpockets to spot and shadow. A boiler exploded. The creator of the Colorado exhibit appeared late one night with a hatchet and destroyed his handiwork, smashing toy houses, decapitating model farmers, and violently harvesting miniature corn, complaining under arrest that he had not been paid for his creation. Hennessy merely advised his guards to be more cautious. The exposition opened late and buckled early because of mismanagement, but none of that was Hennessy's concern. Policing the calm grounds of the vast marvel was a world away from the feudal acrimony of city politics.

Mayor Shakspeare was back in private life, buried in running his family's foundry but keeping a high social profile even though he had accomplished nothing during his combative stay in city hall. His only legacy was the Shakspeare Almshouse, funded by "contributions" from large gambling houses in gratitude for Shakspeare's running all the minor-league card-sanders out of town. Technically, gambling was still illegal, but Shakspeare's almshouse tithe was the closest thing to a gambling license that Louisiana's prohibition would allow.

As soon as Shakspeare's successor was hustled out of city hall, Mayor J. Valsin Guillotte and the "regular" wing of the city's Democratic party, also known as the "Ring," became the new rulers of New Orleans. The police department once again became city hall's private army, and its ranks swelled with specials. Good cops on the force felt their pay was being leeched by these new "deadheads," political appointees collecting paychecks for doing little or nothing. Specials loitered in court hallways, telling tall tales, smoking and spitting, and occasionally beating people up.

Even Chief Boylan's detractors agreed that the police lost leadership when he quit to return to Farrell's Harbor Protection Police in November 1882. Mayor Guillotte's first appointee as chief, Theodore Boasso, served until 1885 when he married a grocer's daughter with a bogus marriage license. When the bride's family learned that Boasso was already legally married to someone else, the enraged young woman found her "husband" and put two bullets in his back. He recovered in prison.

Next came Patrick Mealey, a popular Ring hack, who was already commissioner of public buildings when chief of police was added to his shingle. Mealey's term lasted until the wee hours of 1888, when he was shot in a New Year's Eve saloon brawl. Mealey's political foes were accused of slicing the reins of a horse-drawn cab outside the bar to prevent the wounded man from reaching the hospital.

Ironically, the turmoil was good for Boylan and Hennessy. Police weakness and corruption forced wealthy citizens to hire private agencies to protect their property and commercial interests. When Farrell died in 1885, Boylan renamed their business the Farrell and Boylan Police and Detective Agency, eventually shortening the masthead to the simpler Boylan Agency. Boylan made Dave Hennessy superintendent and let his former detective buy into the firm. Not content to sit at a desk, Hennessy kept busy tracking arsonists and swindlers.

The Boylan Agency was not alone in prospering during the crime-ridden decade. The Shakspeare Almshouse Fund had done good things for the poor and was now doing even greater things for politicians. Money bled away silently until the fund was tapped to buy a city councilman, ending the entire scheme. Thirty-five gamblers were hauled into court, but Lionel Adams, who was serving as Orleans Parish district attorney at the time, threw the cases out. He declared that since the good gentlemen had contributed hundreds of thousands of dollars to charity in good faith, there was no moral reason why they should now be persecuted. The gamblers went free, and the Shakspeare plan died. Gamblers would no longer support it—why pay for protection when the city couldn't guarantee safety from the state of Louisiana?

No publication relayed the graft and bloodshed of Mayor Guillotte's reign with more gusto than *The Mascot*, a weekly scandal sheet featuring tirades against municipal payoffs, or "boodle," alongside advertisements for patented gonorrhea salves. Mayor Shakspeare had once tried to close the paper down after it published an unflattering caricature of him. Compared to Guillotte's crew, however, Shakspeare was a forgotten bore. The paper rained insults on Guillotte and his hooligans. The police were "murderous ruffians," who patrolled polling places "full of cheap whiskey provided by the ward leaders to keep them in a pliable condition." The paper's cartoonist pictured cops as barefoot urchins led by a marionette, whose strings were pulled from city hall. In spite of its irreverent lampoons and self-proclaimed moral rectitude, the truth was that the paper did not respect anyone very much. Its editors thundered against politicians, while playing African Americans, Jews, Chinese, and Italians for laughs.

The *Mascot's* dialect humor column "Miss Bridget Magee's Society Notes" was styled as impolite "fun," but pointed gossip between the lines of its stage Irish brogue could prick as deeply as a hatpin. When "Miss Bridget" indelicately linked Judge William Houston with the daughter of a local lawyer, Houston's politician brother, James, and ex-sheriff Robert Brewster marched into the paper's Camp Street office. James Houston swung his walking stick at the editor, and the guns came out. The *Mascot's* editor was wounded, but he shot a pistol out of Houston's hand, breaking one of Houston's fingers. Four shots found Brewster, who died that night.

Brewster's enormous funeral wasn't the only burial to result from the newspaper's take-no-prisoners coverage of city affairs. In September 1886, *Mascot* writer Frank Waters stepped off an Elysian Fields streetcar to find state assessor Joseph Baker waiting with a newspaper in his fist. "Did you write this?" Baker bellowed, waving a story about corruption in Waters's face.

"Yes, and I stand by every word," Waters replied.

Baker slapped Waters across the face with the rolled-up paper and pulled a gun. Waters fumbled for his own pistol, and although it misfired, the writer shot Baker in the groin and sent him to his grave. Waters, a good-natured young man with tousled hair, would step lightly for the rest of his life for newspapermen had few friends among Guillotte's police. As a matter of fact, Baker had been hanging around the Sixth Precinct station house when the cops pointed out Waters approaching on the streetcar.

A new alliance of Democrats organized to fight Mayor Guillotte and his political machine as the 1888 election approached. Promising reform, the new Young Men's Democratic Association masterfully played up the public's disgust with Ring rule. James D. Houston, who had nearly lost his hand in the *Mascot* office gun battle, was a canny Ring politician, but he jumped ship to advise the YMDA. When the group asked Shakspeare to run again, he was ready.

No one ever accused Joseph Ansoetegui Shakspeare of being tolerant, but he was a public-spirited man, even if his opinions could be as inflexible as the iron and brass hammered out in his foundry. "The Anthony Absolute type with a genius for aristocracy," wrote one bemused reporter. The *Mascot* loved to invent more colorful names for Shakspeare, whose skin was notoriously thin.

Shakspeare had grown up in a hurry after his Quaker father's death in 1850. Young Joseph learned the family business and was managing the Shakspeare foundry by the age of twenty. He kept the business alive during the war and by the time he was first elected mayor in 1880, he was popular and wealthy. He was amazingly stubborn, however, which prevented him from accomplishing much in city hall, where he sat surrounded by a council composed entirely of members of the opposition ticket. His thankless term ended as his twelve-year-old son, Joseph Jr., lay dying. He buried the boy, cleaned out his desk, and went back to his expansive foundry at Girod and Baronne streets, two blocks below the shotgun cottage where Dave Hennessy and his mother lived.

Shakspeare did not disappear entirely from the public spotlight. In 1882 he was chosen to be Rex, king of Mardi Gras. When the next election approached, he accepted the YMDA's mayoral nomination and the assistance of an articulate young lawyer named William Stirling Parkerson, who had a gift for oratory. As a student at St. Stephen's College in New York, he had so brilliantly condemned a fellow student for snitching on drunken classmates that the offender was dunked by a mob, causing Parkerson and others to be suspended. With such high jinks fifteen years behind him, Parkerson now had a successful law practice and the respect of his peers.

The Ring scorned Shakspeare, Parkerson, and the YMDA as "silk stockings." Truly, the YMDA attracted the city's commercial and social elite, and for Ring hacks, that was the problem. It was bad enough that reforms could wither the robust boodle, but the really maddening thing about silk stockings was that they didn't know how *anything* worked. Future Mayor Martin Behrman, a genius of Ring-style manipulation, would remember them as stuffy men who knew everything about Thomas Jefferson and the Roman Empire, but nothing about public schools or garbage collection. Yet after six years of blatant graft and public shootouts, the YMDA's grand promise to kill the Ring found a ready audience.

The polls opened in April 1888 with armed men at the doors, as usual. This year the "Young Men" were the ones carrying weapons. Their guards wore small arms openly, circumventing the law banning concealed weapons, while ensuring that citizens could vote unharassed by Ring special officers. When Shakspeare and his organization triumphed, the *Mascot* howled that the malcontents of the YMDA stole the election by force with the help of James Houston, blacks, and spoiler votes from the dreaded Republican Party. Shakspeare arranged his desk at city hall a second time and offered the post of city attorney to his campaign manager, but Parkerson declined.

Dave Hennessy was not so reticent when Shakspeare offered him the job of superintendent and chief of police. Although Mike Hennessy was back in New Orleans, he was unable to share his cousin's good fortune. Two years earlier, Mike had taken a late Houston streetcar home, and as he stepped into the street, someone shot him to death and vanished into the deep night. Dave and Mike's sisters brought the body home from Texas by train. Dave declared publicly that he knew who killed his cousin, but could do nothing about it . . . yet. If the killer was listening, he could not have been pleased to see Hennessy march back into the New Orleans Police Department with his head held high.

☽

Five

CHAMPION OF THE WORLD

WHEN HENNESSY WAS APPOINTED SUPERINTENDENT AND chief of the New Orleans Police at noon on May 2, 1888, he assumed command of a force condemned as the most corrupt since "the days of carpet bag despotism."

Great things were expected of Hennessy. Even the antipolice and relentlessly anti-Shakspeare *Mascot* felt that the thirty-year-old chief would give the city "a clean police force, there is no doubt, providing he is not hampered or trampled" by politicians.

On a single day three weeks after Hennessy took office, forty-two deadheads were chopped off the police payroll. Despite his lordly demeanor, even Shakspeare had a sense of humor about the purges. He ordered all of former Mayor Guillotte's specials to report to him one morning at 7:00 a.m., dressed in their summer uniforms. Unable to comply because they were issued no uniforms, summer or winter, all the specials were fired for disobeying orders.

The city council agreed to build a new Central Station police complex, which would house police headquarters, detective offices, the coroner, a morgue, and the First Recorders Court in one building. The site was controversial because the council selected a corner at Basin and Common streets, amid blocks of bordellos and slums. Critics worried that lowlife would flee the area, contaminating more "respectable" districts.

Hennessy began overhauling what was left of a police department whose public image and self-esteem were as low as the city's polluted gutters. While the new chief had made a good living with Boylan's agency over the years, the men he now commanded at the police department were being paid less than his father had earned twenty years before. Hennessy nudged the council for raises for his troops. They were issued new helmets and new uniforms. Applicants faced educational tests for the first time in New Orleans Police history and had to pass physical exams for the first time in years.

Discipline was tightened, but there were still public complaints about heavy-handed arrests. Some cops were too free with their clubs and others were accused by the *Mascot* of shaking down prostitutes for protection money. Yet for all the department's remaining faults, Hennessy was creating a police force in whose ranks neither his father nor his cousin could have lasted.

The honeymoon did not last for Shakspeare. In no time, his *Mascot* antagonists were lampooning him as a "lunatic-at-large." Shakspeare limited his interest in crime to acts that played well to his upperclass constituency, such as pushing a Sunday closing law intended to put beer dives out of business. After the state legislature gutted the law, the exasperated mayor asked Chief Hennessy to keep an eye on the dives anyway.

Shakspeare managed a more ambitious feat that autumn after sons of several socially prominent families lost fortunes to high-ball poker, the summer rage in gambling houses. Technically, gambling was illegal. The General Assembly had declared it so nearly ten years before, but neither the state nor the city government bothered to pass any laws to regulate the prohibition. Shakspeare's new law would take effect at 6:00 p.m. on October 3, 1888. Gambling houses would close—all of them. Steady crap games in barrelhouses and baccarat in the city's most opulent sporting palaces would become equal offenses.

That morning as Shakspeare and Hennessy discussed enforcement of the law, a merchant who was a silent partner in one of the big gambling houses blew out his brains a few feet from the gates of the parish prison. Another celebrity of the local faro scene was found dead in his bed a few hours later with an empty morphine vial by his side. Fortunes evaporated as public gaming houses were closed, leaving owners with no way to pay their debts. Of course, a man could still find a game of cards in private rooms, like the Red Light Club, which counted Chief Hennessy as a member.

The Boylan agency's detectives again controlled all serious law enforcement work in New Orleans. In the old days, it was Farrell's security agency with Boylan in the police chief's chair. Now Boylan owned the agency while his young partner, Hennessy, who professed to be staying in public service only long enough to straighten out the ailing city force, was the police chief. Hennessy did not relinquish his share in the Boylan Agency upon becoming chief, and Boylan's critics revived charges that this was a conflict of interest. The *Mascot* accused Hennessy of wanting to keep the department weak, thus "working the old racket" by shunting lucrative private police work to the agency.

The paper's passion for deriding Mayor Shakspeare left it with no qualms about openly attacking anyone serving in his administration. Compared to its direct assaults on Guillotte's men, however, *Mascot* criticisms of Hennessy were vague and scarce. On one occasion "Dave, pretty Dave" was chided for letting a prisoner slip away. Another time "The pet of the Mayor and idol of the Red Light Club" was needled about his reputation as a great detective. Yet for the most part, Hennessy's work at the brand new Central Station escaped the prying, hungry wrath of the press.

The chief, muscular and good looking, with finely parted, almost completely gray hair, wore a mustache like most men. The handlebars diminished a broad chin, but they also hid his mouth. While his eyes might give him away, they had a bemused aspect, preventing anyone from knowing if he was savoring a veiled grin or measuring the distance from his fist to someone's teeth.

Like his father, the young chief was tough and easily angered when criticized. He did not, however, forget his father's failings that had once made him and his mother destitute. While his dad was remembered as a thick-headed political bullyboy with a taste for booze, Dave Hennessy was known as a shrewd, teetotaling gentleman with a wry sense of humor, hard and politely detached from everything but the law. The *Police Gazette* dubbed him "Algeresque."

Hennessy still lived with his mother in a shotgun cottage on Girod Street, two doors above Basin. Fifty years before, the drab neighborhood had been the lower border of "the Swamp," a notorious district where flatboatmen fornicated and drank themselves to death when they weren't robbing or stabbing each other. Girod Street was now a tired and unfashionable backwater crowded by lumberyards and cotton presses. The neighborhood's uptown border was the New Basin Canal, whose dingy waters paralleled Julia Street all the way from its Rampart Street terminus to Lake Pontchartrain. Hennessy's friends urged him to move to a classier neighborhood. "No," answered the chief, who by then had the means to live wherever he chose and was eyeing some uptown property. "My mother is old. I'll stay with her." Besides, the new Central Station was just a short walk away.

Commanding the police force of an American metropolis during the Gilded Age made Hennessy a powerful man in a world dominated by men. The appointment might have collapsed into a paper honor, for he had inherited one of the most dispirited, corrupt, and underqualified police forces in New Orleans history. Fixing the wreck of a department was a role he was well prepared for, perhaps better than those who gave him the job realized. His talents stretched beyond departmental reform and wringing new police helmets out of a parched city budget.

Hennessy's police arrested over twenty thousand malefactors in 1889. Twenty-four murderers were caught, forty-seven stabbings solved, and twenty-eight burglaries were thwarted. Two bigamists and one till-tapper were booked.

Nearly 5,000 simple drunks passed through the precinct houses, while another 2,258 faced the more complex rap of drunkenly disturbing the peace. "Notorious women" arrests numbered 1,991, and 74 New Orleanians were charged with insanity.

Hennessy almost included the boxing "Champion of the World" in his annual arrest statistics, but it was not to be.

When it came to meeting the famed pugilist John L. Sullivan, the chief was no different than any other young man in America, especially one of Irish ancestry, who would appreciate the chance to meet the fighter. Actually Hennessy had more in common with Sullivan's straitlaced trainer, William Muldoon. The strict Muldoon was a former New York cop and champion wrestler who had reclaimed Sullivan from booze and transformed a wheezing, bloated hulk into a solid fighting machine.

It would have been hard for the champion prizefighter and a metropolitan chief of police to avoid each other, even if Jake Kilrain hadn't forced the issue by challenging Sullivan to a bare-knuckles bout. It was agreed that the fight would take place at an undisclosed site near New Orleans, but regardless of where it happened, it would be utterly illegal. Fight fans, "aficionados of fisticuffs," flocked to the city for a chance to see what would be the final bare-knuckles championship contest in the United States.

Throughout Sullivan's July 1889 train journey to New Orleans, governors along the route blustered that there would be no brawling for money in their states. Louisiana's Governor Nicholls and New Orleans Mayor Shakspeare loudly agreed. Reform politicians who couldn't keep the people from buying beer on Sundays and away from gambling tables during the other six days of the week figured they could at least thwart two scrappers like Sullivan and Kilrain.

Sullivan, Muldoon, and their entourage arrived in town and set up headquarters on North Rampart Street, across from the Louisiana Athletic Club, whose members included Chief Hennessy. The champ trained, the chief watched, and state authorities grumbled. Thousands of hungry sports fans arrived in New Orleans to see if there would be a contest, as advertised, at a secret location within two hundred miles of the city. They spent fortunes filling hotels, playing pool, eating oysters, and dropping their suspenders in bordellos to while away the wait. Hennessy blandly told reporters that he had no sympathy for prizefighting, the combatants, or their fans.

Sullivan and Kilrain left New Orleans aboard a hired train at 1:00 a.m. on July 7, disappearing into a sweltering summer night. Chief Hennessy and the U.S. attorney general, William Grant, left an hour later in one of fourteen carriages chartered for the occasion, pulling away from a melee in the Illinois Central station. Over one thousand men who could not afford a $10 fight ticket jammed the depot, swarming around the trains. Blue-coated police were everywhere, poking men from beneath undercarriages with billy clubs. The cops were less successful in getting freeloaders down from the roofs of the cars. As the train steamed out of the station and north toward Mississippi, drunks began firing pistols out the windows, trying to scare the freeloaders off.

Chief Hennessy declared that he would go only as far as the Mississippi state line to ensure that no fight took place in Louisiana. He did not get off the train as expected, but when the locomotive rumbled to a halt in Richburg, Mississippi, and two thousand men scrambled and ran for the hastily erected ring in the morning heat, no one cared a damn if Dave Hennessy was there.

Seventy-five sunburned rounds later, after battering Kilrain into a raw, weeping mess with his bare fists, the puking and bloody Sullivan was the undisputed champion of the world. Sullivan returned to New Orleans and immediately went into hiding.

Two days later, a county sheriff from Mississippi roared into the Crescent City looking for Sullivan. Chief Hennessy accepted the sheriff's credentials, but told him he needed to get a proper interstate warrant from Governor Nicholls. The chief's office crawled with reporters who wanted to know how Hennessy would handle Sullivan when the warrant came.

"I will proceed to apprehend him at once," Hennessy said. There was a grin beneath the wide handlebars. "Mister Sullivan will go to jail, sure, and he will not make much fuss about it either."

"How can you predict this?" a reporter asked, scribbling wildly.

"Well, it's safe to say that Sullivan will come quietly with my men. He knows full well the temper and disposition of the southern people, and he's not likely to put himself in a position to get chilled."

"Chilled?" The reporter's mind jumped, recalling Hennessy's blunt directive about street gangs terrorizing St. Mary's Market: "Don't take them to jail, send them to the hospital or the morgue."

But Hennessy was not in a ruthless mood. "Yes, chilled. I told Sullivan yesterday evening that the best thing for himself while in New Orleans was to keep perfectly quiet, otherwise unpleasant experiences would result to him. I told him that this was not Boston, the Hub of the United States, but plain, matter-of-fact New Orleans—the Crescent City with the young moon for her emblematic designation . . . not so poetical as the 'Hub,' but decidedly more wide-awake. I told him that in this southern clime, a Northerner on a lark or a mauling spree might in turning a corner get a whiff of our peculiar breeze and get a chill. That kind of breeze comes swift when you least expect it and the congealing effect of it upon the blood is uncomfortably and dangerously prompt. No man need whistle too long if he wants to catch a little of that refrigerated air."

"How did Mr. Sullivan react?" asked the reporter, warming to the joke.

"Oh, the big fellow took it pleasantly," Hennessy said. "He replied he would be careful and told his followers he would countenance no bad break on their part. If they wanted to tackle New Orleans policemen and be marched to the lock-up, they could go out and do it on their own hook. He would not commit himself. All I have to do is to say the word 'go' and there'll be some fun. My men are burning to arrest Sullivan."

It was a remarkable performance. No one doubted that Hennessy would love to arrest the champ, who was notorious for busting up property and people while in his cups. Any such spree would be enough to provoke the chief, no matter how chummy he and the champ had become. Sullivan, however, had secretly left town already. The Nashville police would get the Sullivan arrest and the publicity, but with his tongue-in-cheek threat, Hennessy gave the public both a man of the world and an eager servant of the law, a good sport with enough diplomacy in his nature to cleverly keep both the silk stockings and boxing fans happy.

The year 1890 began peacefully. Cops pulled floaters from the river and faced angry dairy farmers whose cows were "arrested" for wandering around the city. One day fourteen-year-old Annie Talbot shot off a pistol outside the chief's Central Station window, sending clerks diving under their desks. Chief Hennessy confiscated the gun, lectured Miss Talbot, and sent the girl home. Then the spring calm was shattered by a strange incident that appeared to be so pure in its criminality that even Hennessy's detractors assumed the police would be able to walk those responsible onto the hangman's scaffold.

☽

Six

IMBOSCATA

As the *Foxhall's* bow cut into the silty, fresh water of the passes early on the fifth of May in 1890, the steamer pushed heavily up the Mississippi, until New Orleans showed through a slip of light in the thick morning dark.

Five days before the crew had left Bocas del Toro to cross the Gulf. Dropping anchor into the blackness the ship waited with fifteen thousand bunches of Panamanian bananas rocking gently below, along with half as many coconuts and smaller cargoes of pineapples, limes, and mangoes. Before the men could lose themselves in the comforts of the city, quarantine crews with carbolic acid would come aboard to exterminate any vermin lurking in the tropical fruit.

The day passed and by nightfall the *Foxhall* was moored upriver at the vast dockland above Canal Street. Stevedores worked late under new dockside electric lamps, carrying J. L. Phipps & Co.'s consignment of fresh fruit ashore. It was past eleven o'clock when the last bushel barrel rolled down the gangplank.

The tropical fruit trade was relatively new to the city, and so were Matranga & Locascio's stevedores, all of whom were Italian by birth, if not by name. Stevedore Gerolamo Caruso had abandoned Palermo years ago and changed his first name to Jim. Handsome and imposing, Caruso had lived most of his thirty-seven years in New Orleans. He never got around to formally becoming an American citizen, but had legally declared his intention to do so, which under Louisiana law entitled him to vote. He had even been an election commissioner in the Fifth Ward. If voting and working in New Orleans made Jim Caruso an American, who needed a piece of paper?

When the *Foxhall's* holds were emptied, the stevedores started for home or a glass of wine. Caruso climbed onto Tony Matranga's wagon. The tired men already perched on the sides of the open spring cart knew each other well. Besides Matranga, Tony and Frank Locascio were there along with Caruso's brother Vincent, who was a Matranga & Locascio foreman. Every time a Central American fruit ship came into port, Vincent would oversee the unloading of a cargo hatch.

Rocco Geraci, another stevedore on the wagon, was a native of Monreale, Sicily, but like the Carusos, he had lived most of his life in New Orleans. So had Tony Matranga, the jowly Poydras Market saloon owner who now worked as a stevedore for his successful brother Charles, who ran the Matranga & Locascio company's office during the day and was now at home, asleep.

The ailing horse jerked the cart toward the French Quarter. The wagon stopped at Dumaine to let Jim Caruso climb down, then crawled on over the cobblestones. The French Market was deserted, except for a few watchmen dozing over covered trays of fresh produce. The horse turned up Esplanade Avenue toward Greek Row, the drowsy neighborhood around Ursulines and Dorgenois streets where the Matrangas lived. Soon the wheels scraped over the tracks of the Rampart streetcar line. The stevedores were weary, but in good spirits. One began to sing and a few of the others joined in as the wagon ambled along under the dense canopy of live oaks.

Not all Sicilian stevedores on the New Orleans fruit docks were as content as Matranga & Locascio's crew. At first, immigrants crowding into the French Quarter ghetto were happy to have any job a *padrone* gave them. They thanked God they were not starving at home, that is until they learned they were being paid pennies compared to the $50 to $75 a month that black and white roustabouts were earning on the cotton and sugar docks. Although the stevedores were illiterate and poor, they were proud men, and not stupid.

Some of the more experienced hands grumbled discreetly that they were paid more when the Provenzano family ran the fruit-unloading business a few years ago. They remembered when the Matrangas made old man Salvatore Oteri, Macheca Brothers, and the other fruit wholesalers a better offer—the Fruit Laborer's Association, the bosses called it. The Sicilian workers may not have recognized the English word *monopoly*, but the men on the New Orleans docks knew the facts of life: the Provenzano brothers were out, Matranga & Locascio were in, and the workers would now get half wages if they wanted to continue to unload green fruit. They toiled, swearing to themselves that the Matrangas were sucking their blood. Lately the Matrangas were paying up slower than ever.

Such things didn't concern Bastian Incardona, the twenty-five-year-old hostler who had worked for almost three of the eight months he had been in America. He slept at Tony Matranga's house and took care of the horse. Like Salvatore Sunzeri, another Sicilian riding on the spring cart, Incardona spoke no English.

The wooded corners at Claiborne and Esplanade converged at the last large intersection on the route home to Greek Row. As the wagon clicked slowly into the clearing, Incardona saw men idling on the corner, probably waiting for a late streetcar. Suddenly the men raised shotguns.

"Here they are, let them have it!" one yelled.

Incardona understood that—the shout was in Italian. He dove under a seat as the guns let loose.

Tony Matranga screamed as a heavy slug hit his right knee and drove splinters of bone into his muscles. Burning shot tore Vincent Caruso's thigh. Sunzeri drew a pistol, but fell when a ball ripped open his hip. As the cart crashed on, a mass of shrieking hinges, Geraci jumped off and fired at the flashes with his revolver. One of his shots hit a dog and the animal fled, yowling in terror.

Police came soon, along with an ambulance and a newspaper reporter. The wounded were taken away and a squad of cops began picking their way through the gloom beneath the live oaks, searching for discarded weapons. The longest shadow in the shrubbery fell from Chief Hennessy, who had been called from his bed.

As the officers stepped carefully through the undergrowth, Hennessy called for carriage lanterns, and behind the jittery kerosene light, the chief and his men moved deeper into the shadows. An officer found the wounded dog in a nearby yard and ended its misery.

By 2:30 a.m. no arrests had been made. The wounded were treated at Charity Hospital, and Tony Matranga lost most of his leg before dawn. A shaken Tony Locascio offered the police a list of suspects, but said he did not recognize the men with the guns. The rest of the stevedores all agreed that they had no idea who had tried to murder them.

When night again enveloped New Orleans, Hennessy's carriage was heard long before it reached the corner of Magnolia and Josephine streets. It was peaceful there, away from the docks and bars, far from the perpetual downtown clatter. The moon silvered oak leaves and picket fences, dropping shadows sharper than those made by the dull streetlight. Wherever moonlight and the weaker incandescence of a lamp ran against a single object, such as the brown body lying in the street, two mismatched shadows angled away or canceled each other's lines.

Hennessy greeted his officers at the crime scene and stooped to examine a small bullet hole at the base of a dead adolescent's skull. The victim was a butcher's helper from Dryades Market. Cops learned quickly that the young man had come down from Baton Rouge to work and was staying with a neighborhood family. There were no witnesses, so police carted off everyone in the household to the Second Precinct.

Hennessy thanked his men and strode toward the house where the boy was living to search it. His officers had followed proper procedure—when in doubt, lock up everybody until someone talks. That usually worked, although Italians would rarely talk, even when they were roughed up. Earlier that day, however, a silence had been broken.

The Matranga & Locascio stevedores identified six men as the shooters— Joseph Provenzano and his brother, Peter; Tony Pellegrini; Nick Guillio; Tony Gianforcaro; and a nervous white-haired man named Gaspardo Lombardo. Chief Hennessy had the suspects arrested, charged, and taken to the Orleans Parish Prison without bail. Quick arrests in a noisy capital case were good for morale and for the department's image, but the chief was not pleased.

When the Provenzanos lost their stevedoring contract to the Matrangas, Hennessy had tried to defuse the tension between the two families by bringing them together. He told them there must be no violence and everyone shook hands.

If the Provenzanos were involved in the shooting, the meeting had clearly been worthless. Hennessy was also weighing more recent signs of trouble. For instance, Italians said to be Jim Caruso's friends had tried to shoot Joe Provenzano outside his grocery at St. Phillip and Decatur, missing their target and wounding an innocent bystander. Provenzano identified several of his assailants, but backed off when the case came to trial. Then a month before, police had arrested two heavily armed men lurking in an empty house near Provenzano's home.

Also troubling to Hennessy was that the Matranga & Locascio employees fingered the suspects late in the morning, hours after first claiming not to have seen the faces of their assailants. Even as the police lineup took place, thousands of copies of the *Daily Picayune* were on the streets, calling the ambush A Presumed Vendetta Upon Which the Wounded Will Shed No Light. The shooting and the Provenzano-Matranga feud were front-page news. Were the identifications a brave change of heart, or was the law being manipulated to settle a private score?

It was an imperfect opportunity, but the chief would make the most of it. After all, Hennessy had developed a reputation as one of the few cops in the nation experienced in dealing with Italian criminals. This was no secret. His friends knew it and so did his enemies.

Seven

FRIENDS, GENTLEMEN, AND CORPSES

A RUNNING GUN BATTLE ON ESPLANADE WAS LESS EXOTIC
for its violence than for the fact that it could not be traced to city politics or
an unhealed older wound, the Civil War. "In the South," Mark Twain wrote,
"the war is what A.D. is elsewhere: they date from it." Even as Twain was pen-
ning a humorous anecdote set in a New Orleans smoking room to illustrate
his point, however, much of the city felt that, for better or worse, modern history began on September 14, 1874 on Canal Street.

When the Civil War ended, New Orleans became the state capital, the
seat of the Republican-dominated Reconstruction government. Many New
Orleans whites condemned Reconstruction as a dark age of draconian restric-
tions and an ungodly ascension of former slaves into a corrupt and ignorant
ruling class. Fatalities on election day, which had been common during the
Know-Nothing terror, returned in horrifying numbers. An 1866 riot at the
Mechanics Institute, briefly the state capitol, claimed at least forty-eight lives,
all but four of them blacks who were murdered in the streets. Nevertheless, the
state constitution of 1868 integrated public schools and abolished—for a
time—the segregation of public accommodations. More significantly, the constitution granted African American men of Louisiana the right to vote, while
simultaneously disenfranchising former Confederate sympathizers.

The street toughs who did most of the shooting at the Mechanics Institute
massacre were considered by local whites to be a less noble crowd than the later
Crescent White League, a paramilitary group formed in June 1874 to oppose
Reconstruction policies. A battle of rhetoric between the league and Louisiana
Governor William Pitt Kellogg escalated that summer, then halted in early September when federal troops seized crates of rifles being secretly shipped into the
city. On September 14, the White League appealed to all citizens to meet at the

statue of Henry Clay in the middle of Canal Street, midway between St. Charles Avenue and Royal Street. Hundreds of armed men arrived by noon, demanding Kellogg's abdication.

Barricades appeared above Canal Street, where a "citizens' army" including thousands of Confederate veterans spent the afternoon behind overturned streetcars, watching the New Orleans Metropolitan Police and U.S. troops assemble at the Customs House. Federal forces led by "turncoat" Confederate General James Longstreet and the Metropolitan Police's chief, General Algernon Badger, trained artillery pieces on the uptown border of the great thoroughfare. The federals were determined not to let insurgents break through to Royal and St. Louis streets, where the St. Louis Hotel was being used as the state capitol. When White Leaguers advanced down the levee, Badger's artillery opened fire, the White League charged, and the city's heart exploded. Badger was wounded three times before a fourth round knocked him off his horse. As he lay bleeding on the cobblestones, a few White Leaguers dashing across Canal Street surrounded him. Some wanted to kill him, but one of their officers intervened to save his life.

Federal reinforcements regained control of the city a few days later, and Governor Kellogg was reinstated. In the intervening days, however, Louisiana was ruled by disenfranchised whites whose pride had suffered the loss of the war and whose hatred of Reconstruction had been simmering for years. The heady glory they felt that week was never forgotten by those who had assembled at the Clay monument.

When Reconstruction was abandoned three years later and Federal troops ended their fifteen years in New Orleans, a strange fraternity drew together men who were on both sides of Canal Street that bloody September day. Badger, a Bostonian who had come to New Orleans with the Union army, remained in the city, married, and was well liked. The chivalric bond between former enemies was withheld from black troops who fought in the bloodbath, but service to either side emerged as a mark of civic stature among whites even as the dead were being buried. This self-perception of nobility would take a century to die.

Captain Joseph P. Macheca had to fight harder than most men for his place in the pantheon of September 14 icons. An orphan raised by the Maltese founder of the Macheca steamship company, thirty-year-old Joe Macheca had led a company of Italians in the White League's charge along the river in 1874. When the daily papers of September 15 gave credit for capturing and saving the life of General Badger to White Leaguer Douglas Kilpatrick, Macheca fired off a public "card," a notice to the newspapers claiming that he had reached the stricken general first and commanded his men to carry

Badger to Charity Hospital. Macheca also claimed credit for capturing the government arsenal and its guards and confiscating government arms aboard the steamship *Mississippi*.

The official White League report gave credit for these feats to other men. It must have galled the stocky Macheca, a proud man who was quick to perceive a slight. Yet he was credited with being of great help in the Battle of Liberty Place, as the White League called it.

A year later, while working for Macheca Brothers, his family's fruit-importing business, Macheca was appointed Bolivia's consul general in New Orleans. It was not his first political role. Some New Orleanians remembered his command of a company of Sicilians during the violently racist Horatio Seymour–Francis P. Blair presidential campaign against Ulysses S. Grant in 1868, when the Ku Klux Klan began terrorizing the South. Young Macheca's men, who called themselves "The Innocents," wore a white cape with a black Maltese cross on the left shoulder. They also carried a sidearm, used to shoot any black man or boy they laid eyes on, and reputedly left a trail of bodies behind them every time they paraded. General James Steedman, Seymour's New Orleans campaign manager, finally forbade Macheca and his group from parading. Steedman was so revolted by killings on his candidate's behalf that when the election was over, he left New Orleans for his Ohio hometown and never returned.

Such open brutality was dimly remembered by May 1890. Macheca still followed politics, but when people looked at him now, they saw a cheerful, luxuriously mustachioed importer of Central American fruit, a partner in his stepbrothers' prospering steamship business. He was a respected veteran of the Confederate army and the Battle of Liberty Place, a wealthy widower who frequently wore a large diamond stickpin in his cravat and lived with five of his six grown children on Bourbon Street.

Soon after Matranga & Locascio's stevedores were ambushed, Macheca stopped in to see General Badger's former errand boy, Chief Hennessy, to voice his concern about vendetta shootings between the stevedores. It wasn't the first time that Macheca had spoken to Hennessy about encountering trouble from the Provenzanos. "It's a shame that crime of this kind always goes unpunished here."

"Don't worry, I have them all in jail," Hennessy assured him.

"Well then, what do you intend to do further?" Macheca pressed.

"Prosecute them to the fullest extent of the law."

Attorney A. D. Henriques, who accompanied Macheca on his visit, said the Provenzanos had been to his office that morning, but he had not met with them. He was on his way to speak with the Matrangas. Henriques said, "I don't know which side to take in this matter."

"Take the Matranga case, by all means," Hennessy told him.

When Macheca and Henriques left, Hennessy may have wondered if they were feeling him out, looking for hints about the investigation's aim. Perhaps not. The three men knew each other well enough to enjoy a chat over a current affair like the vendetta arrests.

Henriques was indeed hired by the Matranga family to help assistant district attorney John Finney prosecute the Provenzano case, with the assistance of former district attorney Lionel Adams who had returned to private practice after a four-year term. The problem was the private detective Adams and Henriques used. When Hennessy heard that Dominick C. O'Malley was involved, he hit the roof.

All of his adult life, O'Malley was a foe to liars and those who tried to outsmart the police, especially if they did it better than he could. A lot of people in the New Orleans criminal justice system rubbed O'Malley the wrong way. The ones he really couldn't stand were the hypocrites.

O'Malley's Detective Agency & Protection Police—the name was a bit grander than his office, but he wisely gave his lawyer associate Lionel Adams prominent billing—promised all the right services in front-page advertisements:

> *Civil and Criminal matters carefully investigated and reported. Uniformed officers furnished day or night on reasonable terms. Missing witnesses found; absent witnesses located; their general reputation investigated; and all matters connected with legitimate detective business properly attended to.*

When O'Malley first came to New Orleans from Cleveland, he worked on the waterfront, accidentally becoming a detective when he recovered some stolen property for his boss. In 1879 he was hired as a "spotter," or informer, for the Internal Revenue Service. Later he would proudly proclaim that he was responsible for more arrests in eight months than were made in the preceding five years. He would conveniently overlook one arrest: his own. O'Malley's IRS boss had him thrown in jail in November 1880, but the charges fell apart.

A pattern of arrest, acquittal, and defiance clung to the detective all his life, interrupted only by an occasional stay in prison or a gunshot wound. The police hated him. During the Devereaux rows, Mike Hennessy drunkenly drew a bead on O'Malley and was fined $10 for the offense, despite two defense witnesses who testified that O'Malley had approached them to arrange Mike's death. While he was chief, Boylan had O'Malley arrested for charging that high-ranking cops were in collusion with waterfront gamblers, but again, charges made by both sides came to nothing. Was O'Malley the most honest sleuth in the Crescent City or the biggest crook who ever put out a shingle?

Some people admired the way he cocked his nose at the fumblings of the city hierarchy. Yet O'Malley's flamboyant behavior caused such strong reactions in others that few inclined a charitable benefit of the doubt his way whenever he turned up on the city's front pages, accused of blackmailing a wayward husband or fixing a court case. In 1882 the *Mascot* denounced him as "cute and unscrupulous to a surprising degree."

O'Malley was too clever a businessman to shrink from such attention. The reputation of being able to get things done, one way or another, was wonderful free advertising. If his business depended on all the scams his enemies accused him of, he must have been a very inept crook, for he was arrested regularly.

"He has always managed to wriggle out of his difficulties unscathed," the *Mascot* noted, adding a warning "to be very careful handling edged tools of this description. The licensed detective often turns out badly enough, but the private one is at best an unmitigated nuisance." The unmitigated nuisance boasted that such accusations were simple jealousy.

Tom Anderson thought he knew envy when he saw it. Anderson did possess a magnificent grasp of the intricacies of human nature, which he would prove a generation later in the next century when his genius for promoting an entire district of bordellos accidentally legalized by the city council would earn him the nickname "Mayor of Storyville." In the year of the Esplanade ambush of the Matrangas, however, Anderson's budding managerial talents were untested. He had his eye on the restaurant and saloon business, where he hoped to become his own boss. Considered to be sincere and enterprising, he was a big, quiet fellow like his chum Dave Hennessy.

Both Anderson and Hennessy belonged to the Red Light Club, a downtown social group whose suggestive name rubbed uptown society the wrong way. The exclusive Boston and Pickwick clubs were not interested in inducting salesmen and merchants into their immaculate ranks. The Red Lights were middle-class successes without social pedigree. Men like Joe Macheca, the Provenzano brothers, Anderson, and Hennessy were all members. They might not have represented the most powerful clans of New Orleans society and commerce, but they were not about to be denied the pleasures of a private club. Although the *Mascot* accused the "sports" among its members of being frequent customers of the city's still illegal houses of ill repute, the club itself was not a bordello. Sex was bought easily elsewhere in the Customhouse Street neighborhood in actual brothels or "parlor-houses." If the name was meant to be something more than an ironic comment on their surrounding neighbors, the working middle-class sports of the Red Lights had a funny way of keeping a low profile. For instance, the group commandeered an entire railroad car for the Sullivan-Kilrain fight and hung a huge scarlet-lettered banner out the windows advertising themselves as the "Red Light Club of New Orleans."

At the club Anderson could talk his friend Hennessy into taking a seat at the card table. The chief didn't gamble, Anderson would say, but he didn't mind a good game of cards. Hennessy would take a pile of chips without putting any money down. By midnight, he usually said good night and left his chips on the table.

One night after Hennessy left, Anderson called Macheca over to play. Macheca agreed but was miffed when the other players asked him to put down cash for Hennessy's chips. "Why don't you stake me sometimes?" Macheca complained. "I suppose you all cater to Hennessy because he's chief."

Anderson thought the barb was odd. It was also ungracious, considering that Hennessy was responsible for saving Macheca's membership in the club. All three men had been members a few years earlier when the old Red Lights dissolved. While discussing potential members for the reconstituted club, some organizers protested that Macheca was spreading rumors about them, that he had a big mouth and was running with bad company. Hennessy defended Macheca. Let him back in, the chief proposed—that way we can keep an eye on him and make sure he doesn't fall in with that crowd when he leaves here at night. Macheca was readmitted and appeared to get along with all the members, even the Provenzanos, who had been dropped as the Macheca Brothers' fruit handlers. Yet one day Macheca told Anderson that he was afraid of Joe Provenzano. Anderson told Hennessy, who suggested a walk down to the clubhouse. When Anderson brought Macheca outside, Hennessy bluntly asked what the problem was.

"I'm afraid Joe Provenzano is planning to do me up," Macheca said.

"Don't worry, Joe," Hennessy said. "The police will protect you. And if they can't do it, I'll protect you myself."

Remembering the promise, Anderson assumed that Hennessy and Macheca were still warm friends. The future Mayor of Storyville put Macheca's queer behavior over the pile of chips down to jealousy and picked up the cards, considering his hand.

Over one hundred murders were attributed to what police, politicians, and the press called "the vendetta" in the years following the Civil War. In January 1889, a mutilated body was found near the New Basin Canal's belt road. A letter in the corpse's pocket contained the name Vincenzo Ottumvo. Chief Hennessy heard that someone named Vincenzo had been murdered elsewhere; now, it seemed, he had a body. Antonio Dema, who lived at the dead man's address, and another man were arrested. Dema's wife, Mary, told police that she saw the men use a razor on Ottumvo. Both suspects were freed when Mary Dema, the only witness, disappeared.

A month and a half later, police entered a garret at the corner of Bienville and Derbigny streets where a trim uniform of the Societa Italiana del Tiro al Bersaglio hung from a portable rack. A bloody footprint stained the floor; bone chips smoldered in the stove. In a rank sack in the corner, the cops found a headless, legless body saturated with coal oil, along with a detached head burned beyond recognition. The body parts belonged to a musician named Giuseppe Mattiani or Maittaino. His wife had disappeared without taking their children, and the abandonment roused their immigrant neighbors. Chief Hennessy himself found the woman walking along Basin Street the next day and arrested her. She claimed that a blacksmith named Charlie Teresa committed the murder, insisted that she had taken no part in it, and stopped talking. Her ten-year-old son was more talkative. At first, he told investigators that his mother's screams awakened him, but by the time the coroner's report was issued a few days later, the boy was scared. "My mother says Charlie will cut my throat if I say anything," he cried. "Charlie visited us often," sobbed the boy, "but only when my father was not at home."

The Italians of New Orleans were horrified by the crime. The *Gazzetta Italiana* denounced the murder and called for a mass meeting of citizens to express their outrage. The *Daily Picayune* applauded the *Gazzetta* and the sentiment of the Italian community.

On June 17, 1890, six weeks after the Esplanade ambush, there was a murder in Matto's wine room in the French Quarter. Ten cards lay scattered on the table where the corpse sat. Police learned that the victim was laughing and calling for a quart of claret he owed his companions for losing the last hand when a shotgun blast from the alley ended the game and his life. The weapon lay on the bar. Both barrels were cut down. One chamber was fired; the other hammer was still at cock.

Reporters scratched notes in the glow of gaslight, struggling with the dead man's name: Vittrano, Vittamo, Vittriano. Nervous Italians lined the wall; no one had seen anything, they said. The cops also questioned an old Frenchwoman they found sitting at the end of the alley. "I saw nothing," she told them, knowing she had not lived to her age by helping the police. Not in this neighborhood. With the old woman, the barkeep and his son, the card players, and a few spectators, the cops had almost a full wagon. Following standard practice, they took everyone in.

Reporters eventually pocketed their notebooks and headed for their Camp Street offices, picking their way down the poor sidewalks of what was known as "Little Palermo." Whenever reporters wrote of them at all, which was seldom, the latest immigrants from Sicily were described as if they were an inexplicable rash that had broken out in the city overnight. The Camp Street newspapers casually detested Sicilians, simultaneously preaching with unconscious irony that any immigrant could be transformed into a good citizen if the foreigner was willing to work. Yet newspapermen were not entirely sure that they hated Italians, for they could make great copy.

When it came to selling newspapers, murders were like found money. Violence among the wealthy was always called a "tragedy" by the press and rarely described as a crime. The middle classes certainly were not above snuffing each other, but scandalous deaths among the gentry or the lurid thrill of low classes slaughtering each other in the ghettoes always produced more sensational stories. Yet newspapermen noticed that explanations were demanded only when the poor killed each other. In a city where dueling was once accepted as an aspect of nobility, it was as if bloody behavior were expected of the wealthy, then dismissed after a good read. Reasons for bloodshed were less easy to uncover in the slums of the French Quarter.

When Americans began arriving in New Orleans in great numbers at the start of the 1800s, the French Quarter had been the epicenter of Creole grandeur for decades. Now, nearly a century later, Creoles were a curiosity, proud human artifacts hounded by tourists who braved foul smells and soggy streets to gawk at the "picturesque types" of George Washington Cable's novels. Into this decay, the Sicilians were coming—eight hundred to a thousand stepped ashore every time a steamer docked from Messina or Palermo, streaming off the ships in solitary bewilderment or in tears as friends and family members met them. They took the worst jobs in the city, just as the Irish and Germans had done before them. They crowded into pestilent quarters no one else would accept and tried to make lives for themselves, often working as laborers on the agricultural farms of southern Louisiana. Like other New Orleanians, some would become killers. Explanations would be demanded. Since explanations were rarely forthcoming from these reticent new arrivals, the press offered a single answer—each murder was the result of a vendetta. Even the musician decapitated by his wife's lover would one day be counted as a victim of an impenetrable revenge conspiracy.

Newspapermen began composing their stories of the latest French Quarter outrage as they navigated the quiet streets leading away from Matto's wine room. The market would awaken soon, between midnight and dawn. Dozing immigrants would pull the covers from their stands and sell newly arrived wares to peddlers, filling the market with dickering. When the sun finally broke out of a gray glow downriver, Italian peddlers would be in every street in the city with tomatoes and bananas and oranges, leading their creaking wagons and calling out to customers.

With the trial of the men accused of ambushing the Matranga & Locascio workers only two weeks away, the shooting at Matto's was a story ripe for
the English-language press. A loud noise makes a good story, and a good story
sells a newspaper. Armed with all the craft of their trade, reporters pondered
how loud a noise a shotgun blast in a dank wine room could be made to
sound. Never lacking self-confidence, they knew it could be deafening.

☽

Eight

THE PROVENZANO TRIAL

ON JULY 15, 1890, THE *Times-Democrat* PRINTED A LETTER
lauded as proof that respectable Italians in the city disapproved of secretive
vendetta killings. The statement, which the editor hoped would "stiffen the back-
bone" of witnesses when the Provenzano trial began that morning, was signed by
prominent representatives of the city's fruit-importing trade, including Michael
and Joseph Macheca, Salvatore Oteri, and merchant Charles Patorno:

> *For a reason appreciated by the entire community we have heretofore been*
> *reticent with respect to the numerous assassinations charged to our coun-*
> *trymen. But we trust that, with the help of the intelligent and inde-*
> *pendent press of this city, we may be able to stamp out forever the horrible*
> *scenes of cold-blooded murder which are charged against our entire peo-*
> *ple, under the delusion that we all favor a settlement of our troubles*
> *through the vendetta.*
>
> *We desire to place ourselves on record as friends of peace and order,*
> *and without meaning to prejudice the case now on trial we trust sincerely*
> *that the witnesses will speak, and that those, whoever they may be, who*
> *have taken part in this midnight assassination may be tried and, after*
> *legal conviction, sternly punished.*

While the letter clearly defended "our entire people," only half of the six-
teen signatories were Italian Americans; additional names suggested that the
fruit industry was united against this particular crime, regardless of ethnicity.
All of the steamship companies and importers who approved the letter had,
over time, used labor controlled by both the Provenzanos and the Matrangas.
As the trial began, despite its declared willingness to let the chips fall where

they might, the fruit industry was implicitly weighing in on the side of the current beneficiaries of its contract work, the Matrangas.

It took less than a day for Dominick O'Malley to be accused of mischief. As a sixth juror was being sworn in, defense attorney J. C. McMahon protested that the private detective was winking and nodding at hired prosecutor Lionel Adams and assistant district attorney John Finney.

"That is nonsense," Finney scoffed. "Mr. O'Malley knows me well enough to know not to wink or nod at me."

"Upon my word of honor as a man, I saw him do it," McMahon said. "Let Mr. Adams deny it."

"Deny what?" asked Adams.

Judge Joshua G. Baker had not observed any improper conduct on O'Malley's part, but said if he did in the future, he would certainly put a stop to it. O'Malley sat back with a smirk.

One potential juror was dismissed for saying he did business with the Provenzanos and thought the ambush was "a trifling matter." Another said that he would not want to be hung and therefore wouldn't consent to hang anyone else. He too was excused. It took two days to find twelve jurors who were not prejudiced against Italians or opposed to capital punishment.

On the first day of testimony, Prosecutor Finney immediately tried to establish the genesis of the "midnight vendetta" against the Matrangas. Fruit importers, including several who had signed the public notice deploring the shooting, testified that they knew the accused as stevedores working for the Provenzano brothers—Joseph, George, Peter, and Vincent—who had lost an unloading contract to the Matrangas. Joseph Macheca claimed that the accused had threatened his brother to get the work back.

"Are you the same Joseph Macheca who shot a Negro and killed him?" McMahon asked when the defense had its turn.

"No, sir, I never shot a man unless it was on the fourteenth of September," Macheca answered, referring to the White League battle on Canal Street fifteen years earlier. "I struck a Negro on the head with a pistol once. I had no ill-feeling against any of the accused, although they threatened to kill me and my brother." Macheca said he remained a friend to the Provenzanos in spite of the threat and had tried to calm the feuding families of stevedores. He had called the Provenzanos to the Red Light Club to discuss the matter after two men were arrested and charged with trying to kill Joseph Provenzano.

"George Provenzano and Joseph Provenzano, Lombardo and Gianforcaro, and eight or nine others were there," Macheca explained. "They said they had the law and the people on their side and it was time to clean the Matranga boys out. All the talking at the club was done by George Provenzano. Joe Provenzano told George, 'Shut up your mouth, you got too much tongue.'"

Salvatore Oteri, the next witness, had been in the steamship business in the port of New Orleans for nearly forty years. He was considered to be a pioneer of the fresh-fruit importing trade and was extremely successful. Like the Machecas, Oteri owned ships that brought the disputed cargo from Central America. The prominent importer knew all of the accused well.

"They worked for me up to two and a half years ago, when an association was formed," Oteri began. "The Provenzanos were discharged and the contract was given to the Matranga crowd—Locascio, Caruso, Tony Matranga, and others worked together. A very bitter feeling existed between the factions, because the Provenzanos had lost a good thing. They'd come to me several times and asked for the work. I told them I was satisfied, and that we had an association and were getting along well. A committee from the Provenzanos in December last stopped in while I was at my work—they were Lombardo, Gianforcaro, and others. They used a few little words, rather hastily. They wanted my work. They said, 'By God, one of these days this will lead to a row.' I told them to keep quiet, one man was as good as another."

The defense asked Oteri which man had spoken the pointed words. "All of them spoke at the same time," he replied. "I had refused them my work and naturally they were angry."

"Did you discharge the Provenzanos for business reasons?" inquired one of the jurors, who were permitted to ask questions.

"I had my work done by the hour and had a good deal of trouble," Oteri said.

The state called the ambush victims next, each telling a similar story of the attack, virtually identical in all but the most minor aspects. Jurors heard of unloading the *Foxhall*, the cart ride up Esplanade, the shouted order in Italian to shoot, and the gunfire. The victims agreed that the streetlight and moon provided enough illumination to recognize their assailants. Climbing onto the stand with crutches, Vincent Caruso pointed to four men—Joe Provenzano, Gianforcaro, Pellegrini, and Lombardo—and accused them of shooting at him. "After the Provenzanos were discharged from the work on the ships, I went to the Red Light Club rooms, and we settled the troubles there," Caruso said. "The chief of police was there."

The defense immediately objected to the witness testifying about what part the chief of police might have taken in the matter, but prosecutor Finney replied that if the chief of police had addressed the feud between the two parties, the jury should be aware of it. When this curious point subsided unexplained, McMahon returned to the night of the shooting. "Did any officer ask you who did the shooting and you said you did not know?"

"No."

Using a crutch to do the work of his amputated leg, Tony Matranga hobbled forward to say that he had no doubt about the identity of the men who fired at him, for he had known Tony Gianforcaro since boyhood and the others for at least four years. He remembered a man coming to the wagon as he lay in it suffering but could not remember what was said. He denied telling any police officer that he did not know who shot him.

Matranga's hostler, Bastian Incardona, claimed through an interpreter that he knew only Lombardo. Incardona said he was too excited to recall how Lombardo was dressed when he raised a long gun to fire, but he'd seen the old man forty times before that moment, mostly buying bananas. Incardona insisted that no one told him to recognize Lombardo in court. Tony and Frank Locascio echoed Incardona's story, testifying that they had distinctly seen the faces of four of the accused.

After police Captain Journée told of cataloging the guns found at the ambush scene, defense attorney McMahon rose and abruptly tried to derail the state's case by accusing prosecution witness Rocco Geraci of murder. "An eyewitness is here, prepared to swear to the affidavit."

Judge Baker hid his astonishment and referred McMahon to the prosecutors. Thinking fast, Finney said it was an inopportune time to bring such a charge and he was not prepared to interrupt one case to begin another. McMahon shrugged. He had done his duty, he declared. If Geraci left the city, it would be the district attorney's responsibility. When the whispering settled, three laborers identified a weapon found near the ambush, a shotgun with a crack in its woodwork, repaired with crude wire wrapping. The men said they had seen the gun in the possession of Joe Provenzano. The defense did not call attention to the fact that one of the witnesses packed fruit in railway cars for the Matrangas and another was a former Matranga employee.

Geraci was next. The object of the unexpected murder accusation said he had known the prisoners for seventeen years and claimed they came to New Orleans with him from Sicily.

Testing Geraci's knowledge of the streets, the defense asked, "Do you live in the vicinity of the place where this shooting occurred?"

"That's too rich for my blood!" Geraci chuckled. The rest of the courtroom laughed with him. "I have not been back at the corner since the shooting and what's more, I don't care to go back there again," he continued, describing the attackers firing a volley, then shooting again as they fled. "When the first shot was fired, I jumped into the grass and saw Guillio and Peter Provenzano run off. I ran after them, almost to the corner. I cannot be mistaken about these two men, for I saw them in the electric light." Geraci testified that he left the hospital after the chief of police arrived, but went to the police station the next day to sign an affidavit identifying the accused.

When Geraci finished his testimony, the defense attorneys asked that he be detained, so Judge Baker asked Geraci to remain. A police captain stopped him when the exhausted court adjourned at 11:20 p.m., but District Attorney Finney told the officer to let the stevedore go. If anyone had charges to make, Finney suggested, they should make them before the recorder or criminal magistrate. A crowd clustered around McMahon, asking whom Geraci had murdered. "I don't know," the attorney hedged. "It was reported around the court building that Geraci had killed a man in Europe." Whoever had supposedly been prepared to swear the murder affidavit against Geraci was nowhere to be seen.

Curiosity seekers were still being turned away from the steamy courtroom the next day when Charles Matranga was called. The well-groomed Matranga & Locascio partner was in his thirties, a confident man with a plain mustache and a faint widow's peak.

"I have known the prisoners for a number of years," Matranga said. "I have never been connected with them in business, but I succeeded them."

"What was the result of your succeeding them in business as far as your friendly relations were concerned?" Finney asked.

"Our relations have not been good. Joseph Provenzano came to me several times and wanted to go into partnership. He said he did not care about his brother. I told him it would not do, for the merchants won't stand it. He said, 'If you don't give me work, there'll be blood shed all over the levee. The merchants will be killed and mincemeat made of all of you.' I told him if he kept his mouth closed it would be better than threatening to kill the Machecas and others." Matranga said that Gianforcaro had similarly threatened to kill Oteri if the steamship owner did not return the unloading contract to the Provenzanos. After the threats were made, Matranga hired a policeman to guard Macheca's ships.

"Do you belong to any societies, Mr. Matranga?" McMahon asked, approaching the witness with some papers.

"I was grand marshal of the festival of the Italian community on the occasion of the celebration of the discovery of America by Christopher Columbus."

"Are you not president of an association of men joined together for the purpose of committing murder called 'The Stilettos'?"

"No, sir. I am not."

With the consent of the prosecutors, McMahon showed Matranga the papers. The first contained a message written in red ink:

We do can business. We are 300 strong of the K.O.T.O. If those brigands who sent you warning and wanted your brother to bring them money at the Old Lake End are found working again on the banana steamers as we saw them on the steamship City of Dallas last trip along with the Poydras Street gang, look out.
Committee K.O.T.O.

The message on the second slip of paper was typewritten:

NEW ORLEANS July 30 1887
One of your noble band was killed and all of you are going to find the
same fate. Beware.
    One of your gang by the name of Ardotto must leave the city. Do not
give him any more work or you will find yourself in trouble. We are still
alive. Look out for us.
K.K.K.
——— N ———
Commander

At the bottom was a red seal representing an owl above a skull and cross-bones, encircled by the inscription "K.O.T. Supreme Council." Three other letters written in Italian were translated aloud:

New Orleans September 1886
Vincent Provenzano and Brothers
We beg you to bring us $1000 at the old lake at the right hand side where
you will find men waiting for it. Let the party who brings it wear a white
handkerchief on his hat, in this way we will know him. You have three
days in which to bring it. If within that time you have not brought the
money, at our first opportunity we will murder you and your brother.
Good by

The next bore a large cross flanked by the words HONORED SIRS and PROVENZANO BROTHERS:

New Orleans
    You had better wake up and think of your outrage against justice if
you don't want to be done up by the mafia.
    Hurry up and do this if you don't want to expose your life for your
infamy.
    Wake up from your deep sleep and remember—or you won't sleep the
second time.
    You are adding to your infamy.
    In time, in time. Your life. . . . . . .

"I should explain that this 'infamy,' this *infamia* refers to an informer or one who discloses things to the police," McMahon said when the translation ended.

To Sicilians in the courtroom, the weight of the word was immediately clear. No one, neither a law-abiding immigrant nor a murdering scoundrel, could commit a perceived *infamia* without putting his life in mortal danger. It simply was not done. The final letter written in Italian was postmarked May 9, 1890, three days after the Provenzanos' arrest. It was addressed to Antonio Giglio and instructed him to deliver it to Vincent Provenzano in the parish prison. It was a secret warning to the Provenzano brothers that the "Stopiglieri Society" planned to kill them.

Prosecutor Finney wasn't interested in the defense's sheaf of blackmail threats. He asked Charles Matranga if he had seen any of the letters before. Matranga said he had not and handed back the dog-eared papers. The brief exchange marked the first time organizations of the Sicilian underworld—the Mafia and its Monreale-based offspring, the Stopiglieri, another criminal society—were publicly mentioned in connection with the Provenzano-Matranga feud. In less than a year, all of the United States would know of their existence.

To cynics working in New Orleans courts, alibis were considered the last resort of criminals. At first, alibis seemed like the only defense available to the accused men. Defense attorneys McMahon and J. M. Pratt's first witness was police detective Antonio Pecora, who had been to a prizefight on the night of the Esplanade ambush. Pecora testified that he saw Joe Provenzano, Tony Gianforcaro, and a third person about Nick Guillio's size on the crowded corner of Canal and Royal streets after the fight around 11:30 p.m. Three other officers testified that they had seen the men in downtown concert saloons, possibly as late as 12:45 a.m. Vaudeville theater employees, a barkeep, and a variety actress placed both the accused and the police witnesses in the saloons at the time of the shooting.

When a recess was called, the defense formally complained that O'Malley was again gesticulating at the jury. Pellegrini and Guillio rose from the prisoners' seats, swearing that O'Malley had gestured to a juror on his way out of the room.

"I haven't seen any improper conduct on Mr. O'Malley's part," Judge Baker said, again. "Under the circumstances, however, I think it might be best if Mr. O'Malley kept out of the courtroom until after this trial." O'Malley grinned and disappeared.

When testimony continued, witnesses recalled seeing the accused men in concert saloons, near Canal Street streetcar stops, or walking home in neighborhoods far from the ambush. As stories of drinking with Joe Provenzano, Guillio, and a deaf-mute boy at the Eden Vaudeville Theatre accumulated, it sounded like the Provenzano party put away a lot of liquor that night.

Pellegrini's sister, Lombardo's daughters, and Peter Provenzano's fellow boarders placed the accused men at home. George Provenzano denied ever seeing the damaged rifle introduced as evidence and accused the man who had linked it to his brother Joe of being a bad character who had once stolen three boxes of macaroni from him. George Provenzano insisted he owned a hunting gun better than the piece of junk produced by prosecutors.

The accused agreed with their alibi witnesses. Pellegrini, a laborer for the Provenzanos when they lost their fruit contract, swore that he was sleeping with his wife and baby at the time of the ambush. Guillio testified that he was drinking in the Eden Theatre with the concert saloon's girls and four friends, including Joe Provenzano until 2:00 a.m. Lombardo told the court through an interpreter that on the night of the shooting, he was at the barber shop until 9:00 p.m., then returned home to find his two daughters sewing shirts to sell to the shops. He went to bed. "I could not have left the house without my children seeing me. What does a man at sixty-two years of age want to go out for?"

Joe Provenzano told of wining away the evening with Guillio, "the dummy," and the Eden girls. Charles Matranga lied in court, swore Provenzano, when Matranga accused him of threatening to soak the levee in blood. Peter Provenzano, who had worked in the family grocery for the past year, denied seeing any weapons in the store or quarreling with the ambushed men. "Jim Caruso and my brother, Joe, had trouble," Provenzano admitted. "I've been on good terms with the Matrangas. There has never been any trouble between the Matrangas and my brothers about the stevedoring work, as far as I know."

McMahon called Joe Provenzano back to the stand to explain the problem with Caruso. "Had that anything to do with the stevedore business?"

"We had some trouble," Provenzano admitted.

"About what?"

"His wife."

Finney spoke up. "Didn't you swear that the trouble was about the stevedoring business?"

"No, sir," Provenzano answered. "It was about his wife. We had some shooting and it was settled."

By the time Gianforcaro took the stand in his own defense, four people had already sworn to seeing him on his way home from Canal Street where he left Joe Provenzano. He woke the boy who looked after his mules when he got home. While the tender drew water and Gianforcaro fed the animals some hay, the bell at nearby St. John's church rang twelve, he said. If Gianforcaro was telling the truth, it would have been impossible for him to have reached the ambush site in time to have joined in the attack.

Contrary to what skeptics were saying about the case, alibis were not all the defense had to offer the jury. A private watchman named Thezan said he had seen Matranga's wagon cross into the intersection from his post a block away. Thezan recalled the occupants being very noisy before the attack. When he ran to the corner after the shooting, the victims asked him to call an ambulance. He said he asked who shot them. They said they hadn't the slightest idea and that the shooting must have been a mistake. Police captains Journée and Barrett questioned Tony Matranga at the hospital five or six hours after the attack. Matranga told Barrett he was suffering too much to talk. One of the first officers to reach the scene recalled asking all three of the wounded men who shot them, and each answered that he did not know.

"A message came that someone had been killed down there," testified Corporal Stephen Boyard, who took the call at the Central Station. Boyard sent word to Chief Hennessy, who met him at the hospital. "As soon as I got there, the chief asked about the shooting. He told Locascio and Geraci to tell me all they knew of the case. They told me they didn't know who'd done the shooting, that they were surprised. They gave me a long list of names of persons whom they suspected. They told me it was too dark for them to tell who did the shooting. After that, I went with the chief of police to the corner of Esplanade and Claiborne streets. There we saw and spoke with Officer Thezan. We searched around for weapons with the light from the patrol wagon. It was dark at that corner and the electric light was not burning then. It was between one and two o'clock and the light was out. We found no guns there. There was no light."

"Not even moonlight?" Finney asked.

"It is very dark there."

Chris Collein, the police captain who had discovered Giuseppe Mattiani's roasted head the previous year, testified that he was ordered to round up nine suspects after the Esplanade shooting. "These six men were arrested and detained. Locascio and Geraci identified them."

"Are you aware that Rocco Geraci has today been arrested for murder?" defense attorney McMahon asked.

"No, sir."

Prosecutor Lionel Adams disappeared into a waiting room and returned with Geraci. "It looks to me as if he has not been arrested."

Finney called Jim Caruso to the stand, held out a large horse pistol found in the Esplanade gutter, and asked Caruso if he had ever seen it before. Caruso said yes, in Chief Hennessy's office the morning after the shooting. "This pistol belongs to George Provenzano," Caruso said. "I used to work for him and at night he would give it to me to watch the shop with. I recognize it by the piece off the handle."

"George Provenzano is not on trial," McMahon objected. "This evidence does not connect the pistol with the accused on trial."

"When this case opened, the state declared that a conspiracy would be proven here," Finney argued. "It is for the jury to decide whether this pistol belonged to the brother of two of the prisoners."

Judge Baker sustained the objection. "The naked fact that the pistol belonged to a brother of two of the prisoners can have no weight against them unless it is traced directly to them."

Caruso continued. "I worked for the Provenzanos two years. George used to give me the pistol in a bundle to put in the ship. The bundle was too heavy and I unwrapped it and saw this pistol."

"Why did you unwrap it?"

"I opened the package because I did not know what was in it and I was afraid of it. I left George Provenzano's employ after he lost the contract for unloading the fruit steamers, because then he had no further work for me to do."

Finney thanked Caruso and declared that the state's case was completed.

The court's evening session belonged to the lawyers. Henriques promised the jury that he would be concise in his summation, but the hired prosecutor put the case against "the Provenzano party" in plain language, and plenty of it, for two hours.

This was an historic case, Henriques said. In past attacks like this one, witnesses could never be found to testify and killers went scot-free. This time the state had willing witnesses, while the best the accused could offer were alibis. Henriques traced the loss of the stevedoring contract and the Provenzanos' harshly spoken attempts to get it back. The feud, Henriques argued, was "the lever and mainspring which brought about this outrage." Henriques reminded the jury that one police witness remembered a moonlit night at the time of the ambush, and that another found two weapons without the help of a lantern. He attacked the testimony of Corporal Boyard, who accompanied Chief Hennessy in an unsuccessful search for weapons.

"Boyard's duty was allotted to him and he knew how to perform it," Henriques scoffed. He accused the cops on duty at the Eden Theatre, the Eden employees, and Detective Pecora of agreeing to a concocted alibi scheme. Henriques claimed that the prosecution had made a clear case with no help from those who should have assisted it—*the police*!

Henriques's partner, Lionel Adams, listened and studied the jury through wire-rimmed spectacles. Hennessy was not going to like this kind of talk, and Adams knew that better than anyone else present. After all, he had defended Hennessy in the Devereaux case. Yet the thirty-eight-year-old attorney had already made his peace with not caring what the chief thought this time.

Adams was the sort of sharp-tongued lawyer to whom respect comes more freely than admiration. He began his career as a "boy wonder" defense attorney by winning a string of sensational cases within months of graduating from

Tulane University in 1881. The first was a tough criminal case in Chicago, where the press called him "the brilliant, beardless lawyer of the South." He came home to win an acquittal for a ship's crew charged with mutiny on the high seas. Adams was soon back in Chicago to defend a ward heeler and alleged gambler convicted of defrauding the city of $700,000 in municipal contracts in a case that caused a national sensation. Adams won an appeal, forcing the state into a fruitless search for a new jury and finally to dismiss the charges. That same year, Adams turned prosecutor in the New Orleans murder trial of the three De Rance brothers. When the De Rances could not come to terms with Adams on a fee for defending them, they told him they didn't need him. Fine, said Adams, who was instantly hired by relatives of the victim to help the prosecution. The De Rances rued their penny-pinching in the penitentiary.

All of New Orleans knew Adams from the 1884 trial of Troisville Sykes, a dandy accused of murdering the fantastically obese madam Kate Townsend the year before. Witnesses thrilled the city with tales of Townsend's psychotic spells, making it easy for Adams and Henriques to convince a jury that Sykes slashed his sugar mama with a bowie knife in self-defense when she came at him with pruning shears. The lawyers made a bundle. Adams became Orleans Parish district attorney later that year, but after a four-year term, he returned to private practice. He and Henriques had fought Finney in the Sykes trial, and tonight all three lawyers were working together, trying to hang the Provenzanos.

After Henriques's fiery summation, J. M. Pratt's defense of the Provenzanos was a flicker. Pratt reminded the jury that the wounded men initially refused to say who had shot them and that a police sergeant had seen Joe Provenzano in the Eden Theatre while the shooting was going on. Pratt spoke for less than half an hour, then sat. It was the prosecution's turn again, so Adams approached the jury and was every bit as rough on the Crescent City police as Henriques had been.

"Gentlemen," he began somberly, approaching the jurors. "Let me remind you of the solemn duty which faces you. It is for you to say whether these six men should live or die."

Adams paused, then continued, "You are called upon to determine whether or not a series of crimes odious to the people of this country shall continue. You are called upon to say whether or not the vendetta of Sicily or Corsica should be grafted upon American institutions—whether midnight assassination should continue to do away with a witness who dares to assert the truth before a court of justice."

It was a miracle that anyone survived the ambush, Adams declared. "What was the defense? An alibi. A 'felon's defense,' as the books say. There were six men living in different portions of the city and yet on this particular night each one of them found someone awake to swear that the accused could not be at the scene of the crime."

Adams fired questions at the jury: Who but the accused had a motive to shoot the Matrangas? If there was no trouble between the families as the Provenzanos had sworn, why would the Matrangas feel compelled to swear away the lives of six innocent men?

"Who has denied what occurred at the Red Light Club, where a settlement of previous trouble was arrived at?" Adams asked the jury. "Is there any doubt that feeling ran so high that in every shadow the Provenzanos saw a murder? Why the interference of the chief of police? Those who believed in assurances they received from the chief of police were waylaid in the dead of night and shot down. This was after the two parties had come together and a supposed settlement was made!"

If the jury wanted to see the custom of midnight murder by shotgun and stiletto stamped out, Adams concluded, it was their duty to find the accused men guilty. If he felt sure of his argument as he returned to the state's table, Adams must have felt even better when he heard McMahon's final plea for the defense. McMahon believed there was a Matranga-Provenzano feud, but proposed that the spat came to a head on May 5 with the men on the cart panicking, jumping down, and shooting each other in the dark.

Finney was gleeful. "A new idea has been advanced by counsel for the defense that these men imagined that they were attacked and shot themselves!" The rest of Finney's closing speech was more restrained and deliberate. He spoke of the difficulty of securing evidence in the case and of the welcome novelty of firsthand testimony. "For the protection of lives and property, the plots of the Mafia must come to an end. It rests with the jury to say whether the vendetta should be throttled or not."

His parting shot was reserved for the practice of the vendetta and Sicilians in the Italian community. "This class of people," he growled, "have been trifling with justice and make the streets of New Orleans their battleground."

Finney meant for his oration to break over the jury like a thunderclap, but any honest citizen old enough to hold a newspaper knew that trifling with justice and turning New Orleans streets into killing grounds were as common as a cup of morning coffee.

Weary reporters did note one oddity: prosecutors had not called any of Chief Hennessy's men or the chief himself. Police officers had testified entirely for the defense.

This peculiar role reversal meant more to some people, including Joseph Macheca who had been pushing Hennessy for results ever since the ambush. Despite what the fruit importers declared publicly about not wanting to prejudice the trial, Macheca in particular wanted the conviction of dangerous men who had threatened him and his stepbrothers, tried to strong-arm their way back to unloading the Macheca Brothers company's ships, and evidently tried to kill the stevedores who did hold the contract. Macheca bad-mouthed

Hennessy around the city before the trial, eventually accusing the chief to his face of helping the Provenzanos. The stubborn and proud Hennessy, who was already angry with the prosecution for using the abrasive detective O'Malley and had by now been accommodating Macheca's assorted gripes about the Provenzanos for two years, furiously told Macheca to mind his own damned business.

Macheca remembered Hennessy's anger every time another cop sat in the witness chair. The chief, who had once promised to personally protect Macheca from the Provenzanos, now appeared to be helping them. If they walked free, there was no telling where this would end. And, Macheca loudly told anyone who would listen, whatever might happen then would be Hennessy's responsibility.

☽

Nine

The Plague of Our Misfortune

Throughout the trial the courtroom was crowded, and the attendance yes-terday was in keeping with that of the previous days. It was noted that none of the wounded men or their friends were present, having absented them-selves upon the advice of Mr. Joseph P. Macheca, who interested himself, with others, to put a stop to the vendetta.

—Times-Democrat, Sunday, July 20, 1890

"All guilty without capital punishment."

When the jury foreman read the verdict aloud, the accused quivered with disbelief. The jury was polled, and as each juror stood to repeat the guilty verdict, tears slid down the faces of the convicted men. Old man Lombardo cried like a child, wringing his hands and wailing his innocence. Court reporters were surprised at how choked up some of the deputy sher-iffs—and they themselves—became as the convicted men's emotions spilled. Only the faces of Joe and Peter Provenzano remained expressionless amid the weeping.

Sheriffs waited until the prisoners calmed down before escorting them to a van outside. Chief Hennessy detailed a squad of men to make sure the way from court to the van was clear. Lombardo broke down and was carried the last few steps to the Black Mariah, a horse-drawn paddy wagon. The driver cracked a whip, and the heavy vehicle lumbered off to the Orleans Parish Prison as newspapermen surrounded the defense attorneys.

"It's wrong to assume that this trial is over," McMahon drawled grandly. "The first scene has just been enacted, but I have good grounds to appeal this to the Supreme Court, which tribunal I am sure will reverse the verdict!"

McMahon's speech sounded foolish to anyone who was aware that he had not reserved a bill of exception—a formal objection to a judge's rulings—on a single legal point in the entire case. Criminal convictions could be appealed on points of law or if the accused could be proven to have been forced to trial without adequate preparation. Because there were no grounds to appeal this verdict, the convicted men could look forward to free funerals in the state penitentiary.

The Orleans Parish Prison was a gargantuan eighty-by-fifty yards wide, a whitewashed monster with a flagstone yard. One of its turrets hung unrepaired and scorched by a lightning strike. Back at the turn of the century, the area belonged to a Frenchman named Blineau who ran a soap factory there. The land was then at the wild edge of the city, where alligators, poisonous snakes, wild game, truant schoolboys, hunters, and runaway slaves were the only living things to be found. Blineau's departure was welcomed by those who lived in nearby shacks, for the charnel stench of his tallow pots had hovered over the land for years.

The prison was completed in 1834. Tremé, St. Ann, Marais, and Orleans streets grew around it as swampland was reclaimed to become part of the city. Yet fifty-six years of housing pickpockets, child murderers, and other malefactors—as well as witnesses to these misdeeds who suffered the unfortunate fate of "safekeeping"—had now passed, and civic reformers were protesting the prison's squalor. The old bastille was crumbling, and more than one city administrator was thinking of razing it, even though such a proposal would have been quickly defeated because no money or political will existed to do the job.

The hard white walls rang with the grief of sobbing children, wives, and parents that afternoon. The prisoners had no complaints against McMahon, Pratt, or the court, but they denounced the prosecutors and O'Malley, whom they accused of loading the trial with perjurers.

"If Camillo Vittrano hadn't been murdered, these men wouldn't be behind bars today," George Provenzano said, visiting his convicted brothers' cell with reporters and recalling the murder in Matto's wine room six weeks earlier. "Vittrano told me just before he was killed that he was called to a private meeting of the Stopiglieri."

"What's that?"

"A stiletto society," Provenzano said. "Tony Matranga's the chief of it. They told Vittrano that if he didn't swear that he saw my brothers and the rest shooting at the Matrangas' wagon, they would kill him. If he swore in court that he saw the shooting, they'd pay him. He said no! They smiled and invited him out to the lake. He said no to that too. He wouldn't give them a chance to stick a knife in his heart! Not much later, they killed him in the wine rooms. The killers were disguised, so nobody in the place could say who did it."

Joe Provenzano tried to cheer his cellmates. "There'll be a motion for a new trial."

"Ain't we got any bills of exception?" Guillio asked.

"Not one," Pellegrini said.

Old man Lombardo and Gianforcaro began to cry again.

"It's pretty hard for a man with three children and a young wife to be taken away from them for something he never did," Pellegrini muttered. "I was at home that night and in the morning on my way to work I was arrested in the French Market. If I had anything to do with the shooting, do you think I would've gone to the French Market to be caught?"

"The jury thought so," a reporter replied.

"Listen," Joe Provenzano snapped. "I don't know anything about this shooting. All I can figure out is that it must have been some laborers who didn't think the Matrangas were giving them a square deal. Right after the shooting, a whole crowd of greenhorns left the city. I don't doubt they did it, but five other innocent men and I are going to spend the rest of our lives in prison for it!"

"What about your shotgun?"

"I swear before God that I never saw that gun before it was brought into court. I don't deny that I carried a revolver for protection because my life was in danger from that gang, but I never used a shotgun. I never belonged to any vendetta gang. All I know about the 'vendetta' is what I've been told by ignorant dagos over whom the dagger hung or who were slaves of the 'society.' If I'd known anything about this case, do you think I would have lived in this prison two months? No, sir, I would not! I would have come out with it. I was on Royal Street at the time of the shooting and we proved it. We all proved that we were not at the scene of the shooting and we were certain of an acquittal. No one thought that we would be convicted."

Guillio's father was trying to comfort his son. "I say to him to tell everything, to get out of trouble," struggled the old man in uncertain English. "He says he knows nothing and I believe him."

"The jury didn't treat us squarely," young Peter Provenzano said. "I hope the truth will come out about this yet and everything will be all right."

The reporters eventually folded their notes and bid the convicted men good night. As they left, one heard the prisoners damning O'Malley and Macheca to hell.

The Provenzanos immediately hired a team of new, well-known lawyers. William Lloyd Evans, a fifty-five-year-old attorney with an enormous soup-strainer mustache, had come to New Orleans from rural New

York as a captain in the Union army. He was a Republican and participated in Reconstruction politics, but unlike the fleeing carpetbaggers, he stayed in the city to develop a law practice. Evans had worked for Italian clients before; he and Lionel Adams were among the lawyers who defended Ardotta and Vasso in the Labruzzo murder case. Both lawyers defended the Hennessys in the Devereaux shooting, but had opposed each other in the Kate Townsend murder trial. Evans and the second team member, his law partner, Arthur Dunn, were notorious for their tempers.

The third new defense attorney was James C. "Judge" Walker. A dour, bearded, native New Orleanian with fierce eyebrows, Walker had served as a private in the Confederate army. When he was hired by the Provenzanos, he was preparing to lobby hard for Louisiana's imminent Jim Crow segregated streetcar law.

The new lawyers quickly obtained news that made McMahon and Pratt's dangerous failure to take bills of exception irrelevant. A deputy sheriff testified that fewer than the one thousand names required by law had been placed in the box used to select potential jurors lottery style. Furthermore, one of the jurors had been on the grand jury. No one needed to speak openly of jury tampering. All that was necessary was a hard technicality: one instance of the rules being broken. The defense had two.

Evans and Dunn would argue that the guilty verdict was contrary to the law and testimony. Considering the number of witnesses who placed the accused men far from the scene of the shooting, the jury had not given them the benefit of the doubt required by law. The attorneys said the jury had unreasonably ignored testimony about the poor state of the street lighting and the obscuring presence of foliage between the light and the attackers. Finally, new evidence would be brought forth, as Evans and Dunn had ten affidavits from police officers, reporters, and people who lived near the crime scene. Each affidavit, in its own way, supported the possibility that the ambushed men lied when they claimed to have seen the faces of the men who shot at them. Whatever his failings, discharged defense attorney McMahon was right about the guilty verdict being only the first act. Act two was about to start, and it was gravely obvious to everyone in court that, whatever the outcome, some people might be doing time for perjury when the curtain finally fell.

Less than three weeks after the Provenzanos' conviction, their retrial motion returned the case to Judge Baker. Adams and Henriques argued furiously against a new trial, but Judge Baker visited the crime scene and inspected the heavy foliage of the live oaks above the Esplanade-Claiborne intersection. When he gave his ruling on August 9, Baker spoke of the difficulty of recognizing anyone at the intersection at that time of night. He emphasized that the "disinterested" testimony of policemen proved that Guillio and Peter Provenzano were not at the scene. There were also two affidavits to consider: outside the Charity Hospital operating amphitheater, the wounded Matranga & Locascio stevedores had told reporters W. B. Stansbury of the *Times-Democrat* and Henry W. Robinson of the *Daily Picayune* that they had no idea who shot them.

"It is not pleasant to me to waste the necessary time nor to listen to a repetition of the former trial with a few additions," Judge Baker concluded. "But under the circumstances, I think that the verdict should not be sustained and I am therefore compelled to order a new trial."

A block below the cottage where the Hennessys lived on Girod Street, a shack made of rough planks sat in the front yard of the Petersen home. Without the few nails holding it together, one good Louisiana thunderstorm would have reduced it to a woodpile. A tin awning slanted low over the wooden sidewalk, bearing the name J. PETERSEN to advertise the coal and wood yard it had once fronted. Some months it was used as a fruit stand, run by newly arrived Italian immigrants who stayed briefly before moving on to more permanent quarters. At the time of the Provenzano trial, three people were living in the hovel: teamster John Beverly lived in the middle quarters with his wife, Rosa Walton; and Emma Thomas lived in a rear apartment, which opened onto a narrow, gated alleyway running to the street. The front room on the street side of the shack was vacant.

The Wednesday after the Provenzanos and their codefendants were granted a new trial, Rosa Walton and Emma Thomas saw a white man in their backyard. That's the second time that man's been here today, Thomas thought.

The man inspected the yard behind the property's large swinging gate. He asked Thomas where he might find the landlord.

She told him to see Mrs. Petersen.

When Theresa Petersen answered the knock on her door, she found a middle-aged man who wanted to rent the shack. That was fine with Mrs. Petersen, but the man needed change, so they went to see Olivia, her daughter-in-law. Olivia Petersen took a $5 bill from the man, who looked to her like an Italian. She gave him two silver dollars from her purse and sat down to write a receipt. "How shall I make this out?"

"Put down Peter Johnson," he told her.

"That don't sound like an Italian name," she replied, dating the receipt August 13, writing the $3 rent figure, and signing her mother-in-law's name.

"Oh, it's not for me. For a friend."

"My stepfather is Italian," Olivia Petersen said agreeably.

The man smiled and said, "Thank you," taking the slip of paper.

Back at the shack, Emma Thomas saw the white man in the yard again. What's he want now? she wondered.

. . .

By the end of the summer, Emma Thomas and her fellow tenants had a new neighbor. They called him Joe, which was fine with Pietro Monasterio, who noticed that Americans thought that all Italians were named Joe.

Nine months earlier, Monasterio was a municipal councilor in the Sicilian mountain village of Caccamo. He was well liked and respected, but times were hard. His shoe shop failed, and he was left with a debt of 450 lire, which his pride would not bear. There was no way to earn such money in Caccamo. Like thousands of other Sicilians, he had only one option—America. With luck he could be home again in a year or two. Few Sicilians could endure the idea of leaving home forever, no matter how hard times pressed them. Some had even made the trip to America and back more than once.

It was nearly Christmas when he left. He wanted to stay for the holiday, but the debt driving him into the world was too pressing. He bid farewell to his sisters and aged parents. He asked his brother, Giuseppe, a priest, to comfort the old ones and promised to write from America. He explained to those of his children who were old enough to understand that he was going away but would be back soon. Until then, they were to behave themselves and help their mother, who had two babies to look after. Finally the shoemaker bid his wife good-bye. She could not help crying, even when he told her that St. Joseph would bring him home safely and that as soon as his debts were settled, he would never leave home again.

On the morning he left, he prayed a last time before the dusty crucifix on the wall of his home and set out alone down the rocky lane. The orange groves in the valley below were barren now. In a few months they would be ripe and full, and flowers would cover the rocky, sunblasted hillsides, all the way up to the ancient castle of Caccamo. Brigands had recently held a merchant for ransom in the ruin. A battalion of troops passed through in pursuit, but did not discover the hiding place. Life was very complicated in such times, thought the former municipal councilor. He fit his bag snugly to his shoulder and walked on toward the sea.

Monasterio found life in America just as complicated as it had been in Caccamo. Work was not as easy to find as he expected, not in a city whose large population of Sicilian shoemakers, tin menders, fishermen, and fruit peddlers was growing. At least Monasterio had a trade, unlike hundreds of Italians arriving in the city with nothing but the strength in their arms and backs to earn their bread. He was able to send some money home, he learned a few English words, and he also moved several times. At summer's end, a friend rented a room for him on Girod Street. Three people lived in the rear of the shanty: a couple named Johnnie and Rosa, and Emma. It was a drab street, not the most beautiful in the city, but not the most dangerous either.

Monasterio knew nothing of the old days of the flatboatmen, when the surrounding land had been called the Swamp and was the most degenerate district in the city. In those days, the police would not go into the Swamp, but now there were always policemen in the neighborhood. One lived across the street with his wife, and the chief of police himself lived less than a block away. In fact, Monasterio repaired the chief's mother's shoes for her.

Monasterio was not the only one to move that summer. Tony Matranga's neighbors, hearing a loud bang and the sound of furniture dragging across a wagon bed, looked out their windows and saw Matranga's house being emptied. The crippled stevedore explained that his brother, Charles, had advised him to move back to his old place near Poydras Market, arguing that the way out to Greek Row was too dangerous. By the end of September, all the Italians would be gone from Dorgenois Street—the Matrangas, Geraci, Tony Locascio, Vincent Caruso, Sunzeri, and the young hostler Incardona.

At the Orleans Parish Prison, the Provenzanos and the other men convicted of attacking the Matrangas and their workers anxiously awaited October 17, when they would go to trial a second time. The hated Geraci arrived in another cell, finally accused of cutting a man in half with a shotgun four years earlier. The Provenzanos fumed as Matranga, Caruso, and Incardona brought Geraci meals at the prison; they cursed when a jury found Geraci innocent.

The French Quarter and Poydras Market bustled in early September as immigrants and migrant workers anticipated Saint Rosalia's day. Sicilians prepared to honor their patroness, the devout young virgin whose bones had been discovered on Mount Pellegrini, the holy mountain looming over Palermo. The families of the men in the Parish Prison prayed long and passionately for *La Santuzza*, the little saint, to deliver them from the plague of their misfortune.

☽

PART II:
SHOTS
IN THE DARK

Ten

THE LONG NIGHT

WEDNESDAY, OCTOBER 15, 1890, WAS A GREAT NIGHT FOR THE theater, if you could get there.

The city streets were misty and cold and pounding rains turned unpaved thoroughfares into long plains of flooded muck. The Academy of Music expected a slow evening.

For all of us, Charles Matranga indicated, handing over a $10 bill at the box office. Theater treasurer Fred Mauberret knew Matranga's guest Joseph Macheca personally and recognized Jim Caruso, but did not know the men with them. He handed Matranga good tickets and change.

The academy's conductor, Armand Veazey, glanced up from his score and saw Macheca settle into an aisle seat as an usher pointed out front-row places to the importer's companions. Signor Pasquale Corte, the Italian consul, also saw Macheca and Matranga. Corte had been in New Orleans for only a few months and had not met the two fruit importers, but knew who they were. The consul only knew the men with them by sight. He would learn that their names were Caruso, Geraci, Patorno, and Sunzeri. He would also learn that they had come to the theater from a meeting with Lionel Adams and Dominick O'Malley, with whom they and Salvatore Oteri discussed their testimony for the imminent Provenzano retrial. In such good seats, the seven men in the front row were hard to miss.

Like the rest of the rain-soaked city, Girod Street was a mess. As Emma Thomas passed Monasterio's door on her way out to the corner grocery, she glanced through his window and saw the shoemaker pacing slowly, one hand hooked in his vest, the other holding a cigarette. The shoemaker looked lost in thought. He was still walking the floor when she returned. Thomas soon realized she had forgotten something at the grocery and headed back out into the gloomy night. This time she stopped for a moment and watched Monasterio through the glass, listening to the rain drumming on the tin awning above. Wonder if he's in some trouble, she thought. When she returned from the grocery a second time, Monasterio was still pacing, alone.

A few hours later, another inhabitant of the shack awoke in a haze. John Beverly turned on his side and saw his wife, Rosa, filling her pipe. Beverly heard a clunk beyond the cracked plank wall that separated them from the Sicilian cobbler in the front room.

"What's that noise?" Beverly asked drowsily.

"Most likely Joe's brother," Rosa said, lighting the pipe. Monasterio always told Rosa that another Italian who visited him was his brother.

The low voices on the other side of the wall continued as Beverly rolled over. Sounds like more than just his brother in there, the weary teamster thought, drifting off.

Across Girod Street in another bedroom, Rheta Thames shooed her two young sons into the bed she shared with them in the front room of their shotgun cottage. She made sure the outer blind doors were locked and decided not to close the inner glass-paneled doors. Then she put out the light and climbed into bed with the children.

As the inhabitants of Girod Street slumbered, Dave Hennessy and Billy O'Connor were approaching, on their way home from the Wednesday night police board meeting. Moments after they bid each other good night at the corner of Rampart and Girod, the entire neighborhood shook from the sound of guns.

Lead ripped apart the weatherboarding of Rheta Thames's room. One ball split the footboard of her bed, inches from her feet. Her children screamed as two spent slugs snapped at the floor. Shots kept coming, perforating the house and chipping the brick foundation. When the din stopped, Thames approached the window, warning her trembling boys not to leave their bed. She pushed open the blinds, and a sharp smell invaded the room. It was dark out there—too much smoke and too much mist to see anything. As she looked into the pungent cloud, the shooting began again and she could hear someone cry murder.

Across the street, John Beverly woke to the sound of shuffling feet.

"Get up!" Rosa cried. "Someone's breaking into the house and shooting into the dago's shop!"

Beverly heard running footsteps as he hurried into his trousers. He and his wife stepped outside, and together with Emma Thomas, they crept toward the small gate between their alley and the street. When Beverly poked the gate open, the banquette smelled of gunpowder. The streetlight at the corner glowed faintly. To Beverly it looked like a red coal. He walked slowly toward the nearly extinct light as Emma Thomas stepped out onto the banquette. She saw Joe the shoemaker standing in his doorway, wearing his underclothes and working slippers, gripping his clay reed-stemmed pipe in his hand. "Emma, Emma, the chief!" Monasterio blurted. "Mama, 'cross street!"

The men who shot Hennessy ran into the darkness. They had planned for him to die on Girod Street, immediately and silently. Instead the chief was struggling for breath outside the Gillis home, about to gasp a word he would later repeat at the hospital, the single word that would turn the city upside down. As Hennessy was lifted into an ambulance, police ran to the attack scene with the epithet *dagos* raging in their heads. They saw the tattoo of bullet holes across the street from the wide open gate to the Petersen yard and charged for Monasterio's door with clubs in their hands.

While Hennessy's neighborhood was jolted awake, the rest of the city was quietly going about its nightly business, subdued by the impossible weather. Heavy rains had canceled General Adolph Meyer's campaign meeting, and someone suggested making a canvass, so Meyer, ebullient politician John Fitzpatrick, Lionel Adams, and their retinue roamed from one waterfront Algiers saloon to the next, glad-handing and talking up Meyer's candidacy for Congress. It was eleven thirty before the weather allowed the drenched campaigners to take the ferry back across the river to the east bank. When the ferry docked, Meyer suggested a nightcap at Leon LaMothe's saloon.

"It's too near midnight," Fitzpatrick said. "Leon's closed by now. What do you say we go to Fabacher's?"

At the German restaurant on Canal Street, Adams spotted his Italian clients, with whom he had met hours earlier. Empty wine bottles covered their table. "I see you've been making a night of it," he said. "Where's Mr. Oteri?"

"He's gone home," Charles Matranga said. "We meant to have oysters when we left you, but the counter was filled so we decided to have supper."

Sensing a chance to extend their political jaunt, Adams introduced General Meyer to the dinner party: Charles Matranga, Joseph Macheca, Jim Caruso and his brother John, Rocco Geraci, Charles Patorno . . .

"I know you!" laughed Fitzpatrick, shaking Patorno's hand heartily. "You look just like your brother!"

"That's what they say," said Patorno, whose brother, Antonio, was a respected former city alderman.

"Of course I know Mr. Matranga and Mr. Macheca well," Fitzpatrick beamed, offering his hand. Adams moved on. "Salvatore Sunzeri."

Sunzeri let the boisterous Americans take his hand and shake it. "I remember you from the Provenzano trial," deputy sheriff Thomas Laroque, one of the members of the campaign party, told Sunzeri. "There was a reporter from the *Times-Democrat* making a sketch of you."

Sunzeri shrugged, and when Patorno translated Laroque's pleasantries for Sunzeri, he nodded.

"Will General Meyer drink with us?" Matranga asked Adams.

Adams thought that was a good idea, so Matranga ordered more wine. When it arrived, Matranga raised a full glass to General Meyer's great success in Congress. The toasts and speeches began.

Minutes later, a cop arrived with word that the chief of police had been shot.

Mayor Shakspeare tried to restore order at the Central Station. Hennessy was alive, but Billy O'Connor's report that "dagos" had shot the chief hurled police headquarters into pandemonium. "Scour the whole neighborhood," the mayor ordered. "Arrest every Italian you come across if necessary, and scour it again tomorrow morning as soon as there is daylight enough. Get all the men you need!"

A squad of police, already combing Hennessy's muddy neighborhood with a rake and lanterns borrowed from the Louisiana Athletic Club, slowly made their way up Girod past the Hennessy cottage, turning left at Franklin. They covered a block before someone fished a double-barreled muzzle-loading shotgun out of the muck. One chamber held seven buckshot; the other was fired. Sam Petrie, a wagon driver who lived on the corner, spoke up. "I heard 'em runnin'. One of 'em slipped and fell out by here."

Officers trolled the badly lit streets, jabbing into submerged gutters, and tracking two sets of footprints to a lumberyard midway up the Julia Street block. There they met John Lannigan, a private watchman guarding the lumberyard. Lannigan said he had heard the shooting while walking his beat. Five men had run past him, he said, including one trying to hide a gun under his coat.

"I asked them, 'What was that shooting?'" Lannigan reported, and one of them replied, "'Me no know.' The three were dagos."

Had he seen their faces? No, Lannigan replied, it was too dark.

When madam Fanny Decker answered her jangling doorbell at 11 Burgundy Street, she found Joe Macheca and five other men smelling of wine and speaking in Italian on her bordello doorstep. It was two o'clock in the morning, somewhat past the peak of business hours, but she knew Macheca.

Decker led her boisterous guests into the rear parlor, which was reserved for better-paying customers and men whose identities were not meant to escape into delicate society. Forty dollars' worth of bottles piled up quickly, but it was all right by Decker if her guests simply wanted to keep it a wine party. Macheca seemed much drunker than his companions. She remarked that they looked like they'd all been having a gay time.

Macheca regaled her with the story of the party's trip to the theater and dinner at Fabacher's. He added that the men had come to Decker's house so that people would know where they were.

"It's too bad about Dave, isn't it?" Decker said, making conversation. News of the shooting was everywhere in the night world.

"Yes," Macheca said. He motioned to his companions, who were on their way to being as drunk as he was. "These are all Dave's enemies."

With the discretion of a good businesswoman, Decker let the comment pass, deciding not to mention Hennessy's name again. Before long, she went to bed and left the noisy party to her employees. Macheca drew a small pistol from his pocket and drunkenly waved it in the air, then tossed it on the floor. Stop being so reckless, he was warned. "Don't worry," he scoffed, "it won't go off—it doesn't have a trigger." Macheca found himself talking to a woman named Hazel Malcolm. To her, Macheca slurred, "I'm glad he's shot."

Decker's piano player, Walter Robinson, knew Macheca, but none of the others, all of whom were carrying on in Italian. Robinson didn't understand them, but that didn't matter, as he was paid to play the piano, not to banter with guests. It was late, but he did his job, even when the Italians remained past the 3:00 a.m. closing time. At a quarter to four, Robinson decided to call it a night. He closed the lid of the house piano and slipped into his coat. When he opened the front door, Robinson nearly stepped on Robert Pollock and two other policemen. Pollock was wrapped in an overcoat and his slouch hat was pulled over his eyes. Still, Robinson knew him instantly. The musician showed the cop into the front parlor and went home.

Pollock stayed for only a few minutes before leaving and crossing the street to join the two other officers, Hevron and Cassidy, beneath a grocery canopy. They waited within clear sight of Fanny Decker's front door. At three minutes to 4:00, Macheca and the others stumbled outside. The party caroused to the corner of Canal and Rampart and talked for awhile before Macheca, Patorno, and the Caruso brothers climbed into a Rampart and Dauphine line streetcar.

The three cops hailed a horse-drawn cab and followed. When the streetcar stopped at Dumaine, Patorno and John Caruso stepped off and began to walk into the French Quarter. Expecting the remaining passengers to get off at Barracks Street, the next stop, Pollock's cab dashed past the streetcar to Ursulines, where the officers scrambled out and hurried to the corner of Bourbon and Hospital, within sight of the Macheca home. They shivered for ten minutes under the damp awning of a corner grocery, waiting.

Macheca and Jim Caruso finally appeared, coming up Bourbon from the opposite direction. The soused businessman and the immigrant foreman stopped at the doorstep of Macheca's house. The police edged back against the grocery, watching and listening.

☽

Eleven

IN MEMORY OF OUR DEAR FRIEND

AT DAWN ON THURSDAY, OCTOBER 16, TWO PAPERBOYS TURNED in a sawed-off shotgun they found in the muddy gutter of the Basin and Julia street corner. Both of the gun's hammers were cocked. Its metal skeleton stock could be loosened by a thumbscrew, allowing it to be folded and hidden. When the boys returned to the gutter with police, they found a half-fired shotgun with a ten-inch barrel nearby. Police were also collecting weapons from Italian immigrants, whose dwellings they would ransack for a week. Frightened Italian men and boys filled the Central Station cells overnight. A fortune teller and over forty peddlers, fruit sellers, and shoemakers were arrested on the streets and in their homes. Fifteen were brought in "on suspicion," but were released as soon as they proved their identities and their names were taken.

Monasterio was the first arrested after the shooting. The gunfire had come from the direction of his shack, and before long his shanty room was full of police. Despite their own dripping feet, they thought it significant that the shoemaker, who had been outside with the rest of the roused neighborhood, wore clean shoes and had put muddy ones under his bed. A reporter took a long piece of paper and pressed it into an oozing footprint in the street. The press reported that the soggy outline encircled Monasterio's shoe exactly. By the time Monasterio arrived at the parish prison, he had been beaten bloody.

Sergeant Joseph McCabe was among the cops who fanned out into the wounded chief's neighborhood. McCabe told reporters that he had heard ten or twenty shots fired from the Central Station blocks away. He saw Hennessy on the Gillis's steps and helped the chief into the house before plunging into the neighborhood in search of the attackers. McCabe, police officer Frank McEntee, and doorman Charles Usher—who worked in Hennessy's office and said he was following the chief home—arrested their first suspect at 1:30 a.m., about forty-five minutes after the shooting. Antonio Bagnetto was the night watchman at Vincent Scaffidi's fruit stand in nearby Poydras Market, which occupied a block and a half of Poydras Street between Rampart and Baronne, three blocks from Hennessy's home. The cops heard that Bagnetto had been absent from Scaffidi's stalls and arrested him with a loaded six-shooter in his pocket. McCabe said Bagnetto suggested the officer should keep the gun. "The Italian said, 'Do you want to be a friend of mine? Take this pistol and keep it for yourself and you will make as good a friend of me as a brother, and plenty of Italian friends. You don't do that . . . you know . . .'"

It would never be clear if Bagnetto's tough talk was a pregnant threat or an attempt to escape a concealed weapon charge. Under the circumstances, Sergeant McCabe took it as a threat.

At the corner of Poydras and Dryades, McCabe and McEntee arrested another fruit seller, forty-four-year-old Antonio Marchesi. An hour later they picked up the bearded vendor's fourteen-year-old son, Gasperi, at the Marchesi home. Young Marchesi had a $100 bill and almost $50 in smaller denominations on him. Sicilian fruit vendors dealt in cash and were suspicious of banks, but any Italian with a $100 bill in his pocket was now suddenly arrestable and newsworthy. Father and son were charged as accessories. The boy was soon released, but would be back in custody in a few days.

Sergeant McCabe got a tip about Antonio Scaffidi, who had been absent from his uncle's fruit stand for most of the night, the same stand where Bagnetto worked as watchman. McCabe headed down Basin Street at daybreak, finding a pistol in the mud along the way. When he arrived at the market, he found Scaffidi sitting in front of the fruit stand reading the morning paper. Scaffidi's Uncle Vincent told McCabe that twenty-four-year-old Antonio had come to work the previous night at eight, somewhat late. He left about ten thirty with the oilcloth used to cover the fruit tucked under his arm. When he returned later, he had the black duck fabric with him. Vincent Scaffidi gave McCabe the oilcloth; the sergeant took the nephew too.

Pietro Natali, a laborer who had just arrived from Chicago, was pushed into a police van at the Illinois Central railway depot. He was pointed out as a "suspicious character" because his clothes were too big for him. Police shook Bastian Incardona out of his sleep at Tony Matranga's oyster saloon at Poydras and Liberty, where he had lived since his boss left Greek Row. Giuseppe Impastado, another Matranga stevedore, was found to be armed with the same heavy revolver he carried when he was charged with intent to kill Joe Provenzano five months before. Impastado was arrested on charges of carrying a concealed weapon and being a suspicious character, but was never charged in the Hennessy attack.

As far as most people knew, Hennessy was still alive, but the city was look-ing hard at anyone with an Italian accent. When the parish prison opened at 9:00 a.m., Peter Provenzano's mother-in-law was at the gate with a bundle of trousers. Deputy Sheriff Tim Dwyer, the prison searcher, ran his hand over the bundle and felt something hard. He unrolled the trousers and four thin files fell out. Criminal Sheriff Gabriel Villere was about to arrest the old woman when the prison clerk explained he was expecting the files. Black inmates were planning to use them to whittle a bone toothpick for Provenzano and needles for themselves.

Police in Mobile, Alabama, learned of the shooting quickly and watched for any suspicious Italians alighting from the morning train. They searched the train, but found no one to question. Two "foreigners" who showed up at the Mobile police headquarters that afternoon applied for a license to peddle candy and in imperfect English gave their address as Lafayette Street in New Orleans, which was near the scene of the shooting. They were arrested, even though they pleaded that they had heard the shooting but knew nothing more. From one hundred miles away, the *Daily Picayune* decided that their shoes fit footprints found in the Girod Street mire. The press was wasting no time lin-ing up suspects for the shocked people of New Orleans.

The first witnesses promised to be the best. Rosa Walton, Monasterio's neighbor, told police that the shoemaker had been visited by two Italians late every night since the weekend. She said they sent her to buy beer for them two or three times. A few nights ago, Walton said she passed the room and saw Monasterio bending and folding a short gun during one of the visits. The men were at the shack the night of the shooting when she went to bed.

This, wrote the press, was what Rosa Walton had to say, but all of it proved to be a false newspaper report, for no one ever mentioned the story again.

A housepainter from Texas named M. L. Peeler came to the Central Sta-tion to volunteer that he had seen the shooting. Peeler said he lived on the sec-ond floor of a house at the corner of Girod and Basin and when the first two shots were fired, he jumped up and went out onto his gallery where he saw a man firing a gun in the middle of the street. "I hallooed to him, 'Don't shoot, stop that! What in the hell are you doing that for?' He fired a shot and from under the smoke from his gun he looked up at me. He fired another shot and I yelled at him, 'Damn you, if you fire, I'll kill you!'"

A woman named Mary Wheeler, who lived in the room next to Peeler, went out onto the gallery too. Peeler said he yelled at her to get his shotgun, even though he did not own one. Hearing this, the man in the street calmly put his gun under his coat and briskly walked two hundred feet to Julia Street, where he broke into a run. Two other men ran past, stooping. Peeler said the first man had been at the corner earlier, about 11:00 p.m. When the shooting began, Peeler said he reckoned the lurker was a cuckold who saw his wife going into a house with another man and was trying to shoot them. Peeler complained that none of the police who came to the scene would go down Basin Street in pursuit of the running man.

"I could've shot him if I'd had a pistol," insisted the painter, who said the man wore an oilcloth coat. That was one of the few things Peeler said that would not be called into question.

Brought to the prisoners' cells, Peeler picked out Antonio Scaffidi from four prisoners. "That's the party I saw on the crossing with the gun in his hand." Peeler said, adding that Scaffidi wore an oilcloth coat. One of the other men running away wore a checked coat. In front of another cell, Peeler identified him as Antonio Bagnetto, who was ordered to put on his coat. "That's the man and that's the coat," Peeler said. He turned to see Bastian Incardona standing white-faced in a cell behind him. "And that's another of the men I saw running away."

J. C. Roe, the Boylan officer detailed to watch Hennessy's house, claimed to have seen the ambush more clearly than Peeler. Roe said he was standing at the uptown corner of Girod and Basin, idly watching a man in light clothing approach from Rampart Street, when three men bobbed out from the gateway of the Petersen shanty with shotguns and a pistol. When they opened fire, the man in light clothes ran and took cover at the corner, returning the fire. Roe said he realized then that the man in light clothing was Hennessy. Roe said he ran into the street with his pistol drawn, but it jammed, and buckshot nicked his earlobe. He said he turned and ran up Girod Street looking for cover and ducked into a passageway as the assassins fired at him. Eight bullet holes were found in the tall picket fence outside the Hennessy home.

Zachary Foster, the laborer nabbed by Boylan officers Roe and Robert Hennessy immediately after the shooting, corroborated Roe's version. He said he had seen the Boylan officer at the corner and saw Chief Hennessy coming. When the gunfire erupted, Foster said he was nearly opposite Roe and saw two men come out of the shanty gateway to fire at Hennessy, who shot back. When Hennessy took cover, his attackers advanced into the street, still firing. Foster said he was escaping down Basin when police grabbed him.

By noon the city knew that the chief was dead. O'Connor's description of the attack, including Hennessy's whisper that "dagos" had shot him, was front-page news. Sergeant McCabe, who also claimed to have heard Hennessy say that his assailants were Italians, filed murder charges against half a dozen immigrants, including Monasterio, Incardona, Scaffidi, Bagnetto, and the elder Marchesi. Zachary Foster was put in the black or "colored" section of the parish prison as a material witness. The Italians were not offered bail, but Foster was held in default of a $10,000 bond, which was an impossible sum for him. When the prison van arrived, two judges and four police guards accompanied it to the prison to make sure no harm came to the prisoners.

Vines of black crepe entwined courtrooms and the Central Station where Hennessy's shrouded picture was placed in the Common Street window. Two crayon portraits of the chief sat on easels in the lobby of the Grand Opera House. Federal agencies and the city's commercial exchanges closed, passing resolutions of mourning as condolences poured in from railroads and the Boylan agency's other commercial accounts. Boylan found over a hundred telegrams of sympathy when he returned from picking out a coffin for his young partner.

Telegrams hummed into New Orleans from all over the country, flooding the mayor's office. The British consul recalled Hennessy's assistance and sent condolences, as did the consuls of Spain and Portugal. Police chiefs in New York, Cincinnati, and cities all over the South expressed their sympathy. Hennessy's friend William Pinkerton, whose telegram wishing the wounded chief a swift recovery lay in the pile of messages, now sent word to order a floral wreath. If there was anything the Pinkerton detective agency could do to help find Hennessy's killers, he said, it was at Mayor Shakspeare's disposal.

Flowers began arriving at the Hennessy home early, crowding the parlor with condolences before there was a body to mourn, filling the house with a tormenting scent of roses and drifting unreality. The Boylan Agency sent a large crescent with a dove nestled in its curves. A mammoth white crescent and star, the city police emblem, was placed nearby. A four-foot-tall cross and crown from Hennessy's fellow members of the Louisiana Athletic Club stood against the wall. When undertakers arrived with the chief's body in the late afternoon, a friend unhooked the dead man's coral necklace and placed it around Margaret Hennessy's neck. Mrs. Hennessy sat silently by the coffin, as light from a silver candelabra flickered across her son's face.

Sympathetic or merely curious people lined the wooden banquettes all the way down to the Rampart Street corner, past the ambush site. Some fingered bullet holes and found traces of blood. Others were allowed to enter the Hennessy home to view the body, but when the noise began to upset Hennessy's mother, cops closed the doors to all but friends and prominent citizens who had known the dead man. As night fell, people on the sidewalks commented on how dark the streets were. It was no surprise that even someone as careful and fearless as the chief could be bushwhacked in such a place.

The chief's dying words had newspapermen chasing every prominent Italian American in the city for a reaction, especially those assumed to have an interest in the Provenzano case.

"I don't want to talk about this," said Michael Macheca, one of Joe's step-brothers and head of the Macheca Brothers steamship business. "I don't want to be mixed up in this affair, but it's deplorable. It is a damnable affair and deserves the severest condemnation. It is strange to me that these killings have been so frequent in past years and nobody has been punished. Men have fallen by the hands of assassins who go unwhipped of justice, but I hope that this case will have a different termination."

Like Macheca, George Provenzano declined to be interviewed. Vincent Provenzano agreed with a suggestion that the killing had been planned to work up public sentiment against his imprisoned brothers. "I wish I could prove that, but I can't," Provenzano said. "Mr. Hennessy was truly a father to us and if I only knew who killed him, I would not take the trouble to convey him to jail." Still facing retrial, the Provenzanos began openly advertising Hennessy as their champion, without proof of the claim.

Frank Romero, an Italian American active in ward politics, told reporters "a man that would shoot a man as Mr. Hennessy was shot ought to be caught and hung." Joe and Peter Provenzano agreed through a grated prison window, calling the killing cowardly and dastardly, adding that the killers ought to be lynched.

Sheriff Villere felt that there was enough anger in the city to warrant heavy security at the parish prison. He had Warden Lem Davis post night guards armed with new double-barreled shotguns and Winchester rifles. Guards checked the cells every half hour. Thirty more men were stationed at the doors of the state arsenal. Most of the Italian-born citizens of New Orleans stayed indoors, as the threats of street characters and word of the panic of arrests spread.

That evening Peeler's neighbor Mary Wheeler visited the Central Station cells. She told police that she had seen the running men but didn't recognize any of the suspects. The streetlight was too dim, but she said she did think that Scaffidi was about the size of the man she had seen wearing an oilcloth coat.

Lannigan, the lumberyard watchman, also visited the cells. A few prisoners looked familiar, but he could not be sure.

The retrial of the Provenzanos did not begin as scheduled that Friday, October 17.

The doors of the Hennessy cottage were opened to the public at 6:00 a.m. and a steady line filed through the parlor until ten o'clock, when police pallbearers arrived. Eight corporals were to place their dead chief in a horse-drawn hearse, but they decided to carry the mahogany casket through the streets to city hall, as bright sunshine filled the sky.

Crowds in Lafayette Square watched as the blue uniforms marched carefully up the stone steps of city hall. Hennessy's men took him to the city council chamber and placed his casket on pedestals above a black bearskin rug. The chief's blue hat, belt, and club were arranged near his head. Hundreds of people came for a look at the waxen face under the glass plate. Hennessy lay only feet from the spot where Jefferson Davis had rested in state a year ago, but the gloom of the Confederate president's funeral was not repeated. Light poured through the open windows, illuminating the blooms of red and purple immortelles. Floral lyres, anchors, and grand broken columns joined simple bouquets left by police officers and their children. Some of the flowers were sent anonymously.

Meanwhile, across town, a gangly, consumptive newspaper seller named Thomas Duffy appeared in the Orleans Parish Prison bull pen, the waiting area between the inner and outer gates. Duffy was a two-bit public nuisance who visited pals in the prison every other day. Today he wanted to see Skip Mealey, the head trusty or "captain of the yard." He also asked for Finch Girard, who was inside for assault and battery and whose prison hobby was kicking weaker inmates in the throat.

Deputies allowed the trio to visit in the reception room. When they emerged, Girard said that Duffy reckoned he could identify that Italian, Scaffidi, as one of the fellows who shot the chief and asked if he could have a look at the prisoner.

Intrigued deputies sent an order inside to the cells for Scaffidi to be brought down. Searcher Dwyer noticed the spindly Duffy putting a hand inside his coat and asked jokingly, "Got a bomb for him?"

A trusty returned with Scaffidi, who shuffled forward curiously. When the fruit seller was a foot from the gate, Duffy pulled a pistol from his pocket, thrust his arm through the bars, and shot Scaffidi in the neck. Scaffidi reeled, then ran, screaming, into the "colored yard."

"Dave Hennessy was my best friend," Duffy shrieked as guards wrestled him to the ground. "If there were seventy-five more men like me in New Orleans, we'd run all the dagos out of town!"

When Duffy's shot echoed off the walls, the entire prison population panicked; Italian prisoners were sure a lynch mob was breaking in to kill them. Duffy was carted off to the police station, while Scaffidi was rushed to Charity Hospital. Like Chief Hennessy, Scaffidi was surrounded by more reporters than doctors as his throat was examined. His hands clutched his bloodstained woolen shirt. He writhed from side to side, asking God why he had been shot. "I'm dying," he cried. "Send for my sister and my parents! I lived here ten years and never was in any trouble. I am a young man, twenty-four years old, and here they kill me like a dog!"

Scaffidi pleaded for a priest. Word was sent to Father O'Neill who was across the street preparing for the chief's funeral. Recorder David Hollander arrived with his macabre notebook, a stenographer, and police detective Dexter Gaster.

"Hello, Judge," Scaffidi gasped through his pierced throat. "You know me, Judge Hollander. Haven't I always been a good boy?"

"Well, Scaffidi," Hollander replied somberly, "I do know you, but my present mission is not to recall acquaintances. I have come to ask you if you think you are going to die and, in that case, if you want to make a declaration."

That was all Scaffidi needed to hear. He had been talking ever since the doctors began bandaging him, and they told him he would live if he'd just stop trying to sit up. His quivering hands jumped convulsively from the bandages to his bloody shirt, then back. When Hollander's stenographer took out a pencil, it seemed as if Scaffidi would never stop talking.

"Oh, yes, Judge Hollander," Scaffidi quaked. "I believe I'm going to die, but I die innocent. Before God, I declare I am innocent! God knows, I don't know who killed the chief. I didn't have a hand in it. I'm innocent. I went home at nine o'clock that night and left at six-thirty in the morning. My wife was sick and I stayed with her. Let me tell you, my dear friends, it's a mistake! I shouldn't be arrested! My wife is in a delicate condition and at nine o'clock exactly she sent for some ham and tea. I heard of it and went home."

"Did you take your oilcloth with you?" one of the visitors asked.

"My oilcloth was over the fruit on the stand. I put it on my arm when I went home and stayed there. It's the truth—I've never been in trouble before! My family have been good citizens for forty years! You catch the right men who were against the chief. *They* killed him. I will help you kill them!"

"Who do you think killed the chief, Scaffidi?"

"The Matranga people were against the chief, I think," he said. "The chief was for the Provenzanos. He wanted to set them free and he was killed by the Matranga men. You catch the right men and by Jesus I'll help you kill them! I'm a friend of the chief. He used to buy fruit from me at the stand—his mother too."

Scaffidi's terror affected those who gathered around him. Yet some sympathetic newspapermen fancied that they could have handled being shot point-blank in the neck with more aplomb. They kept this to themselves for the time being, saving their manliness for their stories.

"I know the Provenzanos and worked for them once," Scaffidi said. "That was long ago. I had no trouble with them. I am a friend of the Matrangas. I mean, I tell them 'good morning' and like that. I'm a peaceable man and I don't have the courage to kill anybody. I am as innocent as when God made me. I wish to Christ I could catch the man who killed the chief. I don't know who had the courage to do it. We knew the chief was a friend of the Provenzanos—"

"We?" Hollander interrupted. "Whom do you mean by 'we'?"

"Oh, we . . . the people . . . the men in this town . . . you know what I mean. He liked them."

This was certainly no secret. Yet the *Daily Picayune* would sketch it as if Scaffidi had stumbled and was not saying all he knew.

"My God, this is hard," Scaffidi said, twitching. "You put me in jail and kill me. It is very hard for a young man. My God, why do you do it?" He continued to protest his innocence. "Catch the head men, don't take the poor men. They are not the ones. I don't know who could do it. I don't know, so help me God!"

The door opened to admit Father O'Neill and two of Scaffidi's relatives. When he saw them, the young fruit vendor burst into tears.

By the time Father O'Neill left the hospital and arrived at city hall, the crowds had become so heavy that police were forced to increase the size of groups allowed to view Hennessy's body. Mayor Shakspeare arrived late, stood sternly at the casket for a moment, then joined a cluster of police commissioners.

Margaret Hennessy's legs failed when she arrived. "My son is gone," she wailed. "My only one!"

"Madam," Shakspeare told her, "you should be proud to have had such a son."

Remembering the stone-faced mayor's loss of his only son, Mrs. Hennessy thanked him and sat quietly beside the coffin as an honor guard of firefighters replaced the police. The psalm *De Profundis* rounded the chamber.

When it was time, Mrs. Hennessy kissed the glass over her dead son's lips and told him she would meet him in heaven. She faltered as Sergeant McCabe helped her down the steps past the long blue lines. "Courage," he said.

The procession to St. Joseph's Church was a mile long, the longest since the funeral of Hennessy's murdered predecessor, Patrick Mealey. As the march left the business district, both the uniformed ranks and the crowds on the banquettes were unusually quiet. It was an eerie silence, broken only by clicking hooves and a low, shrouded drumbeat.

Grand Marshal William Beanham led mounted police, drummers, squads from twenty fire companies, and fifty of the dead man's fellows from the Louisiana Athletic Club. The chief's riderless jet-black horse was led before two carriages full of priests. Hennessy's casket was next, flanked by his closest friends in and out of uniform who wore streamers of white crepe around the left arm of their mourning coats. Captain Journée led a massive foot parade of policemen and over fifty carriages rolled behind, bearing everyone from the mayor to the pupils of the Chinese Mission School who sent a corbeil with a ribbon, "In Memory of Our Dear Friend." George Provenzano and his family rode in the eighth carriage. They were all there—Hennessy's mentors Badger and Boylan, the Red Light Club led by an Italian American named Tony Graffino, and police detectives with their families.

Delegates of African American civic groups filled four carriages. Lawyers, judges, sheriffs, customs officials, court clerks, and stenographers were next, then the politicians. Sharing the twenty-third carriage with Commissioner of Public Works E. T. Leche was Democratic Party kingmaker James D. Houston, the man who shot Arthur Guerin, the killer of Chief Hennessy's father.

Houston was a fixture in New Orleans political life. In past years he had been appointed or elected to serve as criminal sheriff, court clerk, administrator of public improvements, tax collector, and for the past three years, president of the city's waterworks. Despite the mild titles on his résumé, Houston was not a featureless bureaucrat. When someone tried to shoot him outside a polling place during the 1883 election, he returned fire and killed the man. He also participated in the *Mascot* office gun battle that cost Houston's friend Robert Brewster his life. The shooting incidents left Houston unpopular among some New Orleanians, yet friends and foes alike agreed that he possessed one of the shrewdest political minds in the state's Democratic Party.

Like all politicians, Houston went to a lot of funerals, but the chief's funeral was different. Houston recalled a summer day when the man who shot Hennessy's father arrived in Criminal Court and began hollering at a deputy who asked him to remove his hat. Houston, who was then chief deputy sheriff, repeated his subordinate's order. "What business is it of yours?" Guerin retorted, reaching behind his back. Houston pulled a gun and fired, hitting Guerin above the elbow. Houston's second shot hit a door casing and ricocheted into a small boy. By that time Guerin was inside the court railing, where he caught his foot in the matting and fell. Houston's third shot hit Guerin in the small of the back. He lingered for several days, but the bullet in his spine killed him. After securing a change of venue to Jefferson Parish, Houston was found blameless by a jury, which decided there was cause to pull a gun when Guerin reached behind his back. Guerin hated Houston for an imaginary insult, perhaps conceived in one of his "spells," and had pulled a pistol on Houston in court before. Houston faced Guerin down that first time, but took no chances the second time. It was all a long time ago, back in 1871. Chief Hennessy was a fatherless police messenger then, an anonymous boy running messages through the streets of the city. Houston looked at the silent crowds lining the streets, not knowing that he would try to avenge Dave Hennessy long after he had unwittingly avenged the chief's father.

When the cortege arrived at St. Joseph's, the pews were already full. Pallbearers carried Hennessy's remains up the steps of the new church, resting at a black catafalque near the altar and raising their nightsticks in salute. The organ and choir filled the air with the responsories *Libera Me* and *Subvenite*. Incense dropped onto the censer's red-hot coal. Scented smoke and echoes swirled around the dead.

Canal Street was still lined with crowds when the mourners exited St. Joseph's in the waning afternoon. Prominent people walking in the procession got into carriages at Claiborne and rode swiftly after the hearse to Metairie Cemetery, where shadows of dusk stretched across the trim lawns. The hearse stopped at a double row of brick vaults banked by honeysuckle and surrounded by hundreds of floral tributes brought from city hall. Mrs. Hennessy and the priests watched Captain Barrett lift the dead chief's belongings from the coffin as it was pushed halfway into the tomb, crushing rows of red and white roses.

The light was fading fast. Pallbearers placed their white badges on the coffin and Father O'Neill spoke.

"May his soul and those of the faithful departed, in the name of God, rest in peace."

In the hearts of many who saw the casket shoved the rest of the way into the narrow vault, the plea that Hennessy's soul be allowed to rest was less a prayer for peace than a fearful and holy challenge. A wooden tablet was placed over the mouth of the tomb to seal it temporarily. Tom Anderson took a pencil from his pocket and carefully wrote on the tablet, "David C. Hennessy, Died Oct. 16, 1890."

While most of the New Orleans Police were burying their chief, others worked. One squad returned to the Poydras Market neighborhood after the funeral, accompanied by market commissary Dennis Corcoran. Corcoran was everywhere, guiding the police to suspicious Italians. Grocer Charlie Pietzo was arrested because Corcoran claimed to have seen him accepting two guns out of a sack carried by a couple of greenhorns behind his Poydras Street grocery on Monday evening. The grocer had not been seen out of his house since Hennessy was shot on Wednesday night, but this should not have seemed unusual. Many of the city's Italians were staying indoors.

The police also brought in the victims of the Esplanade ambush. Tony Matranga was arrested at his house. While officers waited for a cab to ferry the crippled stevedore to headquarters, A. D. Henriques and Dominick O'Malley arrived at the house. Matranga was carted off as his wife, mother, and children wailed. Police accompanied Corcoran to Vincent Caruso's home where Caruso was at his kitchen table, drinking a glass of whiskey. He was handed his crutches and told he was under arrest. The cops then headed down Basin Street to Salvatore Sunzeri's house, but his wife told them he wasn't home. She invited the officers to check if they did not believe her, so they decided against it and left. Minutes later, Lionel Adams arrived with Henriques and disappeared into the house. They emerged awhile later with Sunzeri and were climbing into a cab when Corcoran and a police corporal spotted them. Adams refused to hand over Sunzeri, insisting that the stevedore wanted the attorneys to bring him to the Central Station. Citizen Corcoran and the corporal wrenched Sunzeri away and took him in by themselves.

Charles Matranga, Rocco Geraci, and Jim Caruso surrendered. Caruso's brother John was brought in on special orders from Mayor Shakspeare. The mayor also ordered warrants for Joseph Macheca, Charles Patorno, and Frank Romero, the man who had said that Hennessy's killers "ought to be caught and hung." Police looked for the three all day, but after one false arrest and rumors of Macheca fleeing aboard a tugboat, which police boarded and searched, the men were not found.

At midnight in the Central Station the mayor raised his hand against a torrent of reporters' questions by the precinct captain's door. "I will tell you this," Shakspeare volunteered, "These dago affairs have gone on as long as can be put up with. They must be stopped and the citizens of New Orleans may rest assured that nothing within human power will be left undone to ferret out all the facts in this particular case and, by showing the Italians that their secrets are not beyond the power of research of an excited and indignant populace, put a stop to their murderous institutions."

Shakspeare and the police hierarchy trooped into the captain's office, where Charles Matranga sat waiting with the door open. Shakspeare grilled Matranga for information, but Matranga protested that he'd have to be crazy to have anything to do with assaulting the chief while the Provenzano case was hanging over his family. Matranga defended his reputation: he had lived in New Orleans for years, he was indebted to the late chief for numerous favors. The door slammed shut.

As reporters craned toward the transom, one of them remembered a visit to Matranga's office during the summer, when a letter accusing Hennessy of being derelict in bringing the Provenzanos to justice arrived at the *Item*. The chief was tight-lipped when reporter Aubrey Murray showed Hennessy the letter, so Murray brought it to the Matranga & Locascio office for Charles Matranga's reaction.

"The chief is not working up the case to my satisfaction," Matranga had said, upset at the mere thought of it. "I don't like the way he's conducting the investigation at all." Matranga hesitated. "I may be able to tell you something in a day or so that will be a great surprise, something which will astonish all of New Orleans. I must speak with Mr. Macheca first, for his permission. I can't tell you today."

"Mr. Macheca?"

"Mr. Joseph Macheca."

Murray was hungry for the story. He tried a bluff, saying he could see Mr.

Macheca himself—but if the matter was that important, could Matranga save him the trip?

"All I will say is that I'm tired of being made out to be a liar," Matranga said angrily. "I won't stand it much longer. My brother lost a leg in this. I'm tired of being annoyed, of this whole midnight assassination business—I want it to stop! *The chief isn't doing his duty*. I've had enough of his humbug and I'm going to tell all I know about this thing."

"Who's making you out to be a liar?" Murray asked.

"I've said all I plan to," Matranga declared.

Murray had no story that day, but maybe his curiosity was being rewarded now. With Matranga in custody and a warrant out for Macheca, at least he could use the interview. An hour and a half later, however, Murray hid his surprise from his colleagues when Charles Matranga pushed out of the Central Station into the early morning darkness, a free man.

Edward Hevron wasn't happy. The scowling sergeant who had shadowed Macheca and Caruso home the night of the murder now looked up a lamppost at the corner of Royal and St. Philip. He would have to shimmy up there.

Hevron cut the stuffed figure down and when he got back to earth, he flipped the effigy over. A card was pinned to its back. It read "Death to the Dagoes."

☽

Twelve

THE COMMITTEE OF FIFTY

BRIGHT AND EARLY ON SATURDAY MORNING, OCTOBER 18, Joseph P. Macheca dressed in his finest suit and took a cab to the Central Station. He was taken upstairs to wait in the dock while an affidavit against him was sworn in the Recorder's Court. His son arrived and they were allowed to speak alone. When their private discussion ended, Macheca was pelted with questions from reporters.

Macheca said he never intended to leave New Orleans, in spite of rumors placing him at the outskirts of town or stowing away on a New Basin tugboat that police ransacked searching for him. "I did not know the police were looking for me last night or else I would have turned up," he said. "If I wanted to escape, I could have left town on one of my steamships."

Hennessy was my friend, Macheca told reporters. He said he had been to city hall to see the chief's remains and followed the funeral procession to the cemetery. Afterward he went to his office to work and then spent the night at a friend's house. When he read the morning *Picayune* and saw that he was wanted, he said he immediately took a carriage to the station. Macheca began to cry. "It's hard to be arrested for nothing," he wept.

When Hennessy's secretary George Vandervoort stared, his eyes were like cold granite. It was commonly assumed that the bristly former newspaper reporter shared more of Hennessy's secrets about the New Orleans underworld than anyone. The first thing Vandervoort saw when he walked into the First Recorder's Court was Joe Macheca crying. It made him insane.

"Your bladder must be near your eyes," barked Vandervoort, who had been one of Hennessy's pallbearers twenty-four hours ago. "You're crying now, but you didn't cry when you said you were glad that 'the son of a bitch' was shot."

"I did not say that at all," Macheca protested. "I swear I did not!"

"You did and I know it. You said it to Jim Caruso at four o'clock Thursday morning. I know where you were and all about it. I know more than you think," Vandervoort retorted.

"I swear I did not say it!" Macheca repeated. "If I did, I hope someone will blow my brains out before I reach the parish prison!"

"Someone might do that yet, and don't be surprised when you get it," Vandervoort said icily. "I know you well and I'll show where you were."

Two hours after Macheca surrendered, Frank Romero walked into the Central Station. The press was now calling him "Nine-Finger Frank" because of his slightly deformed hand. Charles Patorno came in fifteen minutes later and swore that he knew nothing about the murder. He was a New Orleans native, he added, and came to the station as soon as he heard the police wanted him. Although Macheca and Patorno were technically the Matrangas' superiors as their employers on the docks, their relationship with Charles Matranga and their own arrests now firmly associated them with "the Matranga gang" as far as the press was concerned.

Cops were still furiously acting upon orders to grab anyone looking suspicious or "Italian" who seemed to be in the act of leaving the city. Three Italian laborers were arrested at the Canal Street ferry when they tried to cross over to Algiers. Suspicious character charges were dropped when it was established that they were plantation workers, but they were placed under a $250 bond on concealed weapons charges for carrying banana knives.

Detectives returned with George Negelli and Elias Rhoman, the two candy peddlers arrested in Mobile. The men turned out to be a Jewish Pole and a Romanian, not Italians. They were given a safe conduct pass and released. Mayor Shakspeare questioned Tony Matranga for an hour before ordering him sent home by cab.

All day long peddlers, shoemakers, and barbers held "on suspicion" were identified and freed by the police. Meanwhile three carloads of grapes, including two consignments for Macheca Brothers, sat on the wharf, untouched by Italian stevedores who were too frightened to leave home for work. Fruit wholesalers telegraphed their Texan suppliers to postpone shipments.

Italian Consul Pasquale Corte's office filled with immigrants and Italian Americans who were scared or infuriated by the mass arrests and forced searches. Corte was told that detainees at the parish prison were being mistreated. When Corte called on the mayor to complain, Shakspeare told Corte that the parish prison was under the jurisdiction of the criminal sheriff, not the mayor's office. Shakspeare was courteous, but he had other things on his mind.

Poydras Market commissary Corcoran had come to city hall toting a rumor that Italians planned to kill Shakspeare next, then police commissioner Beanham.

Just after noon, Mayor Shakspeare listened grimly as his official notice of the death of Police Superintendent and Chief Hennessy was read aloud to a packed city council chamber. Some councilors had wanted to meet immediately after Hennessy's murder, but Shakspeare felt it would be more appropriate to wait until after the funeral, preventing a riot in the bargain. Shakspeare's anger was blunted by having a clerk read the death notice, but there was no mistaking his mood.

> *The circumstances of the cowardly deed, the arrests made and the evidence collected by the police department show beyond doubt that he was the victim of Sicilian vengeance, wreaked upon him as the chief representative of law and order in this community, because he was seeking, by the power of our American law, to break up the fierce vendettas that have so often stained our streets with blood.*
>
> *Heretofore these scoundrels have confined their murderings among themselves. None of them have ever been convicted because of the secrecy with which the crimes have been committed and the impossibility of getting evidence from people of their own race to convict. Bold indeed was the stroke aimed at their first American victim. A shining mark they have selected on which to write with the assassin's hand their contempt for the civilization of the new world. We owe it to ourselves, and to everything we hold sacred in this life, to see to it that this blow is the last. We must teach these people a lesson that they will not forget for all times.*

Before the council, Shakspeare recalled an incident involving a prominent Italian who had asked for protection from blackmail a decade ago. Because the man would give him no names, Shakspeare could do nothing. Under present circumstances, however, the mayor would see to it that secret assassination societies subsidized by the wealthy and powerful in the Italian community were rooted out and destroyed.

"The Sicilian who comes here must be an American citizen and subject his wrongs to the remedy of the law of the land, or else there must be no place for him on the American continent," he said.

The city council agreed. Motions approved Shakspeare's intention to destroy all secret murder societies for the benefit of both immigrant and native-born citizens. Shakspeare declared that he was next on the list of intended victims, but feared nothing. He got a standing ovation.

The mayor concluded by appointing a group of New Orleanians called the Committee of Fifty "to take action on the very serious condition which confronts us as a municipality."

Later that afternoon, the mayor's secretary, Wright Schaumberg, met privately with Algernon Badger, the police chief maimed in the Battle of Liberty Place who had taken young Hennessy on as a messenger boy, and Henry Warmoth, collector of the Port of New Orleans. Warmoth was one of the best-known men in the city, having served as a governor of Louisiana during Reconstruction. He was a habitual Republican candidate, but perennial charges that he was rallying black citizens to return the state to rule by bayonet kept him collector of customs revenues. The U.S. Custom House employed a large number of Union men whose federal jobs were safe from local recriminations, and among them was appraiser Badger.

Schaumberg, Warmoth, and Badger discussed the *Elysia*, which was steaming toward New Orleans with a thousand Italians aboard and due to arrive early Tuesday morning. The three men decided to quarantine the ship until city representatives could be sent aboard to inspect the immigrants. If any paupers or criminals were found, the *Elysia* would be forced to return them to Italy under the terms of restriction acts. Any Italians found not in violation of such laws would be allowed to land.

Olivia Petersen and her neighbor Mrs. Osberg stood in the parish prison yard, nervously looking up at a line of eight prisoners. Acting on a tip from the Boylan detective agency, Captain Barrett brought the women to the prison to see if they could pick out the well-dressed man who had rented Mrs. Petersen's mother-in-law's shack for Monasterio. The women thought they recognized Joe Macheca, but said they were not sure.

A few minutes after the prisoners returned to their cells, the warden told Macheca to put on his coat and hat and return to the prison office. When he got there, Captain Barrett asked Macheca if he had ever seen either of the two women who stood before him. No, Macheca told the policeman.

"You're the man who came to rent the cottage," Mrs. Petersen said.

"I was never in that neighborhood in my life," Macheca replied. "If I called on you, ma'am, what kind of jewelry did I have on?"

"You wore a heavy gold chain," Mrs. Petersen said uncomfortably.

"Didn't I have a large diamond on my shirt?" Macheca asked.

"I don't know." Mrs. Petersen was visibly indecisive.

"Are you sure this is the man?" Captain Barrett asked.

"I don't like to swear to it," Mrs. Petersen said. Sergeant McCabe dismissed Macheca and called a cab for the two women. He climbed in with them, and when they all reached the Petersen home after a long ride, Olivia Petersen claimed to have regained her composure. Now she was sure Macheca had rented the shack.

The Committee of Fifty convened that night in the city council chamber. The mayor's choice for chairman was Edgar Farrar, a lawyer with perfect social credentials, including memberships in the Pickwick Club and the Southern Athletic Club. The *Mascot* chided Shakspeare for picking a "hothead" for such a sensitive job. No one had any idea how right the scandal rag's editors would be proven, not only about Farrar, but also about others the mayor chose to restore law and order to New Orleans.

Shakspeare's choices of Boylan, Badger, and Judge Robert Davey were predictable. Social lions from the Mardi Gras krewe of Rex and the Boston Club were named, and a dozen White League veterans were also tapped. Maurice Hart, the powerful construction contractor who had seen Thomas Devereaux gunned down, was appointed, as were numerous prominent attorneys and businessmen from cotton, tobacco, hotel, grocery, and wholesale crockery concerns. Shakspeare's committee was a grand meeting of high society and commercial excellence. Their stockings were pure silk.

Like the gangs it pledged to destroy, the committee decided to keep its work secret, and financing would be by subscription. Behind closed doors, committee members were read a petition from thirty-five prominent Italians who denounced Hennessy's murder "in unmeasured terms" and offered assistance in finding his killers. The petitioners sought "to impress upon the committee the difference between Italians and Sicilians" and declared that there were "none of the latter race" in their ranks.

When the hourlong meeting was over, Shakspeare was summoned and listened with satisfaction to the committee's plans while a ruckus started in the hallway outside. Peeler, the housepainter who claimed to have seen the men who shot the chief, was trying to force his way past guards at the door.

Peeler begged for police protection, saying he was receiving threatening letters that promised he would die unless he kept quiet. Shakspeare told the hysterical painter that his life had also been threatened and that his wife and daughters had pleaded with him not to leave his Carondelet Street mansion. Peeler got a police escort home.

"I was never in the neighborhood in question, never saw the lady before this afternoon and never rented any room, either from her or from anyone else in that district," Joseph Macheca told the *Times-Democrat*'s John Coleman in prison. Macheca described his confrontation with Olivia Petersen with careful formality, making sure that Coleman knew that Mrs. Petersen could not swear to a positive identification. "I don't even know where that lady lives, nor have I ever heard of her before."

"Do you belong to any secret or other organizations?" Coleman asked.

"The only association of any character of which I am a member is Pelican Fire Company No. 4."

Macheca recounted his evening at the theater and the late supper at Fabacher's. "While at the restaurant, Officer Sherman gave me the first infor-mation as to the shooting of Chief Hennessy, saying he had been shot in the leg. This fact I immediately communicated to Mr. Lionel Adams, at the same time expressing my surprise and regret thereat. From Fabacher's, myself and friends went to number 11 Burgundy Street, where we remained until 3:30 or 4:00 a.m. At the corner of Rampart and Canal streets the party disbanded, myself, the Carusos, and Charles Patorno taking the same car for our respective homes."

"What were the relations between yourself and Chief Hennessy?" Cole-man asked.

"We were always good friends," Macheca replied.

"Were you interested in the case of the Matrangas?"

"Yes. But only to the extent of putting an end to murders and assassina-tions of any sort in this community."

"Did you ever have any conversation with the chief on this subject?" Coleman asked.

"I did. Shortly after I had heard of the shooting, I called on Chief Hen-nessy in company with Mr. A. D. Henriques." Macheca described their con-versation about unpunished shootings and Hennessy's advice to Henriques about taking the Matranga side. After that, he said, things had gone badly.

"About two weeks after the shooting, I was walking along Canal Street. Chief Hennessy was riding along in his buggy, but getting a view of me, jumped out of the vehicle and came up to me. The first words he said to me were that I ought to mind my own business and not connect his name in any way with the Provenzano-Matranga case. I told him I had heard that he had been helping the Provenzanos to escape the punishment which was due them for their murderous assault upon the Matrangas. To this, the chief replied I was a damned liar, or words to that effect. Then I told him that John Caruso had informed me that he, Chief Hennessy, was paying for the board of the Proven-zanos in the parish prison."

Caruso stood nearby, listening to Macheca's statement to the reporter. "What's that?"

Macheca looked up. "I told the chief that you had informed me that he was paying the board of the Provenzanos in the parish prison."

"Oh no!" Caruso said. "Don't make any mention of that."

"Didn't you tell me so?" Macheca asked.

"Not that I know of."

"You certainly did and you know full well you did," Macheca said, looking Caruso straight in the face.

Charles Matranga, who had been rearrested, was also listening. "Maybe you said that you'd heard it reported this was so," he suggested to Caruso.

"Oh yes, I told you it was reported so," Caruso said. He asked the reporter to leave this out of the story. "It's not important."

"No," Coleman replied. "It's Mr. Macheca's interview and as he considered it important in his statement, it'll have to go."

"When I told the chief what Caruso had informed me, he replied that the statement was untrue," Macheca resumed. "I refused, however, to accept his denial and told him so. In fact, I reiterated to him my belief that he had been helping the Provenzanos. And upon a subsequent investigation, I ascertained to my own satisfaction that he was guilty as charged. Upon my refusal to believe his denial in the matter, he took occasion to inform me again that I had better attend to my own business. I replied that was something which I had always done and we parted."

Macheca added that Hennessy later sent W. B. Stansbury of the *Times-Democrat* to him to ask that the chief's name not be mentioned in testimony in the Provenzano case. Macheca agreed and sent Stansbury back to Hennessy with the message that he hoped he and the chief could remain friends. Macheca pointed out that he lived up to his end of the bargain—he did not mention Hennessy in his testimony. Macheca claimed he saw Hennessy about town twice after their unfriendly parting. Macheca was talking to a woman Hennessy rented some property to on Rampart Street and the chief bade the woman good evening, but ignored Macheca. The prisoner said he last saw the chief about a week before his death.

"I saw him riding along in his buggy as I was coming downtown in a Royal streetcar. Neither of us spoke. I saw him, but I cannot tell whether he saw me or not."

Elsewhere in the prison, reporters crowded around the window of the cell where Guillio, Pellegrini, and Joe Provenzano were locked up for the night.

Provenzano said Hennessy's death was a shock. "We knew him well. We were friends, and he was one of our witnesses. He tried to prosecute us at our first trial, but when he heard all the evidence, he saw we were not guilty."

"Who do you think shot him?" a reporter asked.

"I don't know."

"Nobody knows, but who do you think?" the reported persisted.

"Matranga, sure."

"Why do you think so?"

"Because he was going to be a witness for us and expose them," Provenzano said. "He knew all about Matranga and Geraci. He got some things from Italy about them, and he was going to tell what he knew, and that would break them up. Matranga was the head of the Stopiglieri society."

"What's that society?"

"They're people that work for the Matrangas," Provenzano said. "There are about twenty leaders of them. They're the committee and there are about three hundred greenhorns who've got to do anything the leaders say. I'll tell you about that. When Jim Caruso came to me about four years ago with a letter asking $1,000 for the Mafia or they would kill us, Caruso told me Matranga was the president of it and Rocco Geraci was a leader. Caruso said he had been in it too, but got out of it as soon as he could; that they brought him into the room and he saw Matranga dressed in a black domino, and others were dressed in dominoes, and they made him swear on a skull with a dirk in it. He said he was willing to rob people, but he didn't want to have to kill anybody, so he got out of it.

"I didn't believe Geraci was in it," Provenzano continued, "but Caruso told me yes again. I took the letter to George, my brother, and said I thought we had better pay. George said no, and showed it to some friends. We were in a poolroom on St. Charles Street then. A lot of men wanted to get up a crowd, go to the lake, have us pay over the money, and then catch the fellows. There were about twenty-five or thirty in the crowd. Judge Davey, Mister Mealey, and Ralph Morgan were among them."

"Are there any Italians in the Mafia besides the people who work on the ships?" the reporter asked.

"I don't know. They've got the Mafia Society everywhere. They've got it in San Francisco, St. Louis, Chicago, New York, and here."

"Did you ever belong to it?"

"Me! No, indeed," Provenzano declared vehemently.

"Where does this Mafia or Stopiglieri Society meet?"

"They meet anywhere," Provenzano said, naming the levee and the Back o' Town and Carrollton neighborhoods. "Their headquarters are in Carrollton, I think."

"Weren't you the head of an association?"

"We had a laborers' association when we had the stevedore business and never let any greenhorns in it. All our men were Italians who were raised here, and they were Americans. We had the association to keep up the price for work. We paid 40¢ an hour for day work and 60¢ an hour for night work and Sundays. The men often made $30 or $35 a week, and spent it freely here. Matranga only pays his men 10¢ or 15¢ an hour, and they only earn $5 or $6 a week, and the leaders make lots of money. Their own men hate them, but have to do what they say or get killed. They make the greenhorns do the killing. They pay them $10, $20, or $100 to get a man out of the way, and if the man they order to kill someone won't do it, they have him killed so he can't tell anything to the police."

"They've killed two of our witnesses now," Pellegrini said through the grate. "The chief and Vittrano. Vittrano was going to testify that he was in a restaurant with me the night the Matrangas were shot and they killed him before our first trial."

By the time parish prison guards cleared visitors out for the night, a typical gaggle of fresh inmates arrived: drunks, a wife beater, a woman who had carved another with a knife, and a petty thief called Burnt Finger George. The most famous inmates, however, were not these men and women, nor even the Provenzano brothers and their codefendants. An affidavit filed that morning charged Salvatore Sunzeri with the murder of Chief Hennessy. Joseph Macheca, Rocco Geraci, Jim and John Caruso, Charles Matranga, Charles Patorno, and Frank Romero were accused of being accessories to the killing before and after the fact. They slept that night in prison without the option of bail.

By Sunday the bullet holes at the site of the Hennessy shooting had been counted. Twenty-six pieces of lead had hit the Thames-Dayton shotgun cottage. Another eighteen smacked the house on the corner where Hennessy took cover. All of Hennessy's shots were accounted for. One hit the gate alongside Monasterio's shack. Another hit the shanty wall at floor level. Three more slugs were dug out of the building on the corner.

Arrests trickled off and Scaffidi returned to prison with a bandaged neck. Charles Traina, a rice cutter arrested at the Sarpy Plantation west of New Orleans, was brought into the city. A passenger thought Traina had acted peculiarly in the railway station the morning after Hennessy's murder. The Italian carried a basket and had a bandanna wrapped around his hand. The passenger and a conductor watched Traina as the train headed toward St. Charles Parish. The Italian got off without the basket. When detectives arrived at the plantation, Traina denied having left the place for several weeks, but he was identified as the man on the train. Two other officers found a porter at Grace Episcopal Church, a neighbor of Hennessy's roused by the shooting, who identified Traina as "the short man" running away. The bandanna was taken from Traina's hand, which was found to be skinned.

Sergeant McCabe was promoted to acting captain until the crisis was over. He and Captain Barrett took Rosa Walton and Emma Thomas to the parish prison to see if they could identify Macheca. The two women picked Macheca from the lineup once, then a second time as Macheca was made to don his coat and hat, according to the newspapers. Prison keeper Tom Carey, however, would remember it differently at the trial.

The pressure showed in the naturally edgy Macheca's face. He told reporters that Hennessy had been the Provenzanos' friend, but that they suspected he was about to throw them over and have nothing more to do with them. Macheca claimed to have warned Hennessy to expect trouble between the Provenzanos and the Carusos. After the Matranga ambush on the corner of Esplanade and Claiborne, the chief asked Macheca to keep him posted, which Macheca said he did gladly until he heard that Hennessy was "supporting" the Provenzanos. At that point, Macheca said he ended his friendship with the chief. The parting caused some bitterness, he said, but Macheca had regained his temper and said he considered himself to be Hennessy's friend again.

Coro Groffio's grocery at the corner of Burgundy and Conti streets sat amid a strip of black brothels called Smoky Row. Cribs there were the cheapest in New Orleans, nothing like the fancy bordellos visited by the wealthy and powerful. Any career prostitute who lived past thirty was considered old, and if she managed not to die of disease, there was a good chance she would be found on Smoky Row. Five years before, white passersby had complained of muggings, so police evicted the tough black women, but they soon drifted back into the neighborhood, with the color line blurring to include some white trulls.

That Sunday afternoon, thirty Italian laborers lounged in Groffio's rear courtyard drinking, laughing, and playing cards. It had been a long trip from Chicago, twenty-eight hours by train. The men wanted to relax a little before a *padrone* got them moving again, off to swing cane knives on southwestern Louisiana sugar plantations.

When the doors shattered and the cops charged in, Groffio was so frightened that he ran upstairs and hid under his bed. His customers from Chicago were not as lucky. Some tried to hide in a woodshed, underneath piles of wood. Two crawled up the chimney as the cops beat order into the pandemonium below with their billy clubs. When the violent roundup was over, the police searched the thirty-four prisoners and the courtyard for weapons. Nothing was found.

That same afternoon, three Italian plantation workers strolled down Canal Street, quietly taking in the greatest thoroughfare in the South. As a prank, a passerby told a policeman that the three sightseeing laborers were members of the ferocious Matranga gang.

It wasn't funny to the cop. He followed the Italians for half a block before arresting them. While the joker chuckled, one of the Italians protested that the arrest was unjust. The laughter of a gathering crowd turned to horror and outrage as the cop beat the man bloody on the Canal Street sidewalk.

At seven o'clock that evening, Hennessy's neighbor Officer Dayton and two other policemen knocked on a Julia Street door several blocks from the Hennessy cottage. After getting no answer, Dayton went around to the alley and climbed through a window.

Dayton found his man, another Italian fruit peddler, in bed, which was not unusual at that hour, for most vendors began their day in predawn darkness. The vendor, Emmanuele Polizzi, had been Dayton's and Hennessy's neighbor for four or five months when he lived in the Petersen shack for some time before Monasterio moved in. Dayton arrested the terrified Polizzi in his bed and took him to the Central Station.

Polizzi was terrified. When he arrived at the Central Station, he was asked what his name was. It was taken down phonetically. On his indictment, throughout his trial, and long afterward, the fruit vendor would be known as Manuel Politz.

Poydras Market commissary Dennis Corcoran, still working overtime, produced a black child who identified Polizzi as one of two greenhorns who had delivered guns to Pietzo's grocery. Corcoran and the boy said that Polizzi had then worn a mustache, but must have shaved for his face was now bare.

Officer John Kroper came down to the station saying he had seen a man in a striped suit and pointed shoes running from the scene of the shooting. Kroper and Dayton returned to Polizzi's house and found a striped suit and an old pair of pointed shoes that they took to the station and made Polizzi put on. Yes, Kroper said, this one fell and dropped a shotgun.

There was a mark on Polizzi's right wrist that could have been made by a bullet. The prisoner also complained of soreness in his elbow and arm, and one of his ears was hurt. Polizzi said in broken English that he got the injuries falling from a cart on Monday. He sure was a queer one, the cops thought. He acted like he was drunk.

The police tapped Polizzi's bandaged wrist and asked him if a doctor could prove when he was injured and treated.

"Ah, doctor!" Polizzi said. "Doctor . . . *Bersaglieri*, Old Basin!"

The police searched the Old Basin neighborhood for a Dr. Bagsolari, not understanding that Polizzi was referring to a doctor who tended to members of the Societa Italiana del Tiro al Bersaglio, a local social organization. The press reported that no such physician could be found, implying that the suspect was a liar. Had the Italian invented a fictitious doctor to provide an alibi? It was, after all, a "felon's defense."

Thirteen

The Law Assassinated

CLAIMS THAT THE DEAD CHIEF WAS EVERYONE'S FRIEND clouded the air, from Duffy's hysterical excuse for shooting Scaffidi at the parish prison to Macheca's insistence that he was on good terms not only with the Provenzanos—who, he still maintained, threatened to kill him—and the Matrangas, but especially with Hennessy, regardless of how irritated he might have been with the chief over the Provenzano case. Both the Matrangas and Provenzanos claimed close or at least passable relations with Hennessy, enabling each to reasonably accuse the other of standing to benefit from his suspiciously timed death. If the actual killers had no connection to the Provenzano-Matranga struggle, they must have been smiling.

Accused of murder, Emmanuele Polizzi landed in the parish prison amid drunks, battling prostitutes, Italians arrested with concealed weapons, and a Chinese opium parlor operator. Polizzi's neighbor John Schellang told police that Polizzi had robbed his own wife of $50 and then beat her when she protested. Schellang said he saw Polizzi heading out Julia Street the night the chief was shot, and when Schellang saw the Italian's arm in a sling the next day, he thought nothing of it. He said the Italian always wore a mustache, but he certainly didn't have one now nor did he wear the sling. When asked how he was certain that Polizzi had shaved, Schellang replied that he had read it in the morning *Picayune*.

Just after noon on Monday, police heard that Tony Matranga and Vincent Caruso were fleeing the city. Cops rushed to the fruit wharf to find the two cripples watching their stevedores unload a fruit shipment. They were carted in anyway and eventually released.

Arrests were slowing, but Consul Corte was losing his temper, which was an unwelcome feeling for a diplomat. On Friday evening he had allowed a

Picayune reporter into his office, pleased that the paper editorially resolved that the Italian colony should not be blamed for the actions of its worst element. Corte said he knew nothing about the cowardly killing of the chief, but would do everything in his power to help authorities find and punish the criminals. The consul also lectured the reporter on international immigration law. No Italian was permitted to leave his country without an official passport. Many Italian immigrants arrived in New Orleans without this restrictive document by leaving Italy via other European ports. Corte suggested that a perusal of this law by American authorities would go a long way in reducing the number of lawless characters who turned up in America.

Corte's professorial demeanor frayed over the weekend as scared and angry Italians filled the consulate. The master of the Italian schoolhouse on Customhouse Street protested that one of his twelve-year-old pupils was still in police custody after four days. The boy was one of his brightest students and had an excellent reputation, the schoolmaster protested. The child was no murderer. Why was this happening?

A migrant worker told Corte of being herded to the Central Station with twenty other Italians who had come in from plantations to meet relatives on the *Elysia*. Corte dreaded trouble when the steamship arrived Tuesday with a thousand immigrants from Cefalu, Corleone, and Bisacquino. He again asked Mayor Shakspeare to calm the city, then called for his carriage and visited Governor Nicholls and Attorney General Walter H. Rogers. The safety of the Italian colony must be ensured, Corte insisted to the Americans. It was not right to blame an entire community for the actions of a few bad apples.

In their own way, the city's newspapers agreed.

THE LAW ASSASSINATED, interpreted the *Times-Democrat*, declaring that the killers had not shot Dave Hennessy the man, but Hennessy the chief representative of American justice. "He was universally recognized as one of the best chiefs of police New Orleans has ever had," said an editorial lauding the chief for bringing the police "up to a high standard of excellence" from its previous weak state. "He had rid New Orleans of burglars, thieves and other criminals of that class and was preparing to rid it of Sicilian brigands," who "found American justice in their way in his person; they saw their many crimes abroad and in this country threatened with exposure and punishment . . . and resolved to strike a blow that would teach all officers not to meddle with the Mafia."

Editors agreed that the well-known weakness of the New Orleans criminal justice system allowed the murderers to presume to be able to get away with such a foul deed. The *Daily States* said that Hennessy's death was not an act of personal vengeance, but a blow meant to demoralize the police. To the *Daily Picayune*, killing the city's chief lawman was a declaration of "war between American law and order and Italian assassination." The *Picayune*'s editor warned that if any Italians intended to remain in the city, they had better help find the chief's killers.

Yet all the local papers claimed to stand against persecuting the twenty-five thousand law-abiding Italians of New Orleans who were represented in every social class and stratum of the city's commercial life. "They yield to none in honesty, probity, public spirit, patriotism, and useful citizenship," preached the *Picayune*. "Not to recognize these facts is to be morally and intellectually blind." Crime was not the personal province of any ethnic group, agreed the same papers which were publishing articles on the history of the Mafia as fast as they could get them. The New Orleans *Italo-Americano* strongly denounced the murder, but its shared outrage was barely acknowledged amid the noisy proclamations of the English-language press.

The papers argued against lynching or forming any "vigilance" committee. "It is idle to deny the fact that for some time criminal justice in this city has been far too lax, and murderers have come to believe that with money and influence they can safely defy law," stated the *Picayune*. Yet dealing with "alien murderers" should be left to the mayor. "It is far better to right wrongs by legal methods than to punish crime by violating the law." Editorial indignation over the shooting of Antonio Scaffidi in the parish prison was as unanimous as it was with Hennessy's murder. The *States* railed against Scaffidi's attacker as DUFFY THE ASSASSIN. The *Picayune* begged LET US HAVE THE MAJESTY OF THE LAW—if Italians had killed the chief, it was unlikely that triggermen accomplished the deed without orders from above. Finding the plotters was the real challenge facing the city, the press declared, and when that was accomplished, the Mafia could be banished forever.

Dominick O'Malley was in and out of the parish prison several times during the week following Hennessy's murder, meeting with Charles Matranga who wanted the detective to work on his case. O'Malley was mulling over the request when the silk stockings stepped in. On October 21, he found a note from the mayor's appointed investigative body in his mail:

> *The Committee of Fifty demand that you drop all connection instantly with the Italian vendetta cases, either personally or through your employees. They further demand that you keep away from the parish prison, the Criminal Court, and the recorders' courts while these cases are on trial or under investigation; that you cease all communication with members of the Italian colony; that you cease in person or through your employees to follow or communicate with witnesses in the matter of the assassination of D.C. Hennessy. The committee does not deny the accused the right*

to employ a proper agency, but they do not intend to allow a man of your known criminal record and unscrupulous methods to be an instrument for harm to the public at their hands. By order of the committee.

Edgar H. Farrar, Chairman

A proper agency! By order of the committee! Who did they think they were? The "instrument of harm" sent the silk stockings his own message:

Sir—Your extraordinary communication of this date has just been received. In response I can but say that I propose to conduct the business of my office without instructions from you or the committee you claim to represent. Being unable to discover whence you derive any authority to "demand" that I should obey your behests with respect to the character of my employment, I shall continue to reserve to myself the right to think and act without regard to your wishes. Later I shall have occasion to "demand" at your hands the evidence upon which you have ventured to write of my "known criminal record and unscrupulous methods."
Yours,
D. C. O'Malley

The detective decided that the committee was out to convict someone, anyone, at any cost. He satisfied himself that Charles Matranga was innocent, and took the case.

The mass arrests chilled the city's Italian-born population, with good reason. It was hard enough to make themselves understood without having to explain that they did not murder the chief of police or know anything about it. Life was dangerous for Italian workers, who stayed home even if they could not afford to.

Stevedores kept away from the docks in droves, disrupting port business. When a few wholesale receivers and jobbers told the press that Italians handled fruit quicker and at lower wages than other stevedores, "American" longshoremen were furious, in spite of the accuracy of the claim. The newest immigrants on the docks were certainly willing to work for less than their black and white counterparts. The longshoremen's association rumbled about taking back the fruit work, a relatively new industry it had left to the Italians in favor of unloading cotton, rice, and sugar, which paid more.

. . .

Upriver on the West Bank opposite Kenner that week, a small group of drift-wood gatherers already had a good-sized pile of flotsam stacked on the shore when one of them saw a bulky shape in the brown water. It looked like a log, but they knew what it was. They dragged the floater in and cut open the burlap covering the head and chest. The dead man's eyes bulged at them in cold agony. He was an old man with a grizzly, gray stubble, wearing blue jeans and a red silk throat kerchief. There were finger marks and discoloration around his throat. The tongue was bitten and protruded. The Jefferson Parish coroner said the man had been dead for two or three weeks. The burlap sack was like those used by itinerant peddlers, so it was decided that the man was an Italian peddler who had been robbed of his money and goods and then strangled. Whoever killed him had put weights in his pockets so that the body would not rise from the river. Some speculated he had been thrown into the Mississippi near Sarpy's plantation, where Charles Traina had been arrested.

Captain Journée wanted a full report on the case, but Kenner authorities could find no clues to the dead man's identity. The *Picayune* was circumspect about the floater, who appeared to belong "to the lower order of the dago element. . . . The idea that his death was in any way connected with the Hennessy assassination is ridiculous, as the man had been dead for at least three weeks before the finding of the body." Considering how freely metropolitan papers were stringing together both possible and fanciful leads in the month's more celebrated murder, this was an unusually objective appraisal.

New Orleans cops were still arresting Italians but without luck in having any of them identified by witnesses. Meanwhile, Boylan, O'Connor, and Vandervoort supervised the emptying of Hennessy's office. The chief's mother let Central Station clerks keep Hennessy's picture for the office wall. The photograph stared at the movers with quizzical eyes as three wagonloads of desks, chairs, gifts from Boylan agency clients, and other possessions were carried out. Because the office had been Hennessy's home away from Girod Street, the movers felt as if they were disposing of an entire household.

Hennessy kept his private papers in a black iron safe which had been used at the old station for years, along with a bank box containing a fine collection of stickpins, cuff studs, diamonds, rings, and other jewelry. The papers were said to include his work on the Esposito case, private correspondence, and documents from the Italian government relating to fugitives. When Hennessy's belongings were carted away, a carpet, curtains, and a bare table were all that remained. Everything else was turned over to his mother. Except the documents.

As a grand jury sifted through witness testimony in search of indictments, Mayor Shakspeare's Committee of Fifty plodded noisily into the mystery. One week after the killing, the committee announced that it would hold a mass meeting in Lafayette Square. There was much disagreement over the safety and wisdom of assembling thousands of people outraged by Hennessy's murder, especially with a firecracker like Edgar Farrar on the podium. Feeling was still hot and talk on the streets agreed that one intemperate word could ignite a riot.

Six city councilmen privately told the mayor that they were opposed to the mass meeting and would ban it unless they were sure it would not cause violence. Shakspeare unexpectedly agreed that a mass meeting was a very bad idea. The Italian government was also worried. When Consul Corte telegraphed news of the meeting to Washington, DC, the Italian legation speedily wrote a firm, friendly letter to Secretary of State James G. Blaine. They called the State Department's attention to Shakspeare's proclamation of the previous week, criticizing it as an unjust accusation against all Italians residing in the United States. Blaine telegraphed Governor Nicholls, who refused to say anything until he had time to talk to the mayor.

Shakspeare and Nicholls met for forty-five minutes that Saturday afternoon. Shakspeare told reporters nothing when he left and hurried to the Cotton Exchange. At the elevator, he encountered the councilmen who had visited him that morning and were now on their way to a Committee of Fifty meeting. Shakspeare did not go up immediately; he stepped outside onto the corner of Gravier and Carondelet for a street corner conference with Consul Corte and a delegation of twenty Italian merchants and civic leaders, including suspect Charles Patorno's alderman brother, Antonio, and Father Manoritta, editor of the *Gazetta Catholica*.

The mayor, worried councilmen, and Italians went up to the eighth floor of the Cotton Exchange together. The Committee of Fifty's executive board assured their visitors that nothing inflammatory would be said in public, then its planned statement was read aloud. The Italians were satisfied and left with Shakspeare. When the mayor stepped out of the elevator, he told a councilman, "I went up there to stop this thing. It would have done no good."

Still, editors were uneasy. Sunday papers warned that the meeting was already drawing bad elements. The *Picayune* carried a message from the Committee of Fifty telling the city's Italians that every means would be taken to "allay the popular excitement" and make sure that the "Stiletto Societies" preying upon them would be stamped out. "We believe that the great majority among you are honest, industrious and good citizens and abhor crime as much as we do," read the notice, which sought the Italian community's help. "Send us the names and history (so far as you know it) of every bad man, every criminal, and every suspected person of your race in this city or the vicinity." According to the notice, such information would be confidential, and a locked post office box address was provided.

Despite its reasonable tone, the tension and threat implicit in the appeal were unmistakable. "We hope this appeal will be met by you in the same spirit in which we issue it, and that the community will not be driven to harsh and stringent methods outside of the law, which may involve the innocent and guilty alike."

The call for a mass meeting on Monday, October 27, stood.

The grass of Lafayette Square was already dewy when people began to arrive. At 8:00 p.m., nearly six thousand people stood shifting in the autumn chill as Mayor Shakspeare and the leaders of the Committee of Fifty filed beneath the electric lights on the platform.

Raising his voice, chairman Farrar nominated Board of Trade president B. P. Eshleman as president of the committee. "All in favor of the nominee please respond by saying 'Aye.'"

A broad chorus of ayes resounded.

"Those against?"

"Nay," shouted someone at the back of the crowd.

"The ayes have it," Farrar chuckled and the crowd laughed.

Eshleman accepted, and after a secretary was chosen, Farrar began to read the committee's report as loudly as he could, shouting so that everyone in the square could hear.

The committee, he said, had been convened by the mayor to investigate foreign murder societies and devise means to stamp them out. This mass meeting was called to see if the people of New Orleans approved of such work, and the committee was there to seek the public's mandate to continue.

"Your beloved and efficient chief of police was waylaid at the threshold of his own home and assassinated," Farrar shouted. "Every fact, then apparent and since discovered, shows that the assassination was the result of a widespread conspiracy, and that at least a half a dozen men were personally engaged in the killing. Many more before him in our community have been cruelly murdered, in the same way and from the same cause, and no clue has been obtained as to the assassins. Public excitement rose immediately to fever heat. There was danger of violence and bloodshed which would not discriminate between the innocent and the guilty, and which would bring commercial ruin and disgrace to the city of our homes and firesides."

The committee wanted to repress such violence and to assist the authorities in the Hennessy investigation, Farrar said. It would make sure that the grand jury, the promised help of the Italian government, and the best detectives money could buy would be marshaled to settle the matter once and for all, "to justify the innocent and confound the guilty."

Farrar then said something curious.

"We did not consider then nor do we consider now that any extreme measures are necessary or justifiable against the suspects until all lawful measures have been tried and failed."

Farrar the lawyer may have worked in New Orleans courts too long to have absolute faith in them, or perhaps he was talking tough to the killers, who were likely to hear his words. Whatever Farrar knew or was thinking, the possibility of judicial failure was in his mind. "We owe it to our duty as American citizens to try the law first, and to try it thoroughly. We beseech you to be patient and law-abiding."

The law works slowly, Farrar hoarsely told the crowd, going on to the matter of money. Public donations would be needed, as it would cost at least $30,000 to catch Hennessy's killers. Neither the state nor the city had money for rewards and other expenses, and the customary limited three-month term of each grand jury was too short. More than one grand jury would be needed to finish this case. Italians would help. "We have been promised the fullest cooperation by representatives of the Italian government and the leading Italian citizens and societies, who form an important, a trustworthy, and an honorable portion of our community."

Together the committee and the people would discover once and for all if secret murder societies were operating in New Orleans. If not, the city's name would be cleared of such imputations, he said. If so, the murder societies had to be stamped out at any hazard. The committee would disband if the public showed its displeasure by resolutions that night, but Farrar appealed for the support and help of everyone present.

When he was finished with his prepared statement, he looked directly into the applauding crowd, a well-behaved gathering, much like the YMDA crowds before the last election. The double ranks of policemen on hand were unnecessary, but in the interest of keeping the peace, Farrar introduced only two more speakers.

Colonel A. W. Crandall spoke of the importance of proceeding within the law so that Hennessy's murderers would not escape justice. Crandall asked anyone with hostile thoughts toward New Orleans's Italians to dispel such ideas from their minds. "Some of the most enterprising, progressive, law-abiding of our citizens belong to that race, and they deplore as much as we the foul blot that has been painted upon the history of this city with poor Hennessy's blood. We can no more afford to hold them responsible for the acts of a few bad men of their race than we would be willing to become responsible for the inhuman and cowardly act committed by one of our own nationality upon one of the Italian suspects behind the bars."

The Honorable Charles F. Buck followed Crandall's appeal for patience. A former city attorney, the German-born Buck was a natural choice for Shakspeare's committee. His parents had arrived with the wave of immigrants who followed the Irish into New Orleans. Orphaned at twelve by yellow fever, Buck had worked himself through law school. He was a brilliant speaker who was respected by both friends and political foes alike. One day he would champion immigrant rights in the U.S. Congress.

Buck had no prepared statement, for he was asked to speak at the last minute. When he came to the podium, he spoke of the hideousness of the crime and of the duties of citizenship within the law. When he told the crowd that the reputation of New Orleans depended on temperance and justice, they applauded him. Like Chairman Farrar, Buck did not fear rash action. "There have been occasions before this when the people of New Orleans have come together under trying circumstances, and they have never moved as a mob, and they have never yet moved without a head. They have always been thoughtful and even when driven to death almost, they have obeyed the voice of their leaders and followed only them, not their own passions."

It was a grand statement. Victims of the 1866 Mechanics Institute massacre and other race riots might have considered them to be the words of an amnesiac, but this crowd loved it and applauded warmly. Buck argued for patient investigation and warned against harsh measures.

"Injustice would probably be done where justice was intended and, as has been well-said, the citizens of New Orleans are not meeting here tonight to antagonize or raise a voice against any class of our fellow citizens," he said. "I myself am one of those citizens of America who drew my first breath on the other side of the Atlantic, and it would ill become me to speak a word against one race or nationality from the old country which has come to this land of freedom, of happiness and of prosperity to better his condition—to seek in the new clime and under new skies, under institutions different from their own, freedom, liberty, and better prosperity in life.

"There comes from that beautiful country on the other side which we call Italy," Buck continued, "the country of a mankind who accomplished some of the grandest and most beautiful achievements that the treasurers of art and intellect have ever beheld: where the civilization of the world found its root and had its seat for centuries. And we are not here, I say, to war against that people!

"But if it be true that under the institutions of that country conditions have developed, by which certain portions of a community from a century backward down to the present time have cherished traditions of antiquity and traditions of barbarism, by which they place themselves beyond the law and take the law in their own hands, or do so in associations or organizations of their own and have transplanted their organizations into our midst, it is our duty and our right to see that they become powerless for harm here."

This was all the committee could do, Buck said. He would leave the matter of money to the conscience and sense of duty of every New Orleanian. Cheers blared in the cold air.

"We seek the path of the right, and the right only," Buck concluded. "Let it not be deviated from unless all other means fail, and even then let us under all and any circumstances recollect that the appeal to the law is that which distinguishes American citizens and the American constitution from all other organizations, other methods, and other systems in the world. If such a thing as this had occurred in Russia, or in Germany, or even in Republican France, innocent and guilty alike would be dragged forward and brought to punishment, perhaps without regard to investigation. But in this country, always conscious of the fact that the people themselves are the lawmakers and the executors of the law, we appeal to you who make the law to help us enforce it!"

The crowd applauded Buck long and enthusiastically. As the committee's proposals were shouted from the podium, cheers approved the appointment of the Committee of Fifty to investigate secret murder societies and to devise the means to stamp them out. More cheers resolved that the committee's line of inquiry was supported by the people of New Orleans.

When the speeches were over and Lafayette Square was silent, one aspect of the search for Hennessy's killers had been transformed permanently, as the guardians of public order tried to drag a terrifying mystery into the reassuring realm of certainty. While it was not specifically brought to a vote that night, a single murder theory was now officially sanctioned. By omission, the theory concluded that Hennessy was not killed over an unsavory personal or professional grudge. The timing and appearance of his killers did not suggest a charade, patiently crafted to use the Provenzano-Matranga feud to deflect attention from the actual perpetrators. The conspirators were not paid by the gambling house owners whose lives and fortunes Hennessy had helped to ruin. His security business dealings were not to blame. It was not a political plot. Men whom the chief had personally arrested or kicked off the police force were not responsible, nor were Tom Devereaux's vengeful friends, the St. Mary's Market or Shot Tower gangs, the shady Dominick O'Malley, or any of a quarter of a million New Orleanians who anticipated that the chief of police was about to testify in a notorious vendetta trial. No such possibilities were proposed.

Hennessy was shot down in cold blood by Italians, and with the passing of the public resolutions in Lafayette Square, no question remained in the investigators' minds. No question at all.

The next day the newspapers pronounced the mass meeting in Lafayette Park a great success and implied they knew all along that no violence would occur.

It was a sad fact of New Orleans life that while everyone knew trash caused the gutters to flood and spill filth across the streets during every rainstorm, no one felt like paying to have the gutters cleaned. Mayor Shakspeare had appointed Confederate hero General P. G. T. Beauregard to get the job done, and he tried for a month to raise the necessary money by subscription or city funding, but to no avail. Beauregard quit in disgust, citing poor health.

Gutter cleaning was left to crews from the city workhouse. One such squad was dredging the drain outside the workhouse coffin-making department on Cypress Street, midway between Locust and Magnolia streets, when Patrick Wall tucked his shovel under something heavier than slush. Wall leaned harder and pulled up. Dripping with muck, a sawed-off breech-loading shotgun was at the end of his shovel.

Wall's fellow workers inspected the weapon and one of them, Mike Hughes, found two spent metallic shells in its barrels. Wall wanted nothing to do with the gun, but Hughes considered taking it home and cleaning it. Minutes later, a worker poked a second sawed-off shotgun out of the mud a few yards away, an old single-barreled muzzle-loader. With its iron-frame stock and a hook for hanging it from trousers or a coat lining, the weapon dripped with bad intentions. Both guns were only lightly rusted.

The work gang was staring at the second shotgun when someone wondered aloud if the guns might have killed the chief. A black child crouched where the shotguns were found, picking soggy paper cartridges and buckshot out of the mud with his fingers.

A few days later, the city council passed a motion to make $10,000 available to Mayor Shakspeare for any action he deemed fitting in the matter of ferreting out the causes of Chief Hennessy's assassination. The motion was given to the Budget and Assessments Committee, the same group responsible for finding money to clean street-side gutters.

◡

Fourteen

THE SIBERIA OF AMERICA

AFTER THE MEETING IN LAFAYETTE SQUARE, A PRODIGIOUS
map was ceremoniously unfurled in Mayor Shakspeare's city hall parlor. The
massive eleven-by-fifteen-foot document perfectly charted the entire Hennessy
neighborhood from Poydras to Julia Street, from Liberty down to Rampart.
Red stars pinpointed where bullets were found and black dots represented discarded guns. Drawn by an assistant U.S. engineer and a chief draftsman, the
map would be used by the grand jury, then moved to a courtroom when a trial
took place. It was a splendid piece of cartography, everyone agreed. Mapmak-
ing turned out to be the one thing anyone connected with the state's case did
indisputably well.

Even before the prosecution could decide which suspects to indict, trou-
ble started when Criminal Sheriff Gabriel Villere, administrator of the Orleans
Parish Prison, denied Dominick O'Malley and *Times-Democrat* reporter Frank
Michinard permission to see the jailed Charles Matranga. Villere was a wide
man, a coal wholesaler with hawkish eyebrows and a flat shingle of oiled hair.
He told the court that he only had the prisoners' security in mind after the
Scaffidi shooting. Lionel Adams retorted that Matranga had more to fear from
other visitors than from a reporter and someone trying to help Matranga de-
fend himself. Matranga had a right to confer with his counsel, said Adams.
The state, however, argued that because O'Malley and Michinard were not
lawyers, the right to confer with counsel was not being meddled with.

Judge Marr decided he could not force the sheriff to allow anyone to see
the prisoners. Adams appealed to the Louisiana Supreme Court, arguing that
holding Charles Matranga was an illegal detention kept alive because of the
First District Recorder's refusal—at the request of the district attorney's office—to announce a trial date. The Louisiana Supreme Court rescinded the

ban against Matranga's visitors, ordering prosecutors to set a trial date and get on with it. News of Adams's victory hit the papers on November 17, the same day a scandal concerning the mistreatment of all prison inmates began clattering on Sheriff Villere's square head.

Where and how prisoners slept in the Orleans Parish Prison was complicated. Men and women were separated, then divided into different yards by race, and subdivided again according to whether or not a prisoner could pay for a better cell and allowable amenities imported from "outside." There was nothing illicit about this; it was official prison policy.

Macheca, the Matrangas, the Carusos, Geraci, Sunzeri, and Romero had cells of their own in the "star chamber," the better-furnished second floor of the prison. Each morning they sat down to a huge breakfast brought in by their families. A reporter who visited them one morning found the table filled with a large dish of chicken creole and platters of spaghetti, spinach, potatoes, cold meats, salads, chowchow, and bread.

"I have no complaints with the way I'm treated," Macheca said over the aromatic meal. "The only complaint I have is that our claret was cut off this morning. I presume that has to with the complaints of the prisoners down in the yard. I don't know anything about any mistreatment."

The city coroner, Dr. Y. P. LeMonnier, was asked to examine the poorer Italians in the yard and report to Sheriff Villere. The public report reflected LeMonnier's usual impatience with prisoner complaints. Contrary to various reports about mistreatment of the Italian prisoners, LeMonnier said there was no danger of Antonio Bagnetto's arm needing amputation. A fracture on Bagnetto's left forearm might have happened years before. There were light traces of a bruise on the same forearm, however, which LeMonnier attributed to injuries a month old. As for Monasterio, LeMonnier reported that the cobbler's forehead showed scars, but diagnosed them to be the result of injuries a month to six weeks old. The coroner did not mention that Monasterio and Bagnetto had been in custody for exactly one month. Incardona had a bruise on his left forearm. Antonio Marchesi and another suspect, Loretto Comitz, showed no signs of injuries.

Villere and Warden Davis were elated, but angry. Villere was tired of "persistent efforts being made to censure my administration." Davis said charges of mistreatment were the result of Italians lying to work up sympathy. Monasterio had been brought in already bleeding from a clubbing. Both Bagnetto and Marchesi had grunted in pain when they were first searched and claimed they were beaten on the way to the prison. Davis said he knew everything that went on within his prison's walls, and his men told him he was the most lenient warden in the history of the parish prison.

He admitted it was possible for the prisoners to fight among themselves. "The class of prisoners we have in the yard are not refined, elegant gentlemen of kind and gentle disposition," Davis said. "They are frequently men who would stop at nothing, not even murder, to gain their liberty, and the sternest discipline must be enforced to keep them in subjection."

The toughest inmates often tried to run the prison themselves and assaulted the keepers, Davis said. "Let me tell you about my experience with a big Texas cowboy, as big as Sullivan . . . "

Near midnight on November 20, forty-five days after the shooting, the grand jury returned true bills against nineteen men held in connection with Hennessy's murder. Pietro Natali, Antonio Scaffidi, Antonio Bagnetto, Pietro Monasterio, Antonio Marchesi, Salvatore Sunzeri, Bastian Incardona, Loretto Comitz, Charles Traina, Charles Pietzo, and "Manuel Politz" (Emmanuele Polizzi) were charged with shooting David C. Hennessy with intent to murder. An indictment against Joseph Macheca, Charles Matranga, Rocco Geraci, James and John Caruso, Charles Patorno, Frank Romero, and Gasperi Marchesi charged that they "did feloniously and maliciously incite, move, procure, aid, counsel, hire and command" the other defendants to kill Hennessy. Linked together with a "shooting while lying in wait" charge, which was also a capital offense, all the defendants faced hanging for participating in a premeditated murder if they were convicted.

An amended special report concerned a letter to the grand jury from Consul Corte. The letter had been accepted by Villere and his chief deputy, who waited four days before delivering it to the grand jury. "This letter was supposed to contain charges against the management of the parish prison," the report accused. While the letter was stalled, "the Sheriff was taking active measures to have himself exonerated from blame before the evidence reached the jury." The grand jury left action on the matter up to a judge.

Villere was now being pilloried not by the press or reformers, but by a grand jury. If he thought in his defiant embarrassment that the report officially and unpleasantly closed the matter, allowing him to take his lumps and move on, he was wrong.

Solomon Malaga, an erudite Polish Jew, had just been released from treatment for a fever at Charity Hospital when he was arrested on a trumped up assault and battery charge. At the parish prison, a "captain of the yard" trusty named Gilligan demanded Malaga's money. When the still-recovering Malaga showed that he had none, he got a punch in the ribs and was lashed with a knotted rope. For the next four nights he slept in a freezing cell with no blanket, aching from the beating. He saw Gilligan whip an accused thief, who was beaten until he agreed to switch his brand-new clothes for Gilligan's tattier suit. Malaga also saw Gilligan beat another inmate bleeding and senseless.

When Malaga got his day in court, he was acquitted. The evidence against him was so ridiculous that the judge fined the prosecutor. When Malaga read of the Italian prisoners scandal, he marched into the *Times-Democrat* office with a sworn, notarized statement detailing his own experiences. Malaga had been in America twenty-six years. "I consider the parish prison to be the Siberia of America," he wrote. "I do not think the Russian exiles could be more brutally treated. It is a shame for a liberal and civilized people to permit such outrages in a prison under the protection of law."

Former prisoners and their families came forward with similar stories. Tough inmates like "captain of the yard" Skip Mealey were accused of beating and extorting protection money from weaker inmates. Rabbi Leucht, president of the Prisoners & Asylum Commission and a local philanthropist, visited the prison and got a chilly reception. The cells were filthy. Warden Davis told the rabbi that the prisoners were refusing to work because of the scandal. Davis curtly said he wasn't about to force them to clean the place with charges of mistreatment pending. Rabbi Leucht asked to see Sheriff Villere. Warden Davis angrily replied that the sheriff was never there. As for charges that the prisoners froze at night, Davis told Leucht that he had asked the city for more blankets four months ago and got nothing. The prison was 120 blankets short.

Rabbi Leucht asked to see Gilligan, Malaga's alleged assailant. Leucht expected a ferocious criminal. Instead he was shown an inoffensive-looking mug who stared at him, unwilling to utter a word.

"There's some truth to it," Warden Davis said, audibly more contemptuous of the commissioner than of the convict. "It's not possible to rule so many Negroes with kid gloves. It's necessary to give a fellow the strap once in awhile when he becomes unruly. If I was aware of any officer doing what's been charged, I'd suspend him."

Rabbi Leucht was incensed by Davis's rudeness. He told the *Times-Democrat* that the parish prison was a blot on the community. City commissioner Thomas Agnew got a visit about the blankets. The commissioner said he had gotten no request for prison bedding and even if he had, he would've refused it, for the city had no money for such things.

Sheriff Villere's headache grew. When the *Times-Democrat* tracked him down, the sheriff declared that the subject was closed. The head trusty or "captain of the yard" position had been abolished ever since the charges about the Italians being mistreated became public knowledge.

Villere grudgingly listened to a few questions. What was the city appropriation for the prison? Villere didn't know. Was there any appropriation for bedding? He didn't know. He did know that convicted murderers were issued beds and slept in the hallways to avoid trouble with other prisoners. Witnesses locked up for "safekeeping" and regular inmates were not guaranteed a blanket.

There weren't enough to go around. Prisoners could bring their own bedding. There were no special privileges. All prisoners got the same meal of bread, beans, potatoes, salt meat, and tea. Villere assured the public that the prisoners were very well taken care off. Criticisms of the prison were all lies.

The *Times-Democrat* reporter hurried to the parish prison to see if Warden Davis's answers were the same. When he got there, he found Sheriff Villere's carriage outside. The reporter tried to interview Davis alone, but Villere interrupted constantly. "I told you the answer this afternoon," he steamed. "I'm being bothered to death by reporters!"

Warden Davis looked at the reddening face beneath his superior's slick plank of hair. "I don't want to be interviewed," Davis decided.

"The men are well-cared for here," Villere boiled. "So well treated in fact that when they get out, they want to come back!"

The *Times-Democrat* blasted the prison system, where rumors of torture had escaped scrutiny for years. "It is treatment against which we loudly and righteously declaim when we hear of it practiced in far off lands where the will of the tyrant is the only rule of the country," said the paper, questioning Villere's fitness for allowing the prison to sink into such a state and suggesting that since he had declared himself to be opposed to reforming the system, he should be removed.

Meanwhile, the paper criticized a rumored prosecution plan to postpone the Hennessy case on the grounds that it would be unfair to pen up jurors during the approaching Christmas holiday, with the Mardi Gras season following soon thereafter. Did the city want to be a laughingstock to the rest of the country for failing to proceed as soon as the prosecution was ready with its case, postponing it so as not to interfere with society balls and masquerades?

It was a prophetic criticism. But was the prosecution ready? The delays and sequestered fiddling of the Committee of Fifty had people wondering if there was a case against the men indicted for Hennessy's murder.

The nineteen defendants were scheduled for arraignment on Saturday, November 29. Scant public notice ensured that only a few police detectives, sheriff's deputies, and reporters witnessed the proceedings. Entrances, corridors, and the courtroom were heavily guarded.

The poorer "yard" prisoners were dressed neatly. They were pale and drawn from their month in prison, but only Scaffidi was visibly nervous. Macheca and the wealthier prisoners arrived soon afterward, better dressed and looking healthier. Charles Patorno fidgeted and looked as if he wanted to be left alone. Frank Romero buttonholed everyone who passed to ask what his chances were, while the usually animated Joe Macheca was calm and collected.

After Judge Marr ascended the bench to hear arraignments on the murder charge, Lionel Adams immediately motioned to quash the indictments on the ground that a person who had not been sworn in had attended the grand jury's investigation. Adams and district attorney Charles Luzenberg had already discussed this matter and agreed to argue the motion the following week, which was acceptable to Judge Marr. Adams was collecting his papers to go before Judge Baker in Section B to try to get the "lying in wait" charge quashed, when attorney Fernand Armant rose.

"As counsel for Charles Patorno, I have not been consulted in the presentation of that motion and request that my client be allowed to plead," Armant said.

This was news to Adams, who thought Patorno was his client. Patorno had signed a financial agreement along with the other prisoners, agreeing to pay Adams for their defense. Patorno now wanted Armant alone to represent him. The exasperated Adams struck Patorno's name from the motion. Armant and Patorno still wanted to enter a plea, but agreed to wait until the motions to quash were settled.

On December 6, Adams got all of the indictments thrown out. Luzenberg had taken an unauthorized stenographer into the grand jury room for all but two sessions. Judge Baker ruled that no one but the district attorney and his assistants were allowed in the grand jury room during the questioning of witnesses. He declared the stenographer's presence clearly illegal and quashed the indictments against the Hennessy murder suspects. The prisoners remained in their cells while new indictments were drawn.

On December 13, a new grand jury indicted the suspects in Hennessy's murder a second time, but Adams was not yet finished.

Returning to court on December 16, Macheca, the Matrangas, the Carusos, and the other star chamber boarders were nattily dressed and looked well. Monasterio, Polizzi, Bagnetto, and the others who had been penned in the lower prison arrived unshaven and ragged.

The indictments were read aloud, but instead of entering pleas, Adams stopped the trial again. He pointed out that two members of the grand jury were also members of the Committee of Fifty. Since the committee was convened to prosecute Hennessy's murderers and contributed money toward that end, they had no business being part of a grand jury. Adams motioned to quash the new indictments. He also requested the committee's minutes, records, oaths, and vouchers, as well as all Recorder's Court affidavits referring to the accused. The mayor and committee members fumed. Adams's detractors suspected that he wanted access to evidence the committee had unearthed through its secret work.

Judge Baker ruled that the two men's work with the committee did not invalidate their acts as grand jurors. Adams swung with yet another series of pretrial challenges, all of which were overruled. Adams reserved bills of exception to prepare for appeals, but the defendants were brought before Judge Baker on the murder charge and then taken before Judge Marr to answer the "lying in wait" charge. All pleaded not guilty.

A trial was now inevitable, but the state's case already looked dead. Officially, the prosecution was preparing its evidence, but to New Orleanians, the state's courtroom fumbling and the hazy rhetoric of the Committee of Fifty were uncomfortably familiar. Attempts to bring Hennessy's killers to justice were degenerating into one more maddening bungle. The $15,000 the city council squeezed out of the budget to prosecute the case was answered by nearly a third as much donated to the defense by the local Italian community. The defense lawyers now included not only Adams but former Confederate Senator Thomas J. Semmes, one of the most respected lawyers and men in New Orleans. And by trying to keep Dominick O'Malley from speaking to his clients, the committee had accomplished the incredible and farcical feat of turning the detective into a public martyr.

The *Mascot* teased that the Committee of Fifty's clumsiness ensured that the accused would be old men before any indictments were finalized. "Lorenzo," the *Mascot's* tiny cartoon harlequin whose byline furnished weekly gossip and opinion dropped a cynical tidbit: "It is stated on very good authority that there is no evidence against the Italians but what the defense can shatter. The nineteen accused now in the parish prison will show that they have been arrested solely on the advice of the Provenzano faction." Unless the state came forward with solid evidence, there could be a lingering impression that the indictments were the product of mere spite, added the paper, arguing that police guesswork and the bile of the still-imprisoned Provenzanos should not hang men.

By Christmas, the prison scandal simmered down with Skip Mealey's indictment for robbing other inmates. Tom Duffy was now in prison, convicted of wounding Scaffidi. On New Year's Day, a public fistfight landed Dominick O'Malley and a former special named Roper in front of a judge. O'Malley accused Roper of eavesdropping on his conversations, including an interview with the city's electric lighting inspector. It was a trifling brawl compared to most in O'Malley's life, but the first to reflect his interest in electricity. Particularly electric lights.

The Illinois Central lumbered south through the bayous from the small town of Amite, sixty miles north of New Orleans. Captain Azariah Wilde of the U.S. Secret Service avoided the blinding sunset and studied the face of his prisoner who looked to be about twenty-five years old.

It had been a perfect arrest. Wilde arrived at an Amite hotel early in the day, and in plain view of the guests, he stopped his man. "What's your name?" Wilde asked.

"Anthony Rogers."

Wilde ordered the man to empty his pockets. His wallet contained $105. Picking up the man's derby and feeling a bulge, Wilde ripped open the silk lining and found a handful of crisp $50 bills. Wilde patted the man's vest, ordered him to take it off, and found more greenbacks padding the garment. By the time Wilde ceased ripping, $5,000 had fallen from the suit before astonished onlookers. Wilde hustled his prisoner onto the next train to New Orleans.

Morning papers noted the arrest of notorious counterfeiter Antonio Ruggiero, "a smooth, slick, well-educated Italian speaking English with little difficulty." Captain Wilde told New Orleans police that Ruggiero belonged to a gang of Philadelphia counterfeiters arrested only a few days ago for stamping out bogus silver dollars and was on his way south from Chicago to unload wads of worthless $50 bills during Mardi Gras.

Newspapers warned that Ruggiero's accomplice was in Birmingham before the arrest and might turn up in New Orleans. "He is said to be an Italian also and by others is said to be a Jew," the *Daily Picayune* reported. "He is also supposed to be furnished with a large number of $2 bills which he will attempt to place."

After a preliminary hearing, Ruggiero was unceremoniously thrown into the Orleans Parish Prison. Cops and inmates alike expected him to be there for a while.

Would Ruggiero's capture have attracted as much attention if he had not been an Italian? Any counterfeiter planning to dump $5,000 in New Orleans during Mardi Gras was certainly news.

The Hennessy cloud hung over the city with no sign of clearing. With nothing fresh to enhance bloody scenarios already drawn from "evidence," the murder descended from the realm of sensation into trite daily entertainment. A Royal Street furniture dealer was even running cryptic puzzles about the mystery in his newspaper advertisements. Yet public interest was still strong among the city's Italian-speaking citizens. *L'Italo Americano*'s editor was irritated by the Committee of Fifty, whose appeals for help were aimed solely at the Italian community. Prominent Italian Americans wrote defensive essays such as ARE ITALIANS A MENACE TO THE U.S.? for the English-language press. With the long-awaited Provenzano retrial due to start on January 12, peace of mind was unlikely to return to the Italian community soon.

When the Provenzanos' tenacious new defense team of Evans, Dunn, and Walker drew the second Esplanade ambush trial past the length of the first, spectators wondered if Judge Marr would expire before the end of it. The old, unsteady judge nearly obliged them.

The new trial began much like the first with fruit dealers explaining the Provenzanos' loss of their stevedoring contract and the resulting hard feelings. Joseph Macheca testified he was present when his stepbrother John told the Provenzanos that his contracts were already made and that he was afraid of trouble if he took the work away from the Matrangas. The Provenzanos answered that there would be trouble if he didn't. Macheca said the Provenzanos told him at the Red Light Club last April that they deserved a share of the work because it belonged to them and that they would "fix" the Matrangas if they did not get it. Both prosecution and defense lawyers made sure that Macheca identified himself as one of the men indicted for Chief Hennessy's murder.

On the second day of testimony, Judge Marr suffered an attack of vertigo and was helped out of the drafty courtroom. When Marr recovered and the trial resumed, Charles Matranga claimed he was threatened over the stevedoring work by Tony Gianforcaro and Joe Provenzano on separate occasions during the past year. Under defense cross-examination, Matranga denied belonging to any secret societies. He said he had never heard of any Sicilian organizations formed for the purpose of killing people and did not associate with people of that kind. Like Macheca, he was asked if he was under indictment in the Hennessy case.

The ambush victims similarly denied ever hearing of the Mafia or of any secret society formed to take upon itself the punishment of injuries. Each of them again described the faces of the accused, lit by blazes of gunfire. All denied telling police they had no idea who the shooters were. About the only thing they didn't agree on was whether or not Geraci was singing when the bullets started to fly. Sunzeri testified through an interpreter that he could not have told police he didn't know who shot him, for he did not understand English. Tony Locascio denied pointing out Tony Pellegrini in the lineup because the suspect laughed at him, and Rocco Geraci denied saying "put him in too" when Pellegrini laughed.

As the trial crawled on, the confined jurors complained to Judge Marr that they were freezing at night. Their businesses and families were suffering. The judge requested more blankets from Thomas Agnew, the same commissioner in charge of prison bedding.

A surveyor called by prosecutors offered a map of the ambush scene, showing the nearest streetlight to be 185 feet from the spot where the accused were said to have fired. The jurors told the judge they wanted to see for themselves, so on the night of January 19, the entire court bundled into carriages to visit the crime scene. They arrived in a thick fog, which made seeing faces and figures in the darkness impossible, regardless of the streetlight nearly two hundred feet away. When the jury asked that the accused be lined up on the corner where the shooting came from, Prosecutor Finney refused the request.

Back in the courtroom, the defense opened its case with a student ambulance medic, two reporters, and four police officers, who all testified that the victims said they had no idea who shot them. Corporal Boyard had accompanied Chief Hennessy to the hospital after the ambush. The chief visited the wounded, then told Locascio and Geraci to tell Boyard everything they knew. Boyard went into a room alone with the two men and asked who did the shooting. "They said it was no use," Boyard testified. "They did not know." Boyard asked whom they suspected. He got a list of the four Provenzano brothers, Lombardo, Pellegrini, Gianforcaro, Nick and Salvatore Guillio, and Charles Adorno. Boyard had to coax the stevedores to give him names. "These people," he said, "never give information about their cases." Both Corporal Boyard and another policeman witness told the court that the Esplanade electric light was out on the night of the ambush. So did several neighbors, including one who had passed within thirty feet of the men lingering at the corner without seeing their faces.

Defense attorney W. L. Evans tried to read the Hennessy murder indictments against Matranga, Sunzeri, Incardona, Geraci, and Caruso. All were important prosecution witnesses whose credibility deserved to be attacked, Evans declaimed. Lionel Adams, whose stage-whispers about the credibility of defense witnesses had caused Judge Marr to censure both sides for delaying the trial with their barbs, spoke up. Adams called the court's attention to the fact that two of the "indictments" had been quashed and were no longer indictments at all. Evans instead read the indictments pending against all nineteen of the men accused in the Hennessy case. When he began to read the grand jury's captions to the indictments, Judge Marr told him to stop.

Fatigue hung over the courtroom by the last day of the trial. The lawyers were exhausted and jurors were eager to go home. The accused men were brief in their testimonies, simply repeating their alibis. Prosecutors Finney and Adams called witnesses who had timed carriage rides from the Eden Theatre to the corner of Esplanade and Claiborne. The trip could be made in eight or nine minutes. The witnesses admitted they had never tried it at night. Adams proposed to show the jury that the accused could have reached the ambush scene even if they were in the Eden at the time police officers saw them there. The defense objected strongly, without success.

Lawyers on both sides were aware of impatience with the twelve-day trial and submitted the case to the jury without argument on January 23. An hour and twenty minutes later, the jury returned with a verdict of not guilty. Cheers filled the courtroom. Deputies tried to restore order, but quieting the families of the acquitted men was difficult. Lombardo wept and kissed his lawyers on both cheeks.

"Lying in wait" indictments against the Provenzanos were dropped four days after their murder acquittal. Finney decided that the evidence was not strong enough to warrant convictions on the redundant second charge of premeditation. The Provenzanos and their codefendants left the parish prison, whistling loudly in insult at the Matranga crowd.

The frustrated editor of the *Daily Picayune* did not know where to aim his disgust.

"We do not care to comment on the merits of the case," he sniffed. "The jury has decided it finally." Furthermore, as far as the newspaper was concerned, the verdict wholly disproved the existence of anti-Italian prejudice charged by the city's Italian American press. While the vendetta's code of silence had been broken in the first Provenzano case, the editor felt that the acquittal would return the city to the days when no Italian could be found to testify against another. Now that all of the antagonists in the Provenzano-Matranga feud were free, would the vendetta start anew? What next?

"In the course of a few days, or weeks, or months, or years, the celebrated Hennessy case may come to trial," the editorial continued sarcastically. "The parties charged with his murder are Italians. We know not whether they be innocent or guilty, but from the result of the Provenzano case, if we are to trust all that has been said or commonly believed concerning the vendetta, we may be sure that no Italian can be found to testify against them. It will be a brave or a desperate man who will present himself in cold blood and without prejudice to the bullet or the steel of the vendetta."

Everyone would see soon enough. Attorneys in the Hennessy case agreed to begin the trial the week after Mardi Gras. Judge Baker would preside.

It would be hard to find a jury in so famous a case. Challenges "for cause"—attempts to dismiss jurors on grounds of suspected prejudice—were expected to be numerous. The defense would be allowed 225 challenges. The state was allowed 144. To reduce the number of challenges, two successive trials were planned. Nine of the nineteen defendants would be prosecuted first.

At the parish prison, the counterfeiter carefully watched the Provenzano and Matranga crowds, who hissed and swore at each other whenever they passed in the prison yard. Guards chuckled at the exaggerated grimaces an Italian would make whenever one of his foes came too close.

Without access to the kind of money that would get him a better cell, the counterfeiter remained in the lower prison. He slept on cold stone and ate rancid hunks of meat from slop buckets carried in by trusties. The poorer defendants in the Hennessy case were kept here—Monasterio, Marchesi and his boy, the fidgety Scaffidi, Bagnetto and the rest, including the one the guards called Politz. That one was not right. Anyone could see it.

The counterfeiter's crime made him a minor celebrity in the lower prison, but he volunteered nothing and made no friends. He was friendly enough toward the fool Polizzi. Slowly he began to tell Polizzi things.

These things nearly scared Polizzi to death.

Then, when it was dark, the counterfeiter asked the terror-stricken peddler a few questions.

On January 26, exactly three weeks after his arrest, alleged counterfeiter Anthony Ruggiero was released on a $5,000 bond, which bound him to appear before the grand jury when called. He gave the court a New York address, signed the bond himself, and quickly disappeared, leaving behind the Orleans Parish Prison and the man he had tried to scare out of his wits.

☾

PART III
THE GREATEST LEGAL EVENT IN LOUISIANA HISTORY

Fifteen

WHO KILLA DE CHIEF?

The credit and interests of New Orleans require that these grave matters—scandals as they have grown to be—should be finally disposed of. The innocent accused, if any, have suffered too long already; the guilty have enjoyed undeserved leniency. Let these cases be cleared from the docket before many thousand visitors to our annual festival arrive to wonder at the remarkable skill of our officials in the scheme of "How Not To Do It."

—*Daily City Item*, January 10, 1891

CROWDS ENTERED FROM GENTILLY AND MYSTERY STREETS, lifting umbrellas against the showers and hurrying to the promenades. Rain softened the fairground track, but no downpour could keep the city's aristocrats from their Mardi Gras spectacle.

Knights of the King's Own Royal Guard were young men, gentlemen presumably, "scions of the best families of Louisiana." Identities were carefully hidden from the public. The young knights were the ceremonial bodyguards of His Majesty Rex, King of Carnival, who would reward the winner of the tournament at the Knight's Ball held at the Imperial Palace the night before Mardi Gras. By tradition that was all anyone needed or was allowed to know. The knights donned their chain mail, helmets, and visors, lifted their shields and lances, and nudged their steeds onto the muddy track.

Ivanhoe, Stephen of the Iron Hand, Tancred of the Leopard, and seven others assembled within an elaborate enclosure built especially for them. Each knight would gallop down the track, tilting his lance at rings suspended in air. When the masked riders trotted before the grandstand, their sponsors, whose ranks included Mayor Shakspeare's daughter and other young society women, presented each knight with a streamer of his chosen hue. Last year's Rex and

Committee of Fifty member S. P. Walmsley looked on approvingly. So did James Richardson, another committeeman who would be revealed as the new King of Carnival in a few days. YMDA attorney Walter Denegre was another of the five judges.

When the fanfare sounded for the first tilt, the skies opened. The tournament carried on, with the heavy horses struggling through the soft spreading mire. Water seeped through chain mail, bleeding color from the streamers adorning all the noble young men.

For one observer, the Hennessy murder trial opened with a pun: "It takes a long time to secure even a Baker's dozen of jurymen in a criminal case."

Thickly bearded Judge Joshua Baker looked down to see the man he replaced on the bench now sitting at the state's table. Years before, Charles Luzenberg was the judge and Baker was an assistant prosecutor who tried to convict the Hennessy cousins for killing Devereaux. When Luzenberg resigned his judgeship—to pick up a fat fee for helping Adams, Henriques, and Arthur Gastinel defend Troisville Sykes in the 1883 Kate Townsend killing, gossips whispered—Baker ascended to the bench. Now District Attorney Luzenberg faced Judge Baker. Within a single career, it was possible that any New Orleans lawyer with talent and the respect of his peers might see the criminal justice system from all points around a very small circle.

Luzenberg would be assisted by Evans and Dunn, thus pitting the Provenzanos' champions against the Matrangas' lawyers once again. For the Hennessy trial, however, Adams and the accused hired a man everyone agreed was one of the best lawyers in the South.

Thomas Jenkins Semmes, a member of the exclusive Boston Club, was the Harvard-educated son of a Washington, DC merchant and a distant relative of Confederate naval hero Raphael Semmes. During the Know-Nothing hysteria, Thomas Semmes had bravely spoken out against anti-Catholic violence and attacked the Know-Nothings' American Party. President Buchanan appointed him the U.S. District Attorney for Louisiana. During his term, he prosecuted soldier of fortune William Walker for invading Nicaragua. Everyone knew that Semmes would have had a spectacular national career if the war had not come along. He became a senator in the Confederacy and helped compose its motto, but lost everything he owned during the Union occupation and escaped prison only by applying personally to President Andrew Johnson for a pardon, which enabled him to return home and resume practicing law. Semmes quickly rebuilt his practice and was elected president of the American Bar Association in 1886.

While Luzenberg's mustache and the single tuft of hair on his gleaming forehead made him look like an angry schnauzer, Semmes possessed the sort

of social heft that made people compliment his "capital" bald head. His reputation as a man of honor, brilliant lawyer, and Promethean orator was rock
solid. When New Orleanians learned that he had been hired to defend "the
Italians," many took the news as the latest sign that the city fathers had fatally
bungled the Hennessy investigation.

The trial began in St. Patrick's Hall, a decrepit building on the river side
of Camp Street, across Lafayette Square from city hall. The courtroom was
stuffy and dark, and the acoustics were so bad that jurors often had trouble
hearing witnesses. Even then the city was negotiating a sale of the building to
the YMCA. If the Hennessy murder trial proved anything, people would say
later, it was that selling off St. Patrick's Hall was a wise move.

Expected to be "the greatest legal event in New Orleans history," the trial
opened on Tuesday, February 16, 1891, in an almost empty courtroom containing mostly lawyers and prospective jurors. Seventy-one men were questioned on
the first day, including Jacob Seligman, a tall, middle-aged Baronne Street jeweler.
Seligman said he had followed the case in the newspapers and talked about it but
had formed no opinion. He was accepted by both sides as the first juror.

Few other jurors were found that week. John Berry Jr., a solicitor for a flour
firm, machinist William Leahy, and real estate agent Solomon Mayer were accepted. Walter Livaudais, a young railroad clerk, was chosen on Thursday; another
clerk, Henry Tronchet, and grocery store proprietor Arnold Wille were accepted
on Friday, but the next long day of questioning produced no acceptable jurors.

Buckets of coal disappeared into the potbellied courtroom stove, and the
district attorney's temper rose with the trapped heat. Luzenberg suspected
many talesmen, or potential jurors, of claiming to oppose capital punishment
only to obtain an automatic dismissal. The *Daily Picayune* began to ape
Luzenberg's testiness with jibes about "the scruples excuse," being "afflicted"
with "anti-hanging contagion," and "the talismanic words" jurors spoke
against hanging. Luzenberg was also irritated by numerous citizens who were
unwilling to convict any man on circumstantial evidence in a capital case or
who claimed that newspaper accounts of the murder had given them inflexible opinions about this case. "Newspaper stuff," he snorted.

One day when the district attorney took a break, prosecuting cocounsel
Evans stepped in to grill a promising but stubborn juror. "If the ministers of
the gospel, priests and the high officials of England were to come up here and
swear, would you believe them in preference to the newspaper reports?"

"Yes, sir."

"Well, suppose presidents of banks were to come up here and testify,
wouldn't you believe them in preference to the newspaper reports?"

"No, sir, I would not," the juror replied. The *Picayune* characterized the
dismissed young citizen as "decidedly intelligent."

· · ·

Despite the slow progress, the Hennessy case was stirring again. The Italians and Italian Americans of New Orleans flinched at a newly invented taunt: "Who killa de chief?" Immigrant workers at the Macginnis cotton mill put down their baskets and quit jobs they desperately needed when the shame and bullying became too severe to bear.

When the national holiday commemorating George Washington's birthday approached, Governor Nicholls commanded all New Orleans militias to parade in honor of the country's first president. Washington's birthday fell on a Sunday that year and Nicholls wanted to avoid the Christian Sabbath, so he postponed the parade until Monday. Flags unfurled and drums rolled. The Louisiana Rifles in their tall, white shakos twirled their weapons and maneuvered in Canal Street. Yet the ranks of the Continental Guards, Washington Artillery, and Louisiana Field Artillery were all diminished because the parade was being held in midafternoon on a business day. Only the Italian American Tiro al Bersaglio company turned out in full force for the patriotic display.

Captain Antonio Patorno's smartly uniformed men stopped when the parade before them slowed to a halt. Police were ordered to prevent surging spectators from breaking the flow, but people nevertheless managed to fall into the street. The Tiro al Bersaglio's ranks inched forward as schoolboys began to dog them. "Who killa de chief?" piped the boys.

Patorno and his men stiffened, but maintained their ranks.

"Who killa de chief! Who killa de chief!" the schoolboys chanted.

The children got braver when they saw policemen laughing. A boy dipped his hand into the gutter and scooped up a fistful of mud and let it fly.

The muck hit one of Patorno's men in the neck. The militiaman wiped the filth from the back of his collar and went to the front of the company and held his soiled hand out to Patorno. "Captain, I can't stand this."

Patorno saw shame and anger in the man's face. The cops on the sidewalks were still chuckling. Patorno glanced ahead at the stalled procession and considered returning to the armory. Instead, he faced his men.

"For God's sake," Patorno commanded as more mud flew from little hands. "Don't say a word."

While militias trooped through city streets, a young unemployed molder named Edward Donnegan was sworn as the eighth juror. Unemployed bookkeeper William Mackesy and jewelry repairer Edward Heyob were chosen the next day. Another grocer, William Yochum, was sworn in.

By the time clerk Charles Boesen was accepted by both sides as the twelfth juror, two weeks had passed. Of the 1,200 summoned talesmen, 780 had been examined. More than 300 were excused for opposition to capital punishment, and over 100 more were released because they would not convict a man on circumstantial evidence, especially in a capital case. A dozen were rejected because of their acquaintance with Hennessy, while twice that number was unacceptable because they knew the accused or their families. Eighty-two men arrived at the jury selection with their opinions already set, mostly by newspaper coverage, although some lived in Hennessy's neighborhood or had heard of the case elsewhere. All were rejected. Nearly two hundred were unacceptable because of ill-health, inability to understand English, or reasons unexplained in challenges by lawyers on either side. Fifty-five were rejected because of their prejudice against Sicilians, ranging from hatred to vague feelings of distrust. Many admitted they would not believe uncorroborated testimony by any Italian or defense witness.

As soon as the last juror was sworn in, felony indictments against the accused were read. The indictments promised in formal legal prose that the prosecution would prove that these crimes were not merely contrary to state statute—they were against the peace and dignity of the state of Louisiana.

Early on Saturday, February 28, public seats filled with people waiting to hear the first testimony. Men who arrived too late to be admitted lingered in the halls, creating "a colossal spittoon" of gnawed cigar stubs, cigarette butts, litter, and tobacco spit. Inside, the first nine of the nineteen defendants— Macheca, Monasterio, Polizzi, Scaffidi, Bagnetto, the Marchesis, Incardona, and Charles Matranga—sat in two rows of chairs. Matranga wore a good suit with a red cravat and diamond cluster stickpin. Macheca arrived clean-shaven and wan, trying to look cheerful. Like Matranga, Macheca wore a finely tailored suit and an impressive display of jewelry.

Scaffidi sat to Macheca's left. A well-oiled bang of hair swept above his brows. The young fruit vendor was the kind of flashy dresser some New Orleanians thought of as particularly Italian. He wore a showy scarf pin and massive watch chain, and kept the handsome fit of his blue coat by leaving it buttoned. The press dubbed Scaffidi "the swell of the nine."

Young Gasperi Marchesi sat behind defense attorney Charles Butler, cheerfully unconcerned with the court proceedings. His father sat beside him, visibly more engaged with deep wrinkles carved into the dark skin of his forehead. The bearded fruit peddler was nearly fifty, poorly dressed, and carried a red bandanna like many French Quarter Italians. Antonio Bagnetto was a few years younger than the elder Marchesi. A weighty brown mustache hung beneath his long, turned-up nose. Prison life was taking a toll on Bagnetto. His face looked especially pallid alongside the swarthy Marchesi.

Emmanuele Polizzi's face was expressionless. He was dressed in a red flannel shirt, loud striped pants, and an ugly checked sack coat. His retreating forehead and chin denoted a lack of "self-will" to one reporter. Bastian Incardona's smooth face with its "concave nose" and sparse mustache also created newspaper fantasies of a "weakness of will."

Incardona and Polizzi sat in the front row with the attorneys as did Monasterio. The bearded cobbler was in his fifties, the oldest of the defendants. Wrinkles gnarled the saffron skin beneath his eyes. "His face shows no particular characteristic unless it is hardness and distrust," diagnosed the *Picayune*'s reporter. "Although he says he does not speak English, he took a lively interest in the proceedings and was clearly attentive to all that was said and done."

The cobbler's attention may have been piqued by a fact existing outside the realm of journalistic phrenology: Monasterio was on trial for his life. Police clubs and four months in the parish pest hole left him with no illusions about his situation.

Rain hammered the windowpanes and iron roof of St. Patrick's Hall. Blinds were drawn to deaden the sound of the storm outside, cutting off the winter light and filling the room with the imperfect incandescence of new electric bulbs. Many spectators strained their eyes by killing time with the day's first newspaper editions as preliminaries consumed the morning. Defense lawyers conferred behind a table piled high with at least fifty law books. Cynics decided that the stacked tomes were a theatrical prop meant to impress the jury. The courtroom bustled with police. Captains and stool pigeons alike eagerly whispered advice to the state and deputy sheriffs strutted about the court, running errands. A *Times-Democrat* reporter noted a variety of newsmen on hand, "all studiously endeavoring to look calm and collected, but all trying to give evidence of their superior knowledge of the case by glancing furtively and then long and steadily at nothing whatever."

The mumbling hushed when District Attorney Luzenberg finally called his first witness, Dr. P. E. Archinard. The Orleans Parish assistant coroner had performed the autopsy on Hennessy's body an hour after the chief's death. Archinard described multiple wounds, three of which were mortal. Jurors examined two of the balls Archinard took from Hennessy's body and one that fell out of the chief's clothing. Small birdshot punctures covered the chief's arms, legs, face, and side. All but one ball extracted from the back of Hennessy's right knee had entered the front of his body. Archinard deduced that the bullets came from Hennessy's left, with a slight inclination to the right.

"Would not that have depended on the position of the body of Mr. Hennessy as the direction from which they came?" Semmes asked in cross-examination.

"I can only infer from the character of the wounds," Archinard said. "The direction was so near alike in all of them that I thought they even came from the same gun or from the two barrels of the same shotgun."

Vandervoort, Hennessy's secretary, identified the clothing the chief wore to the police board meeting before the attack. The garments were brown with blood.

"Is this the umbrella he had?" Luzenberg asked.

"Yes," the tight-faced secretary answered. Luzenberg pushed open the umbrella. The fabric was full of holes. The grips of its gold handle were badly cracked. Semmes took the umbrella and inspected it, Adams fitted the chief's bloodied undershirt against his own body, and the jury took their turn with the gory exhibits. Hennessy's clothing was accepted as evidence.

Having established that whoever shot Chief Hennessy had nothing less than murder in mind, the prosecution tried to put as many of the defendants as possible near the chief's home on the night of the shooting.

Newspaper carrier George Mascare said he passed "the shoemaker's" place on Girod Street at about 11:05 on the night of October 15. Light shone through a crack in the shanty's planks and Mascare said he heard voices within, but saw no one. As he came to the corner, however, he saw five or six men standing outside the closed grocery diagonally across Basin Street, two doors from the Hennessy residence. Mascare said he recognized Monasterio and Scaffidi in light cast from the street lamp; he had seen the shoemaker two or three times and was used to seeing Scaffidi in Poydras Market daily. When the district attorney asked Mascare to identify anyone else he saw outside the grocery, Mascare pointed to Antonio Marchesi and Polizzi. Scaffidi wore an oilcloth coat, added Mascare, who said he went around the block twice that night and saw the group each time. He also encountered a man he could not identify who said hello to him with a heavy accent on the corner of Julia and Basin, a block from the grocery.

Adams came at the newspaper carrier fast and hard, wanting to know why Mascare would get off a streetcar at St. Charles, avoid Julia to walk up Girod—a block past a charcoal dealer he planned to see at Julia and Rampart—then change his mind and go looking for the man on Lafayette Street. Mascare said he got off the car because he felt like it. To Adams, this circuitous rambling on a rainy night made no sense, unless it was to conveniently pass the crime scene twice. The pitch of Adams's questions rose. The voices in Monasterio's shed spoke in Italian, in an ordinary tone, behind the closed door? The electric light at the corner was burning brightly and was not sputtering?

Baker stopped Adams, who was nearly shouting at Mascare. The judge told the defense attorney not to speak so sharply to the witness, and Adams apologized, saying he had gotten "warmed up."

Mascare did not look at the shoemaker's shanty when he passed it a second time, but the men were still at the corner and he could see their faces with the help of the streetlight, even though it hung a little higher than the grocery awning they stood beneath. The first person Mascare told about what he had seen was Captain Journée—as a matter of conscience, he claimed. Adams asked if Mascare knew there was a $15,000 reward offered for the capture of Hennessy's killers. When prosecutors objected that no such reward existed, Adams asked if Mascare was aware that the city council had placed $15,000 in Mayor Shakspeare's hands to be used in punishing Hennessy's assassins.

No, replied Mascare, denying he had read much about the case. Adams rigorously questioned Mascare about the electric streetlights at other corners along his route. The light at Girod and Basin was the only one he was able to recall.

"Was anyone produced for you to look at after your conscience troubled you, and you told what you knew to Captain Journée?" asked Adams.

"Yes," Mascare said. "A couple of dozen fellows." Sergeant McCabe brought Mascare to the parish prison. He said he picked out the same three men he recognized by the grocery, but now he wasn't sure if he had picked Monasterio or Marchesi. "It was the bald-headed man," he explained to Adams, pointing again to Marchesi. Mascare said he was sure that he identified Scaffidi at the prison. Adams asked deputies to fetch Salvatore Sunzeri from an adjoining room, where the ten indicted men awaiting the second scheduled Hennessy murder trial were being held.

"Take a good look at him," Adams said as Sunzeri was brought forward.

Mascare admitted he had picked Sunzeri from the prison lineup, but learned he was mistaken. He identified another man at the prison, one who wasn't among the nine defendants seated in the courtroom. After the rest of the suspects were led into court, Mascare said Jim Caruso looked like one of the men on the street corner, but he wasn't positive.

For the first of many times during the trial, Adams returned to the garment Scaffidi allegedly wore. It was an ordinary knee-length black rubber coat, said Mascare; a slouch hat covered Scaffidi's head, not an oilcloth cape. When Mascare left the witness stand, the prosecution called George Zehr, a barber who said he saw Scaffidi in Di Carlo's shoe store near Poydras Market between nine and ten o'clock before the shooting, wearing an oilcloth coat that reached his shoes. Zehr said he was sure Scaffidi wore a coat, not a piece of oilcloth.

Valentine Burke was working in his father's grocery at Girod and Basin, the corner nearest Hennessy's home, and remembered Bastian Incardona coming in around 8:20. The Italian asked for beer and cigarettes, laid two nickels on the counter, and left alone. Monasterio came in an hour later to buy a dime's worth of beer and a loaf of bread as he did every night, then walked home and pulled the door shut behind him. Burke said he could see only a block in the flickering streetlight. The light was similarly of little help to J. J. Driscoll, another Girod Street grocer, the first witness to have actually seen the attack. Driscoll recalled flashes of gunfire coming from the wagon gate along-side the shanty near the corner. The last shots were fired by a man standing on a wooden crossing bridge on the upper side of Basin Street, but Driscoll could not recognize the man's face from a block away. P. Joseph Grillot, owner of a saloon next to Driscoll's grocery, said the shooting got him out of bed, but by the time he reached the banquette, all he saw was smoke.

The first witness to describe the attack in detail was Zachary Foster, the black laborer who had been locked in the parish prison for "safekeeping" ever since the murder. As Foster was walking home from a meeting of the Young Men's Vidalia Association, he passed a Boylan officer, who must have been Of-ficer Roe, the man detailed to guard Hennessy's house. Foster had nearly reached Basin when he saw two flashes in front of a shanty ahead. Two men stood in front of the shed. "They had either pretty big pistols or short guns in their hands." A third man then ran out of the alley, shooting.

They fired at a man in light clothes coming up Girod. When Roe pulled a gun, Foster got scared and ran down Basin Street, eventually looking back to see the man in light clothes coming around the corner, holding himself against the wall and firing his pistol.

He knew now that the man in light clothing was Mr. Hennessy. At first Foster testified that he clearly saw the faces of three men who had shot at the chief. He pointed to Scaffidi, Polizzi, and Antonio Marchesi. Foster said he thought Monasterio, "the one with the beard," was a fourth man whose face he saw indistinctly. Unlike the balding Marchesi's other accusers, Foster was sure all four men wore hats.

Under cross-examination, Foster said the streetlight was only half burning when he reached the corner and his umbrella prevented him from seeing the first shot fired, but he heard it and raised his head in time to see two hands ex-tend to shoot from within the wagon gate. Foster had never seen the defen-dants before that night, but he was willing to swear they were "like the ones" he saw. "They're pretty much like them," Foster hedged. "I wouldn't want to go much further than that."

Dry goods clerk Louis Unverzagt was also on his way home that night and testified that he passed the chief at the corner of Rampart, where Hennessy was saying good night to a man who looked like Captain O'Connor. Unverzagt re-membered hearing the chief's footsteps behind him on the banquette, but saw no one else on the street. He lived a block beyond the Hennessys, and as he reached their house, explosions sounded. Unverzagt ran to his front step, turn-ing to see Hennessy firing at a white man edging around the corner onto Basin

Street with a long-barreled shotgun. Unverzagt said the light overhead was flickering and he could not see the man's face.

Rheta Thames was closer to the corner, but saw even less. Describing the fusillade that ripped into her house, Thames said she threw her windows open after the first fire and saw nothing but smoke. Boylan officer John Petersen, who lived across the street with his mother Theresa, told the court that an Italian cobbler lived in a shed in their front yard; Petersen didn't know his name, but pointed at Monasterio. Petersen described the property and two gates, one wide and one narrow, bordering the shed. Monasterio could leave the shanty by either his front door or a side door opening onto the inner yard. When Petersen came home after ten that night, he said he used the small gate because of the rain. The large gate was closed. A stone the size of his hat was usually pressed up against the gate to keep it shut. Petersen said he jumped out of bed and looked out when the shooting began. The large gate was now open. Adams asked if anyone could push his way inside the big gate. Yes, Petersen replied, there was no security about the place.

Harry Glover lived a few doors from the cobbler and also poked his head outside when he heard shooting, but his upstairs neighbor shouted that the black hostler ought to remain indoors in case of a general arrest. Glover rushed into his yard anyway and saw four men in front of the cobbler's shed, advancing up the street in line with Chief Hennessy, shooting as they walked. Hennessy ducked, then hurried to the corner and shot back. When a uniformed man started toward the chief from Burke's grocery, Hennessy yelled, "Don't come to me, go to the man who's got the shotgun!" The four attackers split up, Glover said: two running up Basin, two heading out Girod. One wheeled in the street and fired a shotgun at the uniformed man trying to help Hennessy. Glover later stood at the corner, watching the ambulance carry the chief away. The electric light was good, he remembered, but not good enough to have recognized Officer Roe's face or those of the running men, one of whom wore an oilcloth or overcoat.

Rosa Walton, who lived behind the Joe the cobbler, took the stand next. She said that through the cracks in her plank wall, she had heard low voices and more than one man walking in Joe's room that night. She smoked her pipe at half past eleven, then went back to bed. A few minutes later, Joe's side door opened and slammed, then she heard the shots. She and her old man Johnny ran out the side door and went to the end of the alley with Emma Thomas. When they got there, Joe was standing in his front door, wearing only his underclothes and shoes. "Emma," he said, "the chief, the chief!"

"Who is the man you call Joe?" Luzenberg asked.

Walton pointed to Monasterio.

* * *

By the time the day's testimony was over, the people of New Orleans could vividly picture men bursting from the Petersen property to kill Hennessy. A few of the defendants—Scaffidi, Polizzi, Antonio Marchesi, and perhaps Monasterio—were identified by Zachary Foster, the only witness so far who claimed to have seen the shooters' faces. But Foster's identifications seemed to wilt under cross-examination.

Perhaps Officer Roe, the Boylan officer whose drawn revolver sent Foster running down Basin Street in a panic, would remember the same scene more clearly.

Sixteen

RUNNING AT MIDNIGHT

IT WAS LATE MORNING THE NEXT DAY WHEN THE COURT CRIER called the names of the accused. As the prisoners filed in, the last man in line burst out in Italian, waving his hands.

"What's the matter with you?" Judge Baker asked Polizzi. Deputies pushed the agitated man into his seat, but Polizzi beat his chest with his fists.

"He wants to speak to Your Honor," Charles Matranga said.

"What does he want to say?"

"He wants an interpreter."

"Well, speak to him and tell me what he says."

Matranga spoke, but Polizzi snapped at him.

"He doesn't want to talk to me," Matranga said.

Judge Baker saw Joseph Macheca speaking to Polizzi. "You talk to him, Macheca."

"He wants to say something to Your Honor," Macheca said. "He wants you to call for an interpreter and then he will say what he has to say."

"Ask him what he has to say," Baker said.

"He says he doesn't want to talk to me."

"Guillio's here," prosecutor James Walker suggested. "He speaks Italian."

Adams turned to Judge Baker and protested, "We would like an opportunity to speak with the man ourselves. He's our client. It is our right."

"Some . . . well speak English . . . write!" Polizzi sputtered in broken English.

Judge Baker removed the jury and sent for an interpreter. "Why do you object to Guillio?" Luzenberg asked Adams as an uncomfortable hush fell over the courtroom.

Adams looked at the district attorney incredulously. "Because he's one of the men prosecuted in the Provenzano case!"

"Any interpreter will do," Judge Baker decided. "If any mistakes are made, the accused, all of whom speak Italian, can call the attention of the court to it." Baker called Adams, Semmes, and Luzenberg to the bench. "Does the defense have any idea what this is about?"

"No, sir," Adams said. "It may be a complaint about his treatment in the prison. I have no idea. Under the circumstances, I think it best that his statement be taken in private. The courtroom is too crowded and whatever he says may cause a disturbance."

Frank Marfese, a Sicilian, arrived and disappeared with Baker into the judge's private chamber with Polizzi and counsel for both sides. Reporters saw or imagined they saw the adult defendants turn pale. Macheca's usual nonchalant smile disappeared. Only Gasperi Marchesi looked oblivious to the disruption as the boy smiled happily at the courtroom spectators.

One reporter rose and, careful not to stray too far, found an Italian who told him Polizzi had said, "I don't want to die."

The delay lasted twenty minutes. Adams emerged first and chatted casually with reporters, but told them nothing. When Judge Baker and the others entered, Semmes announced that the defense team no longer represented Polizzi. Judge Baker said that someone would have to be found to represent the accused and called an hour recess.

"Don't be afraid, nobody's going to hurt you," a deputy sheriff grunted as he pulled Polizzi toward the deputies' office, away from the other defendants. It was agreed that Polizzi would be returned to the prison separately that night and placed in an isolated cell.

Reporters buzzed around Semmes, who would only say, "Quite a sensation here today." Defense attorney Gastinel, who came back from a walk outside the courthouse and sat beside Semmes, was slightly more talkative. "When Polizzi began his statement he said he knew about the case, but afterward asserted that he knew nothing—he was not there, but was sick in bed."

"What do you think of the man's actions, Mr. Semmes?" a reporter asked.

"I think that he's crazy, that the excitement has worked him up so much that it has affected his mind," Semmes replied. "The interview ended without him implicating anyone. Polizzi confesses that he knows all about the case and yet asserts that he is innocent and knew nothing about it. He says there was a meeting near the Poydras Market, that he was in a room and 'divided up the money.' If that's so, how could he be innocent? The whole manner of the man is so singular that I cannot say whether he is crazy or not. His mind is evidently affected by the excitement. It is certainly not clear."

Courtroom regulars were sure the fidgety man had turned state's evidence and would now be tried separately. Five minutes after the other eight prisoners were escorted to their seats, however, deputies led Polizzi to his chair: whatever was said in Judge Baker's chamber had not interested the district attorney enough to grant Polizzi immunity or sever his trial from that of the other defendants. They gazed straight ahead, avoiding looking at him.

Finding a lawyer interested in taking Polizzi's case would take too long, so Luzenberg proposed that Judge Baker appoint someone. Translator Marfese asked the prisoner if this was acceptable and Polizzi agreed. A young lawyer named Charles Theard was appointed to take over Polizzi's defense. A second recess was called until evening, and the doors blew open, expelling rumors from the courtroom. On streetcars, along the docks, in barrelhouses and in private clubs, New Orleanians from the Italian ghetto to the Garden District read that at this very moment Polizzi was dictating his full confession to the Hennessy murder.

Rumors that the prosecution now had a confession capable of destroying the defense case ensured that the courtroom was crammed well before the trial resumed at seven o'clock that night. Sheriff Villere enforced the "no standing" rule, leaving hundreds of people milling in the street. Inside, the newly installed electric courtroom lights were not working, so lamps were provided for the grumbling attorneys and reporters. Oily smoke floated in the airless gloom as spectators strained to see. Luzenberg was asked by reporters if Polizzi's presence in the dock meant that the Italian's statement or "confession" had not been believed. "There are no leaks tonight," the district attorney proclaimed.

Luzenberg called Mary Wheeler, who lived in Peeler the housepainter's apartment overlooking the crime scene. Wheeler jumped out of bed when the shooting started and ran into Peeler's room to see him looking out the window. She looked outside too and saw a man in either an india rubber or oil-cloth coat crouching in the middle of the street firing a shotgun, but could not identify any of the shooters, even though the electric light seemed bright. Wheeler heard someone yell, "Murder, murder, help, help!"

Newspapers would note that Wheeler was a mulatto, but neither prosecutors nor the defense alluded to race while she was testifying. Courtroom tactics shifted when James Poole, a muscular railroad laborer with ebony skin and a small curly mustache, took the stand. Poole spoke very slowly, forming his sentences with painstaking caution.

"On the night of October 15, Wednesday, to the best of my recollection and memory, about eighteen or twenty minutes after eleven o'clock, I was in a place at the corner of Girod and Dryades streets," Poole said. "I was in the barroom part of the place."

"Leave the place and get out on the street," Prosecutor Luzenberg demanded over the laughter of white spectators making fun of Poole's diction.

"I want to show why I was there," Poole explained. "There was in the place at that time a man called Lynch, who was a keeper at the workhouse, and a woman named Charlotte Redmond. Lynch said he was going to take the woman to jail and I was going to see that he didn't. Well, they left the place and I pursued them and, in pursuance of the man and the woman Redmond, I saw Mr. Hennessy at the corner of Rampart and Girod streets. He was departing from a man."

"How do you know it was Chief Hennessy?" Luzenberg asked.

"I knew the chief personally," Poole said deliberately.

Judge Baker interrupted. "Is that the way you always talk? Can't you speak faster?"

"I'm scared, Judge. If I talk fast, I'm likely to tangle myself up." Poole said that when he reached the corner of Girod and Rampart, Hennessy was a block ahead. "It was then the firing commenced. It started, then it paused, then it came quicklike. I saw a gentleman go past at full tilt, you know? He was going fast." The running man, said Poole, was in his shirtsleeves.

"Did you see his face?" Luzenberg asked.

"No, sir, I was scared I would get shot."

Poole said the streetlight was burning brightly enough to see the face of one of the men shooting at Hennessy, but a fog of gunsmoke after the first volley prevented him from seeing the rest as clearly. When Luzenberg asked Poole to pick out the men he recognized, he rose and tipped his outstretched hat at Marchesi. "That's the man, the one with the bald head." Poole also pointed his hat at Scaffidi. "This gentleman was at the corner of Girod and Basin streets on the crossing and fired from there. I don't remember anyone else. That man Marchesi jumped across the gutter and ran to the car track. The other one wore an oilcloth coat and fired from the bridge. I saw him do it."

Poole took a chew of thread tobacco from his pocket and nervously worked the quid into his mouth as Adams approached.

Adams asked how far Poole was from Hennessy when he first spotted the chief and O'Connor. Ninety feet, guessed Poole, who could hear their voices. When the pair parted, Poole noticed a third man, apparently Louis Unverzagt, on the banquette about sixty feet in front of Hennessy.

"Whom were you talking with at three o'clock today in front of the registration office when court adjourned?" Adams suddenly asked.

"I was conversing with some members of the city government."

"You mean three police officers, don't you?"

"Yes, sir."

"When did you ever before mention that a man was in advance of the chief?"

"I never mentioned it before," Poole replied.

"Did you ever *hear* it before?" Adams asked, implying that with or even without police prompting, Poole had invented a memory from Unverzagt's testimony.

"I never heard it, but I saw it," Poole said, adding that he did not know who the man was.

"But you do know the men who did the shooting?"

"I recognize their features."

"When the shooting took place, where was the man in advance?"

"He was at the corner of Girod and Basin streets on the downtown river side. When the firing began brisk, the man in advance of the chief had done passed the secondhand store. He was a colored man and had just reached Burke's grocery."

"You say he was a colored man," Adams said.

"I did not say that," Poole replied.

"There are twelve men here who heard you say it," Adams said sarcastically, meaning the jury, who by now had to be weighing whether Adams was badgering a jittery witness or destroying a carefully scripted performance. Adams asked what Hennessy wore.

"He had on a dark suit and a derby hat," Poole said. "I did not notice if he carried an open umbrella in his hand or not."

"Now the colored man."

"I don't remember the colored man." Poole agreed that he was in court when Zachary Foster testified. Unlike Foster, however, Poole did not recall anyone running to Hennessy during the shooting nor did he see a Boylan officer on the scene. Poole said the oilcloth coat on the man he identified as Scaffidi was light yellow, not black. He was sure it was a coat, despite not seeing buttons, a collar, or anything else indicating it was a garment.

"How could you tell one of the men was bald-headed?" Adams asked, questioning the accusation against Marchesi.

"I could see his full face good. There was no change in the light at all. It stayed lit all the time. Just after the firing it went down again."

"What do you mean by 'it went down again'?"

"It was not lit up before the shooting," Poole said. "When the shooting took place, the light was fully lighted." Two days later Poole joined the mourners viewing Hennessy's body, then moved to St. John Parish the following week. When he returned to New Orleans months later, he said, other state witnesses told him they had seen him the night of the shooting. At that point he went to see the chief of police, who sent him to the prosecutors.

If Luzenberg worried that Poole's methodical manner and race would prejudice the white jury against the state's case, the district attorney felt better about his next witness. John Daure was a young, white barkeep who was walking home from work on the night of the murder. Daure said he knew several of the defendants from a previous job, tending bar near Poydras Market. He claimed he saw everything.

"I heard a shot and later heard other shots," he said. "I saw four or five men start in a fast walk from the shed. One of them, whom I recognized as Scaffidi, whom I had known for two years, stood in a stooping position on the bridge and fired across the street. I saw Antonio Marchesi, the man with the bald head, under the shed. I knew him at the Poydras Market. I recognized also Antonio Bagnetto—that's the man," Daure said, pointing.

"They all had guns in their hands. The last shot was fired by Scaffidi who wore an oilcloth coat. The electric light was burning brightly. I saw others in the vicinity of the shooting. One of them was a boy running on the upper side of Girod Street, between Franklin and Basin streets, and he was going in the direction of the graveyard. That boy was Gasperi Marchesi, whom I have known as long as I knew his father. I could distinguish him from among fifty other boys, as I know everyone about the market."

"Are you absolutely certain that these are the men you saw?" Luzenberg asked.

"Yes, sir."

Adams's cross-examination was white hot. "You work at number 12 North Rampart, for Sidoti?"

"Yes, sir."

"For what class of people does he run the bar and restaurant?"

"For first-class people," Daure replied. "If you come there, you'll be treated well."

"Is it not frequented by prostitutes?"

"No, sir."

"Have you read in the papers about this case?"

"No, I didn't get the time."

"Did you talk about the case?"

"No, sir."

"Do you remember talking about the case yesterday, when you said that when you got up on the stand you 'would not be like the nigger,' and that when Mister Adams asked you something you would not stop and think?"

"I said that, yes."

"What do you mean then, by saying that you did not speak of the case?" Daure did not answer.

"Now," Adams said, "I want you to slap your hands to mark the space between the shots."

Daure hesitated. "Mr. Luzenberg, do you think it proper for me to do it?"

"If the court says so, do it," Luzenberg replied, looking to the judge.

"I see no reason why you should not do so," Judge Baker said.

"I have explained it as best I could!" Daure protested.

Adams bore down. "Other witnesses have done it. You can do it too."

"He has stated to the jury just how it occurred," Judge Baker offered.

Adams would not budge. "We want him to clap his hands."

"Can you do it?" Judge Baker asked Daure.

"I could not do it exactly—"

"Why not?" Adams said.

"I don't remember."

Adams pressed on. "According to your statement, you were fifty or sixty or eighty feet from Carondelet Street when you heard the first shot?"

"I was midway in the block between Carondelet and Baronne when I heard the first shot and started off in a run."

"When you were on the other side of Baronne Street you heard another shot? And you went another block before another shot was fired? And when you got to Dryades Street there was a volley? Then you ran almost the entire block between the firing of the volley and another shot?"

"Yes, sir," Daure answered to each of Adams's questions.

"When you got to the corner of Girod and Rampart streets . . . "

"I heard three shots in rapid succession," Daure said. "These men started to leave. When I got to the corner house is the time they started to leave the shed and move toward Basin Street."

"How did you see the face of any man except the man who stopped to shoot?"

"Because they stopped." Daure said he was at the McDonough School a block from the attack when Scaffidi turned and exposed his face to the light while "the crowd" moved, shooting, toward Basin Street. Daure said he did not pass anyone, white or black, during his run up Girod Street and did not realize the wounded man was Hennessy until he saw the chief at the Gillis house. The chief's back was turned to Daure when the last shots were fired. Scaffidi, he repeated, fired the final shot and wore an oilcloth coat that shone from the rain, making it impossible to determine the coat's color.

Adams could not find Daure's name on the list of grand jury witnesses, but Luzenberg assured Adams that the young bartender had testified. Daure said he first told Chief Gaster what he had seen a month or two after the shooting . . . or maybe it was before Christmas. Or after. He had met with Captain Journée once a week since January. "He told me to tell the truth," Daure said.

Adams made Daure repeat the story of his run. Increasingly flustered, Daure insisted he saw no one else on the street during the shooting, not even anyone at the McDonough School. That sounded unusual to those who had followed the case, for everyone knew that the chief had just said good night to Billy O'Connor on that very corner. Never mind, they thought, O'Connor will clear it up when he gets on the stand.

"How fast can you run one hundred yards?" a juror asked Daure.

"I never measured my time, but I know I am a good, fast runner."

If he was telling the truth, John Daure was not a good runner, he was a great one. He claimed to have run four city blocks during a shooting incident that most witnesses agreed was brief. No one asked him why he decided to run toward a gun battle at top speed when everyone else in the neighborhood—with the exception of police officers—was running away or, at most, poking their heads outside for a look.

A sugar broker named Tessier and a lawyer named Delesdernier were mulling this over when Sergeant McCabe barged into their conversation and warned them that he would not have anyone criticizing evidence outside of the courtroom. The angry cop told the citizens he'd throw them in jail if they kept it up.

☽

Seventeen

TOO BAD ABOUT DAVE

MANY OF HENNESSY'S NEIGHBORS HAD HEARD THE DEADLY fusillade, but most testified they had seen nothing. Prosecutor Luzenberg got a different story from Peeler the housepainter.

When the shots sounded, Peeler said, he came out onto his gallery and looked down to see an armed man wearing an oilcloth coat tied around the waist. The man deliberately fired three times, then stuck his gun inside his coat and walked away. A tall man wearing a striped coat and carrying a shotgun was already running up Girod Street with a stout smaller man. The streetlight, Peeler said, was burning "full blast."

Peeler identified the man in the oilcloth as Scaffidi. Luzenberg asked the housepainter if he could identify any of the other men he had seen. Peeler looked long and hard, then came down from the stand and walked to and fro before the defendants.

"You'd better get on the stand," Adams said. "Test your eyesight. I want him to let the jury see if he can tell a man's face at that distance." The *Daily Picayune*'s reporter made no note of the defense attorney's comment. All the newspaper's readers would know the next day was that Peeler returned to the stand, then pointed confidently at Antonio Bagnetto.

Adams asked why Peeler took so long to identify Bagnetto.

"It was on account of his changed dress," Peeler explained.

Adams got Peeler to admit that he had less time to watch the gunmen from the upstairs gallery than he had just taken to stare at Bagnetto face-to-face. Adams also questioned whether Peeler had been sober enough to open his window and climb out onto the gallery in time to see anything, with or without the help of his neighbor Mary Wheeler. Peeler was adamant, claiming that he saw one of the killers shoot, break his gun to reload, and shoot again.

"Did you see where he got his cartridges from?"

"No," Peeler said. "He had an oilcloth on." Peeler had seen the oilcloth at the police station. He said he thought it did not have buttons like an ordinary coat; it was meant to be thrown over the shoulders and tied.

Adams felt that since Peeler kept mentioning an oilcloth in his testimony, the one confiscated from Scaffidi should be produced. A creased and cracked roll of black varnished duck was brought in and unfurled. It was roughly eight-by-four feet and looked like the tarpaulins used by cab drivers to keep rain off their rigs. Scaffidi smiled as Peeler and the lawyers examined the large piece of plain fabric. Adams asked Peeler to demonstrate how the man with the gun wore it, adjusting the duck around the witness's shoulders. Peeler said he supposed the cloth was held on by a string across the chest.

Peeler thought he remembered someone yelling "help" or "murder," but did not hear Hennessy tell anyone to "catch the other man." He said he told police what he saw at the Central Station the morning after the shooting, he had not seen Unverzagt or Foster, and denied that he had ever accused anyone other than Scaffidi and Bagnetto. In reality, he had initially pointed out Incardona in a cell too.

"I understand you to say that you were sober at the time?" Adams said.

"Yes, sir," Peeler said, adding that he was perfectly sober the night of the crime too. Adams asked Peeler if he remembered his neighbor Mary Wheeler talking to a *Times-Democrat* reporter at five o'clock the day after the shooting.

"Yes, I believe she did say something."

"Didn't she say to them that they ought to let you alone and come back the next day, as you were in no fit condition then to be interviewed, as you were just then getting over a protracted spree?"

"No, sir."

"Was that the size of the oilcloth that you saw on that man that night?"

"Yes, sir."

"It wasn't doubled up?"

"No, sir."

Adams silently hoped the jurors would realize that anyone wearing an unfolded eight-foot tarpaulin would have to be a giant, unless this wasn't the oilcloth Peeler had seen. When Peeler left the stand, Adams handed the rolled duck to a court clerk. "You'd better put this out of sight," he suggested. "They have metamorphosized an oilcloth into a coat and I don't know what it will turn out to be soon."

Ice dealer and former Criminal Court clerk Nick Virgets, who lived across the street from the Hennessys, said he heard the first loud report, a volley, then scattered shots. There was a thick mist on the street when he came out onto his gallery. Three men—two with glistening shotguns—were past him, running for the dark Liberty Street corner. He could not see their faces. He swore at them and told them to stop. When Virgets looked back at the corner of Basin and Girod, he said the light there was "like a red ball of fire" throwing no light. He did not see Daure or any policemen at the corner. "The lamp at that corner is a bad one," the ice dealer added. "It's not unusual for it to go out."

James Price, a Girod Street cemetery sexton, said he heard the shooting from Franklin Street and was twenty feet from its intersection with Girod when he saw two men rounding the corner to run down Franklin in the opposite direction. He claimed to have seen one of them clearly.

"How did you recognize him?" Luzenberg asked.

"From a side face view. I'd seen him before and knew him to be a peddler. He peddled vegetables from a wheelbarrow. He was the man who was dressed in light clothes."

"What did he do?"

"When he was about twenty feet from Girod Street on Franklin, he fell. The gun he carried in his hand was dropped into the gutter. I heard the splash and saw the man get up and run." Price pointed at Polizzi and described another man with a long, dark beard, but said he did not see him among the defendants. Price insisted that he saw the side of Polizzi's clean-shaven face clearly, even though the men were quickly facing away from him, running toward the nearest streetlight at Julia Street, a full block away. When Price later joined the crowd gathering at the crime scene, he said, the Girod and Basin light was out. He estimated the shooting to have lasted three minutes, giving him enough time to stop at police officer John Kroper's house before seeing the fleeing men. The defense chose not to mention that all the other witnesses agreed the shooting lasted seconds, not minutes. When Officer Kroper was called to testify, he said he was asleep in his house on Franklin Street when he was awakened by the shots. He got outside in time to see three men running. Kroper identified the light-striped suit and pointed shoes he and Officer Dayton found in Polizzi's house. Pointed shoeprints had been found on the slimy banquette near the shooting.

"Can you swear that the man with light clothes wore pointed shoes?" Adams said.

"No, sir," Kroper said.

"All you can swear is that these clothes were found in the man's house, and because he was made to run at the station, you think he is the man you saw that night."

"Yes, sir," Kroper said uneasily. He turned to Judge Baker. "I swear positively that these are the clothes that I saw the man have on that night." Kroper repeated that he could only identify the clothing.

"Why did you have the man Polizzi put on these clothes at the station?"

"To identify him," Kroper said. "I picked him out before he put the clothes on."

"And yet you had never seen his face?"

"Yes, sir."

Adams was incredulous. "You had only seen his head and the back of his neck?"

"Exactly, sir."

Poydras Market commissary Dennis Corcoran testified that on the Monday before the shooting, he looked down from his window to see Polizzi and another man pull two guns from a sack and hand the guns to Charles Pietzo, who ran an adjacent grocery. Corcoran said that Polizzi had a mustache when the exchange took place.

"How did you happen to get this man's name?" Adams said.

"I don't know what his name is," Corcoran replied. "I knew him when he lived on Girod Street and can't be mistaken. I took an active part in the arrest, just as any citizen would."

"Even to the extent of taking the accused from his counsel on the street?" Adams said, recalling Corcoran's snatching Sunzeri away on the day of his arrest.

"I didn't know where you were going with him," Corcoran retorted. "Besides, I wouldn't trust you myself."

Adams was ready for the insult. "Mr. Corcoran, have you ever been convicted of murder?"

Corcoran's face reddened. "I was convicted once, but I got a new trial and then I was acquitted!"

"That's all," Adams said dismissively. He knew Corcoran's legal history well, for O'Malley had helped defend the commissary in a past case. Corcoran left the stand, hissing at Adams, "I've got your number! I'll fix you!"

Corcoran's tenant Louisa Ricasner also claimed to have seen Polizzi and the guns. The young black washerwoman said she was sitting on her gallery, heard knocking in the alley below, and looked down to see Pietzo let two "country dagos" into the yard. The smaller one wore a mustache. She said they took two guns from separate sacks and handed them to the grocer. Ricasner told Corcoran about it, and a few days after the chief was shot Corcoran asked if she could identify the men. She said she thought she could and identified Polizzi as the small man with the mustache.

Luzenberg next called lumberyard watchman John Lannigan, who had been on duty near the New Basin Canal. Shortly after shots echoed through the dark neighborhood, Lannigan said he met three men at the unlit corner of Julia and Liberty.

"As I got in front of them I asked one, 'Where's all that shooting?' and he said, 'Me donta knowa.' I looked the three men in the face. They were Italians. When I got three or four feet from the men, the man on the outside started to run and the others followed him. When I got further out, I met two more Italians. I looked them in the face, and as they left, I saw one of them take something from the front of his trousers. I said, 'Hold on, pardner.' The taller man pointed a gun at me and they ran."

Lannigan said he found four of the men at the Central Station the next day. "Scaffidi is the man I spoke to. Polizzi was with him. The third man is not here. I see none of the men I met in the second detachment."

At that point, the ten other defendants not yet on trial were led into court. Lannigan pointed out Sunzeri and Natali as the men he encountered in better light. Lannigan said he was "positive."

Adams stepped in and asked, "Don't you know that man Sunzeri was at the Academy of Music and afterward at a supper at the time you say that you saw him at the Basin?"

"I know that I saw him in the gang."

"And the other man? Don't you know that he was on the train between Chicago and New Orleans that night? You say that he was at the Basin?"

"Yes, sir." Lannigan was positive. Adams draped the oilcloth found at Scaffidi's house around his shoulders and asked if any of the men he met wore such a thing.

"No," Lannigan said. "I would've noticed it. Scaffidi and Polizzi were together, I'm sure of that."

"Did Polizzi have a mustache on that night?"

"Yes, sir, he did have one."

Hennessy's policeman neighbor Officer Dayton, who had arrested Polizzi, said he saw Polizzi daily when he lived in Monasterio's shed, before the cobbler moved in. Dayton described the peddler's wrist as looking like it had been scratched by a bullet and bandaged with a rag. Dayton recalled Polizzi wearing a very short "sort of a mustache." Police investigators who counted the bullet holes in the Dayton-Thames shotgun cottage were the next to testify, followed by the paperboys who found the shotguns on Basin Street. City workers described the weapons they found while cleaning the Magnolia street gutters.

Times-Democrat mail wrapper John Murray identified a ramrod he found under the floorboards of Monasterio's shack the night of the crime. John Beverly echoed his wife's story of being roused by the shots. "When I came out, I saw Joe standing in his underclothes, smoking a pipe. He said to Emma, 'The chief, the chief! Mama 'cross street!' He had fixed shoes for her." Beverly went to the corner, but saw nothing in the bad light. Gunsmith Louis Cook took the stand last. He occasionally shortened weapons for gentlemen who wished to pack guns for long trips and thought whoever shortened the guns raked out of the gutters did a shoddy job.

That night residents of Girod Street awoke to whistling and shouts in the early morning darkness. Sashes rose and windows opened. "What's up?" neighbors asked each other.

Well-known local athlete Louis Knuckles was strapping on his track shoes near the corner of Carondelet Street. There was a lot of public skepticism about John Daure's claim of running three blocks in time to see the last shot fired at Chief Hennessy. Knuckles would try to duplicate the run.

The street was pitch black at that hour, apart from a white knee-high beam of light refracted in steam rising from sugar refinery runoff in the gutter. Three signalers took places along the route as a growing crowd of night characters and cops watched.

A dropped hat gave the signal, stopwatches clicked, and Knuckles tore up the street past the groggy citizens leaning out of their windows. He covered the route in seventy-six and three-quarter seconds.

The *Times-Democrat*'s reporter watched as the athlete huddled with his boosters. What did it mean? Knuckles had run on dry sidewalks, not on slippery wet banquettes. On the other hand, Knuckles had dashed four blocks, while Daure only claimed to have covered three.

A circus, scribbled a reporter before tucking his notes away to the sound of slamming windows.

That afternoon *Times-Democrat* editor Page Baker and his reporter W. B. Stansbury took a cab to the crime scene, where Baker timed Stansbury with a pocket watch as the reporter walked as swiftly as he could to the block beyond Baronne Street. It took Stansbury a minute and a half to reach the spot where Daure said he began to run.

Court was closed on Wednesday for a holiday, leaving the public a full day to talk about the prosecution. There was plenty to discuss. Depending on the accuracy, motives, or sobriety of each witness, the total of defendants implicated as Hennessy's killers ranged from none to three or four or six—Lannigan's impossible identification of Sunzeri pushed the tally to seven. The last shots were fired within the normal reach of a street lamp that was dead, sputtering, or perfectly lit. The attack lasted seconds . . . or minutes, although that seemed unlikely, given the short distance from the Petersen gate to the street corner. And regardless of what anyone thought of the trial so far, the prosecution still had not given the city a reason for Hennessy's death.

New Orleans Police
Superintendant
David C. Hennessy
(*Illustrated American*)

The Hennessy home on Girod Street (*Illustrated American*)

Charles Matranga
(*Illustrated American*)

Pietro Monasterio
(*Illustrated American*)

Antonio Scaffidi
(*Illustrated American*)

Warden Lemuel Davis
(*Illustrated American*)

Criminal Sheriff Gabriel Villere
(*Illustrated American*)

William S. Parkerson
(*Harper's Weekly*)

Girod Street after the murder. Hennessy was attacked while walking past the Thames-Dayton house in the right foreground. M. L. Peeler claimed to have witnessed the shooting from the adjoining upstairs gallery. Burke's grocery is on the next outbound corner. People gather beneath the awning of Monasterio's shack in the left foreground. The walls of the Girod Street Cemetery are visible in the distance. (*Illustrated American*)

Monasterio's shack is in the foreground. To the right of the awning, bullets from Hennessy's revolver were found in the alleyway entrance and feet away in the door molding of the corner building. The large gate to the Peterson property lies past the building on the left. (*Illustrated American*)

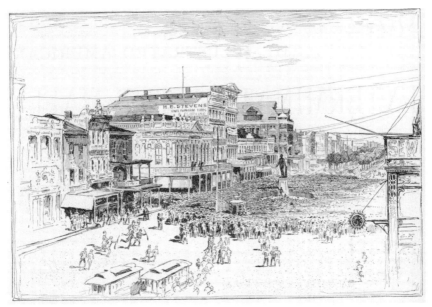

A crowd gathers at the Clay Statue in Canal Street on March 14, 1891. (*Illustrated American*)

The crowd listens to the mob leaders at the Clay Statue on Canal Street. (*Harper's Weekly*)

The bodies of Joseph Macheca (with the Indian club), Antonio Scaffidi, and Antonio Marchesi lying in the "star chamber" gallery. (*Illustrated American*)

Inspecting the bodies of Romero, Monasterio, Comitz, Traina, Geraci, and Caruso in the prison yard. (*Illustrated American*)

Inside the Orleans Parish prison (*Illustrated American*)

The Orleans Parish prison (*Illustrated American*)

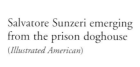

Salvatore Sunzeri emerging
from the prison doghouse
(*Illustrated American*)

AT THE BOTTOM OF IT ALL.
COWARDLY JURIES ARE THE FIRST CAUSE OF MOB RULE.

"AT THE BOTTOM OF IT ALL. COWARDLY JURIES ARE THE FIRST CAUSE OF MOB RULE." The March 25, 1891 cover of the satirical New York weekly *Puck* commented on the lynching, depicting the Mafia terrifying the Hennessy jury.
(Photo courtesy of the Yale University Library)

The Thursday morning rush for seats at St. Patrick's Hall was frantic. A dozen fashionable young ladies were admitted, with escorts, of course. The *Picayune* disapproved. Allowing women spectators in court was already too common in the North and West, complained the paper, which put such a "fad" down to "morbid curiosity."

The prosecution resumed with the Boylan officer who arrested Zachary Foster. Robert Hennessy, no relation to the chief, said flashes attracted him to the scene where he found the chief sitting on a doorstep with his bloodstained pistol in his hand. Hennessy said he later gave the pistol to the chief's mother. A lanky young black man named Amos Scott caused the biggest sensation of the day. Scott told prosecutors that he sold chickens in Poydras Market and claimed to know Bagnetto, Scaffidi, Charles Matranga, and both Marchesis. The Saturday after the murder, Scott said, he saw Gasperi Marchesi in the market, back from prison.

"I say to him, 'Kid, how'd you get out?' He says, 'I told on my daddy.' I asked him how. He says his daddy told him to wait on the corner of Girod and Rampart 'til the chief come by, then he was to go 'head of the chief and run past the house where his daddy was and to whistle. 'Asperi told me and Joe Williams he did like his daddy told him to."

"Did you talk to Scaffidi also?"

"Yes sir. I met Scaffidi about four days before the killing at Poydras Market. He gave me a pistol about this long," said Scott, holding his hands a foot apart. "He told me to go get it loaded for him at a pawnshop on Poydras near Perdido Street. I did, then he sent me to the corner of Common and St. Charles streets, right under the St. Charles Hotel. He told me to go there and find out how much it would cost to go from New Orleans to Mexico. I went there and found that it would cost $61 and I told him so."

Adams eyed Scott, saying, "Where did you come from?"

"New Orleans."

"I mean before you came to court."

"I came from the prison." Scott had been in the Orleans Parish Prison for the past five months. Once before, he said, he had been convicted as an accessory to petty larceny and sentenced to a year in the penitentiary by Judge Baker. Adams asked Scott how he came to know about young Marchesi's whistle. Scott said, "The boy up and told me."

"Did he tell you of his own accord?"

"No, I asked him how it came that he was out."

"What did he tell you?"

"Just what I said. He said his daddy had sent him to the corner and told him to whistle when the chief got in front of the house."

"How did he whistle?" Adams asked.

Scott uttered a short, low note.

"Whose house did he whistle in front of?"

"He didn't tell me."

"How did he explain his being out of jail?"

"He said he got out by telling on his father."

"Whom did he tell?"

"He told me that he told the police."

Adams made Scott repeat Scaffidi's alleged requests to have the pistol loaded and learn the cost of a fare to Mexico. When Adams asked how big the bore of the pistol was, Scott held his fingers apart as if he held a 5¢ piece. Adams asked how much it cost to fill the gun with cartridges.

"It was 15¢, but I told the man that Tony Scaffidi had said to tell him it was for him, so he put it in for 10¢."

"How often did Sergeant Walsh see you at the prison?"

"About two or three times."

"Do you smoke?"

"Yes, sir."

"Chew?"

"No, sir."

"Where do you get your tobacco to smoke?"

"From Walsh."

Luzenberg stepped back in. After establishing that Scott had been imprisoned only as a witness since Hennessy's murder and that there was no charge against him, Scott was excused and freed. His friend Joe Williams was on the stand next. Williams said that normally he minded fruit stalls for Vincent Scaffidi and Tony Tortoricci in Poydras Market and he too was being kept in the parish prison as a witness without any charge.

Williams seconded Scott's story of Gasperi Marchesi's confession. "He said, 'I turned my father. I turned state's evidence.' Yes, he used both sayings. He can talk good English and I understood what he said."

After the afternoon recess, the prosecution questioned two final witnesses about Hennessy's neighborhood. A shabbily dressed man named Samuel Petrie, who lived at the corner of Girod and Franklin where James Price claimed to have seen Polizzi, testified that he heard the shots, running footsteps, and a splash outside his window. He saw plenty of people hunting for weapons, but never saw the men he heard running. Newspaper editor Baker recounted his exercise with reporter Stansbury and the stopwatch. Adams asked him what shape the banquettes were in. They were dry, admitted Baker, who had no idea what they were like on the night of the murder.

Thus far the prosecution had focused only on the forensic details of Hennessy's death, the crime scene, and the alleged triggermen. Luzenberg now proposed a link between the defendants accused of lurking behind the Petersen gate and a man who allegedly hated and feared the chief enough to have him murdered: Joseph Macheca.

Again, the prosecution confidently expected credibility and circumstance to carry their case. Even the first piece of physical evidence the state offered depended on a witness. Olivia Petersen was shown a rent receipt dated August 13. She recognized it and told of renting Monasterio's shanty to the man who wanted a receipt written for Peter Johnson.

"Who was that man?"

"I was told it was Joseph Macheca."

When Adams objected, Luzenberg said, "Well, never mind what you were told. Do you see him here?"

Mrs. Petersen paused, looked slowly down the row of prisoners, and finally pointed to Macheca. "Please rise—that is the man."

Mrs. Petersen said she had written two more rent receipts for future payments and handed the slips to her mother-in-law, who gave a second slip to the renter a month after his first visit. Adams cross-examined her about the man who rented Monasterio's shack. "How was he dressed?"

"In a black or dark suit. Dark clothes and a stiff hat."

"Did he have any jewelry?"

"Yes, sir. A gold chain."

"What kind of shirt did he have on?"

"White."

"Have a pin on it?"

"He might have, but I didn't see it."

Mrs. Petersen's friend Mrs. Osberg said she saw the man who rented the shack come in Petersen's gateway that day. She was not sure she could recognize him, she said, but Luzenberg asked her to try. She pointed to Macheca. "I didn't hear what went on. I think he is the man. He looks like the man."

"Don't imagine," Luzenberg said. "I want you to be sure."

"I am sure. That is the man."

"Did you go to identify him?" Adams asked.

"Yes, sir." Osberg said a police captain identified Macheca by name during the lineup.

The state did not summon Petersen's mother-in-law, but recalled Rosa Walton, who said the man who inspected the yard last August was the fourth man in the row of prisoners, Macheca. There was a rustle in the courtroom. Sheriff Villere commanded the spectators to be silent. Walton said she saw Macheca three times in the parish prison, and each time she identified him as the man who rented the shed: there was no doubt in her mind. Emma Thomas also pointed to the fourth man in the row, saying he was the man who spoke to her about renting the shack. She said that later she saw Mrs. Petersen showing him the room. She watched as he went through the wide gate, inspected the yard, and came out the narrow alleyway.

"Why did it take you so long to identify him?" Adams asked her.

"Because he's changed," Thomas said.

"How so?"

"His mustache was black then. It's gray now."

First Precinct night clerk William Morrison, describing the contents of Monasterio's pockets when the Sicilian was brought to the Central Station, said he found religious pictures, a pocketbook, and papers, including the receipt identified by Mrs. Petersen. The defense wanted to see the pocketbook and papers, so Judge Baker ordered Captain Journée to send for them. Inexplicably, the police never delivered them to court as requested. If any reporters or amateur sleuths noticed that "Peter Johnson," the name on the one receipt entered as evidence, was a phonetic anagram of John Petersen, the name of the landlady's Boylan officer son, none ever mentioned it.

Anyone who knew the two men was aware that relations between Macheca and the chief worsened because of the Provenzano case. The prosecution now picked up the quarrel and attempted to hammer it into the motive behind Hennessy's murder. Patrolman William Cenance, a six-year veteran of the New Orleans Police, testified that he was waiting for a patrol wagon on a French Quarter street corner one night in mid-September when Macheca approached him. They talked of the Provenzanos, who had just been scheduled for retrial. Macheca, Cenance said, accused Hennessy of taking a hand in the Provenzano case and said he could put Hennessy in a box.

Adams asked for a more precise explanation. "The claim of Macheca was that the chief had meddled in the business, doing something he had no right to do. Wasn't that it?"

"Macheca said to me that the chief was deeply implicated in the case, that he could put the chief in a box, and would put him there."

Everyone in court knew that to put a man "in a box" meant to corner him, to "fix his wagon." With Hennessy in his grave, it looked like the talkative Macheca had either made unfortunate use of the popular expression or chosen a veiled threat carelessly.

Macheca's displeasure with Hennessy was no secret. James Kayle, manager of Solari's fancy grocery business, knew Hennessy, Macheca, and Charles Matranga very well. He remembered meeting Macheca on Dauphine Street one midnight not long after the Provenzanos were granted a new trial. Kayle did not recall the exact words, but said Macheca excitedly told him that Hennessy ought to keep his hands off the case. Red Light Club members Isidore Kuhn, Dave Heller, and Tom Anderson recalled Macheca saying that the fruit merchants would hold the chief responsible for whatever might happen if the Provenzanos were released. Macheca was nervous as he always was, Heller said, but not excited.

During a short recess, Joseph Macheca moved to a different seat.

When bordello proprietor Fanny Decker was called, the elegantly dressed madam said she was ill, so she was seated near the jury. Even so, they strained to hear her voice. Decker softly recalled seven men arriving at 2:00 a.m. on October 16 and drinking eight bottles of wine, which was not unusual. "They said they had been to the theater and Fabacher's and had come to see me so that people would know where they were, for they were not friends but enemies of Hennessy. I spoke to Macheca, saying it was too bad about Dave, and he said these were enemies of Dave." She said she remembered Charles Matranga being there but had never seen the others before and did not know if she could pick them out. Only Macheca spoke to her, she said. "I don't know that they left the impression on my mind that they might be suspected."

"What exactly did Macheca say to you about the chief?" Luzenberg asked.

"I said to Joe Macheca, 'It is too bad about Dave being murdered,' and he said, 'Yes. These are all enemies of Dave's.' I said nothing more and Dave Hennessy's name was never mentioned again during their stay."

Decker's piano player Walter Robinson remembered the wine party, but understood nothing of what the men had said, for they spoke in Italian. Officer Robert Pollock described trailing the partygoers and waiting with officers Hevron and Cassidy at the corner of Hospital and Bourbon as Macheca and Caruso approached. "Macheca put his foot on the step of the door where he lives and shook hands with Jim Caruso and said, 'Good night, Jim. I am much obliged to you. I am only sorry they did not do that son of a bitch up right there.' Then I spoke to Cassidy and asked if he had heard what Macheca had said—"

"Never mind that," Luzenberg interrupted quickly. "Tell us what was done." Pollock recalled Macheca walking to the corner with Caruso, who lived elsewhere in the French Quarter.

Adams had Pollock repeat their parting words. "Macheca said, 'Good night, Jim. I am much obliged to you'?" Adams asked.

"Yes, sir."

"'I am sorry that *they* did not do that son of a bitch up'?"

"'I am sorry that they did not do the son of a bitch up.'"

Sergeant Hevron's story was the same as Pollock's. "We didn't want them to see us and they spoke very low," Hevron said. "As Caruso passed me, he raised his umbrella. He didn't know me and Pollock said to him, 'Hello, Jim.' He said hello and went out toward the river."

Adams approached Hevron, his thin voice incredulous. "Macheca spoke loud enough for you to hear half a square off?"

"About half a square."

Luzenberg did not call Hevron and Pollock's companion, Officer Cassidy, and neither did Adams. Not even the press questioned if Cassidy also heard Macheca "speaking low" from half a block away.

The afternoon was rough on Macheca's frayed nerves, but even he was relieved when the district attorney announced that the state's case was complete. After four days and over fifty witnesses, no one else would testify against the defendants.

Adams rose to ask Judge Baker the question all of New Orleans was asking. "Is the state going to put Officer Roe and Captain O'Connor on the stand, their names having been mentioned in the testimony?"

If Baker was as curious as the rest of the court, he was too professional to show it. "I can't control the state in that matter," he said.

"I have to address them through the court," Adams said, explaining why he was asking the judge instead of the prosecutors.

"No," Luzenberg answered. Roe and William O'Connor, the two Boylan officers nearest Chief Hennessy when the bullets flew, would not testify.

"We don't want the state to close until we have had a chance to cross-examine the witness Daure," said Adams, who had no intention of letting anyone forget Roe and O'Connor. He muttered under his breath, loud enough for everyone to hear, "No wonder they aren't putting them on the stand. They'd knock the sprinter's story silly."

The courtroom was cleared for the day. Outside on the sidewalk, Antonio Patorno was beaming. "They did not connect my brother with the case at all," the former alderman and Tiro al Bersaglio captain said happily. "He simply went out with the supper party, but was not aware that he was going out for any purpose but to enjoy himself!"

Inside St. Patrick's Hall, George Vandervoort passed Dominick O'Malley on his way from the courtroom.

"Vandervoort, I'll make you a small bet that not one man you've arrested will be convicted," O'Malley taunted, loud enough for everyone in the filthy corridor to hear. "What do you say?"

Hennessy's secretary kept walking, garnet-eyed and silent.

The *Daily Picayune* appraised the case and agreed with the state that Polizzi, Marchesi, Scaffidi, Monasterio, and Bagnetto were identified as the parties who did the shooting. Macheca was identified as the man who rented Monasterio's shack under an assumed name. All anyone said about Bastian Incardona was that he had been in the neighborhood. The only charge against Charles Matranga was his irritation at Hennessy's interest in the Provenzanos' defense and complaining that "such humbug would have to stop."

Still, the public expected a conspiracy to be proved or at least explained, but this had not happened, wrote the *Picayune*'s trial reporter. It was true. Five months of publicity and grandiose speeches about secret murder societies, vendetta slayings, and blood oaths amounted to nothing in the trial. Where was the plot? No one in New Orleans had expected the prosecution to rest so quickly.

☽

Eighteen

HE ALWAYS CRAZY

THE MAYOR TOSSED A LETTER ACROSS HIS DESK TO REPORTERS. In bad French, the letter threatened Shakspeare and his secretary with death if the Italians were convicted.

"We've received so many such communications that they've become an old chestnut and are generally consigned to the wastebasket without ever being read through," Shakspeare said brightly. "Some of them are quite amusing as works of art, written in red ink and profusely embellished with skeletons, cross-bones and coffins. I think that while some of these letters may be written for purposes of intimidation, most of them are silly jokes."

Boys and men loitered outside the parish prison as early as 8:00 a.m. to follow the prison van to St. Patrick's Hall. Crowds spilled from the courthouse steps across the street into Lafayette Square, while double ranks of cops guarded all the entrances.

Polizzi could see the throngs clearly from the driver's bench. He had spent a quiet night at the prison, but it was assumed that he was still afraid of the other defendants because of his alleged confession. He was allowed to ride to court sitting alongside the driver. Inside St. Patrick's Hall, he was led through Luzenberg's office to the sheriff's private office overlooking Camp Street.

A delay over the attachment of absent defense witnesses stretched into an hour. The unexplained holdup was too much for Polizzi who bolted for the sheriff's window. One of his hands smashed a pane as deputies pulled him back.

Polizzi kicked and struggled. "I make a big mistake!" he wailed, tearing at deputies' hands as they forced him down onto a cane settee and handcuffed him.

"You trying to kill me! Damn you, damn you!" Polizzi screamed.

"Everyboda saya crazy," a reporter wrote as Polizzi mumbled. "Jacka, negro, Giroda Streeta, my frien. He my witness."

"What Jack?" the reporter asked.

Polizzi looked up, his eyes widened, and he sprang forward and grabbed for the reporter's gold watch chain. Deputies wrestled him down.

"He is speaking about fifty things at a time," explained John Cefalu, the court's new translator. "He talks about the city where he lives in Italy. He said he went home that night and went to bed, and the next morning somebody told him the chief was shot, and then they came and arrested him."

"Does he talk sensibly?"

"No," Cefalu said. "He talks about fifty things at one time."

"This is the same way he acted the night he was arrested and when we had him at the station," said George Vandervoort, who stood nearby watching Polizzi writhe on the settee. Polizzi spoke faster and faster.

Who killed the chief? Cefalu asked Polizzi in Italian. "How do I know," Polizzi screamed back. "I was at home! My wife said they killed the chief and I'd better leave the city, and then they arrested me!"

Nothing was accomplished. While Charles Theard was trying to calm his client with Cefalu's help, both sides agreed that too many defense witnesses were absent for the case to go on. Attachments were sent out for missing witnesses, and court recessed until the afternoon. When the jury and defendants returned, the entire court watched Polizzi enter from a side door, without handcuffs, surrounded by four deputies. He came to his seat . . . and kept walking. The deputies grabbed his arms and pointed at his chair, but Polizzi yelled and wrenched his arms free. He was pushed into the chair and held as he wriggled and shouted.

"Mr. Sheriff, put that man in the dock," Judge Baker ordered. Deputies pulled Polizzi to his feet and wrestled him out of the courtroom.

Theard approached Judge Baker and said, "Do I understand Your Honor to mean that the trial will go on without the presence of my client?"

"The trial will go on without his presence if he obstructs the trial. It will go on with his presence if he behaves himself," Judge Baker said. "From what has taken place heretofore and from what has taken place now, I should judge that you will have a great deal of difficulty in managing him. If in your opinion there is any possibility of making this man keep quiet during the trial, I shall be very glad."

Theard left the courtroom and tried to talk to Polizzi with Cefalu's help, but it was no use. Polizzi told Cefalu that he did not want a lawyer.

"But you have one," Cefalu said in Italian. "You asked for one and the judge got one for you."

"The lawyer might be good for you, but I don't want him or any other," Polizzi said. "I only said I wanted one to please you and the judge!"

"Do you think he's crazy?" Theard asked.

"I don't think so," Cefalu answered.

"You won't help me!" Polizzi shrieked at Cefalu. "You're one of *them*!"

Theard wearily reentered the courtroom and asked to be released from the case. The court-appointed attorney saw no point in trying to represent a client who would not trust him.

"He tells me that he desires the services of no lawyer and that he never did at any time," Theard told Judge Baker. "He wants to leave to the court alone the question of his guilt or innocence. That is a matter he insists upon."

"Have you explained to him that the court has no right to try him without a jury?"

"Yes, sir, I have."

"And he says that he does not want you as his lawyer, and that he does not need any lawyer to represent him?"

"Yes, sir," Theard replied. "He wants his communication to be made directly to the court. Your Honor will appreciate, and I hope the counsel on both sides will appreciate, my embarrassing position in these proceedings."

Theard was allowed to quit the case, so the relieved young lawyer picked up his hat and left. Judge Baker assigned the duty of calling witnesses on Polizzi's behalf to the other defense attorneys. As the next witness was called, John Rocci, an elderly, wealthy cotton buyer, volunteered to help. He was much respected within and outside the New Orleans Italian community, whose ten cultural societies he was trying to rally into a federation. He had also condemned Hennessy's assassination in the New Orleans press, differentiating "true Italians" from "members of the Mafia." Judge Baker let Rocci try to calm Polizzi once more.

Five minutes later, Polizzi, pale and quiet, entered the court with Rocci. Again he refused to sit.

Rocci could not communicate with Polizzi. "Judge, the man is crazy. He is mad with me, though I never saw him before. The man is out of his mind and I think if he is kept quietly and alone until tomorrow morning, he will be all right again."

"Take him out of the courtroom." Judge Baker apologized to the jury. "I think it will be necessary to send for the city physician and have that officer examine the mental condition of the prisoner. That being the case, it will be impossible to go on with the case today."

Reporters surrounded the bewildered Rocci as the court dispersed. "The man is out of his mind," Rocci said. "He told me I had dined with Hennessy. I never dined with Mr. Hennessy in my life. He is very much excited and continually mentioned the name of Ruguza, but heaven only knows who Ruguza is. He asked me the name of the chief of police and I told him Mr. Hennessy. He then said that he was not with the party who killed the chief of police, that he had nothing to do with those who killed the chief. At times he spoke Italian very imperfectly and I could not make out what he said. He spoke about the Provenzano and Matranga affair, in which he seems to have been connected in some way."

The deputy fingered his broken watch chain. Polizzi had ripped it apart in another dash at the window.

"He says if he is guilty, he is willing to hang," Cefalu said. "In fact, he would hang himself, but he wants the others to hang with him."

Did Polizzi belong to this Mafia everyone had been reading about since the first Provenzano trial? asked a reporter.

"He hasn't said anything about it," Cefalu replied. "He isn't making sense. He's had enough of all the others and he doesn't want their lawyers. He doesn't want any lawyers. Then he says he was in trouble in Bryant, Texas, and a lawyer got him free. He wants that lawyer." Cefalu shook his head. "He wants Oteri and the other fruit dealers to make up a big bunch of bananas. They must be made of pure gold. They must be sent to his uncle, Salvatore Toro, in Palermo. He wishes he never left Sicily."

Anything else?

"He wants his wife. And he wants the girl he loved before he was married. Both of them are to dress in pure white."

Speaking to reporters outside St. Patrick's Hall, Polizzi's common-law wife, Lana Rosa, said she had been summoned to court, but was now told that Polizzi had changed his mind and did not want to see her.

"It's nothin'," she told reporters, shrugging. "He always crazy. Pretty soon he be alright, no more trouble."

"Isn't it true that you and Polizzi lived in the shanty on Girod Street and moved out to let Monasterio in?" a reporter asked.

She shook her head. "We live there, but then we live downtown, then on Julia Street. Me and him in house on Julia Street when the chief shot. He go to bed at seven thirty that night. I hear about the chief in the morning and tell him. He never leave the house before that."

Inside, all the prisoners were in the dock except Macheca who was in the sheriff's office, talking with his lawyers. A reporter asked if he had seen fresh newspaper accounts of Polizzi's purported "confession" accusing Macheca and the Matrangas of being leaders of the Mafia.

"These are all lies," Macheca yelled at the reporter. "I am a good citizen! This man is out of his mind."

The Black Mariahs returned late that afternoon, and all the accused men except Polizzi were driven away. One of the vans returned for Polizzi. The van was quickly surrounded by a noisy crowd as Polizzi descended the courthouse steps, halted, and would not budge.

Amid catcalls, Polizzi was wrestled to the van by six sheriff's deputies and thrown in head first. As the wagon rolled away, Polizzi jammed his fingers through the round grate and looked out just in time to see a funeral procession passing nearby. He stared out at the hearse and its raven train, then disappeared suddenly. The guards could feel the man inside the van beating at the walls with his fists.

He was quiet when they reached the prison. He was no trouble until he reached the stairway to the cells where he tried to break free and was restrained. When he was calm again, they began the walk up to the condemned cells on the third gallery where the prisoner was now confined, alone.

John Daure got up early Saturday morning and went to his Poydras Street barber for a shave. He spent a nickel on the new *Mascot,* and while waiting for his tender whiskers to be removed, he found his name in the latest story about the Hennessy trial. Spruced up and pleased with himself, he headed to court, passing Poydras Market on the way.

Italian fish vendor Tony Rabito spotted the young bartender and called out to a neighboring stand, "Hey, Cosgrove, here's that expert runner."

"Hello, Rabito," Daure replied. "I'm in the *Mascot.*"

"For *what?*"

Daure was surprised by Rabito's hard tone. "For being a witness in the Hennessy case."

"I hope you'll do as well in that suit you're in down by the Civil District Court. Then that man you're a witness for can pay what he owes me," Rabito snorted, referring to a legal tangle unrelated to the Hennessy case. "You're a great liar. You should be in a $10,000 suit."

"Everything I said I can prove," Daure said. "I have witnesses for it!"

"I suppose you got $1,000 for your story," Rabito said. "I don't care. I have no brothers or relatives in the case. If the fellow wins at the Civil Court, then I get what he owes me. That's all I care about."

The beardless bartender complained to the district attorney about Rabito's jibes when he arrived at St. Patrick's Hall, but Luzenberg had more important matters to attend to than Daure's jitters—including Daure's testimony.

First, Luzenberg called coroner LeMonnier to testify that Polizzi was not insane, but "laboring under intense excitement." Polizzi sat quietly to one side, twisting a handkerchief in his fingers and shuffling his feet whenever Judge

Baker left the room. His new lawyer John Q. Flynn and Father Manoritta of the *Gazetta Catholica* sat with him.

Luzenberg recalled Daure, who told the court he did not recall the condition of the Girod Street sidewalks on October 15. Then Luzenberg came to a more delicate subject—Daure admitted telling Captain A. Kalinski of the Fire Insurance Patrol that he knew nothing about the Hennessy shooting.

"You told him that you did not see it, nor anyone involved in the firing?" Luzenberg said.

"Yes, sir," Daure said. "I was scared."

"Explain what you mean by 'scared.'"

Adams protested strenuously, but Judge Baker allowed the question.

"I knew how touchy these men were and when I went before the grand jury, I was afraid," Daure said. "I said nothing about what I knew to anyone. When anyone would ask me what I knew, I would not say anything or give any satisfaction. I was living right in the center of them and was afraid they would do me the same thing." Daure said he lived with his parents and feared for their safety. When Daure stepped down and Luzenberg announced that the state's case was done, Adams immediately called Captain Kalinski.

Kalinski, a friend of Hennessy's, said he remembered seeing Daure at Cuneo's oyster saloon shortly after the attack. Daure told him the chief had been "done up." What chief? Kalinski asked. Daure told him he'd seen a flash, ran to the scene, and saw the wounded chief lying on the Gillis floor. "He said that he heard the chief say to O'Connor, 'The dagos did it—'"

Adams objected.

Judge Baker instructed Kalinski to testify only about what he himself knew. Kalinski knew very little.

Adams excused Kalinski and concentrated on establishing alibis for the defendants who had visited the Academy of Music on the night of the murder. Oteri recalled being in Adams's law office with several of the men early in the evening, as did Adams, who was sworn in as a witness. The academy's ushers and treasurer, conductor Veasey, police Captain Journée, and Consul Corte all testified to seeing the defendants in the theater. General Meyer described his campaign jaunt in Algiers and the late dinner at Fabacher's. He was sure he had seen all the men except perhaps Sunzeri. Others remembered talking to Sunzeri, who didn't understand them, and politico John Fitzpatrick recalled telling Charles Patorno that he looked like his brother. Patorno and John Caruso testified on their own behalf that they were with the restaurant party. Adams called Sunzeri and asked permission to read a document into the record, but Luzenberg inspected the paper and objected. The jury was sent from the room.

Adams argued that the prosecution was trying to make a conspiracy case against the accused, in which the motive for Hennessy's death was his discovery of something about the accused that made them murder him. "That is, that he had some proof with reference to the men who were witnesses to the Provenzano case which induced them to take him off," Adams said. He wanted to show that Sunzeri had come to America with his passport and an honorable discharge from the Italian army, but Judge Baker ruled that these would only be pertinent if the state endeavored to prove a conspiracy.

Incredibly, in the face of five months of rhetoric from the mayor and the Committee of Fifty, not to mention the criminal conspiracy theory about to be advanced by members of his own prosecutorial team in their final statements and later still by police officials, District Attorney Luzenberg declared that he had no intention of doing such a thing.

Because an early adjournment was expected that afternoon Captain Journée sent for the prison van so that it would be on hand if needed. When the van arrived and the driver went upstairs to look for Journée in the crowd, he noticed a revolver sticking out of Dominick O'Malley's hip pocket. The driver tapped O'Malley on the shoulder and informed him that he was in possession of a concealed weapon.

O'Malley told the cop to take a walk.

The driver pulled O'Malley out of his seat and led the detective out into the smoky din of the hallway. As O'Malley was pushed toward the stairs, he slipped the revolver deftly from his pocket and started to pass it to a man in the crowd. The driver spotted the maneuver and snatched the gun out of O'Malley's hand.

"Where's your warrant?" O'Malley snapped.

O'Malley was formally arrested in the street where the detective refused to get into the patrol wagon. "You can take me down in a hack," he said.

The driver smiled and pointed at his van. "This conveyance is provided by the city for the use of rich and poor alike."

Back in the courtroom, conductor J. D. Farrell of the Illinois Central Railroad said he remembered the day Chief Hennessy died. Farrell's train rolled into New Orleans that morning with seven Italians on board, and he said he thought Pietro Natali was one of them. Luzenberg pressed Farrell, but the conductor would only say that he was not absolutely positive Natali was the Italian he had seen on his train.

Illinois Central labor gang boss Joseph Salavoni told the court that Natali worked for him in Chicago. On the night of October 14, Natali drew his pay and told Salavoni he was leaving for New Orleans. Salavoni's brother Tony agreed this was true and produced his paybook for the week, showing that Natali did not stop working in Chicago until the thirteenth. A Chicago grocer also remembered Natali leaving on the fourteenth.

• • •

The Champion of the World was adrift. He and Muldoon had been on the outs since the Kilrain fight and the Champ slid back into the bottle, putting on pounds. He was an actor now. It was a lucrative business, and he liked it. All he had to do was follow the script, go a few rounds in the course of the melodrama—the fight was written in for him—and soak up applause.

The "Honest Hearts and Willing Hands" tour brought John L. Sullivan back to the city he had fled after the Kilrain fight. The play was doing fair business at the Grand Opera House. Before the Saturday matinee, the Champ decided to see for himself the men who killed the police chief who had befriended him. He had already visited Hennessy's grave. It sickened him.

There was a stir at the back of the courtroom as Sullivan was ushered through the crowd to a seat inside the bar. He watched silently as translator Cefalu questioned Joseph Ivalosa, an Italian laborer who had traveled to New Orleans by train. Natali was with him, said Ivalosa. They arrived on October 16. Natali was called. Cefalu asked when he arrived. October 16, Natali said.

The Champion of the World decided he had seen enough. He emerged from his too-small seat and left after five minutes of testimony.

In another New Orleans courtroom, O'Malley pleaded not guilty to a charge of carrying a concealed weapon. O'Malley insisted he was sitting quietly in court when he was told that the chief of police desired to see him. When O'Malley asked why he was being arrested, the reply was "for being a dangerous and suspicious character." The detective said he foresaw what effect even a little commotion would have on the Hennessy case jury, so he went along quietly.

The judge told O'Malley he would have ample opportunity to tell his story when the case came up.

O'Malley's eyes flashed. "If the police propose to continue this sort of work, then Your Honor had better get a lot of blank bonds ready, for it's likely I'll be arrested again pretty soon."

"I saw the witness Peeler on the afternoon of October 16," *Times-Democrat* reporter W. J. Leppert told Adams back at St. Patrick's Hall. "He was drunk when I called at his house at the corner of Girod and Basin streets."

"Were you not informed," asked Adams, "that this man was not in a condition to be seen—that he was getting over a protracted drunk?"

Luzenberg objected furiously that this was hearsay, not a material question. "The afternoon of the next day had nothing to do with the shooting!"

Adams held his ground. "We claim that he was drunk on the night of the shooting and on the morning when he identified the men he saw." Judge Baker ruled that it was legitimate to question Peeler's condition.

"Mary Wheeler came in while I was interviewing Peeler," Leppert continued, "and said that I should pay no attention to him, that he had been drunk and that he hadn't fully recovered yet. I reported the interview correctly. I didn't put in that he was drunk because I didn't think it was material."

Luzenberg silently worried that it might be very material indeed and got the newspaperman to admit that he was at Peeler's house at half past three in the afternoon. "I don't know his condition between eight and nine on the morning of that day," Leppert agreed.

When St. Patrick's Hall emptied that afternoon, one of the last spectators to leave was O'Malley, who had been sitting in court with a fresh revolver tucked into his pocket.

☽

Nineteen

CLOCKS AND BABIES

PEOPLE STOOD OUTSIDE ALL DAY MONDAY, HOPING TO GET inside the packed courtroom where Polizzi's new attorney John Flynn was asking for a continuance of one day, hoping that his client might relax and become more rational away from the trial.

Judge Baker assured Flynn that the court did not hold him responsible for his client's conduct, but refused to grant a continuance. The trial was three weeks old, Baker said, and the jurors were eager to finish. There had been ample time over the weekend for Polizzi to calm down "if he chose to." Judge Baker said he would not interrupt the trial, but promised Flynn extra time later if he thought it would be necessary for a proper defense.

Now that alibis existed for the wealthier defendants, the defense moved on to the less well-heeled of the accused, the men newspapers were calling Matranga's and Macheca's "tools." The jury would not have to decide if these witnesses were sober or if their eyesight was keen. No one accused them of incompetence because of the color of their skin. None had been imprisoned without charge for months by the same district attorney's office which wanted their testimony before they would be freed from "safekeeping." All the jury would need to consider, particularly in the cases of Bagnetto and Scaffidi, was whether the alibi witnesses were telling the truth or lying.

Otto Stille told the court he worked at Borey's Poydras Market coffee stand and was off duty the night Hennessy was shot, but went down to the market just for fun as he always did. Stille said he saw Antonio Bagnetto cleaning apples between eleven and eleven thirty that night. Luzenberg tried to cross-examine Stille about his buying a $12 gold watch around Christmas, but stopped when Adams began to protest. Sixteen-year-old Muncy Meyer said he was at the market too that night, watching a fruit stand for his uncle, just across the aisle from Bagnetto. Meyer said he remembered Bagnetto watching three stands at the market from nine o'clock until the time he was arrested.

Peter Smith, a waiter at Weaver's coffee stand, testified that he saw Bagnetto minding the stalls before and after eleven o'clock. "A colored boy told me a shooting scrape was going on and I ran to the telephone at a white man's request and telephoned to the station that Hennessy was shot," Smith said. "When I telephoned, Bagnetto was there. He was near a basket, on a barrel." Smith said he heard about Bagnetto's arrest the next morning. "I told several people that Bagnetto couldn't have been there because he was at the market," Smith said under cross-examination. "I told Weaver, who advised me to keep my mouth shut as I'd get into trouble. I told several people, but they all told me to keep quiet."

Salvatore Matranga, his family's handsomely bearded seventy-two-year-old patriarch, struggled onto the stand with a cane and testified through an interpreter that on the rainy night of the murder, his feet were wet, and he got up just before eleven o'clock to exercise his stiff limbs. When he heard shots, he looked outside. He said his tenant Antonio Marchesi came out into the yard and asked if he had heard the shooting. Matranga said Marchesi's son, Gasperi, appeared and walked out front to the hydrant, but the father stayed in the yard. Matranga's daughter, Pauline Conda, who also lived in his house at Lafayette and Howard, four and a half blocks from the shooting, testified that she was nursing her sick baby when the shots were fired. She said her husband went out on the gallery while she gave their child a bottle and heard Marchesi say something to her husband in Italian.

The defense called Wallace Behan, an architectural draftsman, who had surveyed the distance between Joseph Macheca's doorstep and the Bourbon Street corner from which Sergeant Hevron and Officers Pollock and Cassidy watched Macheca and Jim Caruso. The surveyor said the distance was 123 feet. After this, Judge Baker called a recess. The defense attorneys, feeling confident that a jury might feel that forty-one yards was a long way to overhear someone express happiness over any "son of a bitch being done up," enjoyed their lunch.

Court reconvened with the alibi testimony of Henry Iff, who testified that he relieved a friend at Weaver's coffee stand at 11:25. From then until at least two o'clock in the morning, Iff said, Bagnetto was guarding Sidoti's fruit stand.

Iff seemed to think that everything—being roused for his midnight to noon watch, hearing that the chief was shot—happened at 11:25.

"How are you sure of the time?" Henriques asked, trying to steady Iff's stumbling.

"I looked at the clock, because I knew I'd be questioned right here."

Luzenberg jumped on this. "How did you know you'd be a witness?"

"I knew it."

"When you looked at the clock, Bagnetto had not been arrested?" Luzenberg asked.

"No, sir."

"No one had been arrested?"

"No, sir."

"And you looked at the clock just because you knew you'd be questioned about it?"

"Yes sir."

Luzenberg sat down, unimpressed.

The defense recalled Olivia Petersen, who said she remembered a newspaper reporter, Stansbury, calling on her on the same evening she visited the parish prison.

"Did you not tell him that you were not sure that you could identify the man as the one who had rented the shanty from you?" Adams asked.

Mrs. Petersen denied this and began a rambling description of Stansbury's visit. Judge Baker asked her to confine herself to the identification.

"I said that I could identify him, but that my friend Mrs. Osberg was not positive about it," Mrs. Petersen said.

Stansbury also remembered the Petersen interview. "She said she had been to the prison and had identified a man. She was almost certain it was the man, but would not swear to it—she used three or four expressions to that effect. In fact, she was laboring under excitement and someone in the room called her attention to the fact that it would be dangerous for her to talk, because I was a newspaper reporter."

"What exactly did Mrs. Petersen say?" Luzenberg asked.

"She said that she believed that Macheca was the man who rented the house, but she was not willing to swear to it."

"Do you have your notes from the interview?"

"She was excited and I did not take any notes, because I knew it would frighten her and I would not get what I was after."

Adams and the defense attorneys pushed ahead, alternating alibi witnesses with attacks on the prosecution's identifications. Parish prison keeper Tom Carey remembered Rosa Walton and Emma Thomas visiting the parish prison, but said that they did not pick Macheca from eight men marched out in their shirtsleeves. Carey said that Thomas only identified Macheca when he was brought back wearing a coat and felt hat, alone. Prison searcher Tim Dwyer testified that he saw Carey line up the prisoners for M. L. Peeler. "This man," Peeler said, pointing to Salvatore Sunzeri, who had spent the evening with Macheca's roving party.

Antonio Scaffidi's sister, Josephine Soledano, testified that he came to her house at nine thirty on the night of the shooting and told her that his wife was having a miscarriage. Soledano roused an old woman who lived in her house, and the three of them set off out Rampart Street. When they passed Perdido, she said they met a police officer whose name she did not know. City police Officer Frank McEntee was asked to stand, and she said, "Yes, that's the man we saw." Soledano said she stayed with her sister-in-law until five thirty in the morning and Scaffidi was there the whole time, sleeping.

Midwife Cusa Paticina, a tiny woman with dark, wrinkled skin testified in Italian through Cefalu. She told the court that Scaffidi and his sister came to her house that night after nine o'clock. After the three of them picked up Scaffidi's mother at her house, passing an oyster opener and a police officer on the way, they all went back to Scaffidi's where she found his wife in the throes of a miscarriage. Paticina said that from the time she got there until Scaffidi left at six in the morning, he was never out of her sight. He left with a folded oilcloth under his arm.

"Ask her if she could be mistaken," Luzenberg told Cefalu. No, the midwife answered.

Peter Fulco, the oyster opener, testified that he had seen the old woman with Scaffidi, his mother, and his sister at Rampart and Perdido about nine thirty. Officer McEntee testified that he had seen the group around nine thirty too, and not only did he see Scaffidi with the women—McEntee said Scaffidi *spoke* to him.

A twenty-year veteran of the regular force, McEntee said he had known Antonio Scaffidi for seven of those twenty years. Riled by this testimony, Luzenberg demanded to know if Scaffidi wore an oilcloth.

"I don't remember," McEntee said. "I thought he had. I believe he had a coat on, a citizen's coat."

"I wouldn't expect he had a policeman's coat on," W. L. Evans shot from the state's table. Bearing down on the witness stand, Luzenberg asked, "Now Mr. McEntee, within the last three weeks have you not on more than one occasion in Judge Evans's office in Commercial Place, in this city, in the presence of Mr. Dunn, informed him that you met Scaffidi in company with two or three ladies and that he wore an oilcloth coat at the time?"

"I thought so . . . I didn't exactly say that he had one on. I said I thought so."

"Did you tell him positively?"

"That I thought so. But I didn't tell him positively."

McEntee had helped arrest Bagnetto and both Marchesis on the night of the shooting and later brought prosecutors George Zehr, the barber who claimed to have seen Scaffidi wearing a long oilcloth coat in Di Carlo's shoe store between nine and ten o'clock. As far as the defense was concerned, however, an officer producing a witness in the course of his duties did not mean McEntee vouched for what Zehr said in court nor did it negate McEntee's claim to have also seen Scaffidi with his family and the midwife within the same hour-long period. Adams implied that the prosecutors originally planned to call McEntee as a state witness, but dropped him as soon as they learned that he might furnish Scaffidi with an alibi. "They knew all the time that you claimed to have met those people?"

"Yes, sir," McEntee replied. "I told Judge Evans."

"And you had been summoned as a state witness?"

"Yes, sir. I was."

Boiling over, Luzenberg said, "I want to know exactly what the stenographer has got down! I just want to draw Your Honor's attention to it, in order to lay the foundation for another prosecution against this officer in the interest of public justice and truth!"

"I object," Adams said, protesting Luzenberg's implication that McEntee was lying.

"I would have not allowed the statement to be made," Judge Baker said, "but it was made before I had an opportunity to stop it."

Scaffidi's last alibi witness was his fruit stand owner uncle, Vincent, who told the court that his nephew, Antonio, arrived at Poydras Market about 6:00 a.m. with an oilcloth used to cover the stand from rain. Antonio laid the folded oilcloth on a barrel and was arrested an hour later. Adams offered more than alibis to undercut the testimony against Scaffidi. He called the ticket agent for the Texas & Pacific Railroad, who explained that fares to Mexico City—the destination Scaffidi allegedly asked Amos Scott to look into for him—were $52.75 for first class and $38.25 for second class, not $61. There was a ticket office at the location Scott claimed to have visited, but it was for the Louisville & Nashville, which sold no tickets to Mexico whatsoever.

Adams also sniped at Mrs. Petersen's identification of the well-dressed "Peter Johnson" and called officials of the Macheca Brothers steamship company to the stand. They testified that Joe Macheca was in the habit of wearing a flannel shirt and a straw hat at work, and kept his watch in a side pocket. When the busy California fruit season hit the company in August, Macheca alternated as a weigher and generally wore flannel. No one remembered particularly what he wore on August 13, the day the Petersen rent receipt was written.

Ten character witnesses spoke on Macheca's behalf. A grocer, a reporter, merchants, and a U.S. District Court clerk who served with him in the Confederate army testified to Macheca's good reputation for peace and quiet. So did popular saloon owner Leon LaMothe, a close longtime friend of both

Hennessy and Macheca. Police detective Antonio Pecora, who had testified in Gianforcaro's defense in the Provenzano trial, spoke for Macheca. "I am a detective and have been so employed for 25 years," Pecora said. "I have known Joe Macheca from boyhood well. I have seen him daily. I also looked upon him as a peaceful and quiet man and never heard anything against his reputation."

As the day ended, jury foreman Jacob Seligman told Judge Baker that the jury wanted to visit the scene of the shooting. Baker agreed.

The sequestered jury was closely guarded and their drafty quarters were searched daily. Newspaper reports of attempted jury bribery nevertheless swirled around the trial. Chasing rumors, the *Times-Democrat* tracked down several rejected talesmen, including one named Anglade.

Anglade didn't want to talk about it, but finally told the reporter that a middle-aged man with a mustache had visited his office a week and a half ago. "He told me there would be a big stake in it if I could get selected as a juror," Anglade said. "I resented this and told him that if I went on the jury, no money could bribe me. Then he left."

"Can you remember anything else about the man? If he was well or shabbily dressed? The color of his mustache?" asked the reporter.

"Not a thing, I'm afraid . . . he wasn't an Italian. I'm certain of that." Anglade had seen the man around the city several times, but doubted he could recognize him again.

"Do you know if anyone else was approached?"

"The man may have been joking," Anglade retreated, uneasy about talking to the press. When the reporter persisted, Anglade said that other talesmen had been approached, but he did not know their names.

On March 10, four hundred fifty feet of levee caved in at Vidalia, Louisiana, under the rising spring flood of the Mississippi, the first of the lower river levees to break that season. In New Orleans, the defense would rest.

Polizzi arrived in court on Tuesday with his red drawers showing and his face picketed with stubble. A rosary sagged from his mouth, the crucifix hidden inside pursed lips. John Rocci helped the haggard prisoner to his seat.

Nine more prominent businessmen testified to Joseph Macheca's good character including former Mayor Guillotte, a city councilman, presidents of a railroad and a bank, two judges, the deputy collector of the Port of New Orleans, and a congressman. Adams called Jim Caruso to the stand and asked, "When you parted with Joseph Macheca on the morning of October 16 did he say to you 'I'm much obliged, but I'm sorry they did not do the son of a bitch up altogether'?"

"No, sir" Caruso replied.

When the defense called the first of several witnesses to testify to Scaffidi's peaceable reputation, Polizzi slid onto the floor. "Scaffidi! Scaffidi!" he screeched, spittle flying. Deputies took him behind a door within earshot of the court proceedings. Flynn, Polizzi's lawyer, tried unsuccessfully to halt the prosecution of his client by asking that a commission of experts be appointed to examine Polizzi's mental state. An examination had already been made, Judge Baker responded. Flynn argued that the examination was not thorough, but Judge Baker ruled that if Polizzi was convicted, a medical commission would be appointed to settle the question of his sanity pending further proceedings. Flynn's first witness was Polizzi's "Doctor Bagsolari." Dr. Hugh Kelly, the Tiro al Bersaglio's physician, testified that he remembered treating Polizzi for a sprained right wrist three days before the murder. About a week later, Kelly said he read in the papers that police were looking for "Dr. Bagsolari" and realized who they meant.

Prosecution witnesses had a mustachioed Polizzi delivering guns to Pietzo's grocery the same day Dr. Kelly treated him, but Polizzi had no mustache when the doctor saw him. Five of Polizzi's neighbors agreed, testifying that the peddler never wore a mustache. Lama Roma, Polizzi's common-law wife, testified through interpreter Rocci that Polizzi was sleeping with her between eleven and one o'clock the night of the shooting. Luzenberg wanted to know if Roma knew that the man she had been living with for five years was accused of the murder of Chief Hennessy. "Of course I do!" she replied.

The magnificent voice of Thomas Semmes boomed through the courtroom. "This closes the case for the defense. All that remains is for the jury to visit the scene of the shooting."

Before that could happen, Luzenberg wanted to question rebuttal witnesses, including Toby Hart, Peeler's boss. Hart testified that the painter worked for him on October 15 and was sober all day. Hart admitted, however, he did not know what Peeler's condition was at eleven o'clock on the night Hennessy was shot or on the next day after 8:30 a.m., when the painter asked to be allowed to go to the police station. John Probst, one of Peeler's fellow painters, testified that Peeler had one beer on the fifteenth and was sober that afternoon, but Probst similarly could not say what Peeler was like that night. Luzenberg had himself sworn as a witness for the prosecution and testified, "On the morning of October 16, I was at the Central Station. I suppose it was nine o'clock. Peeler was there and he was as sober as I was." Luzenberg's self-examination was followed by three women, all neighbors, who testified that they saw Scaffidi's wife in front of her house the morning after the shooting. Although Luzenberg was trying to portray the story of her miscarriage as a hoax, one woman remembered that Mrs. Scaffidi was crying.

Commissary Corcoran was recalled and told Luzenberg of passing through Poydras Market at ten o'clock on the night of the shooting. Bagnetto, said Corcoran, was not at any of the four stands he was employed to guard. "I look around whenever I fail to see Bagnetto about," Corcoran told Adams under cross-examination. "I don't work both night and day usually, but there has been a lot of stealing." After Corcoran stepped down, Judge Baker asked the jurors if they still wished to visit the scene of the murder, and they said yes. Baker instructed that they would be able to move about the site freely but were not to ask questions or enter into conversations while on the scene. As the court emptied, Polizzi sang a Latin hymn and a song about the patriot Garibaldi.

The Hennessy case courtroom was silent, but later that afternoon Chief Gaster, talesman Anglade, and others went before a grand jury investigating the rumors of bribery that were being published as fact in the press. The grand jury composed three findings or indictments, each accusing an unnamed person of attempting to bribe the Hennessy jury. The spaces for the names of the accused were left blank.

That night police cordoned off the Girod and Basin intersection. The electric light drooping overhead sputtered and blinked and every fifteen or twenty minutes, the light disappeared completely for a few seconds, then sparked back to life.

Judge Baker's carriage arrived first, followed by the attorneys, jurors, and deputy sheriffs. A full police patrol wagon and two vans—one holding Polizzi who was singing and yelling, another carrying the rest of the prisoners—brought up the rear. Girod Street's electric streetlights burned brightly as the carriages approached Hennessy's neighborhood. As the lead vehicle reached Baronne Street, the light two blocks north near the Girod Street cemetery went out. The fluttering light at Basin, however, continued to burn.

Police held hundreds of sightseers back when the carriages stopped outside Monasterio's shack. Residents left their doors open to watch the jurors walking in the street, silently looking up at the galleries and inspecting the banquettes. Suddenly the Basin and Girod light went out, plunging the intersection into darkness.

The blackout lasted three minutes.

When the lamp flickered back on, Adams said he wanted everyone to be aware of the length of the long block reaching to Julia Street, so the court carriages rolled off uptown. It was even darker there, where few streetlights were burning. The light at the corner of Franklin and Julia flared up to its proper brilliance as the procession approached, and it stayed lit.

A small group of men came out of a saloon on the corner. "There they are," hollered a voice. "Say, find those dagos not guilty, will you?"

As the jury rode back to court, the police cordons were removed. Corcoran and Peeler strolled among a crowd of amateur criminologists who found and touched bullet holes in Burke's grocery. Mrs. Petersen told reporters that the man she identified as Macheca had wanted to rent the entire shanty, not just the front portion where Monasterio lived. The man offered her more money to evict her black tenants in the rear apartment, but she said she refused until she knew whether or not Rosa Walton could be persuaded to leave.

"Why didn't you say anything of this in court?" a reporter asked.

"They didn't ask me," Mrs. Petersen said. While she was talking to reporters, Mrs. Petersen recognized someone passing whom she said she had not seen in fifteen years. Reporters took this as proof of her power of recall.

Meanwhile, Corcoran thought he knew why the light was so temperamental. Electric light inspectors had raised the lamp the previous Monday, pulling it two feet higher and five feet farther from the Peeler gallery than it had been on the night of Hennessy's assassination. Neighbors and cops on the beat agreed. Corcoran said that the glass plates were removed from three sides on the lamp, leaving a dirty pane to shine on Peeler's residence.

"It will burn very brightly and for a long time," Mrs. Petersen agreed, looking up. "Then it won't."

"Much was expected of it," the *Times-Democrat* wrote of the suspended lamp. "But like the mother's pet when attention is attracted to its accomplishments and when it is expected to do its best, it not only did not come up to expectations, but was painfully disappointing."

☽

Twenty

IN A BOX

PROSECUTOR JAMES "JUDGE" WALKER SWEPT ACROSS THE
courtroom, promising to stick close to the testimony, but there *was* the
Provenzano trial. There *were* Macheca's threats, heard by his fellow members
of the Red Light Club. "Joseph P. Macheca declared—as was shown by the evidence of Kuhn, Heller, and others—he declared that if the Provenzanos were
granted a new trial, every fruit merchant of this city would hold Mr. Hennessy
responsible for their future actions.

"Not alone did a policeman say this, but three gentlemen like yourselves.
Then comes Officer Cenance. He was waiting for a patrol wagon. Mr.
Macheca comes along and says that Mr. Hennessy had been meddling in the
case, that he had better keep his hands off, or he would put him in a box. *And
he is in a box today.*

"What could the chief of police do to force a new trial?" Walker scoffed.
With eyes blazing—and Adams interrupting with objections—Walker read aloud
Macheca's prison newspaper interviews about his irritation with the chief. There
was the confrontation with Hennessy over allegedly paying the Provenzanos'
board at the prison. "That statement of Macheca's was as much as to tell the chief
of police that he was an accessory after the fact to the shooting of the Matrangas!"
As he pictured Macheca renting Petersen's shack for Monasterio, Walker asked the
purpose of the "Peter Johnson" alias? Why didn't Monasterio rent the shack himself? Hadn't Polizzi lived in the shed? Could the human mind conceive any scenario other than Hennessy walking home "with Monasterio watching him,
catlike, and waiting for the moment when he could spring on his prey?"

The assassins had been identified, Walker continued. The light was
good—Mascare, Grillot, Driscoll, Glover, Peeler, Wheeler, and others testified

so (in reality, Grillot had said no such thing). Why was the oilcloth at Scaffidi's house and not lying over his uncle's fruit at the stand? Who were the people Rosa Walton and John Beverly heard whispering in the cobbler's room? Why had Macheca told Fanny Decker that he and the others wanted their whereabouts known on the night of the murder? The defense provided no answers to these questions, Walker said, and the evidence was overwhelming and damning.

Walker moved on to Jim Caruso, who denied Macheca had said anything about being glad the "son of a bitch Hennessy was done up." Who contradicted Officers Hevron and Pollock about the cruel words on Macheca's doorstep? It was Caruso, who was on trial for his life!

"Now, gentlemen," Walker said to the jury, "you have been amused by people who went there with a tape line and found that it was 123 feet, and they argue that because that was the distance, the officers could not have heard the words. It is just like the buttons on Scaffidi's coat or the pin on Macheca's necktie. Hevron is not on trial. Pollock is not on trial, but Caruso is!"

Walker told the court that he did not believe a word of the alibis, meant to hide the work of a band of organized assassins.

"When such things can be and the chief of police to whose protection the lives of our wives and children are entrusted can be shot down at the foot of his mother's door, perhaps the same thing can happen to you or me. Here is the chief of police, killed in a metropolitan city. Are our laws powerless? Are our police without authority to check such outrages? Can anyone conceive the ends to which these assassinations will be carried? It is for you to say. The city's reputation is at stake!"

Applause overcame the courtroom as Walker returned to the state table. Judge Baker slammed his gavel and asked that no one applaud either side.

During Walker's speech, Thomas McCrystol and James Cooney were arrested at 11:00 a.m. on a warrant from the grand jury for jury tampering. Detectives had seen both men entering Dominick O'Malley's office. Reluctant to speak to the press, Cooney suggested that the accusations were probably a case of mistaken identity.

"The jury is called upon to say whether these men shall live or die. I feel keenly that responsibility," Henriques began. The somber defense attorney asked the jury if it could find proof of any conspiracy in the evidence. He criticized Walker for implying that inconsistencies about physical evidence such as Scaffidi's oilcloth did not matter. "The proof, not of one side, but of all sides, is the basis on which your verdict must rest."

When George Mascare was asked to identify the shoemaker Monasterio in a prison lineup, Henriques asked, why had he pointed to Marchesi? Henriques did not believe Mascare's story of his rambling route to see a man about some coal and doubted that a man hurrying up a banquette on a rainy night would notice a slight ray of light like the one Mascare claimed to have seen through a crack in Monasterio's shack. If Mascare saw everything he claimed, how could he keep it in his breast while attending the wake at Hennessy's house and for six days thereafter?

The barber George Zehr, Henriques said, was asked if he knew the difference between an oilcloth coat and a simple oilcloth, and Zehr said yes, Scaffidi wore a coat in Di Carlo's shoe store the night of the shooting. When Sheriff Villere brought in the confiscated oilcloth entered as evidence, it was certainly not a coat.

Zachary Foster said he saw three men clearly, after testifying that the shooting came from hands outstretched from a shanty alleyway. But Henriques said he was most interested in another part of Foster's story. "When he got to the secondhand store, he turned around and saw the Boylan officer drawing his pistol. Where is that officer he says came over and Hennessy said, 'Don't come to me, go after the man with the gun?' Was the officer so errant a coward that he fled? I ask again, where was that officer? If he was there, why was he not brought here?"

Henriques belittled Foster, waving the witness's race and the bloody shirt of the Confederacy in the white jury's face. "There is a saying that the colored troops fought boldly, and Zachary Taylor Foster—whatever his name is—was no exception to the rule. As honest men, will you believe him? No, I know you will not."

In an age when newspapers reported the testimony of black New Orleanians below the legend (COLORED), the implicit racism of Henriques's strategy was not unique.

"When Foster saw the shots coming, hot and fast, he ran," Henriques said. "He ran as soon as the first shot was fired. He ran like a quarterhorse and had he not been arrested, he would not have been a witness." Henriques bashed ahead. "Great God, here is a man testifying against the lives of nine men—nine lives hang in the balance! Gentlemen of the jury, remember your oaths! Your intelligence is equal to mine, and you can believe or refuse to believe. Can you believe Foster?"

The expected testimony of Harry Glover, Henriques said, "was loudly heralded. Now here was the honest witness who was going to tell it all." Yet Glover identified no one—he ran into the street at the sound of the shooting, but it was already all over. He was honest enough to admit that he had only seen the murderers' backs. Henriques asked the jury to contrast Glover's "conscientious" testimony with James Poole's. "They are both Negroes," the lawyer began. "Poole is a grammarian. He don't use ordinary language and common phrases. This high-strung Negro, who swallowed a grammar and a Webster's Dictionary, spit it out that night." Glover swore he saw the chief with another gentleman at the corner of Rampart and Girod streets. Who is the man? Henriques asked the jury. Was it O'Connor? Why was he not here? "Where is he now?"

Poole, Henriques said, saw sleeves in a yellow oilcloth but did not know if it had sleeves. The witness could not make up his mind whether the man he saw by Burke's grocery was white or black. "But it may be claimed that this is not important," Henriques added, needling the prosecutors.

After witnessing "this fiendish deed, this murder, this assassination," Poole left town for St. John's Parish without saying a word to anyone. "He returned in two months and by divine inspiration, the acting chief of police found out he was an eyewitness," Henriques said scornfully. Henriques's ridicule included John Daure. "I don't care how fast Mr. Stansbury went over the space, Daure could not make it again in thirty seconds," he said. Now that the jurors had visited the crime scene, Henriques asked them if Daure could have seen Gasperi Marchesi fleeing from three dark blocks away, or if Daure could have run the distance in time to see everything.

"Mr. Hennessy showed his bravery that night," Henriques said. Yet this able chief whose job it was to recognize and recall faces did not identify the accused, nearly all of whom lived in his neighborhood. Prejudice against the accused because of their nationality was great, Henriques cautioned. Out of hundreds of talesmen, only a few unprejudiced men could be found. Henriques picked *Wharton on Crimes* from the books stacked on the defense table and quoted a passage about the effect of community prejudices on testimony. Without acknowledging any irony, Henriques repeated a separate passage alleging the lack of credibility of black witnesses. If all Negroes who testified to lies were locked up, Henriques read aloud, there would be none left to give the evidence. Who could believe Poole or Foster?

Henriques shoveled questions at the jury. Would Peeler really sleep with an open window on such a miserable night? Why couldn't Mary Wheeler identify Scaffidi if Peeler was telling the truth? Why was Olivia Petersen's mother-in-law not produced if she had witnessed Macheca's alleged rent transaction? "If this were a conspiracy to kill the chief, do you think Macheca would put his head in the lion's mouth? The woman from whom the room was rented has a Farrell policeman for a son, an officer resided opposite, and the chief of police resided opposite!"

Henriques asked the jury not to let prejudice get the better of them. Pietro Natali was en route from Chicago, the state offered no evidence against Charles Matranga, and Incardona's only crime was buying beer at Burke's grocery.

Why was Sunzeri charged with shooting the chief when so many witnesses had seen him elsewhere? The men who swore that Bagnetto was in Poydras Market were not Italians. The state knew that Officer McEntee saw the Scaffidis and chose not to put the policeman on the stand. And what was so extraordinary about Mrs. Scaffidi crying in her doorway after her husband's arrest, especially in light of her miscarriage? The state would have disproved the miscarriage story if it were a lie. No guns were found in Monasterio's shed, yet the shoemaker was arrested, his property was seized, and the shanty was nailed shut. Marchesi and his son had two witnesses, including Salvatore Matranga, a taxpaying citizen.

"The state entered the contest with $15,000 blood money," Henriques concluded. "In view of the general inequality of position, the law insists upon the reasonable doubt being given the accused."

Until now Henriques's cocounsel Charles Butler had been given little to do for the defense. This day he got his chance. Speaking without notes, he asked the jury to think about time.

Butler believed that the witnesses who guessed the shooting lasted no more than twenty seconds told the truth, as crimes like this were done hastily to escape the hands of the law. Mascare's circuitous route to buy coal at 11:00 p.m. in such bad weather was impossible, and what about his claim to have heard talking in Monasterio's shed and a moment later to have seen the shoemaker on the opposite street corner? And who had Mascare identified as the shoemaker? Marchesi.

"He went to Rampart and Basin streets and recognized a man who said 'hello' as an Italian," Butler said. "By the simple word, he says 'That man is an Italian,' and that man, he thinks, is Jim Caruso, who was in an entirely different place."

Unverzagt said he did not pass Zachary Foster as he ran out Girod Street, but it was impossible for the two men not to have passed each other; Glover saw neither Foster nor Poole in the square. Butler quietly spoke of those who had been closest to the shooting. "D. C. Hennessy ought to have known Scaffidi and Bagnetto. Polizzi used to occupy the Monasterio shed. He knew these three men well. He lived until nine o'clock the next morning. Did he attempt to identify a single man?"

Butler also wanted to know why Officer Roe and Captain O'Connor were not summoned by the state to testify. He thought the answer was that they would have destroyed John Daure's story about his run, which was a physical impossibility. "He must have run like lightning," Butler said, adding that Daure claimed to have seen Gasperi Marchesi, but Glover had not seen the boy.

Butler reminded the jury that Poole put a yellow coat on Scaffidi, while everyone else agreed the assailant's oilcloth was black. Poole then sent Scaffidi up Basin Street, while everyone else had him running out Girod toward the cemetery. "Mr. Price identified Polizzi running ahead of a tall man on Franklin Street, towards Julia. Price was some distance from the corner, and from Franklin to Girod to Julia is 479 feet long—and there is no light at Franklin and Girod," Butler said. No wonder the state introduced "a model policeman who could swear to anything required" like Officer Kroper.

"I never heard anyone swear as Officer Kroper did," Butler marveled. "He recognized Polizzi from the back of his neck and the clothes he wore. These are the kind of people you, gentlemen of the jury, are asked to believe."

As Butler was finishing, Prosecutor Evans sent for Hennessy's bloodstained clothing, and the gory package was placed on the state table alongside the murder weapons. The afternoon was dark and nasty, increasingly similar to the night of the Hennessy shooting. As Evans prepared his notes, the weak electric lights cast a yellow pallor over him, and he started his argument so softly that no one in the room but the jury heard his first sentence. "Counsel on the other side asked why this community has raised such a howl," Evans began. "It was because the people of New Orleans have seen the veil raised. The people raised a howl because of this most hellish and devilish assassination. It is time to howl when a representative of the law can be foully murdered. I join in the howl. When women and children are sleeping in their rooms and bullets are flying around them, it is time to howl."

Adams objected, causing Judge Baker to agree to stop Evans if he went beyond the line of evidence again.

Evans said he had nothing against Charlie Matranga and Joe Macheca. On the contrary, they were personal acquaintances of his, and Evans bore them no malice. He did not know the others, he said, but he bore them no grievance, and yet it was his duty to present the jury with the truth of the conspiracy. He dismissed Henriques's assault on the prosecution witnesses. "Every witness who could not identify one of the defendants was an angel from heaven in the eyes of counsel for the accused. Anyone who identified a defendant was fresh from the mouth of hell and a liar."

Evans told the jury that Officer Roe and Captain O'Connor were not summoned to avoid any charges of this being "a police case." The state wanted the case to be proven by the testimony of the people, both white and black. Mascare's only crime was being a poor boy who got off the streetcar too early. Zehr the barber swore to seeing Scaffidi wear the oilcloth in Di Carlo's shoe store, Evans said, and while Di Carlo was in court every day, the defense never called him to deny this. Foster told the truth, Evans insisted, and Adams had tried to confuse the "ignorant" but truthful Poole.

"The defense complains this is a police case and in the same breath ask why O'Connor and Roe are not placed on the stand," Evans told the jury. "The state did not advise the defendants to do this thing and cannot run the case to suit them."

Before Judge Baker stopped him to adjourn for the night, Evans spoke about America.

"There is no place on God's earth where foreigners are received with more welcome, but this is no place to plant assassination."

No one pointed out to Evans that many of the defendants the city knew as "the Italians" were, in fact, Americans.

☽

Twenty-One

THE BEST OF A BAD CASE

THE GONG ON MAYOR SHAKSPEARE'S GATE CLANGED IN-
sanely. It was 3:30 a.m. The night watchman found a woman at the Carondelet Street gate demanding to see the mayor.

Mrs. Shakspeare came down to see what the woman wanted.

"I live downtown," the visitor stammered. "I just had a dream in which His
Honor was crowned king. I jumped in a cab and rushed right here to tell you!"

Mrs. Shakspeare understood. When Dexter Gaster was made police chief
in January, an eccentric claiming to be the real chief descended on city hall,
demanding to know where his paycheck was.

"A spirit told me to tell him," the woman babbled. "It was a vision!"

"I'm most grateful that you've come," Mrs. Shakspeare said graciously.
"But I'm afraid that the mayor is so weary from his duties that it would be un-
kind to rouse him at this hour. I will tell him of the kingly honors to come. I
promise."

Later that morning there was a dash for courtroom seats. Taking up where he
left off in his closing remarks the night before, Prosecutor Evans spoke of the
electric light at Girod and Basin and of witnesses who remembered it burning
brightly. Evans charged the defense with wanting to abbreviate the time of the
shooting, but, he said, it had taken time to shoot the chief to death.

In reference to the Matranga ambush and the resulting Provenzano trial,
Evans could understand why Charles Matranga was interested in the case, but
what was Joseph Macheca's interest in the affair? There must have been a secret

tie between the Matrangas and Macheca, Evans said, with Hennessy condemned to death by some secret tribunal whose sentence was carried out.

"I shall have to ask you to discontinue this line of argument," Judge Baker warned.

"Very well," Evans replied, then chose his words as he sketched the enmity between the chief and Macheca, whose interest in the Provenzano case and falling out with Hennessy all came from Macheca's own mouth in the published interview with *Times-Democrat* reporter John Coleman. Evans constructed an ambush scenario in which the Matrangas and their workers moved back to Hennessy's neighborhood to surround him, and Macheca's duty was to hire the shanty.

Evans saw Olivia Petersen as "a lady of great intelligence . . . of wonderful self-possession." She knew Macheca was an Italian, she said; she saw it by his eyes. "Gentlemen of the jury, look you at that man's eyes and see if there is not something peculiar about them," Evans said.

How could the jury meet its God and its people if it acquitted Joe Macheca? asked the prosecutor. Macheca declared himself Hennessy's enemy in the house of prostitution and on his doorstep. "He spoke from the bottom of his heart," Evans railed. "And the only sorrow in his heart was that 'the son of a bitch wasn't done up right there'!" Jim Caruso's denial and a tape measure were the only defenses. "What's to become of the law-abiding portion of our people if you do not convict these assassins? Are we to turn our country over to Sicilian assassins?"

"I must caution you, Mr. Evans," Judge Baker interrupted. "You are again proceeding outside the lines of evidence."

Evans then turned on the other defendants. Would the jury turn Polizzi, Marchesi, Scaffidi, and Monasterio loose? Evans reminded the jury that Poole saw someone in white shirtsleeves run past—that was the young barkeep Daure. Poole identified Marchesi, and Daure identified Marchesi's son. Why was old man Matranga exercising at night? Why was his daughter up? Because of her baby?

"This was a wonderful baby," Evans scoffed. "It woke up at just the right time and made Mr. Conda go out and see Marchesi. It was a great night for babies and clocks."

Otto Stille supported his mother and himself on only $18 a month, but could treat himself to a gold watch after "learning what he knew" about Bagnetto, Evans said, implying that the witness had been bought and coached. The alibis for Scaffidi were "rotten," Evans concluded. If Scaffidi hadn't worn the oilcloth, why was it at his home instead of covering the fruit stand from the rain? Watchman Lannigan did not see it on Scaffidi, Evans charged, because the fleeing man had already folded it to enable him to run faster.

"You must do your duty," Evans told the jury finally. "Let us preserve the law and the law will preserve us. We must be true to ourselves, our God, and our country."

Polizzi's defense attorney Flynn called himself a lost sheep in this case, a pygmy among legal giants. Flynn's self-effacing words might have scared his client if Polizzi was in any condition to understand what the young lawyer was saying. But Flynn, tougher than he made himself out to be, also enjoyed an advantage: he was defending one client, not eight.

Throwing down the gauntlet to the state, Flynn observed that Daure and Peeler identified Polizzi, but there was not a single line of *evidence* to prove their claims. If Polizzi had lived in Monasterio's shanty and was part of a great plot as the prosecution claimed, why did the plotters not leave him there?

Flynn called Mascare the state's "mascot" and charged him with testifying in "whimsicalities." Why did the young paper carrier keep mum to his *New Delta* colleagues and to the police? "His testimony was a tender morsel for the state," Flynn said. "Let them enjoy it, but I trust you gentlemen will give it its proper value."

Pointing to Polizzi, Flynn said, "As for my client's mustache, I could have shaved it off, but I wanted to see if this hirsute appendage could be mistaken for a mustache."

Polizzi, whose upper lip displayed a meager scrub, began to stamp and clap his hands loudly. Deputies pulled his arms back.

Zachary Foster was not sure he had seen Polizzi, said Flynn. Most of the witnesses saw only a running man in light clothes. Price swore that he recognized Polizzi from light on the side of his face, but if any light whatsoever reached the dark Girod corner from distant Julia Street, Flynn noted, it would have fallen on the left side of the running man's face as he turned the corner, not the right side visible to Price.

"This is not a light suit!" Flynn said incredulously, holding Polizzi's gray suit in front of the jury. "They went out the day after the shooting and arrested everybody. Every scrap that looked like evidence was taken up and men offered for the sacrifice. Should men be hanged for such evidence?"

State witnesses had Polizzi running with Bagnetto up Franklin Street and running with Scaffidi out Basin Street, a block below Franklin, but he could not be running in two places at once, Flynn pointed out. "The light-clothes witnesses" and watchman Lannigan could not both be correct.

"I think Dr. Kelly is better able to speak on the subject of a sprained wrist than is any member of the police force," Flynn proposed, referring to the mark on his client's wrist. Even if Polizzi carried guns to the Pietzo grocery, he said, no connection was ever made between those guns and the crime. Flynn wondered why Louisa Ricasner had seen two sacks of guns there, while Dennis Corcoran saw only one. "I caution you as to the testimony of Corcoran, our Dennis," Flynn added. Corcoran said he had taken prisoners away from their own counsel because he did not trust the counsel, yet Corcoran had once been tried for murder. Flynn said he would leave it to the jury to decide whom to believe.

"There was but one Italian testifying for the defense and that was the woman with whom Polizzi lived," Flynn concluded. "The woman swore positively that between eleven to one o'clock, he was sleeping with her in the bed.

"Look only at the cold facts," Flynn advised the jury in closing. "If you do, you will agree with me that insofar as Polizzi is concerned, this is a very bad case of mistaken identity."

Lionel Adams rose. If the fate of his unhappy clients depended on Thomas Semmes's eloquence to quiet forever the charge of Dame Rumor, Adams said he would feel better. Unfortunately, Semmes was ill and might not be able to appear.

If he had time, Adams said, he would thank the judge and the jury properly for their kind attention. If there were time, Adams would compliment two of the prosecutors for their conduct in the case. If there were but time, he would attack the other representative of the state, who declared his friendship with Charles Matranga and Joseph Macheca in one breath and in the next arraigned them in terms so far beyond the bounds of professional courtesy that the judge was forced to stop him.

"We might deprecate the unfortunate allusions made to the character of the money which has reached our pockets," Adams added acidly. "We might be tempted to ask whether in other pockets might be found money stained with the blood of a Matranga, of a Caruso, of a Sunzeri, and I might go a step further, gentlemen, and mention another name, but I do not consider that professional fairness would permit allusions to the dead or the past."

Yet time spent in gracious compliments was time taken from the defense, Adams continued, letting the question of whom among the dead he might be speaking hang in the air. It was time for a discussion of the facts.

If a witness was responsible for Incardona's indictment by the grand jury, where was that witness in this trial? "Who here has mentioned the name of Charles Traina? Who has mentioned Loretto Comitz?" Someone's sworn testimony placed these men under indictment, Adams pointed out, but not one witness had spoken against them in court.

"What is this premise that Roe and O'Connor were not put on the stand because they do not want conviction on police evidence? They wanted a conviction based on the evidence of the people. And forsooth, you have seen 'the people' they depend on—Zachary Foster and Emma Thomas and Rosa Walton, the commissary of the market, the penitentiary bird Williams, and Amos Scott." No one in court missed the fact that all the witnesses Adams was maligning, except Corcoran, were black and poor. "Police not good enough? Oh, no!"

The state proposed that Joseph Macheca hated the chief of police so much that he hatched a conspiracy to "take him off," Adams said. Macheca rented the Petersen shed and placed Monasterio in it to watch the chief, then he hired the Marchesi boy to sit at Rampart and Girod and alert the men in the shanty of the chief's approach. Monasterio, Adams said, would be able to point the chief out to the assassins and say, "Yes, that is he," and then, according to plan—.

"At this point we are left indefinite," Adams shrugged. The state's witnesses could not agree on the spot where Scaffidi allegedly stood shooting nor could they agree in which direction Hennessy's killers ran, away from a supposedly bright streetlight.

"Take the witness Mascare," Adams said. When Mascare walked up Girod Street, he claimed to recognize three men—Scaffidi, Marchesi, and Polizzi— speaking Italian under the awning of Burke's grocery. "There cannot be any mistake as to Scaffidi. He was too close to be mistaken, possibly three or four feet from him. Yet when he passed three to four feet from him, Mascare saw sleeves in this and saw it buttoned up," Adams said, motioning to the enormous rectangle of plain oilcloth.

Adams dismissed Mascare's story of getting off the streetcar at St. Charles to see a coal dealer. If this "twisted" story was true, Adams said, Mascare walked five and a half blocks in the rain, got within half a block of the coal man's home, and suddenly decided the dealer might be at the New Basin instead. "So rather than walk less than half a square to see if he was at his house, Mascare preferred to walk all the way back to the Basin and, not finding the man there, go all the way back to his house." After "this objectless walk in the rain without an umbrella," Mascare went home.

Adams accused Mascare of deliberately lying throughout his tangled story. There was the electric light at St. Charles where he got off the streetcar. Mascare first said that the electric light there was bright, then shifted to say he was sure that it was bright because he was watching where he stepped, and finally admitted that he didn't know if there was an electric light there at all. Mascare couldn't recall any other lights in the neighborhood, but for some reason was certain there was one at the corner of Basin and Girod. Mascare was the state's secret witness, Adams complained, implying that the paper carrier's testimony had been bought.

Zehr swore that he saw Scaffidi in Di Carlo's well-lit shoe store, wearing an oilcloth coat with sleeves, a coat that nearly reached his feet, Adams recalled. This was at 10:00 p.m., yet Officer McEntee swore to seeing Scaffidi heading home with the women at nine-thirty. "The state asks why we did not produce Di Carlo here to deny it," Adams said. "The state is a little inconsistent, gentlemen. Whenever an Italian witness is produced, we are not to believe Italians swearing for Italians. But when he is not produced, we hear 'You could have . . . why didn't you'?" The reason Adams did not bother to call Di Carlo was plain, Adams said: Zehr would not or could not remember any of Di Carlo's customers but Scaffidi.

Adams returned to the mysterious indictment against Incardona, against whom no evidence was provided. "Who is the missing witness? Is this a Roe or another O'Connor who must be put out of the way so that Daure and Foster and Poole must be believed?"

Adams methodically compared the testimony of the state's witnesses. He agreed that J. J. Driscoll was credible, recalling Driscoll's opinion that the light at Basin and Girod was a bad one. Unverzagt said the light was flickering—he recognized no one and saw no man in an oilcloth. Not even Zachary Foster saw an oilcloth. Harry Glover testified that he saw the last of the shooting from a quarter of a block away, and although he recognized Chief Hennessy, he could identify no one else, but Daure claimed to have seen the entire incident in perfect detail from blocks below where Glover stood.

From the same window, Adams continued, Wheeler and Peeler placed the man in the oilcloth on opposite sides of Basin Street. The man's back was to Wheeler, she'd said, and the oilcloth was buttoned and its tails flapped, showing a white lining. Wheeler said nothing of Peeler ordering her to get his gun, the command that supposedly made the assassin turn his face to Peeler. "Peeler was present when Mary Wheeler told reporter Leppert he was drunk. She did say it, but he was too drunk to hear." If Peeler was sober, Adams asked why Wheeler was not recalled to contradict the reporter.

No one saw shots fired from the middle of the street but James Poole, who identified Marchesi, Adams said. Not even Daure, who "recognized" Marchesi from the Shakspeare Foundry two blocks away, saw this. Poole said he thought the black oilcloth was yellow and never made up his mind as to whether the man under the shed was red, black, or white. "Then," Adams said coolly, "we have Mr. Daure."

Daure, who first placed himself at Girod and Carondelet, but then placed himself half a block closer when he saw the flashes, ran over wet and broken pavement, always going at full speed and never losing sight of the shooting. "He knew little Gasperi Marchesi because he saw him at the market," Adams said. "I defy the learned district attorney to read one line of his direct examination that will show that he recognized this party except by his clothes." To ask for the jury's belief in seeing at such a distance, Daure swore that young

Marchesi turned. That was how Daure saw the boy's face; that was how he saw all the faces—all the men Daure identified turned to see who was after them. Adams said he found it odd that Mary Wheeler, looking directly down upon the crime scene, could not see any faces because the attackers were all fleeing without looking back in Daure's direction. Even stranger, Adams added, was that the only man Daure did not recognize was the city's chief of police.

Adams sorted through discrepancies as the day wore on. According to Daure, the big gate at Monasterio's shanty was closed when he got there, the door was shut, and no one was standing outside. Not Walton, Beverly, Thomas, or Monasterio. Ridiculing the ubiquitous Corcoran with a double-edged wisecrack that might apply to his daily wages or hunger for a piece of the $15,000 investigation fund, Adams called the commissary "a man with a history and a record, a man so earnest in giving value for the city's money that he watches the market night and day." Wheeler, Peeler, Price, and Virgets all differed on the number of men and weapons. Mascare, Poole, Daure, Zehr, and Wheeler saw an oilcloth coat; Peeler saw an oilcloth strip; and Unverzagt, Driscoll, and Foster saw no oilcloth at all. Besides, Adams asked, how could *eight* men be identified on sworn testimony if three, four, perhaps five figures were seen shooting at Chief Hennessy?

It didn't matter to him, Adams said, whether Macheca rented the Petersen place—surely Joe Macheca, Hennessy's friend, would personally go to rent a room across the street from the chief's home to house assassins, and this bright man Macheca would give Monasterio the receipt so that it would be found on the cobbler after his arrest. Why use Monasterio at all? Adams asked. Didn't Macheca already know Hennessy's habits as well as anyone from their membership in the Red Light Club? Why not use Polizzi? Hennessy knew Scaffidi and Bagnetto. "When he was shot down, what did he say?" Adams asked. "Not 'Leave me, but catch Polizzi' or Monasterio or Scaffidi or Marchesi or Bagnetto, but 'Leave me and go after the man with the gun!'"

What about Gasperi Marchesi? If the boy made a confession to Captain Journée about his father, it was not heard in the case. Either Gasperi lied to Williams and Scott about turning on his father or those two were lying.

"Admit that Macheca and the chief fell out," Adams offered theoretically, returning to the fruit importer. "Admit what Macheca said at the Red Light Club, that if the chief interfered and got men out who had waylaid others, he would be responsible. Was that such a terrible thing?" Macheca would not say such a thing if he truly planned to kill the chief, Adams said. "The other side tried to make it appear from Macheca's statement that Hennessy had been tried by some secret enclave, was sentenced, and that Macheca was picked out to do it."

"I thought this was an improper line of argument," Luzenberg dryly reminded Adams. Judge Baker cautioned the defense.

Adams proposed that there was nothing unusual in Macheca's irritation over hearing that the chief was paying board for the Provenzanos, the men accused of trying to kill his friends, the Matrangas. And now this remark was tortured into a threat against Chief Hennessy.

Two officers claimed to hear what Jim Caruso and Macheca said on Bourbon Street, yet the third officer with them had not been put on the stand to corroborate it. And even if Caruso had used the expression, what of it?

"Unfortunately, Mr. Hennessy had enemies," Adams said, looking sternly around the court. "Hundreds here today used the same expression about him. Because these men went to a woman's house and had wine, and because Macheca said they were enemies of Hennessy, the jury is to hang them."

Bringing his defense of the chief's alleged assassins to a close, Adams said, "I take the liberty of saying to you gentlemen that I knew Mr. Hennessy long and well. I knew him in the days when over his life the clouds hung darkest and in his holiday time of power, when parasite friends gathered about him.

"And I say without any reference to an effect on your judgments, but make the assertion so that I can reconcile my conduct here with my relations with the dead man, that if anything had occurred from the commencement of my relations with any of these defendants to give me any suspicion that he had been connected in any way with this foul assassination, I would be the last man to address you here on his behalf."

Suffering from a severe cold, Thomas Semmes arrived to join the defense, saying that the evidence had been analyzed, so he would make but a few general comments.

"I wish to say that it is the proud boast of Americans that this is a government of law and not of men, and we administer the law fairly and justly to all citizens," Semmes began. "The appeal has been made to you to vindicate the law. If the learned gentlemen meant to vindicate the law as applicable to any individual, all right, but they seem to think that in the person of Mr. Hennessy was the embodiment of the law, and the attack on him was an attack upon the law." Since Hennessy was not engaged in any police duty at the time of his death, Semmes said, his death should be viewed as the death of an ordinary citizen, even though the crime was magnified because of Hennessy's office. Were there not other crimes as great? "What of Jack the Ripper, who created a worldwide reputation by his assassinations? And he is yet to be discovered."

Semmes noted that none of Hennessy's neighbors except Peeler claimed to be able to identify the shooters in the bad light. The shooting took twenty seconds at most. No one could have seen it. It was impossible for John Daure to have run in time to see it. "I throw out the testimony of all the people who profess to identify those men," Semmes declared, the sonorous voice choked by his cold. There was too much conflicting evidence, made weaker by the conspicuous absence of O'Connor and Roe.

"I am totally incapable of making a speech because I have a fever, but I felt it my duty to come and give you some general views on the subject—my duty toward these men—and to show by earnestness in their behalf that I am extremely anxious that the law should be applied fairly and justly in this case."

The most famous lawyer in Louisiana spoke for nineteen minutes, then went home.

Like Semmes, district attorney Luzenberg said he did not want to tire the jury by going over the evidence again, so he began by dismissing the charge against Bastian Incardona.

Luzenberg reviewed the testimony of the state's witnesses for forty minutes. This was a murder trial, not a contest of skill between lawyers, he said. The evidence was that the light was good and these men—Luzenberg pointed to the double row of defendants—were identified. Minor discrepancies were to be expected, he said, for no two people, not even jurors, remember a thing the same way.

Luzenberg admitted that he would not have believed Williams's and Scott's stories about Gasperi Marchesi if John Daure had not corroborated it. He ridiculed Iff, Bagnetto's alibi witness, for looking at the Poydras Market clock "because he knew he would be a witness."

"It is time for this thing to stop," Luzenberg insisted. "It is time that the city's good name should be saved." Could there be any doubt that these men were doing the bidding of their masters in killing the chief?

"As to prejudice, none exists with us," the district attorney said. "We do not care if the accused are Italians or Irishmen or Germans or Frenchmen, or any other race. We only know them as human beings on trial for their lives." Aiming his finger at the pile of sawed-off shotguns, Luzenberg boomed, "These things must not be used in this city! They are not an American institution. If these accused did this act in the way witnesses said they did, you must be men enough to say so. If you have any reasonable doubt, say it.

"If the guilt of the accused has been proven beyond a doubt by representatives of a government whose majesty had been trampled in the dust, then as a fellow citizen interested with you in upholding the law, as a priest in the temple of justice, I demand justice of you!"

The final arguments ended with Luzenberg's closing, and Judge Baker immediately told the jury to find Charles Matranga and Bastian Incardona not guilty, for no case had been made against them. Baker instructed the jurors on their duties for half an hour. When he finished, Adams asked Baker to instruct the jury that they could bring in guilty verdicts to some defendants, not guilty to others, and mistrials to the rest if they desired. The judge complied, and the jurors stood to leave. No one else in the room moved. The public apparently expected an immediate verdict.

Luzenberg and the other prosecutors settled back into their chairs, looking pleased that the trial was over. The judge adjourned the case, telling the jurors to get a good night's rest before deciding anything.

Charles Matranga and Bastian Incardona looked relieved. They had been declared innocent by the judge, but would have to return to the parish prison until the jury formally returned a verdict.

As a dense crowd watched the prison van roll away, the corner boys began their taunts.

"Who killa de chief?" they brayed.

The last of the day's *Daily States* special editions announced, LIONEL ADAMS MAKES THE BEST OF A BAD CASE. A verdict was expected quickly, the paper told New Orleans, "guilty or otherwise." The other city papers were more cautious.

☽

Twenty-Two

THE JURORS' ANSWER

As ITALIANS ACROSS AMERICA PREPARED TO HONOR KING Umberto of Italy on his forty-seventh birthday, gaily colored flags appeared in New Orleans on the Ursulines Street flagstaff used to announce the arrival of fruit ships. St. Joseph's Day, March 19, the holy observance of one of Italy's most beloved saints, and the patron saint of immigrants, was less than a week off.

The rest of New Orleans had no idea what the flags and fuss were about.

On Friday morning, March 13, an hour after the courtroom doors opened and the crush of spectators dispersed in a run for seats and the Matranga, Caruso, and Locascio families arrived and found places, a deputy sheriff faced the crowd and ordered, "Everybody out of the building, gentlemen. Nobody allowed to remain except representatives of the press and members of the bar!"

The sullen crowd rose and a few influential citizens managed to remain, but Judge Baker's precaution of clearing the building was taken seriously. At 10:00 a.m. Sheriff Villere telephoned the parish prison and told Warden Davis not to bring the prisoners to court, but the van was already on its way.

As soon as the van reached St. Patrick's Hall, the sheriff ordered it to return to the prison. Shouts, jeers, and whistles erupted from the ejected citizens outside the court—the departing van meant that no verdict had been reached overnight.

Inside, the lawyers, doctors, and other professional men who had managed to finagle their way within the bar waited, smoking cigars and joking.

A stranger would think it was a groundless rumor that twelve men are closeted upstairs deliberating whether nine men should live or die, mused the *Item*'s reporter. As laughter ricocheted in the hollow room, a physician called the gravity of the occasion to a lawyer friend's attention. "Doctors and lawyers are looked upon as the worst people in creation anyhow," the attorney replied, "the only difference being that our mistakes are published while yours are buried!"

The predicted quick verdict did not come, and the morning passed with no word from the jury room. For the local newspapers there was little to do but rewrite the history of the case. Adams had made the best of a bad case said the *Daily States*, but before Luzenberg's "magnificent argument," the defense "melted away like snow beneath the rays of the noonday sun." Rumors were "as thick as flies in the summertime," said the *Daily City Item*. Although a verdict had already been reached at one thirty that afternoon, those reading the two o'clock edition of the newspapers on the steps of St. Patrick's Hall did not know it.

Sheriff Villere called the prison, and the Mariahs returned to court by a roundabout route. Vandervoort ordered extra police to watch over the crowd outside, and when word leaked that the prisoners had arrived, noise and excitement on the steps grew.

The courtroom was cleared of the curious professionals who did not belong there, then the prisoners took their places in the dock. Charles Matranga looked concerned but without anxiety, now that he was cleared. Yellowed emerald light filtering down from windows near the courtroom ceiling tinged Joe Macheca's taut face a deathly shade of green. The acquitted Incardona and the others were pale and nervous. Only Gasperi Marchesi looked calm and unconcerned. Polizzi looked frightened out of his mind, but everyone was used to that by now. A cordon of officers stood behind the prisoners, ready.

At 2:23 p.m., the jurors walked in, looking down. Only one raised his head, as if to see if the courtroom was crowded. After foreman Jacob Seligman informed Judge Baker of the verdict, the judge sent the jury back to its room to put it in writing.

At seven minutes to three, Judge Baker was given the jury's decision, which he read carefully for a full minute. At last, he looked up at Seligman.

"As I understand it," Judge Baker said, "you wish to enter a mistrial as to Scaffidi, Polizzi, and Monasterio?"

Seligman bowed his head, nodding yes.

Passing the verdict to the minute clerk, Judge Baker said, "Please read it."

"Bastian Incardona, Charles Matranga, Antonio Bagnetto, Antonio Marchesi, Gasperi Marchesi, and Joseph P. Macheca—not guilty."

A disapproving murmur coursed through the room.

"Quiet!" Judge Baker commanded.

The standing prisoners sank back into their seats, Macheca rubbing his eyes with his fingers. Then the defendants were marched into the sheriff's office, where friends and reporters awaited them.

"The verdict is a just one, for I am an innocent man," Charles Matranga said to reporters. Monasterio and Antonio Marchesi paced, conversing, while

Bagnetto stood in the doorway, smoking his pipe. "I did not even know the chief," he said in Italian.

When Macheca was asked if he was happy, he replied, "Yes, I have but one thing to do now."

"What's that?" the reporter asked.

"To find the man who rented Monasterio's shack."

"You were not so fortunate," the reporter said to Scaffidi who was smiling.

"Oh, I'll get out," Scaffidi said confidently.

"But Polizzi says you killed the chief."

Scaffidi's smile broke, and with a nervous laugh, he walked away.

"You're glad to get out, eh 'Asperi?" the reporter called to young Marchesi, who was romping around the room. The boy smiled. "Well, don't do any more whistling," someone joked.

"Oh, he don't whistle," said Bagnetto, who stood nearby. "He wasn't the—" Bagnetto stopped suddenly, then disappeared.

In the Section A courtroom, Polizzi sat alone, flanked by two deputies. After the verdict, he behaved exactly the same as he had before. He looked completely mad.

The prisoners were returned to the parish prison to spend the night. The six acquitted men were technically still accused of "lying in wait," but without a murder conviction upon which to base the charge, release was now certain. Luzenberg admitted that he would be forced to drop the "lying in wait" charges because he could not try the men twice for the same crime. Although the sheriff suggested the jurors leave by the side door, they hesitated. "We might as well face it now as any other time," one said, and they went out the front door.

As they hurried through, the crowd on the steps muttered, and reporters shot questions at them. "We had a reasonable doubt," foreman Seligman said.

"How much did you get?" shouted a boy.

Friends surrounded juror Charles Boesen as he broke free from the crowd telling him they could not believe he had agreed to the acquittal. "I'm sorry I couldn't please the whole community," he said, "but I had to do what I thought was right."

"The state made out a poor case," juror H. L. Tronchet said. The city will be outraged, a reporter told him. Tronchet smiled grimly as he said, "I'm able and ugly enough to handle the consequences."

When Judge Baker came out and was asked his opinion, he shrugged and said he had none. Luzenberg, who was not so reticent, said he was dumbfounded and shared "the universal consternation" of the community. Evans said despite suspicion of the jurors, the state never expected a miscarriage of justice given the evidence and public sentiment about the case.

Dominick O'Malley stood nearby, joking with reporters.

* * *

Disbelief over the verdict spread across the city like a forest fire, flaring, then subsiding to smolder no less dangerously under the surface. The bright flags flying in the French Quarter in honor of King Umberto were interpreted as a sign that Italians were rejoicing over the verdict. Many were, feeling that their maligned community itself was now acquitted. The city's Italian-language newspapers printed congratulations.

District Attorney Luzenberg might be silent because of his position, but others were angry. A secret meeting of half a dozen leading citizens was scheduled for four o'clock at William Parkerson's Commercial Place law office, but before long, the office was jammed with dozens of men.

The jurors were the only key to understanding the verdict, and the press was not about to leave them alone.

At his home, Jacob Seligman told reporters that the jury respected Judge Baker, who had instructed them not to convict if there was a reasonable doubt—and the state did not convince them beyond a reasonable doubt. The doubts, Seligman explained, resulted from the absence of Roe and O'Connor, men who were "at the very shooting." There was the refusal to produce the entire contents of Monasterio's pocketbook. Peeler seemed nearsighted and claimed to have his window open on a rainy night, and none of the jurors believed John Daure. When asked if he believed the alibis, Seligman replied that the jurors had sworn to give as much credence to the Italians as to other witnesses. They believed old man Matranga over Poole who was the only witness in addition to Mascare to confidently identify Antonio Marchesi. Mascare, Seligman said, was "too wonderful" a witness for a jury to believe.

What did he think of the talk of jury bribery? a reporter asked.

"I have no reason to think that any man on the jury was bribed," he said. "They seemed to act squarely, plainly, conscientiously, and frankly, and I saw no signs of corrupt influence." Seligman emphatically denied being approached before the case. "I was anxious *not* to get on the jury. I was snatched up with hardly any questions put to me, so I had no chance to escape."

Seligman and the others had not heard of "Polizzi's confession" until after the case. As to the mistrials of Scaffidi, Polizzi, and Monasterio, he declared the jurors were equally divided with no hope of reaching a conclusion. They pledged to each other not to reveal how each had voted. Seligman said his conscience was clear.

Charles Boesen would say little and Edward Heyob refused to talk at all.

He had voted with a clear conscience, he said, and "didn't give a straw" what the public thought. Arnold Wille said there was no chance of bribery with a deputy sheriff literally sleeping against the jury room door every night. A *Daily Picayune* reporter found armed family friends guarding William Yochum's hysterical mother. There was talk of mobs and vengeance against her boy! God was punishing him for leaving her to run the store alone! When she ran to the corner to ask a policeman for protection, the cop replied, "Madame, the jury has done its part. Let the people now do their part." When he was sure of the reporter's intentions, Yochum presented himself, saying he was sorry he served on the jury, but did not know how to get out of it. Mrs. Yochum fainted.

Reporters provoked other jurors into talking by throwing rumors of bribery at them. The bluff Tronchet, now worried, said some of his fellow jurors were illiterate and did not understand the charges. He said he thought no case was made against Macheca, but was adamantly opposed to acquitting the three men who got mistrials. John Berry agreed in this, although he revealed that doubts wore down his first impulse to convict all of the accused.

William Leahy was so disgusted by the ignorance of his fellow jurors that he'd sat in the corner alone and told them he would agree to whatever they decided. He said he believed some of the accused were guilty, but the identifications were unreliable. O'Connor and Roe were not called, and the jurors thought it was strange that Monasterio's pocketbook and a second rent receipt were never produced. Captain Journée said he had them at the station, but never brought them to court. Leahy said the jurors also doubted the existence of any "Mafia society."

He added that the state's case was conducted "more like a persecution than a prosecution." Slips of paper were constantly passed to the state table during jury selection, and the jury saw state witnesses being prompted. Leahy said he was sure no one had been bribed to serve on the jury to help the defense. If anyone was interfering with jurors, Leahy thought it was the state—when Prosecutor Evans addressed Seligman and Livaudais once by name during his lengthy summation, jurors wondered if their conversations were secretly being fed to the prosecution for the purpose of addressing their specific doubts in court.

Walter Livaudais, the youngest juror, shared Leahy's anger at his "ignorant" fellows. Livaudais said he lay on his bed while the others played cards. If there was any bribery attempt, he was sure he would have seen it. "There was not one they agreed on at first pop," said Livaudais, who was afraid he had lost his job as a railroad clerk because of his three-week absence.

Smoking a cigarette outside of his home, juror Edward Donnegan told a reporter he would say nothing because of his pledge. When the reporter tried to use the gossip of bribery strategy to get him to talk, Donnegan bristled. "The only man I've got to answer to is The Man Above!"

The reporter persisted. "I *knew* this!" Donnegan said in disgust.
"Knew what?"

Donnegan said he expected the jury to be "assailed" this way. This was not what the reporter wanted to hear. Because Donnegan would not play along, the reporter described him as "evasive . . . a denizen of the First Ward . . . decidedly of the 'tough' persuasion."

As the oldest juror, unemployed accountant William Mackesy was urged by the others to act as foreman, and when he refused, they chose Seligman. Like Berry, the Confederate navy veteran said he initially thought all the defendants should be convicted. The absence of Roe, O'Connor, and Mrs. Petersen's mother-in-law who had seen "Peter Johnson" take the rent receipt, however, changed Mackesy's mind. "My wish was to send all the men back to the prison and let another jury settle their case: let the state have another chance to present the testimony. That was why I held out for a conviction all the time."

If Mackesy was dead set on convictions, why did he vote to acquit the men? the reporter asked.

"Well, after the deliberations the evidence seemed so contradictory that I thought it best not to be too hard," Mackesy replied, balancing his little girl on his knee. "Then when we went out to the scene Tuesday night, we saw how hard it was to identify anyone by the electric light. Then all the lights were burning. The doors of all the houses were open, yet when we sent Sheriff Villere off to the banquette about forty feet away, although we knew it was him, we wouldn't have been able to swear to it. I'd sooner let a hundred guilty men escape, if there was a reasonable doubt, than let one innocent man go to the gallows."

Persuaded by a reporter to break his pledge not to reveal the mistrial vote, Mackesy said that he, Mayer, Berry, Tronchet, Wille, and Yochum were for conviction; Seligman, Livaudais, Leahy, Donnegan, Heyob, and Boesen were for acquittals. Although Mackesy begged the reporter not to use the names, the reporter would print them anyway.

There was joy in the Italian neighborhoods. Now the suspicious talk would stop; the acquittals freed everyone from months of shame. Two ecstatic men sent an American flag up a French Quarter flagpole beneath an Italian flag. When the American flag was reported to be hanging upside down, Italian Americans winced. The rest of the city heard the story and was ready for war.

When Sheriff Villere and Warden Davis spoke with the happy prisoners, Charles Matranga said he was grateful to the judge for ordering his acquittal. The Caruso brothers hoped they would be tried and released soon. After all, ten of the defendants still awaited trial. Macheca said he was relieved, and for the first time since his arrest, he actually looked cheerful.

At six o'clock, the prison gates were locked, and by nine, most of the Hennessy defendants were in bed, sleeping soundly.

Polizzi sat among the empty cells reserved for the condemned, alone in the blackness, listening to the bats rustling in the eaves.

At midnight the *Times-Democrat* received a slip of paper:

> *MASS MEETING!*
> *All good citizens are invited to attend a mass meeting on SATURDAY, March 14, at 10 o'clock a.m., on the steps of the Clay Statue to take steps to remedy the failure of justice in the HENNESSY CASE. Come prepared for action.*

The same note, signed by sixty-two of the men who had met in William Parkerson's law office, was delivered to every newspaper in New Orleans.

That night, Charles Heyle, chief clerk of the parish prison, heard a horse-drawn cab stop outside the quarters he shared with Warden Davis. The cab stopped and Heyle could hear footsteps outside the door. He rose from his cot, but was not quick enough to catch whoever was examining the Tremé Street door.

Half an hour later, the cab returned and Heyle again tried to catch sight of the mysterious visitor, but failed. He would tell Sheriff Villere about it first thing in the morning.

☾

Twenty-Three

FEET OF CLAY

DOMINICK O'MALLEY INSPECTED THE CALL TO THE CLAY Statue and saw the names of salesmen, lawyers, sugar and cotton factors, and a few high-society types from the Pickwick Club. S. P. Walmsley, last year's Rex, was there, along with Omer Villeré, president of the Louisiana Poultry & Livestock Association, and Commissioner of Public Works E. T. Leche. Pistol-packing *Daily States* reporter J. C. Aby and *Times-Democrat* city editor T. D. Wharton were on the list, along with half a dozen old White Leaguers and nearly as many from the Committee of Fifty, including Edgar Farrar, John M. Parker Jr., George Denegre, James Lee McLean, and John V. Moore, former aide to White League general Frederick Ogden. C. Harrison Parker, owner of the *New Delta*, and his editor John C. Wickliffe had signed. So had James D. Houston and George Denegre's YMDA attorney brother, Walter. And of course, O'Malley noted with contempt, Mayor Shakspeare's former campaign manager, William Stirling Parkerson.

Despite his bluff behavior, there was enough tension in the city for O'Malley and his wife to have taken the precaution of sleeping at a friend's house. Now he was in his office, surrounded by friends and half a dozen shotguns.

When he was done with his newspaper, O'Malley went down to Canal Street and bought more shells, finding the avenue no busier than usual for a Saturday morning. He dropped by court to have his concealed weapon charge continued, then returned to his office. Finally, tired of waiting, he and two friends decided to go down to the Clay Statue.

* * *

"Rise people of New Orleans!" railed the *Daily States*. "Alien hands of oath bound assassins have set the blot of a martyr's blood upon your vaunted civilization! Your laws, in the very Temple of Justice, have been bought off, and suborners have caused to be turned loose upon your streets the midnight murderers of David C. Hennessy, in whose premature grave the very majesty of our American law lies buried with his mangled corpse—the corpse of him who in life was the representative, the conservator of your very peace and dignity."

Sicilian killers put Hennessy in his grave and American agents set them free by bribing the jury, said the paper. And the jury? HERE THEY ARE! screamed the *States* headline above a story listing the name and address of every juror.

All the Saturday papers expressed frustration and anger. When New Orleanians awoke to find the *Daily Picayune* calling the verdict "a thunderburst of surprise" and wondering how a conspiracy to murder Hennessy had managed to intimidate the Committee of Fifty, possibly bribe the jury, and shroud the truth in "impenetrable gloom," no wonder people were frightened. Fiascoes in the courts were common, but the Hennessy verdict was being sold as something more insidious.

Yet even as the *Picayune* assailed the jury system and the verdict, it swept the call to the meeting to a bottom corner of the March 14 editorial page. "The expressed object of the meeting is so indefinite that we have no idea what it is intended to do," wrote the editor, who would have preferred a well-considered statement of precisely what the committee intended to remedy and what steps it might take. The editor said he did not expect violence. No, "the names of the gentlemen who signed the call would seem a guarantee of peaceful intentions." The editor said he counted on leaders of the meeting to abstain from fiery oratory and to keep the peace. "Let there be no race prejudice in this business," he added, worried that a race war against Italians might break out.

He titled his editorial AT THE FEET OF CLAY.

A worried Joe Macheca read the newspaper notice and asked deputy Richard Stevenson what he thought it meant.

"Don't worry about it," Stevenson said. "If they hold a meeting at all, it won't amount to anything."

Not a soul could be found on the streets around the parish prison. Sheriff Villere looked out and saw a few boys sitting on a woodpile, but no one else. This reassured him, but he asked the night guards to remain to assist men from the day shift in case of trouble. Chief clerk Heyle and thirteen other deputies nailed five heavy wooden planks across the Tremé Street door, sealing it diagonally with a fifteen-foot board.

On the way to his office in St. Patrick's Hall around ten o'clock, Villere began to feel uneasy, so he went to the Central Station instead. "How are things at the prison?" Chief Gaster asked the sheriff.

"Quiet," Villere replied. "But I would like some guards in the event of an attack."

Gaster, who had been out and about in the city, saw the same faces at Lafayette Square that loitered there during the trial, but no one else. The chief asked friends on the streets what they thought. They assured him there would be no trouble. Still, Gaster had sent out an order at nine thirty, commanding the entire police force to assemble at the Central Station. "They are on their way here," he said, looking at the clock. "I have only a small force on hand."

O'Malley was not prepared for what he saw when he arrived at the meeting site. As many as eight thousand people milled around the bronze figure of Henry Clay looming over Canal Street. Mule-drawn streetcars were stalled by pedestrians, traffic was stopped, and movement was impossible. O'Malley walked at the perimeter of the crowd, returning disdainful looks aimed his way.

At precisely ten o'clock, a shout sounded from the St. Charles edge of the crowd. William Parkerson, John Wickliffe, and the Denegre brothers led the signers of the meeting notice through applauding citizens to the statue of the Great Pacificator. Men made way for them inside the railing, where they stood silently for a moment, surveying the crowd.

"Give us a speech!" a man shouted.

Parkerson stepped forward and took off his hat as people clapped. Many knew his mellifluous voice from the YMDA campaign. Parkerson told the crowd that he had come to the Clay statue to denounce the most revolting crime in the annals of any community.

"I desire neither fame nor name nor glory," he cried. "I am a plain American citizen and as such, as a good citizen, I am here. I am here to say that things have come to such a crisis that talk is idle! Action—*action* must be the thing now."

Tremendous cheering greeted him. The law had been defied, murderers must be given their just desserts, and the jury had failed, Parkerson shouted. "I ask you to consider fairly and calmly what shall be done. Shall it be action?"

"Yes! Let's go!"

"We are ready, these gentlemen and I, to do what is necessary—to lead you. What shall it be? Do you want us as leaders?"

The crowd roared its approval, but Parkerson raised his hand. "There is another viper in our midst. And that is Dominick O'Malley. I now, right here, publicly, openly, and fearlessly denounce him as a suborner and procurer of witnesses and juries. Men and citizens of New Orleans, follow me! I will be your leader!"

Parkerson stepped aside, making a space for attorney Walter Denegre. "On September 14, 1874, such a crowd as I now see before me was assembled here to assert the manhood of the Crescent City," Denegre shouted. "I propose to see that you do the same today."

The Hennessy jury was bought, Denegre charged. "The law has proven a farce and a mockery. It now reverts to us to take upon ourselves the right to protect ourselves. Are we to tolerate organized assassination? Not one of those jurors told the truth! They were bribed, and bribed by whom? By that scoundrel D. C. O'Malley, than whom a more infamous monster never lived. The Committee of Fifty have already told him to leave town without avail. More forcible action is now called for."

Denegre had no idea that the infamous monster was watching him, leaning against the window of the Crescent Billiard Saloon and listening to the speech.

"If they want him so bad, there he is," someone said of the sneering detective. The billiard saloon's manager came over. "Would you mind moving?" he asked politely. "If they shoot, I don't want my window broken." O'Malley chuckled and stepped aside.

"I am not after the Italians or Sicilians as a race," Walter Denegre proclaimed from the statue. "But I want every man who murdered Dave Hennessy punished! I am with you. Are you with me?"

"Yes!" answered the crowd.

"As a member of the Committee of Fifty, I have come back to tell the people that the power they delegated to us to employ has failed, and that the committee is powerless. We have come back to lay the matter again before the people and to say 'Citizens of New Orleans! The committee is helpless, the courts are powerless. Now protect yourselves!' There is no point in wasting words!"

The manager of the Crescent Billiard Saloon looked for O'Malley as Denegre stepped away from the railing, but the detective was gone.

John Curd Wickliffe felt the rumble and reached for it. "When the people meet in Lafayette Square, they meet to *talk*," the *New Delta* editor began. "When the people meet under the shadow of the statue of Henry Clay, *they meet to act*!" The rumble grew. "Within the walls of the parish prison are confined a number of men declared innocent by a jury of the murder of Chief Hennessy. Are those men to go *free*?"

The rumble crested and exploded throughout the city center. The mob was so loud now that Wickliffe was forced to stop, then bellow to be heard: "Is the execrable Mafia to be allowed to flourish in this city?"

"No!" roared the crowd.

Wickliffe was not a Louisiana native, but a Kentuckian lawyer who affected a mantle of gentry. A West Pointer, admirers called him. Wickliffe had actually been expelled from the U.S. Military Academy at the end of his freshman year for sloppiness, lack of discipline, and swearing in front of an officer, but the men waving rifles and pistols in front of the Clay monument looked at him and saw a trained military leader.

"Fall in under the leadership of W. S. Parkerson! James D. Houston will be your first lieutenant and I, J. C. Wickliffe, will be your second lieutenant. Are you ready?"

"Yes! Hang the dago murderers!"

"Then come on!" The failed cadet had his command; the cheers could be heard blocks away.

During a beat of silence in the melee, a voice from the crowd yelled, "Shall we get guns?"

"Yes," Parkerson answered. "Get your guns and meet us in Congo Square immediately!"

Parkerson, Wickliffe, and the others descended from the monument and joined their committee. Those in the streets silently began to fall in, three and four abreast. The tramp of feet could be heard as the cheering died, and a military cadence resounded against the facades of Canal Street as the mob rounded the feet of Henry Clay, turning toward the prison.

Police detectives Antonio Pecora and Richard Kerwin saw a *Times-Democrat* reporter hop into a horse-drawn cab and jumped in with him. Onlookers saw the newspaperman and knew he was on his way to the prison. "It's a reporter! He'll warn them, stop him!"

"No," cried others, who did not see the detectives in the cab. "He's all right. Let him alone."

When the detectives arrived, they told Warden Davis what was coming. His clerk hurriedly rang the Criminal Court, where Sheriff Villere was discussing the mass meeting call with Judge Baker. Villere bolted from the court, running across Lafayette Square to the mayor's office where Consul Corte and Attorney General Rogers were in Shakspeare's parlor, waiting for the mayor to return from a doctor's appointment.

One look at the flustered sheriff told Consul Corte all he needed to know about rumors that a mob in Canal Street was planning to kill the prisoners. Rushing immediately to the governor's office the Italian consul pleaded with Governor Nicholls to protect King Umberto's subjects, on the streets as well as in the prison.

Nicholls listened patiently, with the commander of a local militia garrison standing silently by his side. "I cannot take cognizance of the matter without an official request from the mayor," Nicholls replied at last. "I am merely the governor. I am not in charge of the city. Any request for the militia must come officially from Mayor Shakspeare."

The consul was frantic.

"Wait awhile," the crippled governor urged. "I'll see what I can do."

Shouts and approving cheers cascaded from the windows of private clubs as Parkerson led the way up Canal Street. Ladies waved their handkerchiefs from above, but below, women and children were shoved aside in the surge toward Rampart Street. The head of the mob marched in perfect order, but those who followed were pushing and jostling their way through hundreds of Saturday shoppers who had watched the speakers with little interest from the sidewalks, never imagining this.

When Deputy Henry Villere, the sheriff's brother, looked up Royal Street and saw the mob passing, he ran. At Burgundy he leaped aboard a work wagon ambling back to the prison. By then, the head of the mob was there too. A man jumped into the wagon and pressed a pistol against Villere's head. "Get off!" the man demanded.

As the crowd flowed toward Congo Square, very few guns were brandished. Some men unbuttoned their overcoats and withdrew Winchesters, but most of the mob, with the exception of the well-armed leaders, looked harmless. The parish prison's working-class neighbors did not seem to be aware of the intent of the procession. They looked on from sidewalks and galleries, cheering and applauding as if they were being treated to a circus parade.

Spectators commandeered beer and grocery wagons along Orleans Street and turned the vehicles into grandstands over the protests of the drivers. Grocers stood on the sidewalks, hollering at people to get the hell off their shop awnings. Rooftops were dotted with onlookers trying to get an aerial view of what was beginning to look more like Mardi Gras every minute. Deputies who lived in the neighborhood left their homes and sprinted to the prison. When the deputies snapped the prison's gate shut behind them, the crowd jeered.

The banquettes in front of the prison were filling with people from every class and race in the city, overflowing across the open square between Tremé Market and Congo Square. Officers from the Fourth Precinct tried to clear the sidewalk, but they gave up. A deputy sheriff pushed a man away from the entrance and found a pistol leveled at his head. "I've done all I can," the deputy said, raising his hands and backing off.

"Your place is out in front of that crowd!" a bystander who had friends inside the prison shouted at a cop. "Your duty calls you there and that's where you ought to be!"

"You go out there and see how long you last," the cop replied. Then the crowd parted to let Parkerson, Houston, and Wickliffe through.

"Open all the cells," Warden Davis ordered.

Pandemonium overtook the yards as prisoners poured out of their segregated blocks, then milled in bewildered terror before running back into cover. Joe Macheca ran up to guard Tom Carey. "Please for God's sake, hide us!"

"I have to lock up the women," Carey said. "Hide in the water closet and I'll be back to see what I can do for you." Carey relocated the female prisoners in a different part of the prison. When he returned and let ten Italians into the Women's Department, he did not see Macheca.

The prison mascot, Queen, was a lame mongrel whose struggle to navigate the yard endeared it to both the inmates and the guards, who built a doghouse under a stairway in the Women's Department. It wasn't much of a doghouse, just a dry-goods box three feet square with a hole cut in the front. Salvatore Sunzeri and Pietro Natali somehow managed to cram themselves inside. "There's no more room!" they yelled at Charlie Pietzo when he tried to follow them. Pietzo huddled behind the box, beneath the staircase.

Meanwhile, several miles away, the telegraph officer at police headquarters took a dispatch from the precinct house nearest the prison. The message read: THE JIG IS UP.

James Houston picked armed sentries from the mob and posted them to prevent anyone from leaving the prison. When Clerk Heyle came to the front gate to face the men outside, they demanded the keys to the gate, whose iron bars were an inch and a half thick.

"Wait a moment, gentlemen," the chief clerk stalled. "The sheriff's on his way down."

"Wait, hell!" someone shouted. "If you don't give us the keys, God damn you, we'll shoot you all and break this gate down!"

Others in the mob, circling the prison looking for an alternative to the impregnable front entrance, came to the small door on Tremé Street, Captain Davis's private entrance that Heyle and the sheriffs had boarded shut from inside.

Thrown cordwood slammed against the apartment door. A brawny black man found a heavy cobblestone and drove it against the wood. The sound of hammering came from the other side as prison guards tried to drive the loosening nails and spikes back into the walls.

The half-smashed door fell in on Captain Davis's bed, disintegrating it as a cheer rounded the steep prison walls to the front gate and floated back in broken echoes. Drawn revolvers ringed the broken door when Parkerson arrived and sentinels let the leaders pass. Men left in the street who would not be denied a part in the action pushed their way in, filling Warden Davis's chamber with too many bodies. The crowd found two rifles and two shotguns, all loaded, in the bedroom, then pried open the warden's armoire. A young man snatched a bright Smith & Wesson from the shelf and waved it in the air. "Now for the dagos!" he hollered.

The vigilantes found Davis in his office. The warden appeared remarkably cool for someone who had moments ago been shouting panicky orders at everyone. "What do you want?"

"We want the dagos. Where are the keys?"

"I don't know where the keys are" Davis said.

"Take the son of a bitch out and hang him!"

Parkerson entered and said, "We don't intend to do you any harm, gentlemen, but we must have these people."

One of Parkerson's well-dressed companions was less genteel. "God damn you, we'll take you all out and hang you if you don't give up the keys. Who has them?"

"I believe Deputy Andry has them."

A dull boom sounded from the warden's bedroom, as an ax fell against a closed, bolted, iron-ribbed door. None of the men in the mob knew where it led, but they were getting nowhere with the prison staff. The pounding echoed into the prison and out to the bull pen, where the mob trying to force the thick bars of the front entrance suddenly fell silent.

Deputy Stevenson waited nervously behind the bolted door as six of the Italians ran up. "Go back! Go back!" Stevenson yelled.

John Caruso did not listen. He ran into the "white yard" and hid in a cell full of non-Italian inmates. Charles Patorno and Charles Matranga headed toward the Women's Department, while others ran upstairs. Finding no way out, they came downstairs again, running for the women's yard.

"Please, give me something to defend myself with," Rocco Geraci begged a deputy.

"I'm sorry," the deputy replied.

Wickliffe appeared in the Tremé Street door, frantically waving a rusty revolver that looked as if it hadn't been fired in years. Leche was at his side with a shotgun, as were W. W. Crane and former White Leaguer H. L. Lewis. The three were letting selected men inside if they showed a firearm and declared themselves ready to use it.

"Silence!" Wickliffe commanded hoarsely. "There has been a miscarriage of justice," he hollered, reviewing the Hennessy case and declaring the need for "cool action." Young Marchesi would not be touched, he ordered. Those who had gotten mistrials would be saved for another court. "The men who have not yet been given a trial we will let alone, but we must kill those who were acquitted, and those men are Joe Macheca, Scaffidi, old Marchesi . . ." Wickliffe's memory failed. "And the others. The two men whom the state said there was no evidence against, we must not harm."

Crane and Lewis saw a *Times-Democrat* reporter in the crowd and waved him forward. "Yes," they assured him cheerfully. "You'll get it all."

The reporter stepped inside and found the assault party stalled in Captain Davis's chamber, steadily battering away at the door separating them from the prison yard. They could hear men crying out for help on the other side of the impediment, which made them attack the door harder. A cheer reached the street when the iron door finally split open.

Parkerson and Charles Ranlett, both carrying shotguns, led the way inside. "And now for business," said a man following them with a Winchester.

Another man, blocking the Tremé Street doorway with a shotgun, announced, "We are now in possession of the jail. We will bring the murderers downstairs and in broad daylight we will have a public execution. The law will be vindicated."

Guns were about to fire on panic-stricken prisoners jammed into the first cell the mob encountered when prisoner Pat Keenan threw his arms across the open door. "These aren't the men you want, these men are only here for short sentences!"

The mob turned and hurried out into the deserted prison yard. One young society gent saw a face in an upper window and called out, "There's Scaffidi!" He raised his revolver and fired. Those around him poured a fusillade of rifle and shotgun fire into the window. Lead spattered everywhere, raising a cloud of dust from the whitewashed facade. A ricochet hit police sergeant Edward Hevron in the neck. Hevron picked the bloody splinter out with his fingers.

Warden Davis rushed into the yard, begging the mob not to shoot indiscriminately and the leaders agreed. Heading for the stairs leading to the upstairs galleries they met a tall man wearing a light overcoat and carrying a breech-loading shotgun who shouted, "Half you fellows go upstairs and the rest follow me!"

Even though it touched none of the men for whom vengeance was meant, the fusillade had a strange effect on the hushed crowds surrounding the prison. Shouts of "They're at it!" flew into the air, along with laughter and horrified shrieks. Many thought the prison guards and vigilantes were shooting each other. Alley whores ran up and down the banquette, laughing "Give it to them, death to the dagos!" Men threw their hats into the air and cheered themselves speechless.

Not everyone joined the carnival. Women paled and wrapped their arms around each other, weeping silently as the gunfire came; men in the crowd set their lips and stared as the streets around them tapped into the ecstasy of bloodlust.

Frantically looking for an exit, Macheca and Marchesi ran down a cramped gallery to a door leading to the execution room and the rest of the prison. It was sealed with a steel lock.

Macheca grabbed a small Indian club prisoners used for exercise and began hammering desperately at the lock.

"He's one of the bastards!"

Crying and beating on a locked grate doorway, trying to reach the spot where he last saw his father, Gasperi Marchesi tried to run, but heavily armed men grabbed him.

"Wait, don't kill the boy," Parkerson said. "Let's spare him. It'd be a shame for men to kill a youngster. His share in the crime may be less than that of the others."

They took the boy to the second floor and pushed him into an empty cell where he crawled under a cot and lay shivering and moaning.

Twenty of the vigilantes moved on to the star chamber, now deserted. They were about to return to the yard when, through a gallery window, they spotted Scaffidi, Macheca, and old Marchesi crouching behind a pillar near the execution room door. Men crowded around the gallery's other grated windows, training gun barrels on the brick pillar.

"We've got 'em! Kill them!" A locked gate and a second door cordoned off the gallery, separating the mob from the hunted men who called out, asking to be spared. Scaffidi stepped from behind the pillar, begging for mercy.

A rifle ball hit the young fruit peddler above his right eye and tore away the top of his skull. He screamed, his arms rising as he fell.

Antonio Marchesi panicked and began to run, but there was nowhere to go. Tripping over Scaffidi's body, Marchesi sprawled headlong on the floor. When he tried to get up, buckshot riddled his forehead and shoulders. The bleeding man struggled to his feet and stumbled down the gallery.

Macheca hammered desperately with the Indian club, loosening the bolts around the steel lock. The mob was yelling for the key to the gallery. If he could dislodge the bolts—

Macheca whirled as the outer gallery gate behind him swung open with a crash and a rifle shot cracked beneath the low gallery ceiling. Macheca stepped away from the door and fell to the floor, a thin line of blood trickling from his nose onto his white shirt.

Marchesi staggered to the inner door keeping the mob away and tried to hold it shut. The howling men outside were fumbling with a bundle of keys.

When the bolt slid and the door was shoved open, Marchesi leaned back against the wall. Blood coursed from his bare forehead, matting his hair bright red and covering him from head to foot.

As a man lifted a shotgun to Marchesi's chest and pulled the trigger, Marchesi grabbed at the muzzle and pushed. His fingers disappeared in a pinkish spray.

A second executioner discharged a shotgun into Marchesi's chest as the peddler tried to cover his face with his mangled stump.

After Marchesi fell, the mob left Macheca, Scaffidi, and Marchesi for dead. Prisoners shrank into their cells as armed men trundled back downstairs.

"Where are the dagos?"

"In the Women's Department," croaked the inmates.

Finding the prison's telegraph key unguarded, detectives Kerwin and Pecora tapped out a message to the Central Station: The prison is surrounded by five thousand people. Send every available man.

The fully manned Fifth Precinct patrol wagon galloped up Tremé Street, and as it reached St. Ann, the crowd at the prison pelted the police with rocks. Captain Collein saw guns being drawn on his men as he called out for order. Go back, he was warned. The patrol wagon retreated.

The tall man in the overcoat and his companions were about to batter down the door of the white women's cell block when one of the confiscated keys arrived. The armed men ran inside, past the shadows of cell No. 2.

This yard was also deserted except for an old black woman in the corridor. They ordered her to tell them where the Italians were. "They went upstairs, boss," she said, trembling. A door slammed above, followed by the sound of scurrying feet.

"Come on," Ranlett ordered. The men went up, but found the second floor deserted. Three of the men began to have second thoughts about what they were doing and remained upstairs. From a railing overlooking the yard, they could see Ranlett's tall figure reenter the empty square below.

As Ranlett and three others advanced across the yard, Frank Romero, wearing a derby and a brown worsted shirt, darted from cell No. 2. "Please don't kill me!" he cried from behind a brick pillar. Monasterio, Comitz, Traina,

Geraci, and Jim Caruso ran clumsily out of No. 2, heading for the corridor door just a cell away.

The tall man in the overcoat swung his shotgun to his shoulder and fired both barrels at once. Romero's head exploded as his body somersaulted forward and landed limp on what was left of his face.

Standing in a doorway, the old woman inmate was wringing her hands and shaking her head as the Italians fell to their knees and begged for a chance to live.

Loretto Comitz died from a load of shot in his brain with four more wounds staining the tinsmith's dark shirt as he crumpled to the flagstone. As Comitz fell, Charles Traina peeked out from behind a brick pillar and ten buckshot hit Traina's chest, opening his heart. Another round ripped his face, and he fell, his lips and nose streaming.

Big Jim Caruso made a dash for the corridor. He did not make it past Romero's motionless feet, where a bullet in his neck slowed Caruso just long enough for the guns to fire a full volley. Blood poured from dozens of wounds, quickly paling his corpse even without the help of a pumping heart.

Rocco Geraci fell by the corridor door. He swayed on his knees, then dropped. Behind him, Pietro Monasterio tumbled back against a cell door, groaning from a bullet in the back of his neck.

Two men with Navy Colt revolvers ran forward, saw Geraci's legs moving, and fired a .44 slug that split his shirt. The legs stopped twitching.

The window in the corridor door suddenly smashed open. A bright revolver appeared and four shots popped, three of them hitting Caruso and one leaving Traina shuddering. A second gun poked through the window, then a double-barreled shotgun. Both were spent on the bodies.

Ranlett reloaded his shotgun, but the firing had stopped. He walked up to the bodies and put a last load of shot into Caruso and Traina. The corpses bucked. "Let's go," he said. "They're done for."

Men continued to cluster around the scene, treading in crimson puddles and turning bodies over with their shoe tips.

"Which is Macheca? This one?"

"That's Romero. Nine-Fingered Frank."

"Shoot the son of a bitch," someone said, but no one fired at the still body.

Others in the killing party who had found Antonio Bagnetto shouted at him, "Who killed the chief?"

"I don't know!" Bagnetto raised his palms, mutely begging for mercy.

"Let's hang him," a man suggested, producing a thick coil of rope. When he saw the rope, Bagnetto tried to break free, but he was held fast. He tucked his chin into his chest to prevent the noose from being slipped around his neck, but he felt a sharp pain as a knee drove into the small of his back. He straightened for an instant, just long enough for his captors to hook the rope around his throat. As they tried to drag him toward the street Bagnetto thrashed in the doorway and set his feet against the sill. He was wrenched into sight of the cheering mob.

As Ranlett's group stood around the pile of bodies inside the prison, Monasterio's bloody hand strained for the wound in the back of his throat.

"Give him another load," an elderly man said, but none of the men with blood-spackled shoes felt like shooting the dying cobbler again.

"I've got a gun," a young man said. "Will this do?"

"Yes," said the old man. "Anything will do for the son of a bitch. Shoot him again."

The young man held out his revolver saying, "I haven't the heart to kill him. Here's the gun. Do the job yourself."

The old man snatched the gun away and shot the cobbler. Eventually Wickliffe arranged the men viewing the bodies into a military file with shouldered arms and marched them outside into public view.

Polizzi huddled in a ball under the rear staircase to the second floor, his eyes gripped shut against the cries and gunfire, but hands found him and pulled him to his feet. Hands with guns.

Dragging him out of the prison, men kicked and yanked him down the narrow lane of Tremé Street to the corner of St. Ann. A thin cord dropped from the lamp post, hung by a young climber who adjusted it over a crossbar below the gaslight frame. The cord closed around Polizzi's neck, and he struggled as men began to pull. The cord cut into his neck as he began to rise—then the cord broke. The crowd moaned with disappointment as Polizzi hit the ground. Someone found a clothesline, and soon Polizzi's strangling face came into view above the heads of the crowd as he was pulled upward again. His untied hands flailed at the rope until he caught it and began to pull himself up.

The boy perched atop the street light punched Polizzi in the face, forcing him to lose his grip. He fell and dangled by his neck, but his fingers found the clothesline again.

The men managing the rope lowered him and bound his hands with a piece of the broken cord. The struggling man was lifted a third time, and his body convulsed as bullets entered him, leaving puffs of blue smoke in the air. The bound figure writhed and swung, a moving target for the shots that ended his life.

Nine men, three blacks and six whites, dragged Bagnetto's bleeding body down the cobblestones of Orleans Street by a rope around his neck. The noisy crowd parted, but not widely enough to prevent anyone from kicking or beating the badly wounded man with canes and sticks. By the time his captors reached a leafless tree on the far side of the neutral ground median, Bagnetto looked dead.

At the top of the tree a man took the rope and adjusted it over a rotten limb, and as other men pulled, the prone, blood-spattered frame began to rise. Bagnetto's legs were easing off the ground when the dead limb broke and the already shattered body collapsed onto the brown grass.

Once his tormentors found a stronger branch, the fruit vendor was soon hanging above the approving heads of the crowd. The man who adjusted the rope climbed from the tree and as he descended, he kicked Bagnetto in the forehead, hard.

Tom Carey looked around the women's yard, hoping for a sign of Italians the mob had missed. Spotting the tiny doghouse, the deputy looked in and recognized Salvatore Sunzeri. "Come out!" Carey ordered.

As Sunzeri extricated himself from the box, men ran toward them shouting, "He's one of the dagos! String him up or shoot him!"

Carey stepped in front of Sunzeri as a crowd gathered, yelling in return, "This man has not been tried. The killing of this man would be a deliberate murder."

Wickliffe, who was inside the prison again, saw the confrontation and ordered Sunzeri to be held in a small shed opposite the pile of bodies near the corridor. Meanwhile, Pietro Natali was being pulled out of the doghouse by his feet and Carey spoke up again. "Wait there, it was proven in court that this man was in Chicago when Chief Hennessy was killed. Let him alone!" The men dragged Pietzo out from behind the doghouse, and he and Natali were hustled off to the guarded shed.

Outside on the Tremé neutral ground, Parkerson was trying to tell the mob that the Italians were dead.

"Where's Charles Matranga?" someone called out.

"I do not want him touched," the lawyer told the demanding mob. "No, no, the judge ordered him acquitted and it was proper that he should not be hurt. Nor Incardona. Nor the boy."

"O'Malley! We want Dominick O'Malley!" others shouted.

"You shall have him," Parkerson assured them. "I pledge you my word he shall be punished."

The demand for O'Malley's death was so loud that Parkerson had to stop speaking, and he and Walter Denegre slipped back through the crowd to the prison. Trying again, Parkerson clambered up into a window and waving his hand, beseeched the crowd to be quiet.

"Bagnetto, Scaffidi, Polizzi, Joe Macheca, Monasterio, and Marchesi are dead," he said. The crowd cheered. Parkerson did not mention the other five dead men, none of whom had been tried in court. "I have performed the most painful duty of my life today."

Calling for O'Malley's head, the crowd wanted Parkerson to go after the jurors too.

"If you have confidence in me and in the gentlemen associated with me, I ask you to disperse and to go quietly to your homes," Parkerson said. Although the crowd cheered him, hundreds were still bellowing for O'Malley.

"Tell them to go home and if we want them, we'll call them together again," George Denegre suggested.

"You have acted like men," Parkerson shouted. "Now go home like men!"

"O'Malley! We want O'Malley!"

"I pledge to you that O'Malley will be dealt with. Now take my word for it. Mob violence is the most terrible on the face of the earth! I called you together for a duty. You have performed that duty. Now, go to your homes and I will call you if I need you. God bless you and the community."

Parkerson was lifted into the air and carried down Tremé Street as the chant for the private detective's blood continued. Women waved their handkerchiefs as the attorney passed onto Rampart, followed by James Houston and those who had guarded the front gates during the killing.

It was eleven o'clock, only an hour after the meeting on Canal Street.

"The crowd has started toward Canal Street with Parkerson on their shoulders," an *Item* newsman breathlessly reported by telephone. The dispatch was misheard, causing the paper to print that the people carried *carcasses* on their shoulders.

Joe Macheca stared at the world with cold, astonished eyes. Still clutching the splintered Indian club, his other arm rested across Scaffidi, whose shirtsleeves were spattered with bits of his protruding brain. The coroner, Dr. LeMonnier, could not find a wound on Macheca, whose nose and lips were only lightly smeared with blood. "Perhaps he died of fright," LeMonnier theorized. The coroner eventually discovered a hole the size of a coin below Macheca's left ear. LeMonnier carefully removed part of the skull and found the slug.

Incredibly, Antonio Marchesi was not dead. He lay where he had fallen, gurgling and emitting red bubbles from his lips and nose. Black blood covered his face, sealing his eyelids, and his powder-burned stump lay across his chest.

"This man is still alive," LeMonnier said, wiping his hands and heading for the stairs. "We will proceed to the other yard, where I understand six more bodies are lying. Probably by the time we're through with them, Marchesi will have expired."

Tom Duffy, who was still doing time for shooting Scaffidi the previous autumn, arranged the bodies with the help of Skip Mealey, the trusty indicted for beating and robbing the Italian prisoners.

LeMonnier found Monasterio alive, but the cobbler died moments later. Jim Caruso's long, stiffening corpse contained forty-two bullet wounds. The dead man's mouth was open in a grotesque snarl of decaying teeth. The men who died around him lay in congealing blood, some with their heads propped against the wall, still wearing their derbies. Hundreds of spectators wandered into the prison, as if every man in the city was coming for a look—rich and poor, black and white and brown. No Sicilians were seen.

Police patrol wagons rolled up from every precinct in the city as officers began to clear the sidewalks. At the corner of Tremé and St. Ann, souvenir hunters were busily ripping bits of Polizzi's waistcoat and flannel shirt from his suspended corpse. His torso was soon bare, revealing a greenish hue spreading beneath his skin. The tree used to hang Bagnetto was white, completely stripped of its bark and branches by the curious sightseers.

When LeMonnier finished his work inside the prison, he and his jury were told that the bodies of Polizzi and Bagnetto had been cut down and taken to the Fourth Precinct Station, which greatly annoyed the coroner. Police explained that they needed to clear the streets, so the coroner tucked his foolscap paper under an arm and stomped off to the station house.

Running down Rampart Street a few blocks away with a piece of the rope used on Bagnetto in his tiny fist, a young boy passed an Italian fruit vendor.

"This is what we use for the Mafia, see!" he shouted, flashing the rope in the peddler's face.

"Are they going to kill me?"

Gasperi Marchesi was on his knees, crying. Strange men sat him on a cot.

"What have they done to my father? Have they killed him? My poor father, he didn't have anything to do with it, neither did I. We were home asleep. Is my father dead?"

"Your father has been shot."

The boy fell back on the cot, wailing. "I am all alone in the world! I have no one to protect me! Who did they kill?"

"They killed every mother's son of them," a prisoner said, pointing outside to the police taking Bagnetto's body down from the tree. "If you go to the window, you can see your daddy hanging."

Whipped by the wind, the high river was lapping over the levee at the French Market landing. Stalls were deserted; only a few Sicilians guarded their oysters and fruit as inconspicuously as possible. The Italian ghetto was silent. Children who normally played in the miasmic streets were kept indoors as their parents waited for the coming slaughter of the entire neighborhood. The celebration of King Umberto's birthday, which had been mistaken for rejoicing over the acquittals the day before, would not proceed. By nightfall, the only Italian flag still aloft in New Orleans flew from the masthead of a Macheca Brothers steamship.

"They tried to kill me too," Gasperi Marchesi sobbed. Newspaper reporters assured him he was safe, which calmed him somewhat.

When they asked if what Amos Scott and Joe Williams had said about him in court was true, the boy replied, "I said nothing to them."

Recognizing an Italian gentleman from court entering the room, Gasperi threw his arms around the man's neck. "Is my father dead?"

"The last time I saw him, he was well," the man fibbed, forcing a smile in hopes of getting information from the boy. "I guess you won't whistle any more, Gasperi."

The boy knelt. "So help me God, my father is innocent. I know nothing about the killing, and my father was in bed with me that night."

In fact, the boy's father was still alive. Jesuit Father O'Leary was on the gallery above, trying to save the horribly wounded man's soul. Antonio Marchesi breathed softly all afternoon as men watched. No medical aid was given to him.

Mayor Shakspeare said he was never asked for help to protect the prison and by the time he reached his office, it was all over. The mayor exhibited a telegram from William Pinkerton, who denounced the verdict in the Hennessy case as "a blot on the fair name of the City of New Orleans, second only to the Hennessy murder." He also had a telegraph from Shreveport, offering to raise a defense purse for the mob if one was needed. "Hurrah for New Orleans," it read.

Some of the businessmen who took part in the killing returned to work that afternoon at the Cotton Exchange, which quickly drafted a resolution endorsing the actions of its fellow citizens. After all, the administration of criminal justice in the city was "deplorable" and juries were bribed. What else could be done? The Board of Trade, the Stock Exchange, and the Sugar Exchange passed similar resolutions during the afternoon.

* * *

Consul Corte was distraught. After a call came in that three prisoners were lynched at the prison, he ran there as fast as he could. He passed through the mob returning from the prison to find corpses hanging above the streets. The consul did not enter the prison.

When Corte returned to the consulate, his secretary burst into his office, pale as a ghost. The mob had yelled "Kill the Italian!" at the secretary, who had took refuge in a store.

Soon the consulate was crowded with the parents and families of the dead men, who wanted the bodies, help, and advice. Corte told them to lock themselves in their homes, then the consul cleared his office and went to look for Governor Nicholls again with his people's demands and his own gathering fury.

A deputy sheriff watched in disbelieving horror as the blood-caked body of Antonio Marchesi rose and gasped for breath, but air would not come through the hole in Marchesi's throat. He convulsed and dropped back to the floor. Half an hour later, at 7:32 p.m., Marchesi finally stopped breathing. It had taken nine hours for him to die.

In the charged darkness, Parkerson again stood before the Clay Statue, flanked by Houston, Wickliffe, and members of the Committee of Fifty, and told a cheering multitude that they had wiped a stain from the city's name. The covenant to rid New Orleans of thugs and assassins had been carried out.

"How about O'Malley?" the crowd called.

"O'Malley will be attended to," Parkerson answered. "O'Malley cannot live in New Orleans."

By then it was 9:00 p.m. and the people were asked to return to their homes. Wickliffe assured them that "their committee" was not yet dissolved. "It will remain together until the moral atmosphere is cleared and New Orleans is once more safe. As the machinery of law is powerless, the people must act for themselves, but under the direction of the leaders chosen by them. And that action must be had not under the canopy of darkness, but in the broad open light of God's blessed day."

Nothing would be done that night or any other night, said Wickliffe, claiming he feared that mob rule might result.

By 10:30, the crowds melted away. Dominick O'Malley, who was reported to have been captured seven times that day, was nowhere to be found.

Twenty-Four

I Can't Arrest the Community

⏾

Before the sun rose Sunday morning, someone crept into John Purcell's stable, disturbing the mule. Thinking the animal belonged to Purcell's neighbor Dominick O'Malley, the intruder butchered it with an ax.

Father O'Leary performed last rites on the unclaimed body of Antonio Marchesi. After a Mass, Marchesi, Monasterio, and Traina were laid in plain boxes and buried in potter's field. Comitz would have joined them there, but his distraught wife begged $25 from a woman she did domestic work for so that the dead tinker could have a proper funeral. Scaffidi's family wailed over his body. Geraci was buried by his uncle. Only Polizzi's common-law wife and a black woman wept over his grave in Cypress Grove Cemetery. Bagnetto's family sent his lone hearse ahead and met it at Louisa Street Cemetery, avoiding the press. Romero's wife had a simple service at their home, and his body was placed in the Tiro al Bersaglio's tomb in Metairie Cemetery, not far from Chief Hennessy's remains.

The bodies of Joseph Macheca and his friend Jim Caruso were carried into St. Louis Cathedral as the grand choir sang for their families. Vincent Caruso struggled inside on his crutches, laid his head on his dead brother's chest, and sobbed. None of Macheca's fellow members of the Pelican Fire Company No. 4 attended his funeral, but the pallbearers included Judge Anthony Sambola, a prominent New Orleanian. The judge helped carry Macheca's gold-and-silver-trimmed coffin to a St. Louis Cemetery No. 1 crypt, mulling over the fact that potential jurors who had claimed to oppose capital punishment and were thus excused from sitting in judgment upon Macheca were among those who killed him.

While the dead were being buried, New Orleans authorities were busy explaining themselves.

Police Chief Gaster said he was sure beforehand that the meeting at the Clay Statue was called only to denounce the verdict. When asked what he intended to do about the lynching, he replied, "I can't arrest the community." Attorney General Rogers said he believed the grand jury would act on the matter "firmly, justly, and fearlessly."

District Attorney Luzenberg was criticized for allowing Jacob Seligman to serve on the jury after it was revealed that Luzenberg possessed an affidavit from an Oliver T. Nobles, who had sworn that while shopping in Seligman's jewelry store a week after the Hennessy murder, he heard Seligman say he would try to influence fellow jurors if he was chosen to serve on the Hennessy case. Nobles further charged that he and a man named Westcoat were discussing capital punishment in Seligman's store on a subsequent day, and when Westcoat declared himself opposed to hanging, Seligman agreed, saying that he would try to prevent the accused from being executed if he got on the jury, for the Hennessy murder was no worse than the killing of Thomas Devereaux. The affidavit was signed and dated February 21, halfway through the jury selection.

Learning of the affidavit during the trial, the *Times-Democrat* interviewed the district attorney privately, and Luzenberg explained that Westcoat utterly disclaimed Nobles's charges. Anyway, he said, the affidavit was filed after Seligman was impaneled to serve, making any action impossible. Luzenberg told the reporter that he discussed the matter secretly with Judge Baker, with lawyers from both sides present. The newspaper decided not to publish Nobles's uncorroborated story.

The day after the lynching, however, the Nobles affidavit was secret no longer. Reporters from the newspaper found William Pries, who was supposedly present at the second conversation at the jewelry store and said that one night a month before, Pries and Seligman found themselves in the same streetcar.

"After a pleasant salutation, the conversation turned on the Hennessy assassination and I expressed myself, deploring the killing of an excellent officer and a man I had every reason to regard as my friend," Pries reportedly claimed. "I said that I believed the citizens would have to take the matter in hand. I felt that way all along. Mr. Seligman's remarks were to the effect that Mr. Hennessy's character was bad: that he was a member of the Red Light Club, where men gambled and associated with notorious women, that he was not an angel, and that his loss was not as deplorable as some people are trying to make it out." Pries told a Boylan agency officer about the conversation after hearing that Seligman had been selected as a juror. Summoned to court, Pries quietly admitted to prosecutor James Walker that the conversation took place well before the trial, not after Seligman's selection. The prosecutor thought for a moment, then dismissed him.

Now the press threw the whole Nobles-Pries episode in Luzenberg's face. The vexed district attorney would explain his actions more than once, insisting that interviews with Pries produced no information that would justify action.

If Luzenberg's harshest critics held him responsible for the outcome of the trial, no one questioned his integrity. The verdict and lynching put the jurors in a more dangerous situation. Four men were grabbed by a crowd as they hurried along Villere Street. "Yes," admitted one, "I'm Jake Seligman, but for God's sake, give me a square trial!"

Luckily for the hunted juror, a court officer who was nearby summoned the police and Chief Gaster ordered Seligman set free as soon as the crowd dispersed. The nervous foreman disappeared, and rumors had him escaping by train to Cincinnati or Mobile.

Juror William Mackesy, who publicly demanded that the grand jury clear his name, said he suspected other jurors of making up their minds before sitting on the case, but he would not give names. He said that he was for hanging all the defendants, but was talked out of it. Walter Livaudais also demanded an investigation of his reputation.

Jurors weren't the only ones feeling threatened. Defense witness Henry Iff, who had testified to looking at the Poydras Market clock because he knew he would be a witness for men who hadn't even been arrested yet, said that he was confused and excited in court. He said he meant to say that he merely looked at the clock to see if it was time for him to go on watch.

Everyone connected with the Hennessy trial was pressed to explain his conduct by the city's newspapers, which tried to keep pace with the public's desire to make sense of the chaos. The Sunday evening *Daily City Item* congratulated a newsboy for selling seventeen hundred copies of its Saturday edition, whose front-page editorial claimed that Sicilians had been imported for the sole purpose of increasing the voting power of their class. The paper also claimed to have visited Father Manoritta, editor of the *Gazetta Catholica*, who said he had hidden all morning for fear of the mob. He showed the *Item* reporter a letter he received on March 10, a warning in broken English to stay away from the court. It was signed "La Mafia." Father Manoritta was sure, the paper reported, that it was from the Provenzanos and that a more suitable verdict in their trial would have done more to eradicate the Mafia.

"Surely your vocation will protect you from harm," the reporter said.

"You don't know these men," Father Manoritta smiled nervously. "They would like to see all priests in hell."

Father Manoritta showed the letter to Chief Gaster, who read the stage-Italian threats to "stay at homa and not goa to courta" and told Manoritta it was a prank. The priest was relieved, but the chief stationed a man at Manoritta's house anyway.

No police were stationed at the Italian consulate, where Consul Corte was having difficulty composing his report to Baron Saverio Fava, Italy's minister in Washington.

"It is true that among the Italians indicted there were some bad men, but it is also true that some of the charges against them were unfounded," Corte dictated. "I certainly do not understand why the authorities, instead of trying to prevent the massacre, consented to it, if they did not indeed instigate it. The evening before the massacre, the yelling and stone-throwing of young loafers indicated that something worse was about to happen. The violent articles in the morning papers left no doubt as to what steps were to be taken."

A loud hammering shook the side of the consulate. Corte's secretary went to investigate, but found no one outside. Of course not, Corte thought. Last night pranksters rang the doorbell until the shuddering wire broke. His wife was terrified, and their friends and servants were staying away.

Corte simply could not understand why the prisoners had not been removed from a place where they faced certain death. He wondered why no order was given to disband the mob when the first Winchesters were passed out by the mob's organizers. He would report his helpless appeals, the massacre, and everything that happened at the consulate afterward. He did not add names—there would be time enough for that when the mob leaders were arrested.

As Corte completed his dictation, he heard someone destroying the consulate's rear gate.

That night Warden Davis led the way up to the third floor of the prison, to a chapel where all condemned men were blessed before execution. The warden hoped his prisoners would be able to rest better if they were not forced to sleep next to the vacant bunks in their cells. Sunzeri, Incardona, Pietzo, Patorno, John Caruso, and Charles Matranga did not sleep. They stared and cried.

District Attorney Luzenberg was smoking a large Havana cigar in his office Monday morning when the *Daily States* found him. Luzenberg said he would drop remaining charges against Charles Matranga, Bastian Incardona, and Gasperi Marchesi later that day.

New rumors that Hennessy's murder had been planned at a meeting on North Peters Street began circulating. What about Polizzi's supposed confession that Macheca and Jim Caruso attended a meeting where Hennessy's murderers were chosen by lottery and paid $100 each with a promise of more? Was it true that Luzenberg was unable to make the excited Polizzi understand that he would not be freed even if he told the truth about the murder?

"Rest assured of one fact," Luzenberg said, laying aside his cigar. "If Polizzi had said anything that would have warranted the prosecution to use him as a witness, he would have been placed on the stand. His story was a rambling and disconnected one and we did not place any reliance on it."

The *States* printed Polizzi's rumored confession as fact anyway. "This confession, however, was not taken down in writing," the *States* explained, trying to circumvent the fact that the district attorney had given reporters no information whatsoever. "Consequently the full scope of it will never be known."

When Luzenberg went to court later that morning, reporters hounded him to release Polizzi's statement.

"What I have to say in this matter, I will say in court," Luzenberg snapped. "I do not propose to make the newspapers my associate counsel."

Attorney General Rogers was succinct, then silent. "My duty," he said, "is to act now, not talk." Governor Nicholls would reveal nothing about his correspondence with U.S. Secretary of State Blaine about the lynching. Consul Corte was slightly more forthcoming. "It was a truly regrettable affair," said the consul, adding that he had reported to his government about the deaths of Traina, Monasterio, and Marchesi, all of whom were Italian citizens. "Italy will demand satisfaction for her subjects and the ringleaders of the mob will have to be indicted, even if they be later acquitted by a jury."

"Or else the entire Italian fleet will steam up the river," one reporter added to his story, embellishing the consul's statement.

Unlike tight-lipped government officials, the Provenzanos went straight to the press, furious over Father Manoritta's claim that "the Provenzano faction of the Mafia" was threatening him. Joe Provenzano wanted the priest arrested, but Chief Gaster advised him to go to the newspapers instead. While George Provenzano was denouncing the priest as a disgrace to the community and raving that citizens should have killed Charles Matranga when they had a chance, George's brother Joe was a few doors away at the *Item*, offering an almost verbatim tirade.

If Father Manoritta knew anything about the Mafia, Joe Provenzano charged, it was from the priest's intimacy with Tony Matranga's family. Provenzano claimed his own knowledge of the underworld came from Jim Caruso's description of his induction into the New Orleans Mafia, whose black-robed leader Charlie Matranga held a skull in one hand and a dirk in the other, making Caruso swear to follow all rules of the society. Having sworn, Caruso was informed that the society's main object was to kill its enemies. Provenzano said Caruso offered him advice when his family got the extortion letters entered as evidence during his brothers' first trial. In thanks, Provenzano said he advised Caruso to give up his fruit stand and come to work for the Provenzanos as a foreman of stevedores, but only on the condition that Caruso have no more to do with the Mafia. Caruso agreed, saying he had just been chosen to kill some-one—he would steal, but not kill. Provenzano said that he and Caruso went to the nearest church where Caruso swore an oath never to associate with the Mafia again. Caruso got the new job as stevedore foreman, but Provenzano said he surmised that Caruso reneged on the oath and went back to work for the Matrangas out of fear that they would kill him.

If Caruso had actually taken a foreman's position with the more successful Matrangas because he simply didn't want to go back to being a fruit peddler, Provenzano did not say so. Instead, he accused Geraci of being a Mafia leader and called Sunzeri and Polizzi "society" members. All of this Joe Provenzano claimed to have learned from big Jim Caruso, the same man who had pointedly testified against Provenzano and his brothers during their murder trial.

At the parish prison, Charles Matranga was preoccupied with more recent events.

"The crowd was in the room and I could hear the men walking around, asking for the prisoners," Matranga said quietly to reporters. He sat in a circle with Incardona, Sunzeri, Natali, Pietzo, Patorno, and John Caruso. Matranga had escaped by making his bed and slipping beneath the mattress. "I had my crucifix in my hand and placed it to my lips. I kissed it three times and asked God if I was guilty to let them find me. But I was innocent and He did pro-tect me."

"The crowd didn't want any of you," suggested a reporter. The survivors replied that they were afraid the mob would lose control, for after all, several innocent men had been shot. Matranga asked the reporter to write again that Judge Baker had declared him innocent.

"Luzenberg says he will enter a nolle prosequi for you."

The prisoners looked up, wordless.

Later that day, Luzenberg dropped all charges against Charles Matranga, Incardona, Natali, and Gasperi Marchesi. After Judge Marr ordered the men released, a grave Lionel Adams came to the prison for Matranga at noon. The remaining accused men remained imprisoned and listened as Joe Provenzano's accusations in the *Item* were read to them.

"Provenzano says that he has never been connected with the Mafia," read the reporter.

"Yes, that's true," said John Caruso, who suddenly seemed to be annoyed with himself for speaking.

The reporter continued aloud. "Sunzeri is a member."

"Oh!" Sunzeri knew enough prison English to understand this. John Caruso translated as Sunzeri denied belonging to the Mafia or even knowing of its existence. Caruso also denied knowing anything about the existence of the society, swearing by St. Joseph.

"St. Joseph, alleged patron saint of the Mafia," wrote the reporter.

The prisoners were left wondering what might still happen to them, while others in New Orleans were already beginning to cast the day of terror as a historical event.

William Parkerson was a celebrity. Telegrams arriving from Texas, New York, Mississippi, and towns across Louisiana congratulated him and promised to help if such action was ever contemplated again. Parkerson passed these warm wishes along to the New Orleans newspapers, which printed them alongside a "Mafia threat" in fractured English sent to Parkerson's office. With the lynching over, Parkerson proclaimed that the mob's leaders would continue their work under the name Committee of Safety. Assuring the public that Warden Davis's destroyed furniture would be paid for, he did not mention the guns stolen from Davis's quarters.

Leading the mob was "a great and terrible duty," Parkerson said. Praising the forbearance of the crowd, the young lawyer said that nowhere else could justice be righted and normal life resumed in less than an hour with no rioting in the streets. To Parkerson this proved that New Orleans was "the most peaceful and law-abiding city in America." It was a unique situation, he felt. The jury was tampered with, the state's case was certain, and acquittals were contrary to the evidence. Even the American flag had been insulted.

"How could it be borne longer?" Parkerson wondered aloud. "Can any man who loves the government established by the framers of our Constitution say that the people of New Orleans have done wrong?" The newspaper editors of New Orleans were quick to agree. LET US HAVE PEACE, the *Daily Picayune* advised. While accepting the "fait accompli," the paper applauded "the marvelous self-control of the people" for accomplishing the lynching without letting it turn into a citywide riot. Authorities were warned to make sure the unquenched "mob spirit" did not erupt again. "Danger still threatens."

When Hennessy was murdered, the New Orleans press had seen itself as the voice of temperance, speaking out for the rule of law even as authorities were stumbling all over the case. Few newspapers openly printed that it was an open-and-shut case for the prosecution, and premature conviction of the defendants on the pages of the city's more respected papers was avoided by their editors, who consistently advocated reason, law, and patience.

This magnificent facade crumbled in the gale of the lynching. The press immediately closed ranks with the prominent men who had stormed the prison and all talk about the rule of law was forgotten. For the best men in New Orleans to have taken such drastic action, the press now wrote, they must have had extraordinary provocation. If Chief Hennessy had not been killed by plotting Italians whose acquittals were bought by jury bribers, the lynching would have been indefensible. Had the people not acted, the murderers would still be free.

With the help of the press, the mob's perception of the Hennessy killing and the righteousness of its remedy were chiseled deeper with each passing day. Only the *Mascot* would refuse to fall into line with the rest of the Camp Street press establishment, knowing that the silk-stockinged reformers who controlled the city government had proved their worthlessness as guardians of public order beyond anyone's worst imagining.

No one tried to count how many things might have turned out differently if Hennessy had died without uttering a word.

☽

Twenty-Five

RUMORS OF JUSTICE

Five thousand people <u>did</u> <u>not</u> call at Armbruster's, 204 Canal, corner Rampart, to select a piano this week, but those that did buy, certainly got bargains. Another special sale Monday. Every piano fully guaranteed for six years.

—*Mascot* advertisement, March 21, 1891

"YOUR NAME IS VERY MUCH BEFORE THE PUBLIC JUST NOW," began a reporter from the New York *Tribune*.

"Yes," Parkerson said, smiling. "We had a thirty-minute experience on Saturday. The most wonderful thing about it is that it was over so soon. I take more credit for that than anything else."

Parkerson appeared reluctant to talk, but explained that he had taken no more than a good citizen's interest in the trial—until the verdict was announced. He said he found a crowd of people waiting for him at his office that afternoon, and they met again that night to elect him chairman and sign the call to meet at the Clay Statue. The group also decided to follow the public's wishes in the morning.

"Meaning that you would be ready to slay the prisoners?"

"That was the feeling, we understood, of the public pulse." Parkerson described the meeting on Canal Street before "a muttering mob of many thousands of people" and the march to the prison. "The women were crying and the men cheering. It was the most terrible thing I ever saw, the quiet determination of the crowd. There was no disorder."

Parkerson said he saw the six prisoners shot outside cell No. 2. "The intention had been not to shoot any of them, but when my men were inside, about fifty of them, they got very furious, and after the first taste of blood it was impossible to keep them back."

"If you didn't mean to shoot, why did you take the guns?"

"Because we didn't know what kind of resistance we might encounter from the officers in charge . . . from anybody. We meant to get into the prison and we would have torn it down brick by brick if necessary." Parkerson said he would have defended Charles Matranga and "another" with his life, for Judge Baker had declared them innocent.

"Didn't it strike you as not courageous to shoot the lot of unarmed men in a hole?" asked the reporter.

"Well, there was no doubt about the courage of any man in our party," Parkerson said. "Of course, it is not a courageous thing to attack a man who is not armed, but we looked upon these men as so many reptiles. Why, I was told that on Friday, after the verdict, the Italian fruit and oyster schooners along the wharves hoisted the Sicilian flag over the stars and stripes and the prisoners themselves had a champagne supper."

"Were you filled with pride and exultation?" asked the reporter.

"No, sir, I regretted very much the necessity. I regretted that so painful a duty had been forced upon me."

"But haven't you met one violation of the law with another?"

"No, this was a great emergency, greater than ever happened in New York, Cincinnati, or Chicago," Parkerson replied. "I didn't act through a sentimental or personal interest in Hennessy. I knew him well and asked Mayor Shakspeare to appoint him. He was a fine man and an efficient officer and we felt that when he was killed there was no telling which one of us would go next.

"While the Mafia confined itself to killing its own members," Parkerson continued, "we did not resort to violence. But Hennessy's killing struck at the very heart of American institutions. The intimidation of the Mafia and its corruption of our juries are to be met only with strong measures. Moreover, I recognize no power above the people. Under our Constitution, the people are the sovereign authority, and when the courts, their agents, fail to carry out the law, the authority is relegated back to the people who gave it. In this case, I look upon it that we represented the people—not the people of the United States, perhaps, but the people of Louisiana. This is a thing with which the United States has nothing to do. It is a question of state government entirely, since the state controls its own municipalities."

"Don't you think your example may encourage mob law?"

"No, I don't," he replied. "The emergency was an extraordinary one. We couldn't wait to have the laws against jury packing revised. If a man spits in your face or slaps your face, do you sit down and wait for the law to redress your grievance? It is not in human nature to do it. It isn't in my nature, or yours, or that of any good citizen. The theory about turning the other cheek when one is smitten is all very well, but when the cheek is smitten, the blood boils."

"Then you don't think Christianity and American civilization are reconcilable?" asked the reporter.

"In some cases it doesn't seem so."

Parkerson said he expected no more disorder, for Mayor Shakspeare was in control of the city. "I don't apprehend any trouble myself, except from the federal authorities. It is true, they say, that these men were the subjects of foreign potentates. But I understood that they were just dumped here and that their own governments were glad to get rid of them."

"Massacred!" charged Stefano Malata, editor of *L'America*. The Sicilian-born editor's voice climbed to a shout as he spoke to a mass meeting of Chicago's immigrants. "Our countrymen have been massacred! The outrage has no comparison in the history of any civilized nation!"

Malata told the crowd that he had no sympathy for vendettas. "But I insist on right! Why did New Orleans authorities allow Parkerson to assemble thousands of citizens and harangue them to the point of frenzy and murder? The magistrates declared the accused innocent. The assassins were not Italians, they were American citizens!" The Chicago mass meeting passed a resolution:

> *We, Italians by birth, Americans by choice, assembled in mass meeting, unanimously protest against the cowardly and lawless act of the New Orleans mob, aided by the tacit consent of the local authorities, and demand of the Federal Government satisfactory reparation, the severe punishment of the leaders, who were active in breaking the laws guaranteeing the right of citizenship and hospitality.*

Resolutions denouncing the lynching were drafted in immigrant communities across America, in places such as in Kansas City and Pittsburgh where the Mafia was known to have few friends. Pittsburgh's Italian Americans had sent $100 to the defense fund and now resolved to demand action from the U.S. government in case the state of Louisiana should let the matter go.

New Orleans papers called this a "threat."

"In what world are we living?" wondered *Il Progresso Italo-Americano* in New York. "Where is the much-boasted reverence of the American for the constitutional laws of his country? Why is the verdict of a jury in a capital process a farce, a joke, a play, that they should make beasts of themselves and others?"

Yet New York was quiet. When a *Times* reporter asked Italians on the streets their reaction to the lynching, many shrugged.

Washington, DC, however, could not talk about anything but New Orleans. A former California congressman said he thought the lynching was a unique case. Besides, he noted that Chinese were massacred in Wyoming without any reparations to their government. The congressman said he thought the Italian government would have a tough time turning the lynching into an international incident, but he was wrong. The Italians were burning.

After Italy immediately protested to the State Department, Secretary of State Blaine expressed horror at the mob's actions and promised to inform the Italian government what action President Benjamin Harrison would take. With this, Italy's delegation in Washington stopped talking to the press. So did Secretary Blaine, but in his dispatch to Governor Nicholls, which was made public, Blaine deplored the massacre and told Nicholls that the Italian government claimed three or more of the dead men as subjects of the King of Italy. He pointed out that U.S. treaties guaranteed the subjects of friendly foreign governments the same protections under the law as American citizens.

"The President deeply regrets that the citizens of New Orleans should have so disparaged the purity and adequacy of their own judicial tribunals as to transfer to the passionate judgment of a mob a question that should have been adjudged dispassionately and settled by rules of law," Blaine wrote. "It is the hope of the President that you will co-operate with him in maintaining the obligations of the United States toward Italian subjects who may be within the perils of the present excitement, that further bloodshed and violence may be prevented, and that all offenders against the law may be promptly brought to justice."

Offenders against the law? The mob's champions were incensed. If Blaine was against crime, they said, what about murder? What about bribery? The secretary of state—the rest of America—didn't understand.

The Creoles of New Orleans hated George Washington Cable for writing about them, and when he deplored the parish prison lynching from his new home in Massachusetts, the author of *The Grandissimes* made a fresh class of enemies in his abandoned hometown.

New Orleanians quickly learned what the rest of the world thought. Few American newspapers had covered the Hennessy trial, but when one of the largest cities in the country found itself ankle-deep in blood, no one wanted to be caught without an opinion. THEY ARE WITH US! trumpeted a New Orleans daily, which was not entirely true. Before the Hennessy case fell from front pages around the nation, more than one hundred newspapers and dozens of magazines would comment on it, with over half condemning the lynching. There was no geographical pattern to the condemnations or hurrahs, as southern papers were among the harshest critics of the mob. The Charleston *News and Courier* condemned this "most unsightly blot on the civilization of the country," while the Houston *Post* said the disgrace belonged to New Orleans alone.

Many editors repeated William Parkerson's argument that this was a unique situation in which a multitude of provocations moved the people of New Orleans to act out of necessity. The Portland *Oregonian* said that laws were entitled to no special reverence. When the law protected society, "it is worthy of all respect and obedience. When it fails, it is a dull, broken, and worthless tool, to be thrown aside and superceded by any agency at hand."

The Montgomery *Advertiser* and San Francisco *Examiner* blamed the jury, the *Boston Globe* blamed the city, and the *New York Times* was sure that the lynched men were

> *desperate ruffians and murderers. These sneaking and cowardly Sicilians, the descendants of bandits and assassins, who have transported to this country the lawless passions, the cut throat practices and the oathbound societies, are to us a pest without mitigation. Our own rattlesnakes are as good citizens as they. . . . Orderly and lawabiding persons will not pretend that the butchery of the Italians was either "justifiable or proper." There is no room for argument about that, for before the argument begins we must grant the postulate that our civilization and our patiently constructed system of criminal jurisprudence are failures. Yet while every good citizen will readily assent to the proposition that this affair is to be deplored, it would be difficult to find any one individual who would confess that privately he deplores it very much.*

The *Times* clearly did not consult any Italians before bestowing its cynical benediction, for Italians did not think the parish prison incident was butchery—they knew it was. Outrage thundered into the Washington office of Italian Prime Minister Antonio Starabba, Marquis di Rudini, as Rome's press and Italian American newspapers cabled denunciations. Fear and anger set immigrant communities across America on edge. There were mass meetings in New York. Italians in Nashville cabled their sympathy to New Orleans and their anger to Washington. The Italian consul in Chicago asked his countrymen to be calm and confine themselves to dignified protests, while the London *News* said it shared Italy's indignation, but that the jail should have been left intact for jury bribers. "Americans," it said, "are at once the most patient and the most impatient people in the world, and when they have grown tired of any grievance, they move to their vengeance with the swiftness of a hawk."

Throughout it all, New Orleans papers held fast. The *Daily States* called the lynching a "purely local" and "awfully sublime" act of punishment, warning Secretary of State Blaine and the Italian government to mind their own business. Meanwhile, newspapers sold like hotcakes. Copies of the *Times-Democrat* were going for the astronomical price of 50¢ each in Jackson, Mississippi. The press worked hard to keep the story alive by publishing every new and old story about the Mafia it could get its hands on, often mangling details in its haste. Under a front-page headline MAFIA CRIMES, the *Item* described twenty-two murders involving Italians over the previous forty-five years, which was a meager record of mayhem for a city whose murder rate matched or surpassed the same number annually. Under the circumstances, however, it was rich fodder for editorials favoring stricter immigration control and a boycott on tourism in Italy. A Mississippian sent William Parkerson a handsome set of gilt-decorated horns. For want of a better address, the horns were delivered to a New Orleans newspaper.

Although the people of Dallas read that the Mafia had killed Joseph Shakspeare, the mayor, who regretted and endorsed the lynching in the same breath as a "crusade of the good against the bad," was touchy, but far from dead.

"I did not know anything at all about the movement to break into the prison on Friday night and I was not at the meeting," Shakspeare insisted to reporters. "In fact, I was dining with Governor Nicholls. The next morning when I saw the call, of course, I knew something would happen."

Shakspeare said he was at the Pickwick Club during the riot, attending to private business. Did he regret not taking any action to prevent the lynching?

"No, sir," Shakspeare said testily. "I am an American citizen and I am not afraid of the devil. These men deserved hanging. We expected disagreement and had made arrangements for a retrial. When I heard of the verdict, I was frozen to my seat."

"Couldn't you have punished them by lawful means?" a reporter asked.

"They were punished by lawful means. The men who did it were all peaceable and law-abiding. The Italians had taken the law into their own hands and we had to do the same. It was what they did in Italy. The Mafia got too strong for them and what happened? The sovereign took hold of it, the King. Here the sovereign also took hold of it—the people."

"Do you anticipate any new uprising?" Shakspeare was asked.

"No, but if I or my secretary were touched, and anybody belonging to us, our people would take it up and there is no telling where the thing would stop," he replied.

"You approve of Saturday's work?"

"Certainly. I think that fifteen months from now the Italian population will be thanking us heartily for what we have done."

"The Italian consul complains that you have treated him discourteously," the reporter said.

"I can tell you," Shakspeare retorted, "that the Italian consul is himself in pretty bad company. At least so I'm told. That little priest—what's his name? Manoritta is a bad man. The consul had better look out. He complains that he was molested. I have sent him a policeman and I guess he would protect him. I would stand up for the law-abiding Italians fast enough, you can be sure. But these boatmen out here in luggers, why, they hoist the Sicilian flag above the stars and stripes and one fellow, they say, trampled the American flag under foot.

"This is my second term as mayor," Shakspeare added, "and the last time I'll fill a political office. I want to lead a quiet life and be respectable. I am a good American!"

If the lynching and its defenders accomplished nothing else, the violence stopped any questions over why the promised truth about a ballyhooed Mafia conspiracy was absent from the Hennessy trial. Theories offered by Hennessy's friends provided tantalizing hints that provided no lasting illumination. William Pinkerton declined to dispute that the Provenzanos were involved in the Esplanade ambush, but added that Hennessy had refused a request from Macheca to convict the Provenzanos with the help of perjured "Mafia" testimony.

"During the summer, he sent to Italy and got the records of all the witnesses who had testified against the Provenzanos," Pinkerton said of his dead friend. "He dug deeper into the order than any outsider had ever dared and when he was up here to see me in October, he said he had the evidence to uproot the Mafia in this country. He had ascertained facts that would have uncloaked their organized band of assassins and would have sent a great crowd to the penitentiary for perjurers. . . . Chief Hennessy told me he believed O'Malley had told Macheca and Matranga they must get Hennessy out of the way or go over the road."

George Vandervoort had spent Saturday morning pacing in front of the prison, unable or unwilling to do anything about the carnage inside. When the press caught up with him later, Hennessy's secretary said that uprooting the Mafia in New Orleans had become the chief's life's work after the Esposito affair ten years earlier. To Hennessy, Mafia members were always "Sicilians," or "dagos," never Italians. Vandervoort told reporters that the chief unearthed a great deal of dark information about Joe Macheca, whom he considered to be a troublemaker. One day Hennessy blurted out some of what he had learned and threatened Macheca with state prison. This, Vandervoort said, was probably what cost the chief his life.

Vandervoort said that Hennessy's attempt to keep peace between the Provenzanos and Matrangas was sealed with a drink at the Red Light Club.

Hennessy learned, however, that Macheca rushed outside after the Matrangas and told them that they were fools, that the Provenzanos would never live up to their promise, and that Hennessy was helping them. The secretary said that when the Matrangas were attacked on Esplanade, it looked like Macheca might be right. Hennessy sent to Italy for records about the Matrangas and planned to expose them by testifying in person at the Provenzanos' retrial, said Vandervoort, who called Tony Matranga the head of the New Orleans Mafia. Rocco Geraci was their "bulldozer," he said, a killer who had put two men out of the society's way. Frank Romero was a hanger-on at the courts and a politician in charge of keeping greenhorn labor in line. When an assassination was planned, Vandervoort said Romero would run a lottery to select the killers. Jim Caruso was involved too, he added.

Vandervoort said he advised the chief to get affidavits from his Italian confidants in case some harm should come to him. He also advised the chief to station three good men in his neighborhood. He said Hennessy laughed, but shortly before the date set for the second Provenzano trial, the chief received a letter in good English warning him to stay away from the window of his office, where he could be seen sitting most nights. It advised him to take a bodyguard with him whenever he walked home, for there were plans to kill him because of his threats against the Mafia.

If Pinkerton's and Vandervoort's claims of documentation about the Mafia, the Matranga family, and the lynched men existed, however, no such evidence had been presented during the trial nor did they offer it now.

Asked by reporters about Dominick O'Malley, Vandervoort replied, "Well, I won't exactly say that Hennessy and O'Malley were enemies." He would say that the two men had no use for each other, although this was hardly news to anyone who knew them. Hennessy suspected O'Malley of either inspiring press attacks on the chief's integrity or writing the attacks himself, Vandervoort said. O'Malley once told an evening paper that it was not necessary for a chief of police to be a murderer, sniping at Hennessy over the Devereaux shooting. When Hennessy learned of O'Malley's involvement with the Esplanade ambush trial, Vandervoort said, the chief was furious. "He told the force that it must ferret out the perpetrators of the crime, but must not join hands with O'Malley. He told Matranga he did not approve of O'Malley's methods and would not work with him. If the police or the chief could help Mr. Adams, the lawyer, it would do so. It would never work in unison with O'Malley. It was but a short time before Hennessy was stricken down that he told me if he was ever to be killed, it was his firm belief that O'Malley would have a hand in the job."

The shadow play pitting the Provenzanos against the Matrangas soon resumed, clarifying nothing for anyone wondering if one of the families might be the "real" Mafia. Tony Matranga lifted his stump onto a dining room chair and called Joe Provenzano's charges against his brother, Charles, and the lynched men ridiculous. If Provenzano had all of this damning information about Caruso and Geraci belonging to the Mafia, why didn't he mention it during the Hennessy trial when it would have done the prosecution some good? he asked. Why did he wait until they were dead? "All I know about these men is that they were good workmen while they were with me," Matranga said. "I never inquired into any of their private business." He said Jim Caruso never told him anything about belonging to the Mafia. If Caruso had, Matranga insisted, he never would have hired the man, unlike the Provenzanos.

Matranga defended himself and his brother who had been in New Orleans since he was three years old. "Charlie went to an American school and has grown up with American boys. He had a good business. Why should he get mixed up in such things? No, sir, it's lies, all lies done to hurt us in our business . . . look at this leg. The Provenzanos shot it off." Tony Matranga called Joe Provenzano a liar and denied belonging to the Mafia, if there was such a thing. He swore it on the head of his old mother, who stood by his side with the rest of their family.

The Provenzanos continued their own public relations offensive with Joe Provenzano complaining to the archbishop of New Orleans about Father Manoritta's assertion that the Provenzanos, not the Matrangas, were mafiosi. The priest publicly apologized, and now denied knowing anything at all about the Mafia beyond the unfortunate fact of its existence. He had "supposed" Joe Provenzano was involved, he now said, and only said so in confidence to a reporter. But Manoritta was still nervous, and he laughed out loud when told that Provenzano accused him of intimacy with the Mafia through the Matrangas.

Father Manoritta was not backpedaling alone. The *Daily Picayune* publicly apologized to Charles Luzenberg for making unfounded charges about jury foreman Seligman and the Nobles affidavit. It was a wise move because the district attorney was threatening to sue. Luzenberg had since become legal advisor to the grand jury responsible for investigating the lynching and the charges of jury tampering. Charges against all of the surviving Hennessy case defendants had by then been dropped. But if Luzenberg originally considered them guilty of murdering Hennessy, no one questioned why the lynching now made the accused men any less culpable for the chief's death. Nor did anyone wonder aloud how Charles Traina, Loretto Comitz, Frank Romero, Jim Caruso, or Rocco Gerasi could have been aided by jury tamperers, considering that they were shot to death before their cases reached court.

Amid the growing din of accusations and recriminations, someone finally bothered to talk to Billy O'Connor and Officer Roe. In light of Seligman's comments about their absence from the state's case, a reporter wanted to know why the two lawmen nearest to the attack on the chief had not testified. O'Connor refused to be interviewed, saying he was Hennessy's friend then and he was Hennessy's friend still, even though the chief was dead. Go ask Luzenberg why he didn't call me, said O'Connor.

Officer Roe was congenial, but no more helpful. The Boylan agency officer said he had not even been summoned as a witness. Everything he knew about the case had already been published. "The state probably forgot me altogether," said Roe, part of whose ear was missing as a result of the ambush.

☾

Twenty-Six

BLOODY LENT

JOHN L. SULLIVAN WAS IN TEXAS. HE APPROVED OF THE LYNCHING,
but was unhappy. He sent $250 to the Hennessy monument fund. "He was
my friend and they have buried him in one of those ovens in the cemetery,"
the Champ complained. "I want him to have a decent grave and a tombstone."

The dead could not defend themselves. With so few of the living able or
willing to tell the truth, reputations were split like kindling. New York detectives again claimed credit for the Esposito capture, riling Thomas Boylan.
Joe Macheca was denied credit for saving General Badger by an anonymous
source, who said that Macheca's company of Innocents would have bayo-
neted the stricken soldier if it weren't for the chivalry of White Leaguer Douglas Kilpatrick.

There was still no sign of Dominick O'Malley. Hooligans smashed his
wife's flowerpots and uprooted her garden; their two dogs were poisoned. The
detective was scheduled to pursue a libel suit against the *States* in court on
Monday morning following the lynching, but never appeared. Under the circumstances, the judge gave his lawyer a continuance.

Meanwhile, O'Malley's past troubles with the law were dug up by the papers. Two Cleveland detectives said they remembered him as a boy sneak thief
from a tough waterfront neighborhood. In 1875 young O'Malley had been
sentenced to the workhouse for stealing a load of iron. Fifteen years later, in
November 1890, O'Malley returned to Cleveland to persuade Judge Martin
Foran to make a character statement for him. Taking the iron was a boyish
prank, O'Malley told the judge. He and a friend used the iron as ballast for a
boat they used to raid a vineyard. Judge Foran remembered such an incident
and agreed to look into it. When Foran pulled the court record, however, he

found that O'Malley was sentenced in January when the lake was frozen solid and the vineyards were bare. Skating that winter was said to be "excellent."

New Orleans is calm, Consul Corte cabled to Rome. Corte wrote that none of the lynchers were arrested yet, but he hoped it would happen that very day.

Marquis Rudini, Italy's grandly whiskered premier, read the dispatch and instantly cabled Baron Fava in Washington, informing Fava that the murderers *would* be arrested that day. Rudini instructed Fava to present a demand of indemnities and asked that official notification of the mob leaders' arrests be made by the U.S. government. The premier expected the indemnity claim to be accepted "without hesitation."

Adjusting his pince-nez, Fava studied Rudini's cable and quickly drafted a reply. Secretary of State Blaine would be advising President Harrison on the matter within hours, he said. Blaine was requesting full details about the occupations of the three dead Italian subjects and the condition of their families. Fava said he expected this would take Consul Corte at least a week to accomplish. Meanwhile, Fava noted, Blaine was complaining that the U.S. Constitution made the federal government responsible to foreign governments even though it had no power in individual states, like Louisiana.

Mascot columnist Frank Waters was disgusted by the lynching, but his feelings were colored by the fact that attorney Arthur Dunn was one of the prosecutors. Dunn had been close to Joe Baker, the state assessor Waters had killed several years before in self-defense. Kate, Frank's wife, silently endured Mrs. Dunn's insults in public for some time, and she finally told Frank. The usually lighthearted reporter began to drink more than usual and grew morose.

"I've had word that Dunn means to kill me this week, in the dark," he said.

Kate Waters was used to Frank laughing and telling her such rumors were nothing. Now she was terrified.

The threat weighed upon Waters's mind, but he continued his work at the *Mascot*, finishing a tattle in which a husband yanked his wife's false teeth from her mouth to end her insistence on accompanying him to a stag party. Waters turned the gossip into a cheeky meditation upon the role of honesty in marriage. "There are many little things that a man tells his wife and she doubts the truth of," he wrote. "It often happens that a public spirited citizen has an engagement with gentlemen friends to kill an Italian or set fire to a house or initiate a friend into the lodge, but he cannot persuade his dear tootsie-wootsie to believe that there is nothing else on his mind."

Waters spent his second wedding anniversary with a butcher chum. They started with plain seltzer in the afternoon, but beer followed, and by dinnertime they were drunk in the Gem Saloon. They were into their third bottle of champagne when Waters saw Recorder David Hollander and Captain F. L. Crosby of the British steamship *Storm King* having dinner at a nearby table. The writer offered them a glass, which they eventually accepted. Waters brought up the lynching, saying the affair was outrageous.

"This is no place for such a statement," Hollander warned, trying to calm Waters. Hollander tried to give his opinion, but Waters would not listen to any defense of the sons of bitches who led the mob. "I'd face any goddamned one of the curs!"

"Perhaps you'd better not use such language in the presence of a lady," Hollander advised, alerting Waters to a couple dining behind him. When the couple got up to leave, Waters stood and apologized to them.

Just then, Dennis Corcoran walked past the table, and Hollander offered him a glass of wine. Corcoran said he wasn't drinking, but he sat down.

"How many dagos did you hang last Saturday, Corcoran?" Waters asked with a heavy breath.

Corcoran's lips tightened as Waters kept it up. "I'm going to Washington to prosecute everyone who took part in the lynching," he announced, then started condemning Parkerson, Houston, and Wickliffe.

"Judge, you'd better withdraw," Corcoran whispered to Hollander, rising to move to another table. "There might be trouble."

Waters offered Hollander and Captain Crosby another glass, but they refused and paid for their meal. Following them out the door, Waters needled Hollander about the lynching all the way to Canal Street. Frank Waters was drunk as a lord, and it was only seven o'clock.

At a quarter to eleven, Waters leaned into former policeman Scott Wells's face at the corner of Canal and Bourbon. The writer was soused, but calm. Recognizing a local judge, Waters stopped and shook hands with him. While they spoke, Arthur Dunn appeared nearby, talking with friends, and Waters was not so drunk as to miss his enemy.

Suddenly Waters was alone. The judge was walking away, and Wells was going off to Kuntz's saloon with the sheriff of Iberia Parish. Waters saw Dunn crossing Canal Street, heading toward a streetcar.

"Jim Houston is a son of a bitch and I can lick him or any of his friends," Waters yelled when Dunn was twenty feet away.

"Come on then!" Dunn hollered back, flinging down his overcoat and cane. He drew his pistol and started toward Waters with the gun held flush against his leg. Waters fumbled for his revolver.

The lights of Canal Street reeled in Waters's drunken aim. His first shot went wild and nicked the leg of a racetrack programmer standing at a cigar stand. But bullets found Dunn, hitting the lawyer in the chest and hip and bruising his fingers. Waters retreated as he shot, backing into Cluverin's drugstore.

Dunn fired, spattering granite dust from the drugstore's pillar and gashing the brass nameplate. A slug slit Waters's cheek and stopped in his head. Another bullet destroyed his mouth. Waters staggered back over the drugstore step as he and Dunn snapped their empty pistols at each other. Dunn raised his empty revolver and smashed Waters's head so hard that the gun broke into pieces. Waters fell by the drugstore counter.

"I'm hit," Dunn said, limping outside. "Get me a hack."

The police ran in to find Waters gasping for breath with an empty six-shot Colt inches from his hand.

Arrested and sent to an operating room, Dunn was not talkative on the way. "He was looking for it and he got it," he grunted.

The cop watching Waters bleed all over the cab as it raced toward Charity Hospital rapped on the roof. The cab slowed down, then turned toward the Central Station, where the coroner came in the morning.

Intimate friends of Mr. Ben Onorato, who to-day is a lunatic, have, ever since his mind became affected, asserted that it was caused by the Mafia. It is asserted that Mr. Onorato, who was a fruit auctioneer and did a large furniture business, was drawn upon weekly by the society, and threatened to pay over. So frightened did he become that he lost his mind and is in constant dread of assassination.

—Times-Democrat, March 19

Thomas C. Collins, ostracized by his friends for working for O'Malley's detective agency, revealed to the surprise of the grand jury that he was actually a police officer employed by the city.

Collins's former boss Dominick O'Malley seemed to be popping up everywhere. According to one report, O'Malley gave an interview in a Memphis hotel. Another said the detective was hiding in the U.S. Army barracks in New Orleans. Apparently he was in Cleveland too, and Cincinnati, Mobile, Biloxi—minus his mustache—and in Chicago with Jacob Seligman. In reality, Seligman never left New Orleans. Smiling nervously, the foreman of the Hennessy murder trial jury testified before the grand jury investigating the lynching and accusations of jury tampering.

Seligman angrily disputed fellow juror Mackesy's post-lynching contention that "the old men were influenced by the younger ones." Seligman pointed out that these new statements differed from the reasoning Mackesy gave the press just after the verdict was delivered. Seligman said he did not recall saying any of the "cruel and unworthy" things about Hennessy attributed to him, but maintained that even if he had, it would not have prevented him from voting guilty if the state had proven its case. He also dismissed the Nobles affidavit, paying it "no more attention than did the district attorney." Seligman said he asked Luzenberg to tell the public that his brother had desperately tried to get him off the jury when the affidavit first surfaced. Such reticence, he said, hardly reflected a man itching to serve on a jury in return for a bribe.

Judges have the luxury of erring and being reversed, Seligman wrote bitterly in a letter printed by the *Daily City Item*. "A juryman, left to his own resources within the dismal walls of a quasi-prison, remembering his oath, his duty to the state and to the accused, renders a verdict according to the dictates of his conscience, and forthwith he is branded as a wretch, whom the gold of assassins has corrupted; his life is threatened before he is heard, and, fearing violence, he is forced to undergo additional hardships. This is the recompense he receives for serving his country."

Jacob Seligman could have added that he and two of the other jurors were fired from their jobs after the lynching. He had no intention of fleeing, although he was afraid and admitted that the thought had crossed his mind. "Despite the agony I have suffered, despite the vituperation heaped upon me, I would not change my verdict unless the evidence was stronger, for I prefer to suffer these than the torture of the thought of having sent a fellow being to an untimely grave when in my soul and before God I believed him to be innocent of the crime charged."

Popular support from around the country and the world was flowing in to buoy the tense men who stormed the parish prison. Although the grand jury was still in session, emotional support of the vigilantes was evident from California to London. The only New Orleans newspaper to criticize the lynching was the *Mascot*, which hit the streets Saturday, the day after the killings at the prison. Its editors felt the verdict and jury system abuses were outrageous, but derided the mob's leadership and reserved opinion about the "most terrible outbreak of Lynch Law ever witnessed in New Orleans." So far, 1891 had been a disaster for the city. It had been THE BLOODIEST CARNIVAL AND LENT IN THE HISTORY OF LOUISIANA, said the *Mascot*, which was not alone in pointing out that astrologers were claiming to have predicted a season of rage.

One week after the parish prison incident, all of the remaining defendants in the Hennessy case were free. The Italian community, however, was scared, and so were the jurors, who kept wishing aloud that the grand jury would hurry and find no evidence of tampering. Relations between Rome and Washington were tense as Baron Fava waited, William Parkerson was a hero, and Dominick O'Malley had evaporated from the face of the earth.

The ghosts of Antonio Bagnetto and Emmanuele Polizzi were said to be seen haunting Congo Square, the old slave dance ground near the prison.

Nine days after receiving Secretary of State Blaine's alarmed telegram, Governor Nicholls made public his full reply to the federal government. The governor simply told Blaine that the trouble was over and a grand jury was investigating the incident. This was too little for the *Daily States*, which spat red-white-and-blue vitriol at anyone who questioned the wisdom of the lynching. According to the newspaper, the governor had thrown away a perfect opportunity to defend the people of New Orleans, "whose good name and reputation for peace, justice, humanity, and honor have been so grossly assailed by the Italian government, its Minister at Washington, the Italian colonies in this country, and by the American Secretary of State."

Police informer Thomas Collins was rumored to be telling grand jurors the complete details of O'Malley's jury bribery plot. The only thing the tight-lipped grand jury would release, however, was a message exonerating District Attorney Luzenberg for not expelling Seligman from the jury. One factual revelation emerged in the thickening haze of gossip. "Antonio Ruggiero," the counterfeiter arrested in Amite in January, was an Italian American Pinkerton agent named Frank Dimaio, placed in the prison to become intimate with the prisoners. New Orleans waited to hear what Dimaio had learned from the Italians—especially Polizzi.

Baron Fava's patience with Americans was wearing thin. The slaughter in New Orleans was a travesty of international law, he said, and the Italian government was not interested in legalisms about the division of federal and state governments. On Rome's orders, Fava sent Secretary of State Blaine numerous notes explaining the need for the American government to make a positive sign to alleviate some of the clamor of public opinion in Italy. Fava finally pressed the short-tempered Blaine too far.

"It is absolutely impossible for the federal government to interfere with the administration of justice in a single state," Blaine told the Italian ambassador. "I am astonished after your ten years' residence in this country you have not succeeded in impressing upon your government this fact."

Stunned by this personal blast, the baron replied, "I have no reason to reproach myself and you know it. Neither my government, however, nor any other country will be convinced that your internal laws are an obstacle in the way of justice." Revealing that he would be recalled by Premier Rudini if the

Americans failed to act, Fava asked Blaine to convince President Harrison that good relations between the two countries should not hinge on Governor Nicholls's willfulness.

The two diplomats parted, agreeing to say nothing of Rudini's recall threat. Secretary Blaine promised he would contact Baron Fava that evening after dining with the president. He did not keep his word. The next time the Italian ambassador called on the secretary of state, Blaine came out swinging.

"I do not recognize the right of any government to tell the United States what it should do," blustered the American. "We have never received orders from any foreign government and we will not now begin. Please inform Marquis di Rudini that the federal government cannot give the assurances which he requires, and that it is a matter of total indifference to me what persons in Italy may think of our institutions. I cannot change them, much less violate them."

Baron Fava was astonished, but he held his temper.

"The fact is Marquis di Rudini does not give us sufficient time," Blaine complained. "You assure me that four Italian subjects have been massacred, but I have my doubts on that point, as I am informed they were mixed up in some scandalous electoral transactions. Still I don't contest their nationality, but while I ask for time, you want an official declaration on the spot. Well, I will not do anything of the kind and you may do as you please."

"The Italian government does not intend to interfere in the internal affairs of the United States," Baron Fava said stiffly. "Marquis di Rudini does not intend to give any orders to the United States government. The Italian government does not intend to discuss the Constitution of the United States. We ignore the existence of the State of Louisiana so that we might recognize the federal government, with which the treaty was negotiated."

"But that treaty guarantees to Italian subjects the same protection guaranteed to American citizens," Blaine retorted. "Do you ask that your countryman shall have more protection than ours have?"

"Your government is entitled to demand for Italians in America the same protection as is guaranteed to Americans in Italy."

Fava remained in Washington, losing hope that the Americans would redress the New Orleans atrocity. On March 27, another cable arrived from Rome:

> *Ask the federal government to guarantee that the culprits shall be tried and to admit that an indemnity is due to the families of these victims. If these just demands are not granted, give notice that you are going away on a leave of absence from a country where the legitimate actions of the King's representative had proved ineffective.*
> *Rudini*

"Write down the following declaration and submit it to your government," Blaine told Fava, who had informed him of the prime minister's request. Blaine acknowledged a full obligation of American reparations if its treaties with Italy had been violated. The final item he dictated, however, was the sticking point. "As yet no full examination of the case has been made and the law officers of the federal government have not arrived at any decision."

This was too ambiguous for Fava, who suggested a promise of reparations to be arranged when federal law officers finished their inquiry. Blaine refused, explaining that President Harrison agreed that the guilty should be punished, but there would be no such declaration before the investigation was complete. Fed up, Fava cabled Rome on March 31 that he was coming home.

News of Fava's recall flashed through Washington, fueling talk of war. Amid rumors of orders being sent from Rome to Italy's navy, the American press appraised the strength of Italy's substantial fleet. With only one battleship in the entire American navy, the Atlantic seaboard was woefully unprotected, and U.S. Navy officers whose warnings had been rebuffed by a cost-conscious Congress literally said, "I told you so."

Most of the American press interpreted Fava's departure as a purely diplomatic move, a technical tick meant to express Italy's dissatisfaction with Washington's refusal to give assurances about what would happen next in New Orleans. Yet as the days passed, the war scare flushed cheeks with indignation in both countries. Experienced international diplomats agreed that they had never seen anything like it.

☽

Twenty-Seven

AN ASTOUNDING CONFESSION

ON APRIL 1, NEWSPAPERMEN RUSHED TO A NEW ORLEANS street corner where Dominick O'Malley was reportedly hanging by his neck. When they arrived, they found a stuffed dummy swinging from a street lamp. Pranksters laughed at the April fools.

The genuine article surrendered two days later, and after posting $1,000 bond for each of three charges against him, O'Malley stopped at LaMothe's poolroom, went for a haircut, and then walked home. Reporters trotted along as O'Malley declined interviews, promising, however, to give his side of the story soon enough. What about Collins's rumored grand jury testimony about jury bribery? O'Malley would only say that if Collins was tipping off the city about bribes and tampering during the trial, it was strange that none of this inside information was used to prevent allegedly "fixed" parties from appearing as witnesses or sitting on the jury.

O'Malley, who was in a good mood, said that the dead men were innocent. He had interviewed them all, and only Polizzi did not tell the truth. O'Malley insisted that he never would have taken the case at all because of his strained relationship with the dead chief, but the Committee of Fifty's arrogant letter demanding that he keep completely out of the "Italian vendetta cases" prodded him into it.

A week later, he was charged with perjury and bribery. O'Malley and Thomas McCrystol were arraigned together for attempting to bribe one juror; they pleaded not guilty as members of Parkerson's Committee of Safety glowered beyond the bar.

. . .

As Baron Fava crossed the Atlantic, he was accused of faulty translation. Prime Minister Rudini sent a cable to Secretary of State Blaine saying that of course Italy did not expect the lynchers to be punished without due process under the law. All Italy wanted was a *promise* that justice would be done and that reparations promised by the U.S. government would be made to the dead men's families.

Blaine, whose peevish silence was tightened by a spell of the gout, released a steely but detailed reply to the Italian government that quoted the recall note Fava had translated and given him, which *demanded* punishment of the mob and reparations. From now on, Blaine said the State Department would have its own translators inspect diplomatic cables. Blaine also pointed out that while the U.S. government accepted the principle of indemnity if treaties had been violated, he had promised nothing. The indemnity issue would be addressed after authorities in New Orleans settled the question of the dead men's citizenship. Blaine did not tell the Italians, but New Orleans–based U.S. district attorney William Grant was having difficulty figuring out the nationalities of the dead.

As April dragged on with no word from the grand jury, the press entertained the public with tales of the Sicilian Mafia and versions of Polizzi's "confession." The fable of the mutilation of "Reverend Dr. John Forester Rose" returned, as did the New Orleans murders of Labruzzo, Ottumvo, and the cuckolded Mattiani, all of whom were now classified as victims of the secret society that did in Dave Hennessy. Hints were dropped about Dave's claim to know who killed his cousin Mike.

All the New Orleans papers described the lynching in detail, but omitted the identities of the men who did the actual killing, out of fear of vengeance, of the grand jury, and of the federal government. No one examined the irony of *Harper's Weekly*, "Journal of Civilization," reporting that to Sicilians, "the code of 'Omerta' says, 'Evidence is good so long as it does not injure your neighbor.'" Fresh accounts of Secretary Blaine's short-tempered exchanges with Italy lifted the spirits of the mob leaders.

The Hennessy trial jurors went before the grand jury, eager to talk. Mackesy, the grouchy juror who had accused others in the jury room of "being fixed before you got in here," could not be found. Friends said that he had accepted a job as a bookkeeper in Nicaragua, but would return if the grand jury sent for him.

Eventually, U.S. District Attorney Grant completed his investigation, providing background sketches of the dead men that contained the facts the State Department needed to face the Italians. Grant concluded that after all naturalization declarations were taken into consideration, only Traina, Comitz, and Monasterio could be considered King Umberto's subjects. The rest were either naturalized U.S. citizens, natives, or registered voters. Marchesi and Scaffidi had registered to vote on October 3, a couple of weeks before Hennessy's death.

Grant found that Bagnetto had been a sailor, and the Italian consul testified to Bagnetto's and Monasterio's good characters. Grant also learned from Corte that Geraci had killed a man but fled Palermo before he could be arrested, and had been sentenced to ten years' imprisonment in absentia. Comitz was an escaped thief. Polizzi was reported to have been "an unruly character" in Italy and cut a person with a knife in Austin, Texas, before coming to New Orleans. He was the only defendant who had acted unlawfully in the United States.

Although the bribery indictments stood, Grant was not allowed to see any grand jury evidence. On his own, he found nothing to connect the dead men with any bribery of the jury. "I am unable to obtain any evidence connecting these persons with the Mafia, or any other association of a similar character in the city," continued Grant, declining to judge those accused of killing Hennessy. "The evidence is voluminous. Both as a whole and in detail it is exceedingly unsatisfactory, and is not, to my mind, conclusive one way or the other."

When Grant's confidential report reached Washington on April 28, it was conveyed to Secretary Blaine and President Harrison, both of whom stayed mum. Harrison's and Blaine's camps both had their eyes on the White House in the next election and began to wonder aloud if maneuvers were under way to grab credit for settling the flap with Italy. A settlement was expected any day.

While William Parkerson was speaking at a Confederate Veterans Memorial Day ceremony, Italy was shaken by May Day riots. American tourist William Jacques was riding down a Florence street with his daughter when they rolled into the midst of a street battle. Before their driver could escape, stones rained on the carriage. Jacques dove to the floor, trying to protect his little girl from shards of window glass with the help of his umbrella, which was quickly ripped into tatters. A brick struck Jacques's daughter above the temple. The carriage broke free as the girl's blood flowed, soaking her father's suit and his passport, signed by James G. Blaine, requesting safe passage.

An English doctor in Jacques's rooming house who treated the child said she had narrowly escaped death. Somewhat relieved, Jacques asked what the crowd was yelling before the stones flew. "Americans," his driver answered. "Let's lynch them."

As the scarred girl recovered, Jacques was visited by many Florentines who assured him that Socialists or anarchist demonstrators from out of town were responsible. With his driver's translation ringing in his ears, Jacques thanked them without believing a word.

The lynching was still fresh news in America too. A troublemaking *padrone* near Wampum, Pennsylvania, floated a rumor that one thousand Italians were banding together to attack New Orleans. "They want blood," reported the *New York Times*. An Italian laborer declared in a saloon that "those dagos got what they deserved." Someone stabbed him in the back. He blamed the Mafia.

David Hennessy's financial interest in the Boylan Detective Agency expired on May 1, 1891. An attorney was working out a settlement with Boylan for Hennessy's mother, who said she was so pleased with the way Davey's partner was looking after her. Boylan and the rest of New Orleans got a jolt when they picked up their morning papers and read who else was looking after Margaret Hennessy.

According to a story in the *Times-Democrat*, Mrs. Hennessy had been invited to the home of one of her dead son's tenants. Two gentlemen were there. One was a detective, who presented her with deeds to two pieces of her son's property. This was a pleasant surprise, she said, as Dave had always looked after her affairs and while his friends were faultlessly polite, none had ever offered her any advice after his death. The detective promised to look into the matter of a third piece of property uptown, which sounded right to her. Her son had spoken of buying land there. Only when the conversation was over did she learn that she had been talking to Dominick O'Malley and Lionel Adams. If they could help to sort out her affairs, she would be very grateful.

Mrs. Hennessy also told the *Times-Democrat* that former Chief Boylan, Captain O'Connor, and her son's other close friends visited her after Dave's death and requested to see his jewelry box. She said that until then she hadn't the heart to look at it. She watched as they inventoried the stickpins, chains, and rings, and when Boylan picked up a lady's brooch, Mrs. Hennessy leaned forward and held it herself. The brooch was as beautiful as anything she'd ever seen, she said, with twenty-five glistening diamonds. She handed it back to Boylan, who took the entire box for safekeeping with her grateful consent.

When she called at the Boylan agency later to retrieve the box, Mrs. Hennessy said the brooch was missing. She didn't mean to cast doubts on Boylan, who was, after all, so kind to her. And though she had heard that a diamond necklace was given to a young lady to whom her son was said to be paying attention, which she knew nothing about, she was positive about the missing brooch.

Boylan declined to be interviewed on the advice of his agency's attorney, George Denegre, whose story differed from Mrs. Hennessy's. Denegre had handled the succession of Hennessy's estate to his mother: a piece of real estate on Canal, a house on Rampart, an interest in the Boylan agency, some office furniture, and "a little jewelry in a bank box." A month ago, Denegre said he had stopped to see how Mrs. Hennessy was doing and she told him of the jewels. She heard that a Mollie Green had left Dave some diamonds, and Denegre replied that Green's heirs in Chicago had contacted him a year ago, when the chief was still alive. Green's lawyers implied they could get no information from the chief, so Denegre said he asked Dave Hennessy about the diamonds. The chief replied that all of Mollie Green's jewelry had been given to the administrator of her estate. Denegre said he told Mrs. Hennessy that he was sure the diamonds did not exist—he had her son's word. Even if the jewels did exist, they belonged to Mollie Green's heirs. Mrs. Hennessy declared herself satisfied. Now there was still this O'Malley matter. Denegre pointed out that anyone in New Orleans could have done what O'Malley did, which was to copy notarial acts and hand them to the chief's mother. The originals were still filed at the Boylan office.

Lionel Adams refused interviews. The newspapers decided that the jewelry did not exist and declared that the elderly woman's mind was unsettled by her suffering.

The steamship *Plata* lay at anchor off Algiers Point as Marine Hospital surgeons and customs inspectors examined 363 Italian immigrants aboard. Under a brand new federal immigration law approved on March 31, it would be the most rigorous examination the port of New Orleans had seen. Any "idiots, insane persons, paupers or persons likely to become a public charge, [or] persons suffering from a loathsome or a dangerous contagious disease" would be denied entry. So would convicted felons, anyone convicted of a crime or misdemeanor involving "moral turpitude," and those whose tickets were paid for by others.

The immigrants aboard were found to be mostly in good health and cleanly dressed in spite of their long voyage. They walked down the gangplank to begin life in a fearful community, soon to learn the fate of Marchesi and Monasterio who had once slept in the same dank holds of the *Plata* before them.

Meanwhile, an American reporter had found Monasterio's family in Caccamo. The shoemaker's brother, a priest, said that their Pietro was a good man, an educated man who wrote poetry. The priest said the family was destitute and asked if the reporter had any money.

On Tuesday, May 5, 1891, seven weeks after the lynching and over a month after the collapse of U.S. relations with Italy, the grand jury report landed with a dull thud of certainty.

The grand jury was certain that the state had proved its case in the Hennessy trial far beyond any doubt. "Startling" verdicts, coupled with an investigation of tampering, led the grand jury to assume that three members of the jury had indeed been bribed, yet no names were given nor were any of the Hennessy jurors recommended for indictment.

Grand jurors were certain that jury fixing and lack of secrecy were unfortunate facts of life in New Orleans courts. Talesmen in this case were approached during jury selection with comments that "big money might be made by going on the jury and doing right." The comments were always made privately, and if a man rejected the suggestion angrily, the approach was dismissed as a joke, "but surely a well directed one of deep significance" when it came from counsel for the defense, said the report.

Adams and O'Malley were accused of acquiring the list of five hundred talesmen midway through jury selection, in spite of Judge Baker's instructions to keep the list a secret. With the help of "influential friends," O'Malley got the lists of potential jurors as soon as they were drawn, even before the district attorney's office got a copy. The lists were checked against a list in Adams's office, then tampered with. An unnamed jury commissioner delivered the lists to the district attorney's office, stating they were prepared "elsewhere." The lists containing names selected by O'Malley and Adams were then dumped into the lottery wheel. "Truly the business of this enterprising detective agency was facilitated, when 32 names of their selection could be drawn on a panel of 300 jurors from a wheel containing 1000 names," the grand jury report said. Special Officer Collins, O'Malley's supposed employee, was praised for securing most of this information while working undercover.

The grand jury offered no evidence to support these charges, claiming that the secrecy with which talk instead of deeds had corrupted the process created an insurmountable difficulty in securing hard evidence. Nevertheless, it was declared that there was sufficient evidence to justify indicting six men. McCrystol, Cooney, and O'Malley were already indicted. Three other men—Bernard Glaudi, Charles Granger, and Fernand Armant—were accused of bribery attempts.

O'Malley, "the archconspirator," allegedly also sent Collins to the Electric Light Works with instructions for a worker to dim the Girod and Basin circuit before the jury arrived to see the crime scene for themselves, making the light "weak as it was on October 15." The record book for that night was changed to show forty more minutes of weak light than previously recorded.

The grand jury submitted a record of nine cases in which O'Malley had been charged and sometimes convicted of assault or carrying a concealed weapon. It noted two jury tampering charges, which were dropped by Adams during his earlier term as district attorney. Grand jurors, said the report, were "aghast" at the possibilities for corruption inherent in the business relationship between the lawyer and the detective. Unnamed ward politicians wanting power over the office of chief were allegedly behind O'Malley's actions, and this portion of the report concluded with charges that O'Malley visited Jacob Seligman's house during the lynching to warn him.

The grand jury described the Mafia with vague grandiosity, giving its own version of the society's bloody history. The Mafia was now broken and ready to be exterminated, said the report. The "good results" of allowing worthy immigrants into America were praised, but the next Congress was urged to enact even more vigorous entrance laws than the legislation that had just taken effect. "The time is passed when this country can be made the dumping ground for the worthless and depraved of every nation," said the report. Wasn't the success found by Italians in New Orleans worth the price of driving out secret assassination societies and swearing allegiance only to the Stars and Stripes?

As for the parish prison incident, the grand jury had a succinct definition. It was a popular uprising led by "the first, best, and most law-abiding" citizens of New Orleans, pushed into action by an extraordinary situation in which corruption made the law virtually powerless to right the atrocity of Chief Hennessy's murder. "In fact," concluded the report, the lynching "seemed to involve the entire people of the parish and City of New Orleans, so profuse is their sympathy and extended their connection with the affair." The grand jury would not indict the mob or its leaders.

What the grand jury charged but did not bother to explain to a presumably sympathetic public was that after state challenges and dismissals of obviously prejudiced talesmen in the Hennessy trial, the defense had used its allotted 108 peremptory challenges to whittle a select jury of its own choosing. Even if this was true, it was a lot of whittling.

Without publicly offering any proof whatsoever the grand jury accused Adams of stacking the jury with impressionable young talesmen and bought men. Adams allegedly managed this by not rigorously examining the potential jurors, which was a strange accusation. If anyone should have grilled the jurors for fear of tampering, it should have been the prosecution. No one accused the easily irritated Luzenberg of sleeping through the jury selection, nor did anyone seem to notice that the much-publicized "confession" of Polizzi was absent from the report.

State Department lawyers thought little of the report's attempt to excuse the lynching with unspecific allegations of jury fixing. The report might help keep troublesome elements in immigrant communities in line, but its pompous generalities would not please the Italian government. Yet if Washington could prove that the lynched men were Americans, Italy would have no grounds for demanding reparations. The grand jury declared that eight of the lynched men were American citizens; another had declared his intention to become a citizen, thus voiding his allegiance to his native country.

This left two dead Italians. The governments began to fight over the bodies.

When the grand jury report was released, American newspapers repeated their initial approval or condemnation of the lynching. To some, it proved the evils of unrestricted immigration. To others, the idea of a New Orleans criminal justice system so bankrupt that it could be ruled by O'Malley's detective agency on one hand and a mob on the other suggested that anarchy reigned in the Crescent City. The *Albany Express* called the report "an astounding confession of imbecility."

"This is not a legal document," wrote the New York *Post*. "It is the apology of a political committee for an act of revolutionary violence committed by the entire population of a large city and expressed in the inflated rhetoric in which such manifestos are usually couched. It is a confession by a competent authority that the machinery of criminal justice has completely broken down in the State of Louisiana and that crimes of any magnitude have to be punished by a revolutionary tribunal." Nevertheless, the *Post* concluded that other cities would do well to mark the shameful decline of New Orleans so that the "desperate necessity" of mob justice would not be repeated elsewhere.

The Italian American press was uniformly disgusted, but not surprised.

Consul Corte refused to speak publicly about the report, the conduct of the grand jury, or the lynching.

Corte would, however, say that the grand jury summoned him as a witness and had accepted only the portions of his testimony that suited its own ends, ignoring his belief that good men were among the dead. He admitted that two of the men were "criminals in a measure." Comitz had robbed a man at age seventeen and then fled Italy. Under Italian law, he was tried and sentenced for the crime in absentia. So was Geraci, who had once killed a man, although Geraci's brother swore that the killing was in self-defense.

Corte noted that Macheca and Romero were clearly Americans. Monasterio, Traina, and Antonio Grimando (Marchesi) were Italians. The rest had declared their intentions to become American citizens and could even have voted had they chosen to, but Corte said he did not believe that the men had fulfilled legal citizenship requirements. As far as he was concerned, they were Italian subjects when they died.

Corte dismissed the idea that no indictments could be made because of the size of the crowd around the prison. No more than twenty men took part in hanging Polizzi. The rest were curiosity seekers and boys. The consul also had a question—what was police officer Edward Hevron doing inside the walls of the prison when he was wounded if he was not doing his duty?

☽

Twenty-Eight

WAR OF WORDS

THE MOST SOUGHT-AFTER MAN IN NEW ORLEANS WROTE THE story of his life for everyone to read. He began with his humble arrival from Ohio and his first job on the docks of New Orleans as a common roustabout. It was there that he took his first job as a detective, a vocation at which he was so successful that he decided to better himself by working as a private investigator for attorneys. This blossomed into a career that was the envy of every detective in town. It was then, wrote Dominick O'Malley, that his troubles began.

O'Malley's saga of his early triumphs lacked only the odd detail. He boasted of his spectacular record of seizures for the IRS, for example, but omitted his own arrest. According to O'Malley, his real trouble began when petty jealousy over his success caused a city detective to arrest him for being a suspicious character. When O'Malley was acquitted, he was arrested again, this time for vagrancy. Once acquitted, his friends told him to strike back. O'Malley wrote to a grand jury, offering his services gratis to rid the Canal-Front Street levee of barrelhouse gambling taking place under the nose of chief of police Thomas Boylan. O'Malley said he announced that he would prove that the gamblers and police were in cahoots. Chief Boylan had him locked up again, this time swearing to have the troublesome detective locked up for good or run out of town. O'Malley said that Mike Hennessy and another detective swore in court that he was a bad and dangerous man; Chief Boylan testified that he only knew what his detectives told him. Mayor Shakspeare revoked O'Malley's license, but he was acquitted and his license was restored. Regular harassment arrests began, including a blatant setup on a concealed weapons charge. O'Malley said he finally had his pockets sewed shut so that nothing could be planted on him.

In June of 1881 when foulmouthed Mike Hennessy waved a pistol in his face in public, O'Malley merely folded his arms. Hennessy was fined by the court, which put the fat in the fire, O'Malley wrote. Blood being thicker than water, Dave Hennessy took his cousin's side in the matter and began to dislike O'Malley, toward whom he previously had been friendly. When Devereaux was killed, things worsened when the incarcerated Hennessys found out O'Malley was saying that Devereaux's death robbed him of a good friend. O'Malley had no idea how bitter Dave was until he became chief of police.

Friends made efforts to heal the breach between O'Malley and Hennessy over the years, and it seemed like the two would be reconciled, but something always stood in the way. Working for rival detective agencies prevented any peacemaking, even after Hennessy became chief, for Hennessy was still a partner in the Boylan agency when he died.

After the Esplanade ambush, O'Malley was employed by the Matrangas to expose their attackers. The detective wrote that Hennessy responded by hiring counsel to get a new trial for the Provenzanos, which was a serious charge, O'Malley admitted, but he could prove it if necessary. Charles Matranga's friends tried to convince him to fire O'Malley to avoid Hennessy's pique, but Matranga would not do it.

After the cruel and cowardly murder of the chief, O'Malley publicly asserted that the men accused of the crime were arrested solely to defeat the prosecution in the second Provenzano trial. The result spoke for itself, O'Malley said, as none of the men who escaped being butchered in the parish prison still faced charges. And in spite of garbled press stories about Chief Hennessy's correspondence with Italian law enforcement officials and the Provenzanos' foul attempts at slander after their retrial and release, no actual evidence was ever offered of the defendants' bad character, O'Malley argued. The existence of a Mafia or other organized society was not even hinted at in the Hennessy trial testimony. The press was responsible for such talk and the resulting public opinion.

There was more to question about the prosecution testimony. "The negroes Poole and Foster swore to improbabilities," O'Malley wrote, while Scott and Williams manufactured the laughable story about Gasperi Marchesi turning on his father, when the record showed that Gasperi had been released a day earlier than they claimed. Measure the long gun against any sack, he said, and see if Polizzi could have hidden it inside; consider the folly of throwing guns in gutters with the New Basin nearby; think of the suppression of O'Connor's, Roe's, and old Mrs. Petersen's testimonies; remember how the state itself contradicted those who swore that Monasterio fired and ran away. Put aside the public clamor, he said, and, giving every man the benefit of a reasonable doubt, any honest man would vote for acquittal.

It would have been preposterous for Joe Macheca to have gone into Hennessy's neighborhood, O'Malley continued. In broad daylight, to rent a shack owned by the wife of a Boylan officer, only a block from Hennessy's home? Police officer Dayton lived across the street from the shack and knew Macheca well. Macheca had accompanied the chief home and was well known in the neighborhood. Did it make sense? he asked. Besides, Hennessy and Macheca were reconciled, just forty-eight hours before the shack was rented. At the request of friends, they met at the home of Hennessy's Rampart Street tenant, Mrs. Daneel. After Macheca was imprisoned, the detective said, Macheca tried to learn if any of his codefendants were guilty.

O'Malley said he publicly offered his services to the city government after Hennessy's murder and was met with silence and contempt. Instead, Charles Matranga asked to see him, but O'Malley said he refused until he satisfied himself that the accused were innocent. He met with Matranga, but his poor relationship with the dead chief made him balk at taking the case. Then came the Committee of Fifty's bullying letter, then Sheriff Villere's ban, and police surveillance of the defense team. The defense struggled against fearful odds, he said.

O'Malley nevertheless knew plenty about the Committee of Fifty. His information came directly from YMDA attorney Walter Denegre, who opened up whenever one of O'Malley's friends baited the lawyer by vilifying the detective in Denegre's presence. O'Malley said he also knew all about the Pinkerton man in the prison and informed both the sheriff and the defendants about Dimaio even before his arrival.

After the lynching, O'Malley read the papers daily and laughed at his reported presence in half a dozen different states. The Memphis impostor was a good joke. The unjust slaughter in the prison, however, was no laughing matter, he wrote. Not a word spoken during the trial justified suspicions that the dead men were members of a Mafia or assassination society—and it was worth remembering that the Provenzanos had sailed to New York to testify on behalf of the bandit Esposito a decade ago.

O'Malley said he was an innocent man. He would deposit $1,000 in any bank of the Committee of Fifty's choice, allowing it to be paid to Charity Hospital or the almshouse in the event that satisfactory proof was produced to prove the foolish bribery allegations. With this offer, Dominick O'Malley signed his public letter of defense and delivered it to the *Times-Democrat*. The newspaper printed it all on May 7, devoting nearly a full page to the detective's story, but not before contacting Walter Denegre and Thomas Boylan.

The letter was a typical O'Malley performance: proud, unintimidated, self-righteous, contemptuous, and sealed with a challenging wager. It was also composed with his habitually selective memory. O'Malley's declaration that Macheca was intimately known in Hennessy's neighborhood did not jibe with

Macheca's own protests that he was never in the area in his life. The reconciliation at Mrs. Daneel's place, the same home where O'Malley and Adams had recently met with Hennessy's mother, was never mentioned in Macheca's own defensive accounts of his relations with the late chief. Joe Provenzano and Tony Pellegrini were not the only New Orleans Italians to have sailed to New York to testify at the Esposito hearings. Matranga stevedore Rocco Geraci went too.

O'Malley did not mention Thomas Collins once, but Walter Denegre certainly did. The angry lawyer denied ever being a member of the Committee of Fifty and said he would have known through Collins if O'Malley was trying to get information from him. Denegre was being cagey about the committee, however, for his brother George—Boylan's attorney—was a member.

Thomas Boylan freely admitted then and now that gambling went on while he was chief. It was an open secret, he said, but back then he was often called before the grand jury, from which he concealed nothing. The former chief challenged any man to say that he ever received a dollar from the gamblers and praised Mayor Shakspeare for forcing the almshouse contributions from gamblers in lieu of licensing. Boylan said he recalled nothing of the grand jury letter O'Malley claimed to have written to offer his services, but he did recall having O'Malley arrested under a city ordinance and two judges testifying to O'Malley's bad character.

The second most sought-after man in New Orleans also put pen to paper. Jacob Seligman denied any bond between himself and O'Malley as suggested by the grand jury. The most important missive of the week, however, was not penned by an American.

"If, as it is publicly asserted, some members of the grand jury were in the mob and that body is trying to excuse their actions, it does not concern me personally," Consul Corte wrote icily. "But I cannot allow my statements to be altered or partially published with the aim of drawing inference contrary to my deductions."

Out of solidarity with New Orleans authorities, Italy's consul said he had openly told the grand jury that there were more than a few Italian criminals in the city, just as there were plenty of criminals of other nationalities. Corte felt it would be hard to get rid of the bad elements because "most of them are naturalized citizens who have the support of politicians or certain authorities or because extraditions are so costly in the United States." He cited the expense of the Esposito extradition and the heavy opposition to it by the American press. When Corte read what the grand jury made from this candid testimony, however, he felt betrayed. He said they had heard only what they wanted to hear.

The consul's words had the thunder of a man telling off willful liars. He assailed the "agreeable silence, the studied reticence, and other accompanying irregularities" around the lynching, which brought him to denounce the killings to his government. To Corte, it was a simple fact that "an extrajudicial body appointed by the Mayor from the beginning premeditated, as it appeared in its appeal, the killing of the prisoners; that the same body assembled on the night of the 13th of March to take, in cold blood, the necessary steps to kill, for political purposes, defenseless but fearful adversaries; that about twenty parties, among them some representing the law and order, executed said project.

"Innocent Italian blood was shed," Corte concluded. "Not only nothing was done by the authorities to prevent it, but a few officials contributed directly or indirectly in order to accomplish the work, and finally, the names of the participants in the killing, as well as those of the instigators, are of public notoriety."

True to his word, Corte sent this letter to the grand jury's foreman first, then released it to the press on Friday, May 8. The following Monday the grand jury announced publicly that it would not dignify the consul's letter with a response.

Corte was accused of "promiscuous blurtings" and making charges "based on the airiest of street rumors." The U.S. government was said to be demanding his recall, but the State Department snuffed that rumor with a dispatch saying that Corte had done nothing "in derogation of the majesty of the United States government," making those angered by the consul's letter hotter than ever. The tamest thing they could say was that Corte had outlived his usefulness in New Orleans.

While the attacks on Corte intensified, Europeans took a hard look at the way Americans honored their treaties. A Spanish diplomatic journal questioned the wisdom of making treaties with the United States. France considered pulling out of the 1893 Chicago World's Fair. Italian newspapers said that it would never again be possible for any civilized country to make a treaty with the United States based on reciprocal protection of the lives of its citizens. Washington smarted from such charges, and it appeared likely that Congress would examine the lynching to give other countries assurances that it signed such treaties in good faith.

Consul Corte did not begrudge the *Times-Democrat* its harsh editorials. He was, in fact, grateful to the paper for uncovering the parish prison scandal, and he said he didn't mind that they differed about the March 14 incident and its aftermath.

Allowing a *Times-Democrat* reporter into his office as he cleared his desk of unfinished business, Corte said he was going to Rome to report on the lynching, but planned to return. His family would remain in New Orleans; no one was recalling him. Corte, who wanted no mistakes, spoke in French, a language in which he was more fluent than English.

Corte said he had proof that some of the lynched men were innocent and their families were now destitute. He could see no reason why he should be reproached for standing with his people as an Italian. For those who did not believe the Committee of Fifty's intentions were prejudiced, Corte quoted the circular asking the Italian colony's help in learning about the Mafia, promising that the innocent and guilty would suffer alike if the assassins were not uncovered. Corte said he knew the names of the men who took part in the killings in the prison and the role each played. Corte said Gasperi Marchesi had watched his father shot by four men, including Dennis Corcoran.

Weighing a bundle of 250 voter registration forms, the consul said that local politicians pressed the forms upon Italian laborers by promising it would make Americans sympathetic to them. Workers were ignorant of the fact that registering to vote was as good as renouncing Italian citizenship. Polizzi's American citizenship was being claimed on the basis of a signed voter registration form. Yet Polizzi and most of the other dead men could neither read nor write, Corte said. Carmello Larrozo, a professional letter writer for immigrants, had written many letters home for the illiterate Polizzi.

Corte's interview grew by the time it reached the pages of the *Times-Democrat* on May 13. The paper printed that Corte claimed to have saved the lives of the mayor, Wickliffe, Parkerson, and others by telling a dozen excited Italians not to pursue vengeance. Among those demanding revenge were several women who declared themselves willing to kill the mob leaders and dynamite the Pickwick Club with Mayor Shakspeare inside. Corte's infuriated visitors supposedly calmed down when he threatened to reveal their intentions to city authorities, in order to prevent a wholesale massacre of the Italian community, and when the vengeful talk subsided, he promised to look into the matter of indemnities for the dead men's families.

The *Times-Democrat* and the *States* published similar interviews quoting Corte as claiming to have saved Shakspeare and the others. The *Picayune* further reported that Jim Caruso's wife was among the angry women. As soon as the stories were printed, the grand jury dispatched a French-speaking delegation to the consulate to investigate. Their interview was kept a secret.

The Committee of Fifty's final report to the mayor, however, was released to the public verbatim. Drenched in language complimenting the "inevitable" lynching, the committee denied any connection with or advance knowledge of the events of March 14. According to the report, the committee's first mandate was to investigate secret, oathbound murder societies, of whose existence there was no doubt: Boylan, Badger, detective commander Leonard Malone, and Chief Gaster all agreed on this, as did Hennessy who knew more about it than anyone until he was killed. The Provenzanos and Matrangas were the city's two major factions, said the report, and each complained regularly to city authorities about the criminal activities of the other.

The committee declared that Hennessy had written to Rome's chief of police, L. Bertin, on August 12 to ask for the names, records, and photographs of Esposito's band. Chief Bertin responded that he would be happy to comply, but Hennessy shortly became aware that someone in New Orleans knew about the request, even though he told no one of it. Chief Bertin was murdered before he could send the information. Hennessy soon followed him to the grave. "After Hennessy's death and after the arrest of the guilty parties, there was found among his effects an anonymous letter, dated July 23, 1890, informing him that his life had been sworn away by the Mafia, and naming some of the men afterward concerned in his murder."

Inexplicably, the committee did not provide these names in its report nor did it note that the message was dated four days after the Provenzanos' conviction.

Peeved at Pasquale Corte, the committee stated that the consul had said he believed the Mafia was in New Orleans and promised to forward a report with the names of alleged Mafia leaders and over one hundred Italian criminals and fugitives suspected of being in the city. The committee now complained that Corte's promised report never came because the Italian legation in Washington suggested he not release such information.

The final mandate of the committee was to suggest remedies, which included a total ban on immigration from Sicily and "Lower Italy" modeled on the Chinese Exclusion Act. "We have had long experience with these people," the committee said. "There is no reason why they should be permitted to participate in the blessings of a freedom and civilization which they are not only unable to appreciate, but which they refuse to understand or accept."

The committee recommended legislative reforms of the jury system, including shorter duty terms, $2 pay per day, a minimum age of twenty-five, and barring anyone convicted of a crime or misdemeanor from serving. This would diminish the hardship on jurors and improve the quality of the juries, according to the committee's report. The law should be amended to make it a crime to approach a potential juror with a bribe, and Orleans Parish should join the rest of Louisiana in having Criminal District Court judges appoint jury commissioners in a nonpolitical fashion. In an unambiguous slam at Lionel Adams, the committee further suggested that the legislature recognize the existence of "a bar association with the power . . . to try, disbar, and revoke the license of any attorney whose evil practices render him unworthy to remain an officer of the court." The Committee of Fifty also suggested the city handle "dangerous" detective agencies under new municipal regulations.

Mayor Shakspeare and the city council accepted the report and formally discharged the Committee of Fifty with thanks and congratulations. As the council passed a motion to treat Corte's statements "with silent contempt," Shakspeare loudly announced that he would demand the consul's recall. As far as the city fathers of New Orleans were concerned, the lynching matter was closed.

The news reached Corte in New York, as he prepared to board the steamer taking him home. "No one ever came to me and threatened to kill Mayor Shakspeare and the men who led the citizens on the day of the outrage," Corte scoffed on the dock. "If anyone had made such threats in my hearing, I would have promptly denounced them to the city authorities." Gasperi Grimando, who had now formally shed the Marchesi name, accompanied the consul and acted out the killings for reporters, telling the story in heavily accented English. The boy and the diplomat were not the only Italians who had come to New York from New Orleans. Many Sicilians were leaving the city, saying they were afraid they couldn't get jobs and that they didn't like the way people looked at them.

In a final statement released when he was at sea, Corte unleashed a comprehensive attack on every indignity the Italian community in New Orleans had suffered: nocturnal visits, arrests, and searches of peaceable Italians by men claiming to be members of the Committee of Fifty; the inflammatory rhetoric of the committee's call to a mass meeting; and the parish prison scandal, which the mayor tried to hush up by telling Corte that the prisoners were fine. Seven criminal indictments against trusty Skip Mealey showed that things were not fine, but the committee did not like the idea of pressing charges, so the bully went unprosecuted.

It was at that time, Corte wrote, that the Committee of Fifty began to lose members. Shakspeare's claim that the assassins were locked up was belied by the fact that the mayor pressed ahead the request for reward money long after the defendants were arrested. The availability of that money was responsible for perjured testimony like Corcoran's impossible claims against Natali and Sunzeri.

"These statements failing of their purpose because the proof was weak, and the public beginning to see that there were mystifications in the Hennessy case, as well as the Provenzano case, recourse was had to a last expedient which was to affect the entire population." This, wrote the Consul, was the confession of Polizzi. "But when I learned that it was provoked by Chief Gaster, who sent Joe Provenzano to the concubine of Polizzi to induce her lover to make a confession, and when I learned that a prisoner with bad precedents was pardoned for having attempted to obtain a confession from him, to confirm the assertion of the mayor, said confession lost for me all its value.

"When I learned that Walter Denegre had offered Matranga's son-in-law $700, which he refused, to have the naturalized Italians vote for his party; when I heard from the Attorney General in the presence of four persons that Frank Romero was sacrificed by those whom he assisted in politics; when by

Mr. Michinard, a reporter of the *Times-Democrat,* I was formally assured that Peeler, one of the most important witnesses, was completely drunk at the time he said he saw the shooting and recognized the assassins, I understood that there was a great mystification, not on the part of the judicial authorities, but on the part of outsiders. But the public and myself at the time of the verdict ignored these details, and consequently the surprise created by the verdict was a natural."

Corte blamed the YMDA cabal for the lynching. He was extremely annoyed with the way the grand jury misrepresented him. Yet he knew that many Americans had voiced their disapproval of the lynching. The consul sailed for home hoping that Italy and the United States could settle their differences amicably.

As summer began, the incident lost some of its steam. No war had broken out. Diplomats and the New Orleans city fathers were the only ones still brawling. Feelings cooled elsewhere. Commenting on Corte's salvo at the grand jury, for example, the *New York Times* feared that "the exact facts as to the guilt or innocence of those sacrificed to popular wrath, so far as the Hennessy murder is concerned, will never be clearly ascertained." The *Times,* which once wrote with carefree certainty of "bandits" and "the bribed jury," lashed out at a Reformed Presbyterian minister from Pittsburgh for trying to toss labor unions into the same pot with the Mafia. "Whatever may be true as to the Mafia in New Orleans," said a June 3 editorial, "the 'investigation' by the grand jury, judged by its presentment, was a very shallow, prejudiced, and insufficient inquiry, while the conclusion it reached as to the murderers of the Italian prisoners was a willful evasion of duty."

The two nations relaxed, making the grand jury report look inflated and empty, a colorful sack of hot air launched to distract the people of New Orleans from a lack of hard facts and names. Those who doubted the report were left with a maddening mystery, which had thus far bloodied or tainted everyone who neared it. Only conviction of the accused jury bribers could now damn the Hennessy trial acquittals, providing the long-promised key to a still unproven conspiracy.

Twenty-Nine

THE JURY BRIBERS

IF, AS SOME PEOPLE SUSPECTED, THE PROVENZANOS HAD hoped to return to the docks by destroying the Matrangas in the Esplanade ambush or perhaps through a more Machiavellian strategy of assassinating their alleged friend Hennessy to throw suspicion on their enemies, the end result was the same as if they were the innocents they claimed to be.

The Provenzanos were no closer to working on the levee than they had been before the chief's murder. In the wake of Joe Macheca's lynching, the Macheca Brothers company was not going to invite them to unload fruit. Joe and Peter Provenzano, however, continued to harass Macheca stevedores on the Mandeville Street wharf and were arrested. Mayor Shakespeare's anger with the Provenzanos placed him in the bizarre position of defending the Machecas and Matrangas. "This thing must stop, now and for all time," he warned the Provenzanos in a public tongue-lashing. If they continued attacking the Matrangas, Shakspeare said, he would use "every means at my command to wipe from the face of the earth every member of your gang who tries to raise a hand against a person of this community."

The Provenzanos' stevedoring days were over.

"What is the position of the Mafia in New Orleans at the present time, Mr. Shakspeare?"

"They are quiet, quieter than they have been for years. The lesson taught them at the parish prison has had a most excellent effect and I do not anticipate we will have any more trouble with them," replied the mayor, on his way home from a Denver conference. Shakspeare announced that three hundred

Mafia members in New Orleans were slowly on their way out of town after their unforgettable warning.

"I have 20,000 good Italians to protect and intend to do it," Shakspeare declared. "They have for years been dominated over and blackmailed by this society of cut-throats and are more glad than any other class of citizens to be rid of them. You may announce that the reign of the Mafia in New Orleans has ceased."

When Dominick O'Malley was charged with unlawfully opening a letter addressed to prizefighter James Carroll, the touring lightweight said he knew nothing about it, but assumed the government had good reason for arresting the detective to whom he'd entrusted his mail. O'Malley was being indicted on every old and new charge imaginable, but he didn't mind. Also accused of tainting the judicial process were Fernand Armant, John Cooney, Thomas McCrystol, Bernard Glaudi, Charles Granger, and Emile Bagnetto. Tried separately, the men faced a battery of prosecutors paid from the city's $15,000 investigative fund, much of which remained unspent. Little of the money would be left when the trials were over.

Armant's case immediately stalled. The attorney who had defended Charles Patorno in the Hennessy trial now stood accused of attempting to bribe talesman Leonce Burthe, the son of a respected court clerk. Burthe's cousin Edgar White, a deputy sheriff and prison guard, was also arrested for allegedly trying to dissuade Burthe from testifying against Armant. White was so angry that he demanded to be tried immediately without a jury. That, responded the judge, would be improper. Burthe vanished, but was quickly arrested in St. Louis, panicky and broke, making it impossible for the state's cases against Armant or the furious White to proceed. One of two bribery counts against John Cooney evaporated when the state admitted it had mistakenly indicted Cooney instead of Emile Bagnetto because of a shaky description. The other charge was dropped when a talesman couldn't identify who had approached him. He had been told the man's name was Cooney, and for this, the grand jury had indicted Cooney.

Was New Orleans to be treated to a new cycle of judicial bumbling? The public had been assured that the trials of the accused jury bribers would prove beyond any doubt that a conspiracy had thwarted justice in the Hennessy trial and that cash, not the state's inadequate lawyering or the lynched men's innocence, had resulted in the lack of convictions. Again, New Orleanians would get little of what they were promised.

O'Malley and McCrystol asked for a change of venue, and to prove they could not get a fair trial in New Orleans, A. D. Henriques had Parkerson, Wickliffe, Houston, and over sixty other lynch notice signatories summoned. Henriques offered the Committee of Fifty's report and numerous anti-O'Malley newspaper editorials to the court. Parkerson took the stand and told Henriques he was not a member of the mayor's Committee of Fifty, but was involved with the self-appointed Committee of Safety.

"Were you in the neighborhood of the parish prison on March 14?" Henriques asked.

"I decline to answer."

"I do not desire to press such questions."

"Don't worry yourself," Parkerson retorted. There was laughter in the court.

"I am not worrying," Henriques said. "Were you near the Congo Square?"

"I decline to answer."

Parkerson granted that editorials condemning O'Malley were widely circulated. "I believe that in this case where these men are charged with attempting to bribe a tales juror, from my knowledge of the people, that the men can get a fair and impartial trial. I believe the people of this city—"

Henriques had not asked for a speech and tried to interrupt, but Parkerson rolled over him.

"—I believe the people of this city to be the most law-abiding, long-suffering, patient people among whom I have ever lived or with whom I have ever had anything to do."

"Can O'Malley get a fair trial?"

"The fact that he walks through the streets unmolested and casts defiance at the people, and his own statement that the prejudice against him is confined to a few lawbreakers shows that he can get a fair and impartial trial."

James Houston, the mob's "first lieutenant," was questioned about the Committee of Safety's formation in the evening of March 14, hours after the lynching. "On that night or on any subsequent night, was there a resolution passed by that body to kill D. C. O'Malley?" asked Henriques.

"I decline to answer."

"Do you know of a resolution being passed by the committee to kill O'Malley in the event of his acquittal by a jury?"

"I decline to answer."

The Denegre brothers similarly refused to talk about their actions at the prison. After the four Committee of Safety members declared that O'Malley could get a fair trial in New Orleans, Henriques astonished the state by dropping the change of venue motion. More legal haggling allowed O'Malley and McCrystol to be released on bond—their cases were postponed indefinitely.

The first defendant prosecutors managed to try was Bernard Glaudi, who was found guilty of saying to a potential juror, "How would $500 do?" Glaudi admitted saying aloud that there was money to be made in the case, but insisted it was just an observation. After two Boylan officers testified that they saw Glaudi approach potential jurors in court, however, he was convicted, sentenced to a year of hard labor, and required to pay court costs.

Both Charles Granger and Emile Bagnetto pleaded innocent. Henriques argued that no legal basis for their prosecution existed, acknowledging that while bribing jurors was clearly a crime, penal statutes said nothing about potential jurors. Judge Marr ruled that a potential juror was no different from a sworn juror. Prosecutors called talesman Alphonse Labarre, who testified that when his friend Granger got him out of bed one day, Labarre thought Granger was there to pay him a poker debt. Instead Granger asked if he wanted to make $500. Yes, said the unemployed Labarre, whose jury summons had arrived that morning. Granger said there was $500 in it if Labarre could get on the Hennessy case and "work the jury." Labarre said his conscience would not allow him to do such a thing, and Granger left without another word on the subject. Labarre said nothing about the exchange when he was examined as a talesman, because he'd forgotten it. In any event, he was not chosen to sit on the jury.

In his own defense, Granger recalled talking about the poker debt and possible innocence of the Hennessy case defendants, but insisted that money was never mentioned. Granger worked as a cargo checker on the docks for Oteri, Macheca Brothers, Phipps, and other fruit lines. Character witnesses called his reputation "gilt-edged," and while no one spoke of it, Granger came from a socially well-connected family. Henriques, Butler, and Gastinel, all defense lawyers in the Hennessy trial, distinctly recalled Labarre swearing during jury selection that he'd spoken to no one about the case. The jury deadlocked 9 to 3 in Granger's favor. Because the current jury pool might be prejudiced, Judge Marr granted a continuance until September, over the prosecution's protest that Granger deserved a right "guaranteed to every accused by the Constitution—a speedy trial."

Tom McCrystol was less fortunate. Talesman Thomas McCabe accused McCrystol of approaching him twice, first offering him $500 to get on the jury and vote for acquittals, then offering $1,000 for McCabe's jury subpoena. When McCabe refused, McCrystol asked McCabe to persuade his next door neighbor William Mackesy to go on the jury. McCabe refused, but thought McCrystol had visited Mackesy, who did wind up on the jury.

Jailed for bribery with Cooney a few days before the lynching, McCrystol witnessed the slaughter in the prison. That night he nervously promised to tell the district attorney everything he knew about the Hennessy case if Luzenberg would protect him. Luzenberg replied that he had a dead open-and-shut case and would only speak on McCrystol's behalf during sentencing. McCrystol agreed and confessed to bribery. Judge Baker ruled the confession inadmissible, in spite of Luzenberg's assurances that it was voluntary, but when the jury retired to consider McCrystol's case that afternoon, they ordered dinner, found

McCrystol guilty in eighteen minutes, and were gone by the time their food arrived. McCrystol was sentenced to a year in the penitentiary.

On another count, McCrystol and John Cooney were tried together for attempting to bribe F. J. Gormley in a bar next to his plumbing shop. Cooney said he'd heard Gormley was to serve on the Hennessy jury and would do anything in God's world to clear his personal friend Charles Matranga. Gormley did not expect to serve, because he had a family to provide for and could not afford to lose work.

"As far as that's concerned, your family will be provided for," Cooney allegedly said.

"I don't need anyone to provide for my family as long as I'm all right," Gormley replied. Cooney and McCrystol asked the plumber to "let the matter drop" and left. They did not offer him any money.

Police informant Thomas Collins testified that he heard the defendants say they were going to see Gormley and accused them of reporting to O'Malley's office, where Collins was working undercover, but Cooney denied ever working for O'Malley or trying to bribe Gormley, whom he had known for years. He said that Gormley was upset about being summoned for the Criminal Court trial, as he'd just finished jury duty at Civil Court. Cooney suggested Gormley ask the district attorney's office to be excused. "They're smart men," Cooney reflected at the time, "even if Hennessy was no angel."

McCrystol and Cooney were found guilty on June 17. That day Fernand Armant's postponed trial finally reached court, where he faced his neighbor, the elusive Leonce Burthe. Burthe claimed that Armant, Charles Patorno's lawyer, offered Burthe $750 if he would get on the Hennessy jury and vote to acquit. Burthe said the matter came to nothing because he was excused from jury duty, but he later told William Parkerson and the grand jury about Armant's offer.

Prosecutors closed their case against Armant surprisingly quickly. Defense witness Lionel Adams could not recall who challenged Burthe as a juror, but thought it was the state. Adams said his relations with Armant during the Hennessy trial were "somewhat strained." Adams added, "Let me say here that I do not consider myself responsible for everything that was done on the part of the defense in the Hennessy case."

Nine character witnesses accused Burthe of being a habitual liar, and Armant testified that Burthe badgered him repeatedly during jury selection for an introduction to Salvatore Oteri, apparently with the intention of soliciting a bribe. "I told him that I represented Patorno and he was not on trial," remembered Armant, who had heard the rumors about available bribe money but rebuffed Burthe, adding that he did not even know Oteri and was on poor terms with all the defendants except his own client. "I said to him, 'I'm not made out of that sort of cloth.'" When Armant was indicted, it was clear that

Burthe was responsible for the charge. Burthe tried to explain himself to Armant outside the Grand Opera House, saying his father brought him to Parkerson's office, where he was bulldozed into making statements he hardly remembered. "Where did you perjure yourself?" Armant replied angrily. "Before the grand jury, in court, where?" Burthe responded that he had to do something to save himself.

Armant got a mistrial. One of two jurors holding out for conviction said that they all believed he was guilty, but Burthe's unbelievable testimony and bad character caused them to hang fire. Burthe's testimony that his cousin Edgar White drunkenly told him to flee New Orleans fared no better. White testified that he saw Burthe waiting outside the grand jury room. When Burthe asked if it was true that White planned to undercut his testimony and speak on Armant's behalf, White said yes. Burthe protested that it was not his place to do so.

"It is my place," White insisted. "You know you're a liar and a thief. You can't convince me that Fernand Armant offered you $1,000 or $1,500, for a man like you, who would steal, who'd take the money." That night after their argument, White was arrested on his way home from work. When the police told him he was being charged, he thought it was a joke.

Judge Baker stopped the trial, declared the evidence insufficient, Burthe entirely unreliable, and Edgar White innocent. Ironically, McCrystol and Cooney got new trials that day. Upon Henriques's appeal, Judge Marr reexamined the conversation between the two defendants and Gormley. Marr agreed with Henriques's claim that the conversation alone was insufficient evidence to support a charge or conviction. In spite of the suspicious nature of the chat, no deal had been proposed to the plumber.

Of the "gang of jury bribers," this left only Emile Bagnetto, nephew of the lynched Antonio. Bagnetto was accused by David Bonhage, a sparely-built shoemaker. His wife was ill during the Hennessy trial, so instead of eating at home, Bonhage began having his breakfast at Bagnetto's restaurant near Poydras Market. When Bonhage was summoned as a talesman, Bagnetto allegedly brought the shoemaker upstairs and offered over a hundred dollars to help "his uncle or his cousin"—Bonhage admitted he couldn't remember which. Nor could he recall under cross-examination if he was threatened with the penitentiary in Parkerson's office if he failed to testify against Bagnetto.

Bagnetto's recall was clearer. He remembered the morning Bonhage came into the coffee stall and said, "Well, I'm in it."

"In what?" Bagnetto asked.

"On the jury in the Hennessy case."

"Well, Dave, I'm glad to hear it. If you can give my uncle the benefit of a doubt, I shall expect you to do it."

"Well," Bonhage replied, "I'm out for the stuff."

"I have no money to give away, Dave," Bagnetto answered. He never took the bribe-hungry shoemaker upstairs.

The jury took an hour to find Emile Bagnetto innocent.

It was the Fourth of July in Bloomington. When the morning sports games were over, the parades were disbanding, and the patriotic hymns were all sung, crowds moved toward the red, white, and blue bunting adorning the platform. A young woman read the Declaration of Independence aloud. It was time for the oration of the day. Out of a smiling delegation of Illinois farmers stepped the invited speaker, William Parkerson of New Orleans.

Twelve thousand cheers greeted Parkerson. The attorney thanked the people for their hospitality. He complimented the waving fields of green around them, the result of perfect cultivation and earnest toil. Then he spoke about brotherhood and the healing bonds between North and South.

William Parkerson loved America. The President of the United States would know that Southerners loved the Stars and Stripes if he had seen fit to visit New Orleans. The implication was that President Harrison's dim view of the parish prison incident was mistaken. In contrast, Parkerson wished James Blaine would come to New Orleans. "We will show him how we appreciate his genius and admire his Americanism!"

When Parkerson spoke of the noble duty of every American to look to the welfare of his country without desiring any political office—referring to himself—he got the wildest applause of the day. "It would seem as if every mother's son who is born in this land of the free is aspiring for office, and that is not the worst of it. The negro, immediately upon his enfranchisement, thought that he must fill all the positions in the land. And the immigrant, from whatever quarter of the globe he may come, when first he breathes the air of this country, prepares himself for the race. Before he speaks the language, he wants to be making laws. Before he understands the form of the government, he wants to govern. It is a mistake, a very grave mistake, it is a terrible evil, the cause of most of our trouble, and something must be done to correct it.

"For the people who are already among us, there is but one way—the best way to teach anything—and that is by example. Teach the negro, teach the white man both native and naturalized, that what is being done is in the hope of benefiting the community and not in the expectation of getting an office. Teach them there are higher purposes than personal aggrandizement. Show them the dignity of private citizenship."

Parkerson preached for restricting immigration and making it harder to attain American citizenship. The immigrant must be made to feel himself lifted from serf to free man, he said. Parkerson spoke of William Tell, of Saxon kings immortalized in poetry, of Bunker Hill and Valley Forge, of Leonidas and the Spartans. Was American patriotism dead? he wondered. No, it was awakening from its slumber.

As Parkerson mentioned Gettysburg and other bloody names from the war, tears came to the eyes of many who were old enough to remember. The young lawyer praised Grant and Lee equally. "I yield to none in regard for that broad-minded, great-bearded statesman and patriot Abraham Lincoln. In his death, the South lost a great friend. He alone could solve the difficulty of Reconstruction. He alone could reconcile the differences and avoid the bitterness of strife." Patriotism such as this, said Parkerson, covered all the world in the blaze of its glory.

The lawyer from New Orleans thanked the people as he waved to the sea of smiling white faces and stepped back from the podium. He was an authentic hero of a moment, admired by many around the country and, at the same time, despised by many as a coconspirator in a shameful and despicable act, a betrayer of some of the same American ideals he would continue to extol for the rest of his fleeting celebrity.

That summer Cooney was freed, and prosecutors dropped the charge against Armant. McCrystol and Glaudi were still in the penitentiary. The *New York Times* called the latter "a garrulous butcher whose whiskey-loosened tongue got him into trouble." If booze and a big mouth were all that landed Glaudi in the jug, that did not say much for the conspiracy theory.

Dominick O'Malley, the biotype of Parkerson's belief that apathy toward civic duty opened the door to corruption, noisily wished that Charles Luzenberg would either set a trial date or drop the remaining bribery charge. The district attorney had done neither by late August, and he was in no mood to accommodate the abrasive detective.

The truth was that the state's case against O'Malley was in trouble; his indictment was based on the terrified McCrystol's interview with Luzenberg after the lynching. When the court threw out that confession, there was no way to indict O'Malley again unless McCrystol wanted to talk a second time, but by then McCrystol was serving his year in the pen, silently.

With no evidence forthcoming from McCrystol or the expensive dithering of the defunct Committee of Fifty, Luzenberg had no alternative. O'Malley, internationally condemned archconspirator and "suborner of juries," the man the mob had been ready to run up the nearest lamppost, would not spend a single day in jail for his alleged mischief in the Hennessy case. On October 8, as soon as the charge against him was dropped, O'Malley was instantly back in business, loudly threatening to sue Parkerson and Walter Denegre and have them disbarred. Of the accused jury bribers, only Charles Granger's case remained unsettled. On November 27, more than eight months after the lynching, the charge against him was also dropped.

Glaudi's and McCrystol's sentences were the best the state did to prove that the jury system had been corrupted. Without them, the moral fulcrum upon which the slaughter at the parish prison was elevated by its champions would have collapsed completely. *The New York Times* called it "a legal draw."

No one was ever indicted for dealing with any of the twelve jurors who actually weighed the Hennessy case.

The word "Mafia" had rarely appeared in American newspapers before the first Provenzano trial, when the Esplanade ambush still looked like a local curiosity. Because of worldwide coverage of the Hennessy case, however, the word was now familiar far from New Orleans. Testimony in the case exposed no conspiracy by Sicilian criminals or anyone else for that matter, but Mafia treachery was now cited whenever crime involving Italians or Italian Americans occurred, replacing the brigandage and mysterious vendettas of earlier times. When a brawl over the affections of a prostitute turned into a riot between railroad graders and immigrants on the Washington state frontier, the *New York Times* reported that the spurned party was "a sort of king among the Italians," a faro dealer said to have been "driven from New Orleans for his part in the Mafia murders." With the word Mafia now imbedded in the American vernacular, the truth about Hennessy's death and the lynching became increasingly less important than the way the story was used for decades to come.

The pink-sheet Gilded Age tabloid *Police Gazette* feted the chief's career, falsely complimenting him for single-handedly storming polling places to kill black pollworkers committing election fraud. In reality, Hennessy's own relations with the African American community had been good, while Shakspeare's administration was maligned by racists for "stealing" its place in city hall with bargained votes of African Americans, who were nominally rewarded for their political support. From the pro-Italy side, Shakspeare was condemned by one commentator as a typically corrupt Crescent City politician and "a rabid Irish papist"; in fact the starchy mayor was the son of a Quaker father and a Swiss mother. Warped views of the Hennessy case continued to multiply for a century, with details or falsehoods chosen to fit the popular prejudices of each new era.

Senator Henry Cabot Lodge and others warmly recalled the New Orleans incident whenever anti-immigration talk flared in Congress. Yet the memory of the Hennessy murder was not the exclusive tool of bigots, braggarts, and congressmen. Any New Orleanian who felt like insulting an Italian spat out the old question, "Who killa de chief?" The insult took years to die out, and even the children of immigrants, who shrugged off its sting as the city healed, knew well the deeper meaning of the words. Ironically, despite the violence in New Orleans and the best efforts of xenophobic legislators, no significant lull in immigration from Italy to the United States occurred until 1895. In the first decade of the twentieth century, the trickle of migrant workers evolved into a flood as hundreds of thousands of Italian men, women, and children sailed for American ports, hoping to find permanent new homes.

President Harrison settled the indemnity fracas in April of 1892. Without accepting any official or national responsibility for the New Orleans affair, the president ordered 125,000 francs, about $25,000, to be paid from a special contingency fund to the Italian government. The money was to be distributed among the families of the three lynched Italian subjects. There were complaints about the executive path President Harrison took to avoid a fight with Congress over the payment, but the matter was closed, almost. The City of New Orleans still faced lawsuits from six of the dead men's families, including Comitz's widow and the families of Traina, Scaffidi, and Monasterio. In December 1893, Gasperi Marchesi's guardian at a Rome orphanage was awarded $5,000 in damages.

Italy welcomed the chance to get relations between the two nations back to normal. An American ambassador was dispatched to Rome, while six hundred Italian Americans chartered a steamer to meet Baron Fava as he sailed into New York en route to Washington, doffing his silk hat and waving his handkerchief at the welcoming crowd.

On Christmas night of 1892, William Parkerson's doorbell jangled him awake. Realizing that the house was in flames, he roused his wife and they fled. Holidaymakers had spotted the blaze and given the alarm. Parkerson would say nothing about the fire, but friends openly called it the work of Mafia arsonists. One man reported that he overheard an Italian pointing out the house to another as they rode past on a streetcar. Why would Italians point at Parkerson's home unless they had evil intentions?

In the spring, Judge Marr disappeared. The old man took daily walks along the levee. Friends sadly assumed that he had fallen and the Mississippi River had taken him.

The summer was nearly over when Chief Gaster received a note written in dimeshow Italian threatening to kill Judge Marr if a ransom wasn't paid. Resisting an urge to crumple the paper, the chief of police handed it to a reporter instead, saying he thought it was a very bad joke.

Epitaphs:

THE GREAT MYSTIFICATION

As new crimes consumed the years and paperwork on his case disappeared from official files, Hennessy's murder and the story of the men who paid for his death passed into the city's popular mythology. The tale of the Reverend Rose, Polizzi's "confession," and even Gasperi Marchesi's warning whistle became accepted as facts. No one was eager to pick at the scars, so the truths, omissions, and lies began to harden where they lay.

Signor Pasquale Corte was transferred to France. In the traumatic months after the parish prison incident, Frances Xavier Cabrini stopped in New Orleans on her return from building an orphanage in Managua, Nicaragua, and established a branch of her order, giving the Italian immigrant community one of its first relief organizations. Then Mother Cabrini returned to New York and sainthood. The New Orleans Italian American community flourished as the nightmare of 1891 slowly receded.

On June 10, 1893, Captain Azariah Wilde of the U.S. Secret Service retired after thirty-one years on the job in Orleans Parish. He was feted as "a terror to wrongdoers, especially those who counterfeited Uncle Sam's specie and currency." Frank Dimaio, the Pinkerton agent Wilde "arrested" and delivered to the parish prison, traveled to Argentina in 1902 in a vain attempt to arrest Butch Cassidy, the Sundance Kid, and Etta Place. When Dimaio returned, the Pinkertons sent him to the limestone quarries of Ohio and Pennsylvania to infiltrate the Black Hand and the Mafia.

Thomas Boylan retired in 1893, turning command of his detective business over to Billy O'Connor. New Orleans Police superintendent and chief Dexter Gaster, Hennessy's successor, served for ten years until his death in 1901. He was followed by another of Hennessy's officers, John Journée. When Journée's successor, E. S. Whitaker, was fired in 1908 for trying to shoot a newspaper editor, Mayor Martin Behrman filled the vacancy with the stout superintendent of the Boylan detective agency—Billy O'Connor.

Despite his noisy threats against Italian American stevedores, Joseph Shakspeare was hounded by riverfront labor unrest throughout the rest of his term. Contrary to his word, Shakspeare ran for mayor a third time. He lost to Ring candidate John Fitzpatrick in 1892, ending the YMDA's "silk-stocking" reign. True to his word, William Parkerson never held a public office. After a general strike by united black and white levee workers paralyzed the New Orleans docks in 1907, state legislators convened a commission, ostensibly to investigate conditions on the waterfront. Parkerson acted as cocounsel for the Port Investigation Commission, serving its outspoken white supremacist leadership with enthusiasm. James D. Houston died a few years following the lynching, after traveling hopelessly to find relief from a cancer destroying his stomach.

Dominick O'Malley did not accomplish his threat to have Walter Denegre disbarred. Denegre campaigned to bring drainage to New Orleans and spent his last years in Washington, DC, where he served as custodian of the Bureau of Alien Property during World War I. Denegre's brother, George, was buried a few yards from Chief Hennessy beneath a stone inscribed WRITE ME As ONE WHO LOVED HIS FELLOW MEN. When society biographers profiled John C. Wickliffe after the lynching, his youthful expulsion from West Point was not ignored. Yet someone falsely revised the total of his 108 demerits downward to 101, suggesting that a solitary petty point pushed him over the acceptable limit of 100. The mercurial lawyer and hundreds of other New Orleanians by then had ample reason to maintain the fantasy of Wickliffe as a well-disciplined military man. John M. Parker, one of Mayor Shakspeare's police commissioners and a lynch-notice signatory, was a member of President Theodore Roosevelt's fabled 1902 Mississippi "Teddy Bear" hunt and stabbed the captive bear Roosevelt refused to shoot. Parker ran for vice president on Roosevelt's unsuccessful Bull Moose ticket in 1912. He later became governor of Louisiana and an ardent foe of his successor, Huey P. Long.

Lionel Adams went back to the district attorney's office to act as its chief criminal prosecutor for a year and never fully retired. By the end of a long career, his successful conviction rate was over 97 percent.

Dominick O'Malley lived in New Orleans for the rest of his life, tormenting his enemies far into the next century. He continued to dig up dirt for his associate Lionel Adams, and he even bought the *Daily City Item*, flailing at his foes with hyperbolic spite on the same front page where he had once been vilified. He spent a little time selling fish and game wholesale, and he spent a little time in jail. By the time of his peaceful death in 1920, he had been shot, indicted, sued, beaten, arrested, and publicly denounced more than any man in the city of New Orleans.

After his term as governor ended in 1892, Francis T. Nicholls was appointed Chief Justice of the Louisiana Supreme Court, where he served for nearly twenty years. Judge Joshua Baker also ascended to the Louisiana Supreme Court. He outlived them all except Charles Matranga, who remained in the fruit business for the rest of his life. While he was never again charged with a crime, some historians continued to accuse Matranga of being a mafioso long after his death. Margaret Hennessy left her money to a religious order of nuns.

Once the lynching overtook the public image of a martyred police officer, no one paused to ask whether justice for David Hennessy was still due. Abandoned investigations and a lynching were strange memorials for an officer who had devoted his life to the law and thrived on detective work. To the mob's defenders, the outcome may have seemed like rough justice that the chief would have appreciated; to the mob's critics the outcome remained no less obscene. Nothing was settled, but quiet descended on the case.

He was not completely forgotten. The City of New Orleans renamed a street for the dead chief, and a private subscription fund eventually paid for a more personal monument. A square granite base sits atop the grave's grassy hummock in Metairie Cemetery. There David C. Hennessy's epitaph is carved beneath the star and crescent of the New Orleans Police:

His Life Was Honorable and Brave
His Devotion to Duty
was Sealed by His Death

An unscored, twenty-six-foot stone column rises from the tablet, featureless and unscalable. A sculpted police chief's baton and uniform belt grip its apex, the clasp enveloping the symbol in a shroud.

☽

SELECTED BIBLIOGRAPHY

Contemporary daily accounts by the competitive New Orleans press are the best surviving primary source of information about the Hennessy case and the Orleans Parish Prison lynching. Analysis of these period accounts provides both facts and illuminating misinformation. While these voluminous reports are a basis for nearly all scholarship on the case, the accuracy with which the material has been handled since 1891 has varied considerably, with errors often compounded by retelling and the passage of time.

In nearly a century of historical commentary and folktales, the guilt of the men lynched for Chief Hennessy's murder and the inevitability of their fate were seldom questioned. John S. Kendall's 1939 article, "Who Killa de Chief?" provides a good example of such apologias. Italian American historians began analyzing the incident in the 1970s. Such reappraisals include Humbert Nelli's *The Business of Crime* and Richard Gambino's *Vendetta*.

Joy Jackson's *New Orleans in the Gilded Age*, John Wilds's *Afternoon Story*, and John Higham's *Strangers in the Land* provide valuable context for understanding the bloody events of 1890 and 1891. James D. Horan interviewed Pinkerton agent Frank Dimaio almost sixty years after the lynching. The resulting chapter about Dimaio's participation in the Hennessy murder investigation in *The Pinkertons* is colorful, but at odds with the historical record. Raleigh Trevelyan's *Princes under the Volcano* steered me toward press accounts of the Rose kidnapping, which was universally misreported for a century in the wake of the Esposito extradition.

The New Orleans incident will remain a significant subject for social historians examining U.S. immigration history and the Italian American experience. Such studies can be found in Gambino's *Blood of My Blood* and *The 1891 New Orleans Lynching and U.S.-Italian Relations*, edited by Marco Rimanelli and Sheryl Lynn Postman. The latter also includes detailed analyses of the deterioration of diplomatic relations between Italy and the United States in 1891.

NEWSPAPERS
New Orleans:
Daily City Item
Daily Crescent
Commercial Bulletin
Daily Picayune
Daily States
Democrat

The Mascot
New Orleans Crescent
L'Abeille
New Delta
New Orleans Times
Tagliche Deutsche Zeitung
Times-Democrat
New York:
New York Times

ARTICLES

Coxe, John E. "The New Orleans Mafia Incident." *Louisiana Historical Quarterly* 20 (1937): 1067–110.

Karlin, J. Alexander. "New Orleans Lynchings in 1891 and the American Press." *Louisiana Historical Quarterly* 24 (1941): 187–264.

Kendall, John Smith. "Journalism in New Orleans Between 1880–1900." *Louisiana Historical Quarterly* 7 (October 1925): 557–73.

———."Old Days on the Times-Democrat." *Louisiana Historical Quarterly* 33 (October 1950): 406–29.

———."Old Time New Orleans Police Reporters and Reporting." *Louisiana Historical Quarterly* 29 (January 1946): 43–58.

———."Who Killa de Chief?" *Louisiana Historical Quarterly* 22 (1939): 492–530.

"The Mafia and What Led to the Lynching." *Harper's Weekly* 35 (March 28, 1891): 602–12.

Mario, Jessie White (Vedova). "Italy and the United States." *The Nineteenth Century*, May 1891: 701–18.

BOOKS

Arneson, Eric. *Waterfront Workers of New Orleans: Race, Class, and Politics, 1863–1923*. Urbana: University of Illinois Press, 1991.

Asbury, Herbert J. *The French Quarter: An Informal History of the New Orleans Underworld*. New York: Knopf, 1936.

Biographical and Historical Memoirs of Louisiana. 2 vols. Chicago: Goodspeed, 1876.

Castellanos, Henry C. *New Orleans as It Was*. 1895. Reprint, Baton Rouge: Louisiana State University Press, 1978.

Chandler, David Leon. *Brothers in Blood: The Rise of the Criminal Brotherhoods*. New York: Dutton, 1975.

DeConde, Alexander. *Half Bitter, Half Sweet: An Excursion into Italian American History*. New York: Scribner, 1971.

Gallo, Patrick J. *Old Bread, New Wine: The Italian Americans*. Chicago: Nelson-Hall, 1981.

Gambino, Richard. *Blood of My Blood: The Dilemma of the Italian-Americans*. Garden City, NY: Doubleday, 1974.

————. *Vendetta: The True Story of the Largest Lynching in American History*. Garden City, NY: Doubleday, 1977.

Higham, John. *Strangers in the Land: Patterns of American Nativism*. New York: Atheneum, 1965.

Horan, James D. *The Pinkertons: The Detective Dynasty That Made History*. New York: Crown, 1967.

Jackson, Joy J. *New Orleans in the Gilded Age: Politics and Urban Progress 1860–1896*. Baton Rouge: Louisiana State University Press, 1969.

Jewell, Edwin Lewis, ed. *Jewell's Crescent City Illustrated*. New Orleans, 1873.

Kemp, John R., ed. *Martin Behrman of New Orleans: Memoirs of a City Boss*. Baton Rouge: Louisiana State University Press, 1977.

Kimball, Nell, and Stephen Longstreet, eds. *Nell Kimball: Her Life as an American Madam, by Herself*. New York: MacMillan, 1970.

Knappman, Edward W., ed. *Great American Trials*. Detroit, MI: Visible Ink, 1994.

Moquin, Wayne, ed. *A Documentary History of the Italian Americans*. With Charles Van Doren and Frances A. J. Ianni. New York: Praeger, 1974.

Musmanno, Michael A. *The Italians in America*. Garden City, NY: Doubleday, 1965.

National Association for the Advancement of Colored People. *Thirty Years of Lynching in the United States, 1889–1918*. New York: NAACP Press, 1919.

Nelli, Humbert S. *The Business of Crime: Italians and Syndicate Crime in the United States.* New York: Oxford University Press, 1976.

New Orleans Police Department Benevolent Association. *New Orleans Police Department.* New Orleans: NOPD Benevolent Association, 1900.

Niehaus, Earl F. *The Irish in Louisiana, 1800–1860.* Baton Rouge: Louisiana University Press, 1965.

Reynolds, George M. *Machine Politics in New Orleans, 1897–1920.* New York: Columbia University Press, 1936.

Rimanelli, Marco, and Sheryl Lynn Postman, eds. *The 1891 New Orleans Lynching and U.S.-Italian Relations.* New York: Peter Lang, 1992.

Robinson, Elisha, and Roger H. Pidgeon. *Robinson's Atlas of the City of New Orleans, Louisiana.* New York: E. Robinson, 1883.

Rosenberg, Daniel. *New Orleans Dockworkers: Race, Labor, and Unionism 1892–1923.* Albany, NY: SUNY Press, 1988.

Rousey, Dennis C. *Policing the Southern City, New Orleans, 1805–1889.* Baton Rouge: Louisiana State University Press, 1996.

Saxon, Lyle, ed. *Gumbo Ya-Ya.* With Edward Dreyer and Robert Tallant. Boston: Houghton Mifflin, 1945.

Tallant, Robert. *Ready to Hang: Seven Famous New Orleans Murders.* New York: Harper, 1952.

Trevelyan, Raleigh. *Princes Under the Volcano.* New York: William Morrow, 1973.

Van Every, Edward. *Sins of America: As Exposed by the Police Gazette.* New York: Stokes, 1931.

Wilds, John. *Afternoon Story: The History of the New Orleans States-Item.* Baton Rouge: Louisiana University Press, 1976.

INDEX